The Limits of Structuralism

The Limits of Structuralism

Forgotten Sources in the History of Modern Linguistics

Edited by
JAMES MCELVENNY

Great Clarendon Street, Oxford, OX2 6DP,
United Kingdom

Oxford University Press is a department of the University of Oxford.
It furthers the University's objective of excellence in research, scholarship,
and education by publishing worldwide. Oxford is a registered trade mark of
Oxford University Press in the UK and in certain other countries

© editorial matter and organization James McElvenny 2023
© the chapters their several contributors 2023

The moral rights of the authors have been asserted

All rights reserved. No part of this publication may be reproduced, stored in
a retrieval system, or transmitted, in any form or by any means, without the
prior permission in writing of Oxford University Press, or as expressly permitted
by law, by licence or under terms agreed with the appropriate reprographics
rights organization. Enquiries concerning reproduction outside the scope of the
above should be sent to the Rights Department, Oxford University Press, at the
address above

You must not circulate this work in any other form
and you must impose this same condition on any acquirer

Published in the United States of America by Oxford University Press
198 Madison Avenue, New York, NY 10016, United States of America

British Library Cataloguing in Publication Data

Data available

Library of Congress Control Number: 2023930742

ISBN 978–0–19–284904–5

DOI: 10.1093/oso/9780192849045.001.0001

Printed and bound by
CPI Group (UK) Ltd, Croydon, CR0 4YY

Links to third party websites are provided by Oxford in good faith and
for information only. Oxford disclaims any responsibility for the materials
contained in any third party website referenced in this work.

Contents

List of contributors   vii

1. Scouting the limits of structuralism   1
   James McElvenny

2. 'Primitive structures', polysynthesis, and Peter Stephen du Ponceau   11
   Floris Solleveld
   Peter Stephen du Ponceau (1838): *On the grammatical character of the languages of North America, known as Lenni Lenape, Mohican, and Chippewa*   29

3. Franz Boas' 'purely analytical approach' to language classification in the backdrop to American structuralism   51
   Margaret Thomas
   Franz Boas (1920): *The classification of American languages*   70

4. Georg von der Gabelentz's typology: Humboldtian linguistics on the threshold of structuralism   81
   James McElvenny
   Georg von der Gabelentz (1894): *Typology of languages—a new task of linguistics*   102

5. Grammaticalization and the sentimental evolution of Antoine Meillet   109
   John E. Joseph
   Antoine Meillet (1912): *The evolution of grammatical forms*   123

6. Roman Jakobson, language unions, and structuralism in Russia: Encounter or misunderstanding?   139
   Patrick Sériot
   Roman Jakobson (1931): *The Eurasian language union*   159

7. Louis Hjelmslev on the correlational structure of language: The place within the system   205
   Lorenzo Cigana
   Louis Hjelmslev (1933): *General structure of linguistic correlations*   225

8. Émile Benveniste on the relation between linguistic and
social structures: 'Let us then consider that language
interprets society' 267
Chloé Laplantine
Émile Benveniste (1970): Structure of language and
structure of society 288

References 298
Index 324

List of contributors

Lorenzo Cigana is a researcher at the Department of Nordic Studies and Linguistics (NorS) at the University of Copenhagen. Since his PhD on Louis Hjelmslev's theory of markedness, he has been working on structural linguistics, with a particular focus on Danish theoretical linguistics and glossematics, the theory of language developed by Louis Hjelmslev and Hans Jørgen Uldall in the 1930s. He is currently working in the 'Infrastructuralism' project, whose aim is to establish an open-source infrastructure providing the international academic community access to correspondence and manuscripts from the archives of Louis Hjelmslev and other Danish structuralist linguists in a digitized and annotated form.

Andrew Eastman is based at Savoirs dans l'Espace Anglophone, University of Strasbourg. His research focuses on rhythm, prosody, and subjectivity in English-language poetries. He has recently published articles on Whitman's rhyme, punctuation in *Shakespeare's Sonnets*, and Susan Howe's 'type collages'. He is currently working on a study of rhythm and voice in Elizabeth Bishop's poems.

Patrick Flack is Senior Lecturer in the History of Ideas in Eastern and Central Europe at the University of Fribourg. Before taking up his current position in 2021, he was a visiting fellow at the Central European Institute of Philosophy (Prague), the Peter-Szondi Institute (Berlin), and the Husserl Archives (Leuven). He is the author of *Idée, expression, vécu* (Herman, 2018) and *Russian Theory* (sdvig press, forthcoming), as well as the editor of several volumes, including *Hendrik Pos, Écrits sur le langage* (2013), *Linguistics and Phenomenology* (2016, with Simone Aurora), and *Merleau-Ponty and Structuralism* (2018, with Beata Stawarska).

John E. Joseph is Professor of Applied Linguistics in the University of Edinburgh, and a member of the Royal Danish Academy of Sciences and Letters. His work in the history of linguistics includes the books *Saussure* (Oxford University Press, 2012), *Language, Mind and Body: A Conceptual History* (Cambridge University Press, 2018), and his translation of Emile Benveniste's *Last Lectures: Collège de France, 1968 and 1969* (Edinburgh University Press, 2019). He serves on the boards of the Henry Sweet Society for the History of Linguistic Ideas and the Société d'Histoire et d'Epistémologie des Sciences du Langage, and is currently president of the Cercle Ferdinand de Saussure.

Chloé Laplantine is a Researcher at CNRS/University of Paris. She has published extensively on Émile Benveniste's linguistics and poetics. She has edited his manuscript notes on Baudelaire and is currently preparing an edition of his fieldwork notebooks on the Tlingit and Haida languages. She has also published research on the relation between linguistics and poetics in the work of Franz Boas and Edward Sapir.

James McElvenny is a linguist and intellectual historian whose research focuses on the history of modern linguistics. After completing his PhD at the University of Sydney in 2013, he was an Alexander von Humboldt Fellow at the University of Potsdam from 2015 to 2017, and then from 2018 to 2020 a Newton International Fellow of the British Academy at the University of Edinburgh. Since 2020 he is a researcher in the Special Collaborative Research Center 'Media of Co-operation' at the University of Siegen. He is the author of *Language and Meaning in the Age of Modernism* (Edinburgh University Press, 2018) and editor of several volumes, including *Form and Formalism in Linguistics* (Language Science Press, 2019) and *Gabelentz and the Science of Language* (Amsterdam University Press, 2019).

Patrick Sériot is Emeritus Professor of Slavic linguistics at the University of Lausanne. Born in Paris, he studied Slavic and general linguistics at the Sorbonne, with a specialization in the analysis of Soviet political discourse. After receiving his doctorate, he worked from 1985 to 1987 as a researcher at the Centre national de la recherche scientifique (CNRS) in Paris, before taking up the chair of Slavic linguistics at the University of Lausanne in Switzerland. There he specialized in the history and epistemology of Soviet linguistics and philosophy of language. After his retirement in 2014, he worked for four years at the University of Saint Petersburg as an invited professor in the history of linguistics, teaching a course on the comparative epistemology of Soviet and Western European attitudes towards sign and language. His main work is the *Structure and the Whole: East, West and non-Darwinian Biology in the Origins of Structural Linguistics* (De Gruyter, 2014).

Floris Solleveld is a postdoctoral researcher at KU Leuven and is currently finishing a project on ethnolinguistics in the long nineteenth century. He studied philosophy at the University of Amsterdam and obtained a PhD in cultural history at Radboud University Nijmegen with a study of transformations in the humanities around 1800. He has held fellowships in Halle (Saale) and Gotha and was a guest researcher at the Max Planck Institute for the History of Science (Berlin) and Leiden University.

Margaret Thomas is Professor of Linguistics at Boston College in Chestnut Hill, Massachusetts. Her research interests are broadly in the history of linguistics, especially twentieth-century linguistics in the United States. She is the author of *Formalism and Functionalism in Linguistics: The Engineer and the Collector* (Routledge, 2020), and is working on a book about the early years of the Linguistic Society of America.

1
Scouting the limits of structuralism

James McElvenny

1.1 Introduction

What is structuralism? This simple question has no simple answer. The label 'structuralism' has been applied to such a diverse range of doctrines, schools, and methods that any attempt to find a single underlying essence or even to enumerate a catalogue of common characteristics would seem to be doomed to failure (cf. Joseph 2023a). But if we look at this question from a sociological perspective, we can begin to approach an answer: 'structuralism' is the name of a broad intellectual movement that emerged in the early twentieth century and spread throughout the humanities and social sciences, reaching a peak mid-century. Who was part of this movement? Who was not? What spirit animated their work?

These are the questions we ask in this volume. They allow us to survey the conceptual boundaries of structuralism, to see where its borders may lie and how permeable they may be. Our focus is on linguistics, the fertile ground out of which structuralism first sprouted and from which it propagated to neighbouring fields. Within this domain, we take a broadly philological approach and engage in close, contextualized reading of key primary texts that highlight the contours of structuralism. For each text, we provide an introductory essay and critical notes, which together draw out the ideas and methods the text contains, elucidate its intellectual and historical background, and demonstrate its continuing importance today.

Before we embark on our expedition to the frontiers of structuralism, let us briefly explore the formation and expansion of this intellectual movement. In section 1.2, we search for the origin of structuralism in the work of the Prague Linguistic Circle. In section 1.3, we then follow the spread of structuralism from this source to other schools and disciplines. Equipped with this sociological perspective, we turn in section 1.4 to the chapters of this volume, and outline their content and how they can help us to scout the limits of structuralism.

1.2 The emergence of structuralism

First appearing between the two World Wars, and with its highest incidence around the middle of the twentieth century, structuralism was something of an intellectual epidemic, transmitted from scholar to scholar across the humanities and social sciences, mutating slightly in each new host. The epidemic has an identifiable patient zero: the Russian linguist and literary theorist Roman Jakobson (1896–1982). Although there are prior attestations of 'structuralism', it was Jakobson who first used the term in the relevant modern sense, and whose usage spread through contact with his colleagues.[1] In 1929 Jakobson wrote:

> Were we to comprise the leading idea of present-day science in its most various manifestations, we could hardly find a more appropriate designation than *structuralism*. Any set of phenomena examined by contemporary science is treated not as a mechanical agglomeration but as a structural whole, and the basic task is to reveal the inner, whether static or developmental, laws of this system.
>
> (Jakobson 1971 [1929]: 711; Jakobson's italics)

This quotation comes from an article Jakobson published in the popular press reporting on the First International Conference of Slavic Philology. At this conference the Prague Linguistic Circle, of which Jakobson was a leading member, first strode onto the international stage as a defined group with a party line, which they set out in their 'Thèses' ('Theses'; Durnovo et al. 1929). As Jakobson states in his presentation, the central tenet of this new 'structuralism' was to treat each language as 'a structural whole', with the overarching aim of 'reveal[ing] the inner ... laws of this system'. The 'Thèses' expand on this point to assert that the best way to capture the language system is to examine it in its synchronic aspect as a means of expression appropriate to a particular communicative end. The methodological prototype embodying this conception of language and language study was the phonological research pioneered by Jakobson and his fellow Prague Circle member Nikolay Trubetzkoy

---

[1] In the early twentieth century, the term 'structuralism' was occasionally used to refer to the theories of the Anglo-American psychologist Edward B. Titchener (1867–1927; see, e.g., Angell 1907), which he developed from the doctrines of his teacher, the German philosopher and psychologist Wilhelm Wundt (1832–1920). Titchener did not use the term 'structuralism' himself; he generally referred to his own work as 'structural psychology' (e.g., Titchener 1898; 1909). This psychological 'structuralism' has no direct connection to Jakobson's later use of the term.

(1890–1938).[2] The centrepiece of their approach to phonology was phonemic analysis, under which the articulated sounds of a language are categorized as realizations of underlying abstract units—the 'phonemes'—whose mutually delimiting forms define the phonological structure of the language (see Trubetzkoy 1939).

But this conception of language and its related methodological innovations were not unique to the Prague Circle linguists, and indeed they did not claim any priority. The great thinker to whom the chief insights animating structuralism were attributed was the Genevese linguist Ferdinand de Saussure (1857–1913). Although Saussure is not mentioned by name in the 1929 'Thèses' of the Prague Circle, the document itself is constructed around the central theoretical pillars sustaining his 1916 *Cours de linguistique générale* (*Course in general linguistics*): the dichotomies of synchrony/diachrony, langue/parole, and the notion of value.[3] Two similar manifestos from the previous year, both authored principally by Jakobson, make explicit reference to Saussure: Tynianov and Jakobson (1928) summon Saussure in support of a programme of formalist literary analysis, while Jakobson, Trubetzkoy, and Karcevsky (1971 [1928]), in their 'Proposition' to the First International Congress of Linguists, outline an approach to phonological research described in Saussurean terms. Serge Karcevsky (1884–1955), who 'countersigned' the 'Proposition', most likely introduced Jakobson and Trubetzkoy to Saussure: he had studied from 1905 in Geneva and, although he was never enrolled in Saussure's general linguistics course, he took other courses with Saussure and was most certainly aware of Saussure's ideas about general linguistics. In 1917, Karcevsky returned to Moscow with a copy of Saussure's *Cours* in hand; the book was eagerly read within the Moscow Linguistic Circle, which had been founded by Jakobson (see Joseph 2001: 1885).

Jakobson consistently cited the inspiration he claimed to have received from Saussure, even though there are other antecedents that would seem to have had a more immediate influence on his ideas and methods. The modern concept of the phoneme and the techniques of phonemic analysis, for example, are

---

[2] Toman (1995: 144) relates an anecdote from the correspondence of Vilém Mathesius (1882–1945), the principal founder of the Prague Circle, where Mathesius recounts that the password hint for the Circle's bank account was 'The Main Area' of the Circle's interest. The solution was 'the discipline represented by N. S. T[rubetzkoy]'s name', i.e. phonology.

[3] As is well known, Saussure's *Cours* was published posthumously by his Geneva colleagues Charles Bally (1865–1947) and Albert Sechehaye (1870–1946). The published book is based on a combination of Saussure's own notes and student notes for lectures he gave in three courses on general linguistics at the University of Geneva in the period 1907 to 1911 (see Joseph 2012: 632–634).

more directly derived from the work of the Polish linguist Jan Baudouin de Courtenay (1845–1929), who shaped Russian linguistics through his teaching in Kazan and later St Petersburg (see Jakobson 1971; cf. Mugdan 1985; 2014). Indeed, there are respects in which the phonology Jakobson developed in collaboration with Trubetzkoy was incompatible with Saussurean theory. Saussure (1922 [1916]: 166) insisted that 'in language there is nothing but differences *without positive terms*'. That is, each language system is entirely abstract and self-contained; how linguistic forms are realized and even what the forms refer to in the world are completely irrelevant to the analysis of the linguistic system. Saussure would go no further than to say that phonemes are defined by their differences from one another, but Jakobson and Trubetzkoy looked at how these differences are instantiated through 'distinctive features', such as place of articulation or the presence or absence of voicing. Furthermore, in their work on 'markedness', they constructed hierarchies in which some sounds were found to be more complex and less common cross-linguistically, and learnt later by children (see Jakobson 1971 [1939]; Joseph et al. 2001: 19–26).

Deference to Saussure—despite the potentially contradictory details of their own analyses—became a shibboleth identifying structuralists. We might cite the example of Antoine Meillet (1866–1936), one of Saussure's students from the period in which he taught in Paris, who acknowledged Saussure as his master (see, e.g., the dedication 'à mon maître' in Meillet 1903 et passim). It is to Meillet (1903: 407) that we owe the first appearance in print of the famous dictum 'chaque langue forme un système où tout se tient' ('each language forms a system where everything holds together'), a declaration of the holistic nature of languages comparable to Jakobson's 1929 proclamation of structuralism. Similar displays of fealty can be found throughout the literature of the era. Even after structuralism had become endemic across the humanities and social sciences and transmogrified into myriad forms, Saussure remained a defining figure. When Jacques Derrida (1930–2004) first began to deconstruct structuralism in the 1960s, his point of departure was a close reading of Saussure's *Cours* (e.g., Derrida 1967).

Meillet's description of the nature of linguistic systems offers us a window onto the background to Saussure's thought. Although Saussure is so often cited as the great genius conceiving structuralism, his ideas did not appear out of nowhere. Meillet (1903: 407) attributed the insights underlying his dictum to Saussure's first book, the 1879 *Mémoire* on the reconstruction of the original Indo-European vowel system. At the time this book was published, Saussure was still a doctoral student of the Neogrammarians at the

University of Leipzig, and his book was generally considered a contribution to Neogrammarian scholarship (in fact, Saussure was even accused of plagiarizing his Neogrammarian teachers; see Joseph 2012: 242–247). That Meillet would locate central structuralist insights in a work that had been widely regarded as Neogrammarian in character is ironic given the way that many structuralists cast the Neogrammarians as their foil. The Neogrammarians, so it was said, took an 'atomistic' approach to languages, focusing almost exclusively on the historical development of individual sounds without an appreciation of the synchronic systems in which the sounds were embedded. This critique is implied by Jakobson in 1929 when he contrasts the 'structural whole' perceived by contemporary science to 'mechanical agglomerations'; the fact that this was directed at the Neogrammarians is made explicit elsewhere (e.g., Jakobson et al. 1928). Saussure's ideas most certainly matured between the young upstart days of the *Mémoire* and the classical doctrines of the *Cours*, but the fact that his early work could be claimed both by the Neogrammarians and the structuralists suggests that Saussure was part of a gradual intellectual transition rather than the instigator of a revolutionary break.

Espousal of system-oriented thinking accompanied by polemical contrast to the supposedly atomistic approach of previous generations was not confined to linguistics but was in fact a pattern of behaviour widespread among scientists and scholars across many fields around the turn of the nineteenth to the twentieth century. This trend was especially pronounced in biology, medicine, and psychology in the German-speaking world, where it was often—although not necessarily—bound up a with a conservative, traditionalist world view (see Harrington 1996). Even scholars in such sober sciences as physics and pure mathematics settled on the epistemological position of 'structural objectivity' (as it has been called by Daston and Galison 2007: ch. 5), an essentially Neo-Kantian view that sees objective knowledge as being anchored in our perception of the relations between things in the world, as opposed to our being able to know things in themselves. Due to the prestige of German science in this era, such positions enjoyed international currency.

Jakobson was clearly aware of this broader context when he declared in 1929 that structuralism was 'the leading idea of present-day science in its most various manifestations'. He was not alone in this opinion: Jakobson's totalizing claim was later endorsed by the Neo-Kantian philosopher Ernst Cassirer (1874–1945; see Cassirer 1945). Jakobson frequently acknowledged the inspiration he and his colleagues had received from various holistic, system-oriented schools across the arts and sciences. In the sciences, he highlighted the influence of Gestalt psychology on his thinking, and in the arts he pointed to such movements as Cubism and *zaum*, or 'transrational' poetry (see Waugh and Monville-Burston 1990: 3–5). Cubism was characterized by abstract images that sought to capture the underlying structure of the subjects depicted, while *zaum* embraced the creation of new word forms based on onomatopoeia and sound symbolism, a procedure that served to focus attention on the formal structural features of sounds in language. In christening structuralism, Jakobson therefore sought to put a name on what he saw as the guiding principle of the sciences and arts in his day, the dual commitment to holism and systemic analysis.

1.3 The spread of structuralism

Jakobson was not only the first individual to exhibit unmistakable symptoms of structuralism, but also the primary vector through which it spread to others. With the outbreak of World War II in 1939, Jakobson left Czechoslovakia for neutral Denmark, where he spent some months in close contact with the Copenhagen Linguistic Circle around Louis Hjemslev (1899–1965). The Copenhagen Circle had been founded in 1931 on the model of the Prague Circle. The members of the Copenhagen Circle understood their work to be a variety of structuralism, kindred to that of the Prague Circle's, although the Copenhagen linguists tended to formulate their ideas at a much higher level of abstraction and to concentrate on the formalization of theoretical principles (see Rischel 2001).

In 1941, Jakobson finally left Europe for New York, where he became part of the vibrant scene of émigré European intellectuals in that city, and where he taught at the École Libre des Hautes Études, a Francophone university in exile hosted by the New School for Social Research and funded principally by the Rockefeller Foundation. One attentive listener in Jakobson's lectures was another exile academic, the French anthropologist Claude Lévi-Strauss (1908–2009), who adapted the methods of linguistic structuralism that he learnt from Jakobson to ethnography. In his doctoral thesis, which he defended in Paris in 1948 and published in 1949 as *Les structures élémentaires de la parenté* (*The elementary structures of kinship*; Lévi-Strauss 1969 [1949]), Lévi-Strauss applied structural analysis to the classical ethnographic topic of kinship. In the following years, Lévi-Strauss extended his structuralism to annex all of anthropology; the ultimate codification of his theory is his 1958 *Anthropologie structurale* (Lévi-Strauss 1974 [1958]; English trans.: *Structural Anthropology*, Lévi-Strauss 1963 [1958]). Lévi-Strauss' example was emulated by French scholars in psychology, literary studies, and history to the point that structuralism of one stripe or another became the theoretical foundation of the Francophone humanities and social sciences, with an influence felt internationally (see Dosse 1997 [1991]; 1997 [1992]).

After World War II, Jakobson stayed in the United States, eventually becoming a professor at Harvard University. In this capacity, he continued to develop and propagate his brand of structuralism in America. But there was an existing tradition of 'American structuralism', a label that became established especially in the wake of Hymes and Fought's (1981) history of American linguistics in the first half of the twentieth century (cf. Matthews 1993). The American structuralists—led by such figures as Franz Boas (1858-1942), Boas' student Edward Sapir (1884-1939), and Leonard Bloomfield (1887-1949)—occupied themselves principally with the description of the languages of North and South America. To this end, they employed—like their European counterparts—a methodology that had crystallized around the central concept of the phoneme and from there was extended to other aspects of language. Their focus on indigenous American languages invited synchronic analysis, since the vast majority of these languages had had no written form before the European colonial invasions of the modern era and therefore no historical sources for philologists to pore over. As outsiders peering in on languages very different from those built on the familiar 'Standard Average European' model—as it was dubbed by Sapir's student Benjamin Lee Whorf (1897-1941; 1956 [1939]: 138)—the American structuralists had a natural affinity for seeing languages as patterned formal systems. Their task was always to decipher these wholly foreign languages from externally observable clues; they could never rely on their own linguistic intuitions. The penchant for formal analysis became particularly marked in the work of Bloomfield and his followers, who spurned any speculation about 'meaning' or other intangible aspects of language, a form of radical empiricism inspired and supported by their commitment to behaviourist psychology. Bloomfield (e.g., 1933: 139-157) advocated postponing the study of meaning until an imagined future time when science would be more advanced and meaning could be rendered tractable in behaviourist terms (cf. McElvenny 2018a: 156-159).

The Bloomfieldian school came to dominate academic linguistics in America up until the mid-twentieth century, when it was swept away by the so-called 'Chomskyan Revolution', which established the paradigm of generative grammar. In a nutshell, Noam Chomsky (b. 1928) rejected the hyperempiricist, inductive approach of the Bloomfieldians and argued that linguists should turn their attention to the putative mental processes underlying language. He advocated a method of linguistic research that relied on introspection to uncover native speakers' intuitions about the grammatical forms of their languages. Chomsky's call was heard not only in linguistics but also in psychology and other sciences concerned with the human mind, and precipitated the abandonment of the behaviourists' dogmatic empiricism in favour of the more liberal methodology of the modern cognitive sciences. Despite these seismic shifts in outlook, Chomsky and his most loyal followers maintained a single-minded focus on the formal structures of languages to the exclusion of meaning (see Harris 2021).

Whether or not Chomsky's innovations constituted a real revolutionary break or were merely a step in the steady evolution of American structuralism is a controversial matter (cf., e.g., Hymes and Fought 1981; Matthews 1993; Newmeyer 1996). In the broader international context, the emergence of the generative school is of interest because it represents in part a recombination of the European and American strains of structuralism. Morris Halle (1923–2018), Chomsky's collaborator in the development of generative grammar, had been a student of Jakobson's, and Jakobson remained in close contact with Chomsky and Halle after they had established their academic base at the Massachusetts Institute of Technology. Whatever the novelties and nuances of Chomsky's linguistics, he still held the terminological torch of structuralism aloft. His 1957 book introducing the generative paradigm bore the title *Syntactic Structures*.

The role of Saussure as disciplinary totem was less prominent—but not absent—in American structuralism (cf. Falk 2004). Bloomfield (1924: 318), for example, in his review of the second edition of Saussure's *Cours*, cast Saussure not as the great genius who ushered in the modern age of linguistic science but merely as the competent summarizer of the latest ideas in linguistics: 'Most of what [Saussure] says has long been "in the air" and has been here and there fragmentarily expressed; the systematization is his own'. However, in a letter from 1945, Bloomfield vented his irritation at his colleagues' belief that he had not adequately incorporated Saussurean thinking into his 1933 magnum opus *Language*: 'There is a statement going round that de Saussure is not mentioned in my *Language* text book (which reflects his *Cours* on every page)' (quoted in Cowan 1987: 29). Although Chomsky (1966) constructed a genealogy for generative grammar that incorporated such diverse forebears as René Descartes (1596–1650), the Port-Royal grammarians (Arnauld and Lancelot 1660), and Wilhelm von Humboldt (1767–1835), Saussure remained a central point of reference, whether as illustrious ancestor or straw man. The fluctuating status of Saussure in Chomsky's estimation is most visible in his treatment of the Saussurean notions of *langue* and *parole*: over the years,

Chomsky has tried variously to assimilate and supersede Saussure's notions with his own 'competence' and 'performance', and their later equivalents 'I-language' and 'E-language' (see Joseph 1990).

The narrative recounted here in sections 1.2 and 1.3 constitutes the core backstory of structuralism, and allows us to delineate its shape as an intellectual movement. Structuralism began in early twentieth-century linguistics, but it was not confined to this discipline: it grew out of a more general holistic attitude that was widespread in this era, and its central tenets and methods were rapidly taken up and adapted by scholars working in other humanities and social sciences. Continually evolving as it spread from field to field, structuralism exhibited a dizzying variety of characteristics. At the very least, however, we can identify apparent constants in the understanding of phenomena as realizations of systems where *tout se tient* and the accompanying performative invocation of Saussure. With these attributes in mind, we now turn to the task of trying to find the limits of structuralism.

1.4 About this volume

Each of the primary sources around which the following chapters are based presents a challenge to received ideas about where the conceptual and temporal boundaries of structuralism lie. The volume is divided into two main parts. The first part revolves around three texts that attempt to harness the tools of the European grammatical tradition in order to render tractable the radically different structures of non-European languages and, ultimately, to produce a scientifically valid classification of those languages. In the course of these efforts, the texts pave the way for the core structuralist insight that languages are internally structured wholes, which are most profitably examined from a synchronic perspective. We see hints of this insight both well before the structuralist period in the 1838 study 'On the grammatical character of the languages of North America' (Chapter 2) by the French polymath Peter Stephen Du Ponceau (1760–1844) and in the early years of American structuralism in the 1920 'The classification of American languages' (Chapter 3) by Franz Boas. Located temporally between these two contributions, on the eve of the structuralist era, is the 1894 'Typology of languages – a new task of linguistics' (Chapter 4) by the German sinologist and general linguist Georg von der Gabelentz (1840–1893). Gabelentz' essay establishes a proto-structuralist basis for the classification of the world's languages and, in the process, anticipates key elements of the present-day subfield of typology.

The second part of the volume contains four texts from the periphery of European structuralism that re-assess ideas typically taken to be core tenets of the movement. Antoine Meillet's 1912 'The evolution of grammatical forms' (Chapter 5) examines how innovations might enter the system of a language; his answer gives us both the modern term *grammaticalisation* ('grammaticalization') and the foundations of the contemporary approach that the term designates. Roman Jakobson's 1931 'The Eurasian language union' (Chapter 6) offers the most extensive presentation of Jakobson's theory of the Eurasian language area, which occupied an important but underappreciated place in his thought and greatly influenced his contributions to structuralist theory. Louis Hjelmslev's 1933 'General structure of linguistic correlations' (Chapter 7) investigates the oppositional nature of morphemic categories and develops a theory of 'markedness' distinct from that of Jakobson and Trubetzkoy. Finally, the 1968 'Structure of language and structure of society' (Chapter 8) by Émile Benveniste (1902–1976), a student of Meillet's, delves into the enduring structuralist conundrum of whether it is legitimate to postulate a connection between a language and the society of those who speak it. Benveniste's study points out the difficulties inherent in structuralists' longing for the pristine, self-contained linguistic system.

The primary sources showcased in this volume have been selected not only for their usefulness in identifying and critiquing the features of structuralism, but also because of their relative inaccessibility to the mainstream of present-day English-speaking scholars and the resulting lack of attention they have received. Although several of the texts are occasionally cited today as waypoints on the path to contemporary concerns, none is read as closely and understood as deeply as it deserves. The majority of the texts were originally written in French, German, or Russian and appear here for the first time in English translation. In addition to the potential difficulty represented by the languages of the texts, the conceptual schemes in terms of which they are framed often rely on assumptions quite different from those that pertain in current linguistics and allied sciences. The introductory essays and critical notes assist present-day readers in understanding the texts and in bridging the conceptual gap between past and present views. To enable easy comparison with the original texts, in most chapters the corresponding page numbers in the original sources have been inserted in square brackets. The one exception is Hjelmslev's text in Chapter 7, the original of which is divided up into short numbered sections, each consisting of a few paragraphs. Our translation reproduces this structure.

2
'Primitive structures', polysynthesis, and Peter Stephen du Ponceau

*Floris Solleveld**

2.1 Introduction

The *Mémoire sur le Système grammatical des Langues de quelques Nations Indiennes* (1838) by Peter Stephen du Ponceau (1760–1844) has the curious distinction of being widely recognized as a canonical text in the history of Americanist linguistics (and of linguistics in general) without ever having been translated into English.[1] Du Ponceau's work stands out as the first comparative and theoretical study of Native American languages based on substantial empirical material and grammatical analysis; it forcefully argued that the structure of these languages was anything but 'primitive', and that they belonged to a distinctive type of languages, which Du Ponceau called 'polysynthetic'. On these grounds, Du Ponceau can be said to have brought the study of Native American languages to a higher level, and although his central hypothesis that *all* indigenous languages of the Americas have a 'polysynthetic' character has not stood the test of time, *polysynthesis* is still a current—although not undisputed—notion in linguistic typology (Fortescue, Mithun, and Evans 2017).

Du Ponceau's *Mémoire* was the culmination of two decades of collecting and corresponding, editing and publishing from the moment, in 1815, that Du Ponceau, as acting President of the American Philosophical Society in Philadelphia (APS), installed a Historical and Literary Committee there. Throughout, he relied on earlier missionary linguistic work. Observations on the grammatical complexity of specific North American languages

---

* Research for this article was supported by a Postdoctoral Fellowship of FWO Research Foundation—Flanders

[1] A reprint of the French text was published in Leopold (1999). Du Ponceau's *Mémoire* was, however, not included in the thirteen-volume Routledge reprint series *Origins of American linguistics, 1643–1914*, apparently because of the fact it was written in French.

Floris Solleveld, *'Primitive structures', polysynthesis, and Peter Stephen du Ponceau*. In: *The Limits of Structuralism*. Edited by James McElvenny, Oxford University Press. © Floris Solleveld (2023).
DOI: 10.1093/oso/9780192849045.003.0002

had been made by several seventeenth- and eighteenth-century missionaries, such as John Eliot (c. 1604–1690) for Massachusett (Eliot 1666; 1822), Hans Egede (1686–1758) for Greenlandic (Egede 1745), and David Zeisberger (1721–1808) for Onondaga and Lenape (Zeisberger 1827). Along with these, the most important sources used by Du Ponceau and his APS associate, John Pickering (1777–1846) were the information supplied by Du Ponceau's correspondent, the Moravian missionary John Heckewelder (1743–1823), the grammars summed up in Johann Christoph Adelung and Johann Severin Vater's overview of the languages of the world, *Mithridates* (4 in 6 vols., 1806–1817), and the remnants of an earlier collection by the previous APS President, Thomas Jefferson (1743–1826). Du Ponceau's contribution to the study of Native American languages was as a theorist and compiler rather than as an observer: he did not engage in anything that we would now call 'fieldwork', and his contact with Native Americans was brief.

The most important conclusions of Du Ponceau's linguistic research were already presented in his first report to the Historical and Literary Committee (Du Ponceau 1819), along with a list of sources, his correspondence with Heckewelder, and a long ethnographic account and Lenape vocabulary by the latter (Heckewelder 1819a; 1819b). After weighing this evidence, and taking 'a bird's eye view', the three propositions that Du Ponceau 'submitted to the investigation of the learned' were the following:

1. That the American languages in general are rich in words and in grammatical forms, and that in their complicated construction, the greatest order, method, and regularity prevail.
2. That these complicated forms, which I call *polysynthetic*, appear to exist in all those languages, from Greenland to Cape Horn.
3. That these forms appear to differ essentially from those of the ancient and modern languages of the old hemisphere. (Du Ponceau 1819: xxiii)

Du Ponceau defined the 'polysynthetic construction of language' as 'that in which the greatest number of ideas are comprised in the least number of words' (Du Ponceau 1819: xxx); it meant that entire phrases could be expressed in single compound expressions, and that these compound terms were not simply strings of words glued together. That the major native languages of the East Coast and Great Lakes area exhibited such features was well attested by the materials Du Ponceau possessed at that point. That they occurred 'from Greenland to Cape Horn' was more of a stretch; between the writing and the printing of his *Mémoire*, Du Ponceau had already encountered a perceived anomaly in Otomí (López Yepes 1826; Du Ponceau 1838a:

86n). Whether 'polysynthesis' marked a separate and 'essentially different' type of language structure remained subject to debate. Most prominently, Wilhelm von Humboldt (1767–1835), who was collecting materials about the languages of the Americas at the same time and on a similar scale, and with whom Du Ponceau corresponded, never accepted this third point (Verlato 2013: 44ff).

The existence of Du Ponceau's 1819 report in part explains why his 1838 *Mémoire* has gone untranslated. If Americanist linguistics needs an equivalent of William Jones' (1746–1794) foundational 'philologer passage' about the kinship between Sanskrit and European languages (Jones 1787: 422–423), it is in these three points, upon which the *Mémoire* elaborates two decades later. But as a contribution to linguistic theory, Du Ponceau's *Mémoire* is arguably a much richer text than the 1819 report. It makes a number of arguments which are interesting with regard to later developments in American and structuralist linguistics. First, it outlines a comparative approach to languages of what Western scholars then regarded as 'people without history' (Wolf 1982), languages which had no earlier written record—a linguistic approach which could be called 'synchronic' in its attention to structure and function. Second, it makes important observations about phonetic differentiation, that is, which differences between sounds make a difference in meaning and are perceived and distinguished as such by speakers. And third, it advances a theory about the relation between language and thought in which words do not denote ideas, but rather evoke thought complexes which are then differentiated further.

The question is what to make of these analogies. It would be anachronistic to describe Du Ponceau's linguistic ideas as structuralist. Although there is a trail of direct personal and intellectual connections linking Du Ponceau to twentieth-century American structuralism via Horatio Hale (1817–1896), Franz Boas (1856–1942), and Edward Sapir (1884–1939), that is not how these ideas travelled. And while the synchronic perspective of structuralist linguistics was, in its American version, linked to the systematizing of fieldwork and the lack of ancient texts in indigenous languages, what Du Ponceau outlined a century earlier was a comparative approach, not a proto-structuralist theory about sound systems and systems of signs. Ironically enough, Sapir (1921), in one of the central texts of American structuralism, rejected the notion of 'polysynthetic languages' as a separate category. Still, the analogies are there and they are non-trivial, and by seeing Du Ponceau's ideas in their own time we can assess them better as an episode in the history of linguistic thought.

This introductory essay traces the sources, development, and reception of Du Ponceau's linguistic ideas, drawing upon the work of Swiggers (1994; 1998; 1999), Gray (1999), Harvey (2015), Verlato (2013), and Andresen (1990). This also entails emphasizing the less 'modern' elements of Du Ponceau's linguistic thought. Important aspects of the *Mémoire* are a response to and reformulation of French debates from the mid-eighteenth to early nineteenth century about general grammar, the origin of language, the relation between language and thought, and the 'science of ideas' (*idéologie*), similar to how most of Du Ponceau's data are a reformulation of seventeenth- and eighteenth-century missionary linguistic work. Contemporary German scholarship, apart from Humboldt and *Mithridates*, had less influence on Du Ponceau; foundational figures of historical-comparative grammar like Bopp, Grimm, and the Schlegel brothers are not even mentioned. As an *émigré* who had left France before the Revolution, and a younger associate of the American founding fathers, Du Ponceau was distinctly a man of the late Enlightenment.

For reasons of space, the translation only covers chapters I-IX of Du Ponceau's *Mémoire*, the most theoretical part. It leaves out the bulk of the work, Du Ponceau's comparative grammar of Algonquian languages, as well as the appended comparative vocabularies and the lengthy preface. It is in these other parts that we can see how Du Ponceau positioned himself and how he worked with the materials available to him. This introduction will address these matters in a more condensed form; additionally, it discusses Du Ponceau's ideas about phonetic differentiation and the relation between language and thought as they occur in chapters I-IX as well as in Du Ponceau's article on English phonology (1818) and his *Dissertation on the Nature and Character of the Chinese System of Writing* (1838). Other texts by Du Ponceau that it draws upon, apart from the 1819 report and its appendices, are his edition of Eliot's *Grammar of the Massachusetts Indian Language* (with John Pickering, 1822) and his translation of Zeisberger's Lenni Lenape grammar (Zeisberger 1827).

2.2 Du Ponceau and the afterlives of the French Enlightenment

Du Ponceau's *Mémoire* originated as a prize essay for the Prix Volney, awarded on a yearly basis by the Institut National in Paris from the legacy of Constantin-François Chassebœuf, comte de Volney (1757–1820). Volney had bequeathed to the Institut funds for contributions to the 'philosophical study of language'; Du Ponceau had made a previous, unsuccessful submission in 1825 (Robins 1999). But in setting the topic for the 1835 Volney Prize, the Institut all but commissioned an essay from Du Ponceau: *Determining the grammatical character of the North American languages known under the names of Lenni Lenape, Mohican,* and *Chippewa.* With a view to his 1819 report and subsequent activities, there were no realistic candidates other than Du Ponceau—although the eccentric naturalist and polymath Constantine Rafinesque (1783–1840) made an attempt (Boewe 1999).

At the time of writing the *Mémoire,* Du Ponceau was at a certain distance from French debates both physically and mentally. He had left France aged seventeen in 1777 to join the American War of Independence as an aide-de-camp to Baron von Steuben (1730–1794), and was now something of an elder statesman in the United States. His French comes off as archaic and circuitous even by nineteenth-century standards, and his sentence construction is very repetitive—which indicates that Du Ponceau was not using his mother tongue very actively anymore in the 1830s. But there are four clear references to French influences in the *Mémoire.* First, it opens with a reference to Enlightenment polymath Pierre-Louis Moreau de Maupertuis (1698–1759), who had advocated studying the idioms of 'remote peoples' which were based on a different 'scheme of ideas' (*plan d'idées*) (Maupertuis 1752 [1740]: 256). Second, there is the influence of his mentor, Antoine Court de Gébelin (1719–1784), to whom he devotes kind words in his introduction. Third, there is his criticism of *grammaire générale* as an impossible universalist pursuit. And fourth, there is Du Ponceau's use of 'ideology' as a header to the 'purely grammatical part' of his *Mémoire,* which links him to the revolutionary-era group of intellectuals called *Idéologues* to whom Volney belonged. All four will be discussed in this section.

Maupertuis had been among the first to address the problem of the origin of language without reference to God, Eden, and Babel, turning it into a problem of how early humans could form ideas from sensations, link them to sounds, and communicate with each other. This was an important step in the history of linguistic thought, as the debate expanded rather quickly in the following decades. In his *Réflexions philosophiques sur l'Origine des Langues et la Signification des Mots* (published 1752, privately printed 1740[?]), Maupertuis argued that signs initially served to distinguish between different sensations, e.g. *I see a tree* vs. *I see a horse,* but also to make comparisons and generalizations, giving rise to complex expressions—and there were different ways of doing so. It followed that there was 'much arbitrariness' in how signs designated different parts of perceptions, and that 'remote nations' could have built their language on principles radically different from ours (Maupertuis 1752 [1740]: 363).

Court de Gébelin was the author of the unfinished, nine-volume *Monde primitif analysé et comparé avec le Monde moderne* (1773–1782), a highly speculative and rather esoteric work in which he sought to reconstruct the universal language and self-evident, pictographic alphabet of the Ancients. Du Ponceau had been his secretary at age sixteen to seventeen after quitting seminary to try his luck in Paris (Dunglinson 1844: 6–8); and although he did not share Gébelin's 'philological opinions' about 'the primitive language' (Dunglinson 1844: 8), it was Gébelin who introduced him to comparative philology, and from whom he derived the idea that 'primitives' and their languages are not all that primitive. For all its esotericism, *Monde Primitif* was also an Enlightenment project to eradicate false ideas by tracing back words to their natural meanings; and although Gébelin's Greek, Latin, and Hebrew etymologies were largely spurious, that project also involved a taxonomy of language families, the identification of sound shift laws, and a description of the speech organs. On these points, Gébelin can count as a pioneer in the comparative study of language, even if his laws and taxonomies themselves are somewhat arbitrary (cf. Auroux, Boes, and Porset 1981); Edelstein (2010) portrays Gébelin as a key example of what he calls the 'super-Enlightenment', where freethinking drifts off into mysticism.

Grammaire générale was a genre of grammar that sought to analyse the universal logical structure of language, and that put forward the 'science' of general grammar in contrast to the 'art' of mastering a language. The model for the universal logical structure of grammar, unsurprisingly, was French and Latin grammar; it had been so since the foundational *Grammaire générale et raissonnée* or 'Port-Royal Grammar' of Arnauld and Lancelot (1660). In the Cartesian didactic programme of the school of Port-Royal, general grammar likewise served the purification of thought through the expression of clear and distinct ideas and the eradication of wrong ideas. So it did, with a different agenda, in the philosophical curriculum of Étienne Bonnot de Condillac (1714–1780; see Condillac 1775), in the chapters on grammar in the *Encyclopédie* (cf. Auroux 1973), and in the volume on 'universal and general grammar' in *Monde Primitif*. What Du Ponceau (1838a: 53ff) rejects in general grammar is the idea of a grammatical system applicable to all languages, a notion that is unsustainable after comparing the languages of the new and the old worlds. In this regard, it has to make way for comparative grammar, a new, 'beautiful', and 'sublime' science which is only beginning to take shape (Du Ponceau 1838a: 53ff). However, the two are not wholly incommensurable: one could make a general grammar that applies with some exceptions to a certain class or type of languages, and then compare these different types (Du Ponceau 1838a: 54). Phenomena such as polysynthesis, and also dual and trial as they occur in Polynesian languages, are equally part of general grammar and therefore general or philosophical grammar should be refashioned accordingly (Du Ponceau 1838a: 156). What Du Ponceau retains, then, is the notion of a logical structure of language as well as grammar as a means for the clarification of ideas.

Idéologie was a term coined by the French philosopher Antoine Destutt de Tracy (1754–1836) to denote the 'science of ideas', which was at the heart of his programme to reorganize education and the sciences after the Revolution (Destutt de Tracy 1798). The term 'ideology' therefore meant something different for Destutt de Tracy and his associates, the *Idéologues*, as well as for Du Ponceau than it does now. Ideology, as Destutt de Tracy understood it, was an analysis of the relation between ideas and signs and of the associations between ideas. As such, it went back to Condillac and his theory about the origin of human knowledge (Condillac 1746). In the curriculum proposed in Destutt de Tracy's *Élémens d'Idéologie* (1801–1805), 'ideology' was part of a new *trivium* together with general grammar and logic; but the programme of the *Idéologues* also extended to the physical and anthropological study of man, political economy, linguistics, and the history of philosophy. At the Institut National, created to replace the old Royal academies, they dominated the section of Moral and Political Sciences until it was abolished by Napoleon in 1803. Largely neglected by modern historians, they contributed significantly to shaping the 'social sciences', another neologism of the period (Gusdorf 1978). It is in line with the wider programme of *idéologie* that Du Ponceau (1838a: 12) defines the science of language as 'the history of the progress and development of the human mind'.

Du Ponceau's indebtedness to Maupertuis and the *Idéologues* is clear from his prolonged discussion of the relation between signs and ideas, starting from his definition of polysynthesis as 'the greatest number of ideas ... comprised in the least number of words' and ideology as 'the comparative study of the grammatical forms and idiomatic constructions of languages, by which we are taught to analyse and distinguish the different shapes in which ideas combine themselves in order to fix perceptions in our minds, and transmit them to those of others' (Du Ponceau in Zeisberger 1827: 13). This relation between signs and ideas, Du Ponceau argued eloquently in the chapter 'On the Formation of Languages', is far from straightforward:

> It is said that languages are made to express our ideas. They do not express them at all, they evoke them and render them present to our imagination. All our ideas are complex and infinitely divisible; they present themselves *en masse* to the mind[.]
>
> (Du Ponceau 1838a: 80)

But this does not imply that language is lacking in logical structure; rather, Du Ponceau infers from this that language structure is the result of a process of disambiguation for the sake of mutual understanding that occurs in the early stage of the formation of languages. Once established, this structure is virtually inalterable; which is why the languages of India and China are completely different in structure even after millennia of contact. What the languages of the Americas have shown to Du Ponceau is a completely different way of structuring linguistic expressions, one that is equally regular as the structure of Berber, Chinese, French, Latin, or Italian, and yet equally dependent upon the impulses of those who shaped the language in its early stages as well as upon 'climate and other local circumstances' (Du Ponceau 1838a: 84). This conjectural history of the formation of languages comes almost verbatim from Maupertuis (1752 [1740]), with the important difference that Du Ponceau does not presume an initial state of simplicity and one-to-one correspondences; instead, he assumes that languages, like the world, started in chaos (Du Ponceau 1838a: 120).

Polysynthetic languages are one part of Du Ponceau's argument about the relation between language and thought; the other, hinted at in the *Mémoire* and elaborated in more detail in his *Dissertation* on the Chinese writing system, are monosyllabic languages. The leading argument in Du Ponceau (1838b) is that Chinese characters represent words, not ideas, contrary to what Chinese literati professed and European scholars from Fréret (1718) and Amiot (1776) to Abel-Rémusat (1822) had propounded. As a consequence, the Chinese writing system was not a 'philosophical alphabet' but a way of registering a spoken language, like every other writing system. Du Ponceau came to this insight after being presented with a manuscript Vietnamese-French vocabulary and Vietnamese-Latin dictionary (attributed to the Catholic missionary Joseph Morrone, published in Du Ponceau 1838b: 124–375) and seeing how Chinese characters—in which Vietnamese was written—were used for words with different meanings, while Chinese words functioned as loan words.

Both in the *Mémoire* and in the *Dissertation*, then, Du Ponceau was formulating his insights about the relation between signs and ideas with reference to eighteenth-century debates while drawing upon previously unpublished material about non-European languages. By 1838 both the question about the origin of language and the idea of a 'philosophical alphabet' were increasingly rejected as unscientific—the latter also by Du Ponceau (1838a: 25ff; 1838b: 13n)—but that does not diminish the value of Du Ponceau's insights.

By severing a one-to-one link between words and ideas Du Ponceau was effectively studying language as an autonomous structure in which one had to identify the elements that made a difference in meaning.

2.3 Du Ponceau's data and the reformulation of missionary linguistics

In spite of these theoretical reflections, Du Ponceau was more empirically than theoretically inclined. The linguistic work that he admired most was *Mithridates*, Adelung and Vater's collection of translations of the Lord's Prayer and other linguistic data about c. 500 languages and dialects, 'the most astonishing philological collection that the world has ever seen' (Du Ponceau 1819: xix) which 'caused a revolution in the science of language' (Du Ponceau 1838a: 5). He defended missionary linguists who knew indigenous languages firsthand and 'had other things to do than reasoning philosophically' (Du Ponceau 1838a: 48), publishing significant amounts of missionary linguistic work by Eliot, Heckewelder, Zeisberger, and the otherwise obscure Father Morrone to accompany his treatises. Throughout his work, he criticized a priori reasoning about the presumed primitiveness, poverty (De Pauw 1768: I, 140), and irregularity (Monboddo 1773: 347ff) of Native American languages or the lack of abstract terms in them.

> We are now occupied with the search for facts; slowly the veil of illusions that ignorance has given birth to is being lifted, and we are preparing for positive discoveries which a strict logic can extract from the accumulated facts. But the time for positive inductions has not yet arrived; as more facts come to light, they press around us and seem to invite the formation of hypotheses about the origin and formation of human language. But theories and hypotheses have been abused too much already; we need to take pause for a while and continue to assemble facts, and moreover to ascertain them well.
>
> (Du Ponceau 1838a: 49)

Most of the 'accumulated facts' had reached Du Ponceau via Europe, particularly through *Mithridates*. This was largely a critical compilation from previously published sources but contained significant new information about the languages of the Americas. That information mainly stemmed from Alexander von Humboldt (1769–1859), who had collected missionary grammars and vocabularies during his 1799–1804 explorations in Latin America, and from Lorenzo Hervás y Panduro (1735-1809), who had gathered linguistic material from the Jesuit exile community in Italy for his encyclopaedic *Idea dell'Universo* (21 vols, 1778-1787). Before being used by Vater for vols III.2-3 of *Mithridates*, Alexander von Humboldt's collection had already inspired Schlegel (1808) to make a fundamental distinction between 'inflecting' and 'agglutinating' languages and to formulate the notion of 'comparative grammar'. While Hervás only published vocabularies, numerals, and Lord's Prayers in the five linguistic volumes of *Idea dell'Universo*, transcripts of nine grammars obtained by Hervás had reached Vater via the elder Humboldt brother, Wilhelm.

The great advantage that Du Ponceau had over Vater and Wilhelm von Humboldt was the detailed information provided by Heckewelder, from whom he also obtained Zeisberger's exceptionally rich Lenape grammar and seven-volume, 2,367-page Onondaga lexicon along with other manuscripts (Du Ponceau 1819: xlvii-l). Still, Vater and especially Humboldt had enough information about regular, highly intricate word formation in a range of American languages to make the same 'inductions' as Du Ponceau. Humboldt, moreover, had intended to write his own linguistic *magnum opus* about American languages until his attention turned to Malayo-Polynesian in the mid-1820s (Trabant 2012); like Du Ponceau's work, much of his linguistic project revolved around the reformulation of missionary linguistic works.

And yet, Humboldt and Du Ponceau arrived at opposite interpretations of the same grammatical structures. What Du Ponceau called polysynthesis was not a 'veritable grammatical form' for Humboldt (1824), since it did not effect a real 'synthesis' between different elements but rather concatenated and compressed them; he saw it as a particular kind of agglutination ('incorporating': Humboldt 1998 [1836]: I, §23).[2] The difference in interpretation is not due to any lack of information or of grammatical insight, and indeed the *status aparte* of polysynthesis is disputable, but Du Ponceau is right in blaming a certain philosophical prejudice on Humboldt's side (Du Ponceau in Zeisberger 1827: 16). For Humboldt, Sanskrit exemplified the most perfect form of grammatical synthesis, and at the opposite end of the typological spectrum, Chinese represented a different type of 'condensed clarity of expression'; American (and Semitic) languages had a 'less perfect structure' (Humboldt 1998 [1836]: I, §§23-24).

---

[2] For noun incorporation as an aspect of polysynthesis and as a phenomenon in North American languages, see Kilarski (2021: 48-59).

Du Ponceau first used the term 'polysynthetic' in a letter to Heckewelder dated 30 August 1816, thanking him for further details on Lenape morphology:

> [A]s far as my researches have extended, I have found those forms in all the Indian languages from Greenland to Cape Horn. The venerable Eliott's Grammar shews that they exists in the idiom of the New England Tribes, which is believed to be that of the Natick tribe. Crantz [1765] and Egede [1745] prove in the most incontrovertible manner that the language of Greenland is formed on the same *syntactic* or *polysynthetic* model. So are the various dialects of Mexico, as far as I can judge from the Grammars of those languages that are in our Society's library. Indeed, the authors of those Grammars are the first who have noticed the personal forms of the Indian verbs and have given them the name of *transitions*. I find from Father Breton's Grammar and Dictionary of the Caribbee language [Breton 1665; 1667], that those forms also exist in that idiom, and the Abbé Molina, in his excellent History of Chili [Molina 1808 (1776/1787)], has shewn that the Auracanian belongs to the same class of languages.
>
> (Heckewelder and Du Ponceau 1819: 430)

What Du Ponceau meant by 'polysynthesis' was not merely compound words that contain multiple ideas or even entire sentences, such as Lenape *wulamalessohalian* 'thou who makest me happy' or Greenlandic *aulisariartorasuarpok* 'he hastened to go fishing'. This, after all, also occurs in European languages, as in Italian *nolo* 'I do not know' or Latin *morituri* 'those who are about to die', to cite some of Du Ponceau's favourite examples. What made American languages *poly*-synthetic is that they used various forms of synthesis from inflections, particles, affixes, suffixes, and 'linking meaningful particles' to 'inserting syllables and sometimes single letters, to the effect that they awaken an idea of the expression of which that letter made part' (Du Ponceau 1838a: 89). This meant that they shared features with Latin and Greek (inflection), Hebrew and Coptic (particles, affixes), and Chinese ('linking meaningful particles'); but the feature that interested Du Ponceau most was 'ellipsis', here understood as systematically leaving out parts of words.

Ellipsis is the recurrent feature in a range of sample words in Greenlandic, Chilean (Mapuche), Lenape, Massachusett, and Chippeway that Du Ponceau dissects in chapters IV ('General Character of the American Languages', Du Ponceau 1838a: 89–96) and XI ('Formation of Words in Algonquin Languages', Du Ponceau 1838a: 115–147). For example, Lenape *pilape* 'unmarried young man' is a contraction of *pilsit* 'chaste' and *lenape* 'man', while *aulisariartorasuarpok* derives from *aulisarpok* 'he fishes', *peartorpok* 'he is about to do something', and *pinnesuarpok* 'he hastens'. This was not fundamentally different from how French abbreviated personal pronouns, articles, and negations into clitics—indeed, in doing so, the French used 'an Algonquin form' (Du Ponceau 1838a: 122)—but polysynthetic languages used this feature to much greater effect, blurring the distinctions between nouns, verbs, adjectives, adverbs, and pronouns.

One effect of these 'elliptic' contractions was that they also obfuscated the underlying grammatical regularity in declensions (Du Ponceau 1838a: chs XIII–XIV), conjugations (Du Ponceau 1838a: chs XVI–XIX), and grammatical gender (Du Ponceau 1838a: ch. XII). It was possible, Du Ponceau argued, to make oneself understood without polysynthetic forms, 'but the Indians do not like this at all: they call it *women's language*, because this is how Canadians speak who have married native wives' (Du Ponceau 1838a: 245). For the same reason, information from Indian traders and interpreters was bound to be simplified and distorted, and therefore 'they are not the proper sources from which knowledge of the grammar is to be obtained; … it is not so that Indian orators express themselves when addressing their tribes on important subjects' (Du Ponceau in Zeisberger 1827: 19). There is some inconsistency in how Du Ponceau conceives of polysynthesis in this regard. On the one hand, it is a high-prestige register cultivated by chiefs and orators, comparable to how 'Homer and Ossian could compose sublime chants when their languages were not yet written' (Du Ponceau 1838a: 245). On the other, he presents it as a make-do solution to 'say all and express everything' from an early stage of language formation (Du Ponceau 1838a: 199), of which the traces can still be seen (Du Ponceau 1838a: 159). The 'more intelligent' Chinese, by contrast, have achieved a similar elliptic effect by leaving the relations between isolated signs to be inferred, and so their language 'intimates much more than it expresses' (Du Ponceau 1838a: 199). But in both cases, the languages have been constructed with the same aim: to transmit as many ideas as rapidly as possible (Du Ponceau 1838a: 198).

Direct information from native speakers played a limited role in Du Ponceau's studies. In 1816 he had written to Heckewelder that Vater 'had not the same means of ascertaining facts that we possess in this country' (Heckewelder and Du Ponceau 1819: 431), but in total he had four or five encounters with native speakers to this end, and it is unclear whether he left Philadelphia for them. The *Mémoire* mentions 'an encounter of half a day' with the half-Ottawa missionary Abbé Hamelin (Du Ponceau 1838a: 97, 298), from whom he obtained a short Ottawa vocabulary; 'a long discussion with an intelligent and educated Iroquois' (Du Ponceau 1838a: 100, 103n) about whether a certain sound should be spelled with G or K; and a meeting with 'savage Wyandots' (Du Ponceau 1838a: 110) whom he astonished by addressing them in their own language with the help of Gabriel Sagard's *Dictionnaire de la Langue huronne* (1632). Where and when this last meeting happened is not specified ('some years ago'); it could be the same meeting that is described in more detail in his 1819 Report. There, he mentions two Wyandot (Huron) interpreters, Isaac Walker and Robert Armstrong, to whom he 'ventured to ask some questions in the Huron' and one of whom 'recited slowly and with emphasis part of a speech, by which I acquired a pretty clear idea of the modulation of the language' (Du Ponceau 1819: xxxiv–v). They provided him with 'several examples of simple and compound verbs' as well as corrections to Sagard's dictionary, which described their language, to their astonishment, as 'constantly changing' (it was familiar enough after two centuries), 'almost without rules', and 'imperfect' (Sagard 1632: 9–10). Harvey (2015: 5) quotes Du Ponceau's testimony to argue that 'Native knowledge was central to this process [of collecting linguistic information]', which is true in the tautological sense that all information ultimately stemmed from native speakers but not true for Du Ponceau specifically. A more accurate formulation is that Du Ponceau used native interlocutors in a corroborating role, to verify and supplement his written sources and to confirm the hypotheses that he had already developed.[3]

2.4 A synchronic study of language?

Du Ponceau divided his treatment of Algonquian languages into three parts: *phonology*, *etymology*, and *ideology*. Of these, 'ideology' occupies the bulk of the *Mémoire*; phonology and etymology only receive a short chapter each. Still, they represent important parts of his programme, as formulated already in his first Volney Prize essay (Du Ponceau 1999 [1825]). The main argument of the 'Phonology' chapter is that each language has its own sounds which

---

[3] Du Ponceau (1819: xxxiv) recounts a further meeting with two Chickasaw interpreters who convinced him that 'that language, as well as that of the Choctaws, is highly polysynthetic'. Du Ponceau's autobiographical letters describe a much earlier discussion, in 1778, with an Abenaki man who spoke (and sang) fluent French (Du Ponceau and Whitehead 1939: 221–223)

are difficult to pronounce for foreigners, and that Amerindian languages are no exception: the sounds that Europeans find difficult to transcribe are perfectly normal for native speakers. Their 'phonological system' is regular, but not uniform: like each European language/dialect, each Algonquian language has its own system of sounds (Du Ponceau 1838a: 102). Although this notion of a 'phonological system' is not elaborated further, it is relevant to consider it in combination with his observations about how single sounds can stand for entire words in polysynthetic constructions, as Du Ponceau does in his preface to Zeisberger's Lenni Lenape Grammar:

> There are probably principles or rules pointing out the particular parts that are to be selected in order to form the compound locution. Sometimes a whole syllable, and perhaps more; sometimes a single sound, or, as we would call it, a single letter: to discover those rules would require a great proficiency in the language, and at the same time a very sound discriminating mind; qualities which are seldom found united; perhaps also the ear, an *Indian* ear, is the guide which is generally followed; but the ear has also its rules, to which the mind imperceptibly conforms: however it may be, this is an interesting fact in the natural history of human language, justly entitled to the attention of philologists.
>
> (Du Ponceau in Zeisberger 1827: 21)

Most of the argument of the 'Phonology' chapter can already be found in Du Ponceau's first published paper, 'English Phonology', where he argued for a science of *Phonology of Language* that would 'analyse and compare [different sounds], class them according to their respective analogies, and graduate them by an accurate scale' (Du Ponceau 1818: 231). This was an interest he shared with Pickering, to whose *Essay on a Uniform Orthography for the Indian Languages of North America* (1820) he provided substantial input, as well as with Volney, who devised a similar system for the transcription of Arabic and Persian (Volney 1819) and intended the Volney Prize endowment to partly further the development of transcription systems. But unlike Pickering, whose orthography was based on the Latin alphabet (with added diacritics and Greek letters) for practical purposes, Du Ponceau recommended intentionally unfamiliar (Hebrew-like) descriptors for theoretical purposes and drew a sharp distinction between written and spoken language. Accordingly, he warned against taking 'the alphabet of any language ... as the basis of a system of its sounds; for an analysis which proceeds from the sign to the thing signified, can never produce a satisfactory result' (Du Ponceau 1818: 232). This did not imply that English orthography should be changed, because it served well enough to convey what was meant; but a universal alphabet, if not impossible, would have to represent a much larger array of 'all the sounds and shades of sounds actually existing in human language' (Du Ponceau 1818: 231). In line with this, twenty years later, Du Ponceau's *Mémoire* (1838a: 45–48) praises the Cherokee syllabary designed by Sequoyah (c. 1770–1843) not only as an impressive intellectual achievement but also as more appropriate to the spirit (*genie*) of his language than the Latin alphabet.

By 'etymology' Du Ponceau meant not only the historical origins of words, but also the interlingual affinities between them. Since there was no written record of Algonquian before the arrival of Europeans, there was little to be said about etymological derivations or 'mother tongues'; in practice, Du Ponceau's 'etymology' was about identifying language families through clusters of cognate words. This is the purpose of the appended vocabularies: Vocabulary B compares forty-five sample words in up to thirty Algonquian languages and divides these into subgroups, while Vocabulary A shows how Lenape (Algonquian) and Onondaga (Iroquoian) have no lexical similarity whatsoever. The same applies, Du Ponceau notes (Du Ponceau 1818: 87–88), for the Sioux, Eskimo, and Choctaw languages, not to mention those of Mexico and South America. This presents him with a taxonomical difficulty: grammatically all American languages would belong to the same *genre* (genus), but on a lexical level they divide into distinct families. This is a difficulty he acknowledged and left unsolved; the implicit (Linnaean) distinction between genus and family did not explain it away, since in the Indo-European languages it was purportedly the other way round, with large lexical analogies and grammatical differences (Du Ponceau 1818: 87).[4]

Throughout the nineteenth century, the mapping of Amerindian languages and their classification into distinct families was largely done on the basis of vocabularies, from Barton (1797) and Jefferson's half-destroyed collection to Powell (1891). These were, after all, much easier to produce and compare; Gallatin (1836) and Powell (1877) drew up standardized word and phrase lists to this end, distributed among agents, traders, missionaries, interpreters, etc. While Du Ponceau and Pickering edited and translated older missionary grammars, very few new grammars of Native American

---

[4] Confusingly enough, a *genus* is below a *family* in Linnaean taxonomy. A similar distinction between *règne* (grammatically related) and *famille* (lexical) is made in Balbi (1826: 6n), whereas Klaproth (1823: x) asserted the primacy of lexical over grammatical similarities (cf. Solleveld 2020a). Du Ponceau's inconsistency may stem from these sources, both of which were used and recommended by Du Ponceau (cf. Smith 1983).

languages were produced until the foundation of the Bureau of American Ethnology in 1879. Hale (1846: 533–629) extracted as much grammatical information as he could from the vocabularies of Northwest American languages he gathered during the 1838–1842 US Exploring Expedition, with only one somewhat detailed grammatical description of Sahaptin to aid him; Wilhelm von Humboldt's former secretary, Eduard Buschmann (1805–1880), was the only one to identify Amerindian language families on the basis of comparative grammar, in his work on Athapaskan and Uto-Aztecan (Buschmann 1856; 1859). Neither Hale nor Buschmann used the term 'polysynthetic'; John Wesley Powell (1834–1902), who dominated US ethnology and language documentation for decades, did not even include Du Ponceau in his list of 'Literature relating to the classification of Indian languages', ruling that 'The evidence of cognation is to be derived exclusively from the vocabulary' (Powell 1891: 11).

Theory formation about the character of Native American languages all but stalled after Du Ponceau's death. Hale published important theoretical papers in the 1880s as well as a critical edition of the *Iroquois Book of Rites* (Hale 1883a), but nothing in the decades in between; Buschmann, who set forth Humboldt's projects, was not a theorist. William Dwight Whitney (1827–1894), discussing Native American languages rather briefly in *Language and the Science of Language* (1867), turns Du Ponceau's argument about their structural complexity on its head:

> [I]t is the confident opinion of linguistic scholars that a fundamental unity lies at the base of all these infinitely varying forms of speech; that they may be, and probably are, all descended from a single parent language. For, whatever their differences of material, there is a single type or plan upon which their forms are developed and their constructions made, from the Arctic Ocean to Cape Horn; and one sufficiently peculiar and distinctive to constitute a genuine indication of relationship. This type is called the incorporative or polysynthetic. It tends to the excessive and abnormal agglomeration of distinct significant elements in its words; whereby, on the one hand, cumbrous compounds are formed as the names of objects, and a character of tedious and timewasting polysyllabism is given to the language ... and, on the other hand, and what is of yet more importance, an unwieldy aggregation, verbal or quasi-verbal, is substituted for the phrase or sentence, with its distinct and balanced members.
>
> (Whitney 1867: 348–349)

Thus, excessive complexity was turned again into a sign of primitiveness, of extremely 'changeable' languages 'unchecked by culture' and 'destitute of literature' (Whitney 1867: 347–348); Powell (1880: 69ff) made the same argument about the 'Rank of Indian Languages' more extensively yet even more dismissively. In general, with the exception of Hale (1846) and Gallatin (1848), studies of Native American languages after Du Ponceau reverted to Enlightenment notions of language reflecting levels of civilization, mixed with nineteenth-century ethnological notions about language and race (cf. Harvey 2015).

The question is, to what extent does Du Ponceau's linguistics provide a theoretical basis for a synchronic study of language? Many of his remarks—about differences in grammatical structure, the relation between signs and ideas, and 'phonological systems'—acquire a new meaning in retrospect, in the light of later theoretical developments in the late nineteenth and early twentieth century. Robins (1999: 6) argues that Du Ponceau's analysis of the Chinese writing system 'made use of two Saussurean concepts some half-century before Ferdinand de Saussure's active years, that is, the distinction between diachronic origin and synchronic function, and the arbitrariness of the linguistic sign'; Swiggers (1998: 39–40) describes Du Ponceau's typological insights into language form and word formation as 'milestones in the history of linguistic thought'. Still, Du Ponceau's synchronic approach is not defined in polemical contrast to a diachronic approach; rather, it was a matter of expediency for lack of older written sources (Du Ponceau 1838a: 106–107). It was precisely the lack of ancient texts that made Humboldt turn his attention from Amerindian to Malayo-Polynesian languages, after encountering a twelfth-century Javanese epic (Solleveld 2020b); in the report of the US Exploring Expedition, however, Hale (1846: 117–196) would show that a diachronic analysis of unwritten languages is possible by reconstructing the chronological order of Polynesian migrations through sound shifts. But then, Polynesian languages were all clearly and closely related and neatly divided over island groups. Later in life, Hale (1883b) sought to identify the oldest languages of the Algonquian, Iroquoian, Siouan, and Muskogean families based on the principle that these would be the 'most complete in form and in phonology', and then to reconstruct patterns of migration on that basis; but the problem of whether and how these families were related remained.

Horatio Hale's contributions to linguistic thought are underappreciated in their own right. His findings as the expedition's philologist/ethnologist on the US Exploring Expedition, for instance, included not only a comparative Polynesian grammar and a language map of the Pacific Northwest but also a detailed analysis of creolization in the Chinook trade jargon of the Oregon Territory (Hale 1846: 636–644; 1890). In his later work, he formulated a theory that 'the origin of linguistic stocks is to be found in what may be termed the language-making instinct of very young children' (Hale 1886: 191) and used parallel phonetic transcriptions of 'some doubtful, or intermediate pronunciations' to conclude that for some sounds not distinguished in the speaker's language, 'the difference was not in the speaker's utterance, but in the ear of the listener' (Hale 1885: 234), four years before Franz Boas' landmark paper 'On Alternating Sounds' (1889; cf. McElvenny 2019). Although there are clear debts to Du Ponceau and Pickering, who lobbied for Hale's inclusion on the US Exploring Expedition and provided him with instructions (Mackert 1994), these ideas and observations are distinctly Hale's own. The more important point, however, is that these ideas and observations were made possible by studying languages as independent structures with their own organization, emulating the work of Du Ponceau.

The genealogy can be extended further. Hale supervised Boas' fieldwork on Vancouver Island from a distance in the late 1880s; according to Gruber (1967: 32), 'Hale taught Boas how to collect linguistic data and how to use it for ethnological purposes'. Boas, in turn, trained a generation of linguist-anthropologists who contributed to the *Handbook of American Indian Languages* (1911–1941). Although Boas rather traced back his ideas about cultural relativity and the 'inner form' of language to Humboldt (Bunzl 1996; also see Chapter 3 of this volume) and rejected generalizations about 'polysynthesis' in favour of a thick description of individual languages, what became structuralism has more in common with Du Ponceau's agenda than with Humboldt's, which was historically oriented and guided by philological close reading. This does not imply that there is a linear trajectory from Du Ponceau to structuralism; rather, his work represents one parallel strand in the development of nineteenth-century linguistic thought, along with British ethnology, French orientalism, historical-comparative grammar, and the 'Humboldtian tradition'. Most of these strands were part of the reformulation of Enlightenment thought about language, culture, and the study of mankind that took place after the French revolution. And that, in turn, formed the background for the emergence of structuralism and its various strands, American and European, linguistic and anthropological.

On the grammatical character of the languages of North America, known as Lenni Lenape, Mohican, and Chippewa

Peter Stephen du Ponceau (1838)
Translated by Floris Solleveld

Facies non omnibus una
Nec diversa tamen, qualem decet esse sororum[1]

Ovid

Chapter I: Preliminary observations

In order to avoid repeating a lengthy nomenclature, we have given the Lenni-Lenape, Mohican, and Chippewa languages the name of *Algonquin Family*, to distinguish them from those of the Iroquois, Sioux, and Eskimos, and of their neighbours the Floridians. The name *Algonquin*, as well as *Iroquois*, is attested by the reports of the earliest travellers and missionaries; [76] while the Mohicans have almost entirely disappeared from the surface of the earth, and the Lenape are on the point of extinction, the Algonquin nation still exists under its old name as well as under that of the Chippewas, and is spread over a vast territory. Its language is still the means by which different Indian tribes communicate among each other today as it was two centuries ago, as related by La Hontan, Charlevoix, and all the other authors of that period.[2] It is the French of North America.[3]

Therefore we have found it convenient to conserve the old name *Algonquin*, which also has the advantage of fixity and which is not subject, like more modern names, to frequent mutations. The name *Chippewa*, which this nation

---

[1] 'Their faces were not the same, but not that different; they could be called sisters.' (*Metamorphoses* II: 13–14)
[2] Louis Armand de Lorme d'Arce, Baron de Lahontan (1666–before 1716): French explorer whose *New Voyages to North America* (1703) contain 'A Dictionary of the *Algonkine* Language'. Pierre-François-Xavier de Charlevoix S.J. (1682-1761): French Jesuit whose *History of New France* (1744) identifies three North American 'mother tongues', Sioux, Algonquin, and Huron.
[3] That is, the language of international communication.

gives to itself, has already undergone several changes in writing; it is written *Chippewa, Chippeway, Chippaway,* and a recent writer (Mr. Schoolcraft)[4] has told us that they should be called *Ojibways*.[5] The French were right to give fixed and euphonic names to Indian nations. Words, after all, are made to be understood, and not to search in them for etymologies which are always hazardous and most often false. They are made even less to imitate barbarous sounds to which neither the ears nor the organs [77] of speech are accustomed. It is good to know the names that peoples give to themselves in their own language, but it is not essential to imitate them in our own. The Greek called themselves Ἕλληνες; the Romans called them *Græci* or *Graii*. Likewise, we say *Londres* [in French] and not *London, Anvers* and not *Antwerpen,* etc., and by this means a beautiful language is not bristled up by words that nobody can pronounce.

We have observed the special recommendation made to us by the honourable institute 'to indicate, with the aid of grammatical and lexicographical comparisons, what resemblances and differences occur in the designated idioms and in the dialects that could be attached to it', and will follow this direction in our work as much as possible. To aid the lexicographic comparisons that the institute demands, we have added to this memoir an annotated Comparative Vocabulary of more than thirty languages or dialects of the Algonquin family, corresponding to forty-five words of our own language, which we have selected as those found most frequently in collections of this genre; but in spite of our efforts, we have not been able to represent all these words in each of these languages, and we would have [78] presented a lesser number, if we had selected differently. This is because each maker of vocabularies gives those words that please him, and there is no uniform system between them. We hope that the observations we have made in this section, whenever the occasion presented itself, will throw some light on the formation of these languages.

As concerns the grammatical differences which exist between these languages, we are even more at loss. All these languages seem formed according to the same model, apart from some exceptions which do not seem of too great importance. Our task would have been easier if we had to compare them with neighbouring languages, which belong to different families, like the Iroquois, for instance, or the Sioux; and even more so if the comparison had been between North and South American languages, or between those of the New and the Old World. The differences would have been more salient and easier to detect; whereas in idioms of the same family, in languages which one could call

---

[4] Henry Rowe Schoolcraft (1793–1864), geographer, geologist, explorer, and Indian agent, author of *Indian Tribes of the United States* (1851–1857). Schoolcraft's first wife, Jane Johnston (1800–1841), was half-Ojibwa.

[5] Names of tribes have been slightly altered to modern spelling, provided it is recognizably the same name.

sisters, they easily escape the eye of the observer. The greatest number of these differences are in words, and there are few between grammatical forms. What does it matter, [79] for example, that the Italian says *dico*, and the Spaniard, *digo*; that one says *dirò* and the other *diré*? That is not what matters if one does not want to learn speak a language, but only desires to know in what matter and what form it presents ideas to the mind. All the same it is good to cast a glance at the way in which words vary between languages of the same family: it throws a light on their respective formation, and helps to understand it well. Without doubt, this is what motivated the commission to demand *lexicographic* comparisons; besides, the commission may well be assured that we will do all we can to fulfil its views on all points and to merit its high approval, without which hope we would not have undertaken this task.

Chapter II: On the formation of languages

Let us get to the heart of the matter. We will not dwell at length on this chapter, no matter its appeal to us. We believe that some general reflections could be helpful for the application of what is to follow.

[80] It is said that languages are made to express our ideas. They do not express them at all, they evoke them and render them present to our imagination. All our ideas are complex and infinitely divisible; they present themselves *en masse* to the mind: *Catervatim iruunt cogitationes nostræ*.[6] They pass before us with a rapidity that nothing can describe; they change form and intermingle like kaleidoscope figures. Man would fix them as he receives them, but that is impossible; no language, no sign can produce that effect. We grasp a portion, a side, a point, and apply signs which serve to reveal the rest; this is why ellipsis dominates in human language. We make ourselves understood by what we do not say as much as by what we say. This is what makes the difference between languages, as regards the meaning of words and grammatical forms; each grasps what he can of the group of ideas that presents itself to him, and applies a word or a sign which more or less recalls to him the parts of that group. Whoever says *nolo*, for instance, has grasped all at once the idea of free will, of personality, and of negation; on the contrary, who says 'I want not' has only grasped one of these parts and used [81] his words accordingly. It must have been the same at the origin of the formation of languages. They were made as one could, initially without any system; grammatical forms have come later. All we wanted was to understand each other, and we arrived there,

---

[6] 'Our thoughts rush in troops'; probably a paraphrase from St Augustine, *Confessions* X.8:12, about memories: 'quaedam catervatim se proruunt'.

following different roads, because nature did not indicate any preference to another.

> *Opera naturale è ch'uom favella*
> *Ma, così o così, natura lascia*
> *Poi fare a voi, secondo che v'abbella.*[7]
>
> DANTE

Before a language exists, a savage who feels pressed by hunger articulates one or several sounds to which he adds visible signs. All this means: I am hungry, give me something to eat, meat, fruit. In the end, it is his need which he wants to make understood, and wants to demand means to satisfy. It is neither the idea of hunger, nor of eating, nor of meat or fruit which presents itself to the listener, but all this at once and in a confused manner, clear enough, nonetheless, to make him understand what his companion needs. It follows from this that the word which he articulated is neither a word, nor a verb, nor that which [82] we call a part of speech; it is an indicative sound, of which the general meaning is understood, but which the mind has not yet analysed, because the necessity has not yet made itself felt.

Another savage, in the same situation, either repeats the word he has heard, or invents a new one, resulting in two synonymous words. Maybe there will be three, four, or five before people are persuaded to use them with different meanings, bit by bit, but nonetheless rapidly enough, for the need to understand each other is of prime necessity. Everybody hastens, in his way, to improve the language, adding a syllable to a word, putting it either in front or behind, changing or moving a vowel or a consonant, and thereby making substantives, verbs, participles, adverbs, etc., all this without knowing exactly what they are doing; or just as well they leave the word as it is and leave it to the meaning of the phrase in which it is found to determine in what sense it has to be understood. It is largely on this latter principle that the Chinese language is formed, following the first impulse which has been given to the language by those who have first invented it.

It is not always men of genius who have invented the first languages. The man [83] of genius, civilized or savage, is generally modest and does not like to impose himself. It is rarely genius which governs human affairs; most often, mediocrity and sufficiency sit in the highest places. In all congregations of men, there is a class which one could call *makers* or *doers*;[8] persons untroubled by

---

[7] 'That man speaks is the work of nature; but to speak so or so as pleases you, nature leaves to you' (*Paradiso* XXVI: 130–132).

[8] French *faiseurs*: this means both 'makers' and 'doers'.

doubts who acquire an influence that the modest man cannot or cares not to attain. There have been such *makers* and *doers* during the infancy of peoples as there are in our days, as human nature is always the same. To these vulgar men the anomalies and irregularities which can be observed in all languages are due. We do not want to suggest that genius has not sometimes presided over their formation; the Greek language offers us too beautiful an example of the contrary, but even that has its anomalies, partly as a result of mingling with other peoples, but which one can also attribute to the insouciance of *doers* who have helped shaping it or corrupting it after it had been formed.

To be convinced of the truth of all this, one only has to observe what happens in our days: is it men of genius who have introduced in recent years a mass of barbarian terms into the French language which all its analogies, its pronunciation itself [84] repulse and which nonetheless seem destined to stay? No, without doubt, it is the *makers* of our times which the men of talent and genius have not been able to fight with success. It is not in this way that Cicero enriched the Latin language by borrowing words from the Greek.

In this way the difference between languages has been produced according to the character of those who have presided over their formation, modified to a certain point by climate and other local circumstances. This is the origin of analytic, synthetic, monosyllabic, polysyllabic languages, languages with inversions, languages in which the words follow in a more or less natural regular order, inflected languages, languages with prefixed and suffixed particles, and all that constitutes the variety observed among different idioms. The first impulse given by the first *makers* has been followed by those who succeeded them, as man is naturally more inclined to imitate than to invent; this is what gives all languages a manifest tendency to conserve the grammatical character imprinted upon them from the beginning. Chinese[9] has been monosyllabic for four millennia; [85] the languages of India, by contrast, retain the opposite character, although the peoples speaking them are neighbours. This undoubtable fact throws the clearest light upon the origin and formation of languages; but this is not the subject which should occupy us; we have said enough to *make think* those who occupy themselves with this matter, and to explain the phenomena that the languages of the American savages will present to us.

It follows from all that has been said above that chance, caprice, ignorance and a mass of social and personal circumstances have concurred in the original formation of languages and that these have necessarily differed in their

---

[9] [Note by Du Ponceau:] By *Chinese* we mean all the monosyllabic languages of East Asia.

structure and their grammatical forms; the need to understand each other has produced different ways to reach that goal.

This theory of the origin of languages has been suggested to us by the study of those of America, of which the form and the spirit, it seems to us, cannot be explained by any other system. We would have wanted to develop it further, but the design of this treatise has not permitted us; we make no further claims. A cause for the facts that we will present must well be sought. In a matter so little accessible to human intelligence, we can only [86] formulate conjectures, and in such a large field it is easy to get lost.

Chapter III: Of American languages in general

This is yet another subject on which we would like to expand; but we must restrict ourselves to the limits prescribed to us as much as possible. Nonetheless we believe not to wander too far in pointing out that the languages designated to us have common traits with all the others of this continent. When we say 'all the others' we do not mean this to be understood rigorously; it is possible that there are idioms in America which differ as much as Basque and Chinese in their grammatical forms; but if they exist, they have not yet come to our knowledge.[10] All that we know about these languages, from Greenland to Chile, bears the same character, and in all [87] this vast stretch of land, we have not yet been able to discover a single exception to the general system which we will present here.

If we consider human language as part of the natural history of man,[11] the indigenous languages of America, with respect to their structure and their forms, can be regarded as a *genus* which has its species and its varieties, but where the general traits predominate; this is not the case for their etymology. Whereas in the Old World we see, from the banks of the Ganges to the Atlantic Ocean, a mass of idioms differing among each other in grammatical form but in which the words nonetheless are so analogous that philologists have united them in one and the same class, under the denomination of Indo-Germanic or Indo-European languages, we see nothing similar on the American continent. The grammatical system everywhere resembles in the most striking way, but one should not seek verbal affinities, except between those languages that can be called sisters and belong to the same family. There are some exceptions: one

---

[10] [DP:] Since this Memoir has been written, such a language has been discovered, that of the Otomi Indians. See [*Mémoire*] Preface, 70.

[11] That is, 'anthropology' in the pre-twentieth-century sense. Also note that Du Ponceau's erstwhile mentor Antoine Court de Gébelin had written a *Histoire naturelle de la Parole* (1774).

might find in the language of the Choctaw, or in that of the Sioux, some words which seem to be of Algonquin origin, but they [88] are very few in number. The Iroquois and the Algonquins have lived a long time in close proximity to each other; they have fought long wars and have reciprocally adopted prisoners of both sexes that have lived among them. The Hurons, an Iroquois tribe, have been allied with the Algonquin tribes against their common enemies; nevertheless, comparing the languages of these two families, one would find hardly two or three words which seem derived from the same source. To prove this fact, which we find noteworthy, we have added in the appendix a Comparative Vocabulary of 250 words in the Onondaga (Iroquois) and Lenape (Algonquin) languages. We have only found a single word (which means *foot*) which seems to indicate any verbal analogy between these two language families. All the more they differ from Mexican, Chilean, or Peruvian, and yet they are all subject to the same general system of grammatical forms. We make no reflections on these remarkable facts; it is sufficient for us to indicate them.

[89] Chapter IV: General character of the American languages

The general character of the American languages consists in that they unite a great number of ideas in the form of a single word: this is why American philologists have given them the name *polysynthetic languages*.[12] This name suits them all (at least, those that we know) from Greenland to Chile, and we have been unable to find a single exception, so that we feel justified to presume that none exists. With the aid of inflections, as in Greek and Latin; of particles, affixes, and suffixes, as in Coptic, Hebrew, and the languages called Semitic; of linking meaningful particles, as in Chinese; and finally, through inserting syllables and sometimes single letters, to the effect that they awaken an idea of the expression of which that letter made part, and to which ellipsis, which makes the impression, should be added, the American Indians have arrived at forming languages which comprise the greatest number of ideas in the lowest possible number of words. By means of these procedures [90] they can change the nature of all parts of speech, make verbs into adverbs or nouns, adjectives or substantives into verbs; eventually, all authors who have written about these languages with sufficient knowledge, from North to South, affirm that, in these savage idioms, words can be made endlessly. Therefore missionaries have not been wrong to invent some with more or less skill to serve their theological explanations.

---

[12] That is, Du Ponceau himself, in his 1819 Report.

All these languages are more or less regular in their grammatical forms. Their verbs are conjugated through inflections or case endings, and a mass of accessory ideas mingled in by means of slight changes or prefixed or inserted syllables. They have rules for number and gender, and agreement between the different parts of speech; the adverbs are distinguished by their proper forms. In the end, their languages can be submitted to grammatical rules. There are irregularities in these idioms, like in ours; nonetheless, Abbé Molina affirms that there are none in the Chilean language. This seems hard to believe; still, it is possible. He adds that it is not at all divided into dialects, and that it is spoken [91] in its pure form over a vast territory. Such is not the case in the northern part of the American continent.

There are differences in the grammatical forms of these languages, but they are of a secondary nature; the polysynthetic character dominates in all. The formation of words varies according to the nature of the elements of which they are composed. One language has a large number of meaningful particles which it can unite easily; another has auxiliary particles of which the use is subject to rules; yet another takes the syllables as it finds them when it comes to forming new words. There is a noticeable difference in the formation of words between the languages of hunters, fishermen, or nomad peoples and those of sedentary Indians who have received a certain degree of civilization. The latter in general have more method, with simpler elements that are used more artfully; they have a less rude and savage aspect. To show this difference, we will give some examples from the languages of Greenland and Chile. One can see there the same polysynthetic system, varying only by the use of elements of a different nature. [92]

I. *Language of Greenland*

We take the following examples from the description of this country by the venerable Hans Egede, who lived there for twenty-five years as a missionary.[13]

1. *Aulisariartorasuarpok:* He hastened to go fishing.
   This word is composed of the following:
   Aulisarpok, he fishes: the syllable *pok*, which designates the third person singular present indicative, is subtracted, or rather transported to the end of the composite word.

---

[13] Hans Egede (1686–1758), Danish Lutheran missionary to Greenland, author of *A Description of Greenland* (London: Hitch, 1745), from which these examples are drawn (pp. 172–173). I could not determine whether Du Ponceau also possessed Paul Egede's *Grammatica Grönlandica Danico-Latina* (Copenhagen: Kisel, 1760), a far less widely disseminated but linguistically more detailed work by Hans Egede's son.

Peartorpok, he is about to do something. *Pok* is again subtracted, and *iartor* is put instead of *peartor.*

Pinnesuarpok, he hastens. *Pinnesuar* is changed into *asuar,* and the word is terminated by the syllable *pok* subtracted from the first two words.

2. *Agglekiniarit:* Try to write better.

This word is composed of the following:

Agglekpok, he writes. *Pok* is subtracted.

Pekipok, he does better, or improve. The language has no infinitive. Here only [83] the syllable *ki* or *eki* indicates or recalls this word.

Pinniarpok, he tries, he attempts. *Pok* is subtracted, *it* substituted to indicate the imperative mood, the *p* from the first syllable is also subtracted; *niar* or *iniar* is all that is taken from this word.

II. *Language of Chile*

We take the following examples from the interesting description of Chile by Abbé Molina.[14]

1. *Iduanclolavin:* I do not want to eat with him.

This word is composed as follows:

I for *in,* to eat; *n* indicates the first person singular present indicative, thrown back to the end of the word; the rest is made up from meaningful words inserted in their entirety: *duan,* to desire; *clo,* with; *la,* no; *vi,* him; *n,* verbal form transposed from the first syllable, which makes *eating desiring with not him me.*

2. *Pemepravin:* I went in vain to see him.

The author does not analyse this word; all the same it shows how many ideas [94] this language assembles in a single phrase.

It follows naturally from this system that these languages must abound in a species of verbs which we call *circumstantial,* because they join a mass of accessory circumstances to the principal action or situation. We will give

---

[14] Juan Ignacio Molina (1740–1829), Jesuit missionary and polymath, author of *Saggio sulla Storia naturale del Chili* (1776) and *Saggio sulla Storia civile del Chili* (1787), translated together as *The Geographical, Natural, and Civil History of Chili* (1808). Du Ponceau's samples are from the appended 'Essay on the Chilean Language', vol. II, 285–305.

some examples drawn from languages far remote from another, one from the southern, the other from the northern part of the American continent.

III. *Language of Chile*—extract from Molina.

Elun, to give.
Eluelen, being in the act of giving, to be giving.
Eluguen, giving more.
Eluduamen, wanting to give.
Eluyecumen, to come giving.
Ellullen, really giving, in good faith.
Elumen, going to give, to go and give.
Eluyaun, to go giving.
Elumon, having opportunity to give.
Elupan, coming to give, to come and give.
Elupen, doubting whether to give.
[95] *Elupran*, giving without reason, without subject.
Elupun, to pass giving.
Elurquen, seeming to give.
Eluremun, giving without being expected to.
Elulun, coming to give.
Eluvalen, to can give, having the means to give.
Elumepran, going to give in vain.
The author adds *et cetera*.

IV. *Language of the Cherokees.*

Manuscript of the missionary, Buthrick,[15] cited by Jarvis[16] and Pickering.[17]

Cutuwo, I wash myself, I bathe myself.
Culestula, I wash my head.
Tsestula, I wash the head of someone else.
Cucusquo, I wash my face.
Tsecusquo, I wash the face of someone else.
Tacasula, I wash my hands.
Tatseyasula, I wash the hands of someone else.
Tacasula, I wash my feet.
Tatseyasula, I wash the feet of someone else.

---

[15] Daniel Sabin Butrick (1789–1851), Congregational missionary among the Cherokees and witness of their Trail of Tears. For the linguistic use of his notes by Pickering and Du Ponceau, see Kilarski (2021: 226–232).

[16] [DP:] *A Discourse on the Religion of the Indian tribes of north America*, by Samuel F. Jarvis. New York, 1820.

[17] [DP:] *Observations on the language of the Muhhekaneew Indians*, by Jonathan Edwards. D.D. a new edition with notes, by John Pick[e]ring. Boston, 1823.

Tacungkela, I wash my herd.
Tatseyungkela, I wash the herd of someone else.
[96] *Tacutega*, I wash plates.
Tseyuwu, I wash a child.
Cowela, I wash meat.

The nouns are modified according to an analogous procedure. But we have said enough about it to make known the general character of these languages; it is now time that we come to those which are the main subject of this memoir.

Chapter V: Of Algonquin languages

Of this numerous family of languages, the most extensive of the northern part of the American continent, we only have knowledge of around thirty dialects, of which several are already extinct, and others soon will be. All the same, we know that there is a much larger number of them still alive; but we know of no work, in manuscript or printed, which could give us an idea of their structure and their forms; all that we know from those who have visited the peoples that speak them is that these languages belong to the Algonquin family. Ottawa is one of these, and it [97] is only recently, in an encounter of half a day with Abbé Hamelin, mentioned in the introduction of Vocabulary B in the appendix,[18] that we obtained from this intelligent Indian a short vocabulary of his language and some notion of its grammatical forms.

There are few works relating to the grammar of these approximately thirty dialects of which we come to speak. Those of which we have more or less precise notions are Algonquin proper or Chippewa, Lenape, Abenaki, Mohican, Massachusett, and Narangansett, which differs very little from the latter. For the rest, we have nothing but vocabularies varying in length and credibility, and what we have been able to learn from conversations or correspondence either with Indians or with people who have lived among them. Nonetheless, it must be said that these communications facilitate the study of savage languages more than only reading books, which only say what they want to say and cannot respond to any questions other than those foreseen by their authors. By seeing these languages, so to speak, in action, one has the means

---

[18] From the appendix [*Mémoire*, 289]: 'Their language would have been entirely unknown to us, unless we had made the acquaintance of Abbé Hamelin, a young priest-in-training and son of an Ottawa woman. He spent two years in Rome at the College of the Propaganda Fide. Apart from Ottawa, his mother tongue, he spoke French, English, and Italian; we have an Ottawa vocabulary from him by his own hand, which we have used here.'

to form a more correct and more precise idea of them. In spite of these advantages, [98] we are far from believing that it is within our power to give the honourable commission all the satisfaction it rightly demands. We feel the shortcomings of our clarifications, and even more the weakness of our talent. We will nonetheless attempt to fulfil the task imposed upon us.

To proceed with some method, we treat first of all the phonology of Algonquin languages, i.e. the vocal sounds of which they are composed. We pass from there to words, which we consider first from an etymological point of view, and then from that of their formation. Finally, we end with the grammar, following the order of parts of speech, which seems to us the most proper to fulfil the objective that we have proposed.

Chapter VI: Phonology of the Algonquin languages

It must not have been easy for man in the times of the formation of languages to articulate vocal sounds. To be convinced of this difficulty, it is sufficient to cast a glance at the languages with which we are most familiar: [99] nothing is easier to a Frenchman than to pronounce the sounds *u*, *eu*, palatalized *ll*, and yet there are many who cannot articulate that last sound, and replace it by the Greek *y* or the German consonant *i*; but foreigners whose ears and vocal organs are not used to it find it very difficult to bring forth these sounds, and often never succeed. It is the same for French speakers with several sounds in other languages; only in infancy can the exact pronunciation be acquired. In the age of the formation of languages, all vocal articulations, with the possible exception of some vowels, were strangers to man. Several attempts must have been made before a few were articulated, and initially only imperfect sounds were produced. We do not need to turn to savage languages to prove this fact. Ours offer sufficient examples. Why is it that the Spaniards and the Gascons confuse B with V, whereas the Germans hardly distinguish between K and harsh G, D and T, B and P, and often use one or the other consonant indifferently in their orthography? It is in the beginnings of their language, fumbling around, that they settled upon an unsteady sound, a kind of middle sound [100] between those which they confound, and this way of articulating has been reinforced by habit, and has become national.

It is the same among savage nations. A few years ago, we had a long discussion with an intelligent and educated Iroquois, in order to determine whether a certain sound in his language was that of a K or a harsh G; whether one should pronounce *Ganadayé* (village) or *Kanadayé*. The discussion was long, and in the end we decided upon *K*. In printed books, missionaries used both letters indifferently. Zeisberger honestly admits in his Lenape ABC that his printer had no K, obliging him to substitute the letter G for it. Zeisberger was German.

Without doubt, it is this difficulty in articulation which, at the origin of the Algonquin language, has made some of its dialects pronounce the same word with L, others with R, and some with N. In one dialect of the Massachusett language, a dog is called *alum*, in another, *arum*, and in a third, *anum*. In the beginning, once the [101] language has been formed, each must have pronounced the consonant as he could, according to the strength or weakness of his organs, and in separating, each tribe has conserved the pronunciation which it has received from its fathers.

This is also where the sounds unknown to European ears stem from, which would embarrass many designers of universal alphabets if known. We do not speak here of Asia, nor of Africa; America itself presents us with a large enough number that can only be known by the sense of hearing, and which the pen seeks in vain to describe. Such, for instance, is the sound in Quechua and Otomi which Spanish-American grammarians call cc *castañuelas*. This is the letter K doubly articulated from the bottom of the throat, the sound of which, to the extent that it can be described, resembles the noise made by a monkey cracking nuts. Furthermore, the Lenape have a consonantal *ou* like in our word *oui*, but followed immediately by another consonant pronounced without intermediate pause, which should be called the whistled *ou* or *w*, since one must effectively whistle to pronounce it. The same sound exists in Abenaki, but instead of being labial as in Lenape, it is guttural, pronounced from the bottom of the throat. There is a [102] multitude of other strange sounds in the savage languages of America; but we will not stop to describe them, because this is not our aim. We only add that we have heard the majority of these sounds pronounced by Indians with the greatest ease and without the least effort, and that they did not seem to us more barbarous than the barred *ł* in Polish, the Russian *yeru* (Ы), the *ão* and *ões* in Portuguese, and the ע (nghain [ayin]) in Ashkenazi Hebrew. All these sounds are easy and natural to those who are used to it, and their pronunciation softens in usage.

Although the Algonquin languages are all part of the same family, it does not follow that they all have the same phonological system; still they do not differ more among each other than European languages equally derived from one source. There is, for instance, a great difference in the phonology of the four daughters of the Latin language: French, Italian, Spanish, and Portuguese.

The dialects or *patois* of the French language give rise to the same observation. Poitevin [the dialect of Poitou], for instance, has the Italian *c* sound before *e* and *i*. To say *ce garçon* [that boy], the Vendeans say *tchô gârs*.[19] The sounds of Algonquin languages do not differ more among each other and maybe less.

The alphabets of these languages are not generally very numerous; still they are much more so than those of the Iroquois, where fourteen letters could represent all the sounds.[20] More are needed for the Algonquin languages.

The Algonquins do not have extraordinary sounds that we know of, except for the consonantal *ou* mentioned above. Furthermore, that sound does not exist in all idioms; it is not found in Algonquin proper or in Chippewa. Nor does it occur in the Ottawa language: they use the vowel *ou* instead. Thus, where a Lenape says *w'danis*, his daughter (whistling the *w*), the Ottawan says *ou danis*. It is like this in all purely Algonquian languages.

The Algonquins lack the labio-dental consonants *f* and *v*. These sounds are rarely found in American languages, *v* almost never. The sound *f* exists in some Floridian languages, like Cherokee, Chickasaw, and Choctaw; but we do not know it in any language north of the country these tribes inhabit. In the language of the Otomi (a Mexican tribe), the *f* sound is purely labial; the teeth play no part in it. This can be called a *blown f*. The Spanish grammarians call it a double consonant and write it *ph*.[21] Maybe this was the sound of Φ in ancient Greek, since Π was aspirated.

The Algonquins proper or Chippewas have the consonant *z* as we pronounce it [in French]. The Lenape do not: they have the German and Italian *z*, pronounced *ts*. Some have the French *ch*, and several also our [French] *j*, which the English write *zh*. The Chippewas do not have the German guttural *ch* (kh), but the Lenape do. We do not find in any of these languages the vowels *u* and *eu* as in French; they nearly all have the nasal vowels *an* and *on*. The Abenaki in particular and northern tribes in general make them

---

[19] [DP:] In Poitou this phrase is given to foreigners to pronounce: *Tch' est ó tchu tchi a mis tchó t'u tchúre itchi?* 'Qui est celui qui a mis cet œuf cuire ici?' [Who has put that egg to boil here?] This is the *shibboleth* or rather the *ciceri* of the country. It must have caused harm during the Vendée wars. The [nearby] Saintongeais pronounce *eu* instead of *i*.

[20] [DP:] The Iroquois languages can be written with the following letters: five vowels, *a, e, i, o, ou*; three nasal vowels, a, e, o, pronounced *an, ein, on*; and six consonants, *k, h* (guttural), *n, r, s, t, I* and *ou* are simultaneously vowels and consonants, and can be distinguished in writing as *i, j*, and *u, w*. This alphabet has been formed by an intelligent Iroquois of the Mohawk tribe, which the French call *Agniés*. This Iroquois, of mixed race, is an Anglican minister, and knows several languages.

[21] [DP:] See *Catecismo y declaracion de la doctrina cristiana en lengua Otomi, con un vocubalario del mismo idioma*, por el R.P. Fr. Joaquin Lopez Yepes. Mexico, 1826.

much felt. Father Rasles[22] writes them *aṭ* with two points on the last letter. The English, and especially the Germans, rarely mark them out; they write *an, on,* the English sometimes *ang, ong*. We have known an Abenaki who was called *Nia-man-man-ri-gounant*; he pronounced his name as a Frenchman would have done it, only with more force and the final *n* audible.

The Indians of the Algonquin family articulate distinctly; they pronounce the vowels very openly and their syllables are stressed. They have a *pressing* [appuyé] and a *striking* [frappé] accent; the first is placed on long vowels, like in Italian *quando, quello*; but they do not double their consonants, which the Italians call *battere*. The striking accent is placed on brief vowels, like in the English words *èver, nèver*, and the Italian *dirò, farò*. What is most remarkable in their accentuation and what they have in common with all the Indians of North America is the way in which they pronounce the final syllable of the phrase, [106] especially in their orations. They throw this syllable forward with force, in a way which one can only compare to military exercise commands; those who have heard the major of a regiment say *portez-armes* can form a clear enough idea of this way of articulating the final syllable of a phrase or speech: there is a sort of preparation in the preceding syllables.

We have observed that in general the pronunciation of the northern Indians is stronger and harder than that of the southern tribes. Nevertheless Huron seems to us very soft; but Abenaki and the languages of ancient Acadia have something more savage than the other ones that we have heard. The languages of mountain dwellers also seem rougher than those of the peoples of the plains.

Chapter VII: Etymology

What we call *etymology* is the knowledge of words in a language or family of languages with regard to their origins and affinities. This matter cannot be treated for American languages in the same way as [107] for those of Europe. There is no question here of mother languages and daughter languages, for among the more than sixty idioms or dialects that make up or made up until recently what we call the Algonquin family, how to know which ones have preceded the others? How to distinguish the ancient languages from the modern ones? All we can see here are sister languages, and we will never discover the common ancestor from which these languages have grown,

---

[22] Sébastien Râle [Rasles] S.J. (1657–1724), Jesuit missionary and lexicographer whose *Dictionary of the Abnaki Language* was published by Du Ponceau's associate John Pickering in 1833. Rasles was massacred together with an unknown number of Abenaki villagers by New England colonists during a British-Abenaki war.

nor even the immediate filiation of a single one among them. Delaware and Munsee, for example, are two dialects of the language of the Lenape tribe. The third, Unalachtigo dialect is entirely unknown to us; we do not possess even the smallest word of it. What reason, then, do we have to accord priority to one rather than the other? Should we give the first our preference, because Zeisberger and Heckewelder have written about it?[23] But if Vater[24] or Abel-Rémusat[25] or some other genius of that ilk had given us a grammar of the second or third, we should then put that one above the others for the same reason, only because we know it better; and this is not the right way of reasoning.

We cannot say which American language [108] is derived from which. All that we can do is divide them into etymological families, and we do not lack the means to do so.

The striking difference which exists between the words of various language families and the little that they have borrowed from each other, in which they differ fundamentally from those of Europe and western Asia, is the most certain of those means. The Iroquois family, for example, could never be confounded with the Algonquin family. One hardly finds two or three words in both which can be extracted from the same root. Otherwise, their physiognomy is so dissimilar that a slightly trained eye cannot be deceived, which is not at all the case with dialects which stem from the same ancestor, even if that ancestor is unknown. The Comparative Vocabulary of these two families appended to this memoir provides clear evidence of these facts.

There are other distinctive signs by means of which languages of the Algonquin family can be easily recognized. A crowd of analogous words exists in almost all; those which are not encountered in one are found in the other, in composite forms if not in their simple form. [109] True, some of these languages have words which cannot be linked to others; these anomalous words occur mainly in the Acadian languages in the north, and in those called *Pamlico* and *Powhatan* in the south, little known idioms which form the outer limits

---

[23] David Zeisberger (1721–1808) and John Heckewelder (1743–1823), Moravian (Pietist) missionaries whose works on Onondaga and Lenape were Du Ponceau's richest linguistic sources. In 1782, ninety-two of their Lenape converts were massacred by militiamen at their Gnadenhütten mission station on suspicion of siding with the British. Du Ponceau in part developed his linguistic ideas in his correspondence with Heckewelder, which he published as an appendix to his 1819 *Report* along with several texts commissioned from Heckewelder.

[24] Johann Severin Vater (1771–1826), professor of theology in Halle and Königsberg, continuator of Johann Christoph Adelung's overview of the world's languages in *Mithridates oder allgemeine Sprachenkunde* (1806–1817), which according to Du Ponceau 'caused a revolution in the science of language' (*Mémoire*, 5).

[25] Jean-Pierre Abel-Rémusat (1788–1832), leading French sinologist, criticized in Du Ponceau (1838b).

where these languages probably begin to degenerate. This should not appear extraordinary to us; some are entirely extinct.

Still more signs serve to distinguish this family of languages. The personal and possessive pronouns are the same both as affixes and suffixes. *N* or *ni* represents the first and *k* or *ki* the second person; *ou, o, w* represent the third. With nouns they are prefixed; in verbs they are most often put at the end of the word in easily recognizable forms. *Ak, og* are used almost everywhere as signs of the plural. This is enough to distinguish them from the languages of adjacent nations.

By closely examining the second Vocabulary in the appendix,[26] an adequate idea can be formed of how words pass from one idiom to another and of the affinity which exists on an etymological level between the approximately thirty languages of which [110] we have given examples. One can see the same word pass, *per saltum*, from north to south and from east to west, while the same thing is expressed in different words in neighbouring languages. Without doubt, there are subdivisions to be made within this family, but such further classification is not demanded from us and is not part of the aim of this memoir.

The Algonquin languages, like the Huron and Iroquois languages, do not seem to have undergone great changes in the two centuries since they have been known to us. La Hontan's vocabulary could still serve more or less for the language of the Algonquins proper, the Chippewas, and the Ottawas today. Finding ourselves with savage Wyandots (the same people as the Hurons) some years ago, we astonished them by speaking their language by means of Father Sagard's dictionary,[27] far too much deprecated by Charlevoix.[28] They perfectly understood [111] what we read to them, and their interpreter gave us an explication in English entirely in conformance with that of the book in our hand. The author, in his preface, compares the Huron language to that of the Epicérinys [Nipissing] (a tribe now extinct) and of the Canadians or Montagnais [Innu] to show how much they differ from each other. 'The Hurons', he writes, 'call a dog *gagnenon*, the Epicérinys call it *arionce*, the Canadians or Montagnais *alimoy*. "My mother" is *andouen* in Huron and *necaoui* in

[26] 'Vocabulaire comparatif et raisonné des langues de la famille algonquinne', *Mémoire*, 307–411

[27] [DP:] *Dictionnaire de la langue huronne*, by Fr. Gabriel Sagard, Recollect [Friar Minor] of St Francis, of the parish of Saint-Denis. Paris, 1632, 12°. This work is generally bound with *Grand voyage au pays des Hurons* by the same author. [Sagard (1632) was the main source for Lord Monboddo's statements about the lack of rules and abstract terms in Native American languages, in *The Origin and Progress of Language*, vol. I (1773), 347ff. It is unclear whether Du Ponceau's encounter with the Wyandots is the same that is described in his 1819 *Report*, xxxiv–v.]

[28] [DP:] Jesuits and Franciscans were jealous of each in Canada as they were in China. [For Charlevoix' critique of Sagard, see Poirier (2016).]

Canadian."[29] Yet it is easy to recognize *alum, arum, anum*, of which we have spoken in the previous chapter, in *arionce* and *alimoy*, and the Abenaki *nigaous* as well as the Lenape *n'gahowes* in *nicaoui*, varying a bit by the difference between dialects and maybe also by grammatical forms, if not by the author's ear and orthography. It is remarkable that, in this long distance of two centuries, Iroquois and Huron on the one side, and the Algonquin languages on the other, have made no rapprochement by the adoption of words in their respective languages, [112] even though they inhabited the same country and in spite of their frequent communications in peace and in war. This is a phenomenon which seems to us worthy of attention.

Some tribes, however, have adopted several words from European languages. The Micmac[30] greet each other with *boujourti* (bonjour à toi); they call a hat *monchapoug* [French *mon chapeau*], never neglecting to add the pronominal prefix. They have also borrowed English words: they say *blakit* for blanket and *djackit* for jacket.

The Abenaki[31] have also introduced many French and English words into their language. The first were mainly linked to religion: they say *angeri*, angel; *nécommunicousi*, I receive communion; *confesséouiarmé*, to confess; *sancte* (from sanctus), holiday, etc. They also have French words of a different kind: they call copper money *soumarkinak* [French *sou*], a bottle *potanié* [French *bouteille*], etc. Their English words are generally related to agriculture and commerce, like *manni* (money), *kaous* (cow), *ahassou* (horse), *coucou* (kettle, from 'cook'), *pikess* [113] (pigs), *cabits* (cabbage), etc. Finally, according to Father Rasles, they call French wheat *igriskarnar* (English corn).

We will not dwell much longer on this subject, which we have treated in detail in the observations scattered throughout our Comparative Vocabulary, which contains all that we can say about the etymological aspects of these idioms. We also will not say more here about the manner in which words in general are formed in the Algonquin languages, because we believe that this belongs to the ideological or grammatical part of this memoir which follows.

---

[29] [DP:] The Hurons belonged to the Iroquois family, while the Epicérinys, like the Canadians or Montagnais, to the Algonquin, of which the good Father [Sagard] had no idea. [DP quotes from Sagard (1632: 4).]

[30] [DP:] *Massachussetts Hist. coll.* vol. 6 [=Thomas Pierronet, 'Specimen of the Mountaineer, or Sheshatapooshoish, Skoffie, and Micmac Languages' (1797). The manuscript, with 288 Mi'kmaq hieroglyphs presented by Gabriel, an Innu [Montagnais] man, is in the APS Library, Mss. 497.3.P61s.]

[31] [DP:] Rasles, *Dictionnaire abénaqui* [first published in English translation by Pickering (1833)].

Chapter VIII: Ideology

We have now arrived at the most important part of our memoir, the properly and purely grammatical part. We trust that the preceding observations and the two attached vocabularies have achieved, for all we can judge, the aim proposed by the commission; for the lexicographical part, the task that remains is infinitely more arduous. We will nonetheless do what we can to achieve it, [114] not without begging indulgence.

The course that we propose to follow is to treat successively and separately each of the elements which grammarians have considered since times immemorial as components of what we call *speech*,[32] or more precisely, *language*. This division into eight or nine parts of speech is an admirable analysis of human thinking and seems to us even more applicable to the ideas which present themselves to our mind than to languages which endeavour to express them. For there are parts of speech, e.g. the article, which are completely lacking in certain languages; but they are always found in analysing thought, and if the language does not express them, the spirit infers them. Likewise, there are languages in which these parts are conflated in expressions, as the ideas of them are before they are developed through analysis. This can be observed in a striking manner in the languages which we discuss; but it is impossible to carry out an analysis of the forms of these languages otherwise than by analysing the ideas which they recall and render present to the mind. Whenever, in an Indian language, we find a group of ideas assembled and so to speak agglomerated in the form of a single word, [115] it is only through the elements which the word contains that we can understand its meaning. So we apply to ideas those elements [categories] which grammarians have applied to words, and from there we pass to the forms in which they are coated, either separately in an analytical manner, or seemingly confused by means of those polysynthetic forms which dominate more or less in all American languages.

But before proceeding with this analysis, we believe it necessary to give a brief overview of the entirety of those languages which we will discuss.

Chapter IX: General view of the Algonquin languages

In order to form a correct idea of the manner in which these languages are composed, it is necessary to transport ourselves in spirit to the time of their formation. We are not looking for facts here to support a system established a

---

[32] French *discours*; this has wider connotations than 'speech', but Du Ponceau is talking about parts of speech.

priori; on the contrary, we are searching for a theory which can lead us to the origin of those [facts] we have before our eyes. It is from the facts existing at present that we draw the consequences [116] without which it seems impossible to account for the cause of their existence. No doubt we may be mistaken; we do not pretend to know the past any more than we know the future; but we believe in the power of reasoning and sound logic to give us an account of things that we have not seen ourselves; this power, in truth, is very limited, but we can approach its limits to a greater or lesser extent, and since the aim of our theory is only to make known what exists, no matter whether it is true or false, it will always have fulfilled our intention.

We therefore suppose our Algonquins in the midst of their forests, like the *mutum et turpe pecus* of which Horace speaks,[33] not yet possessing the use of speech. They are endowed, as they are today, with exquisite physical senses; they have keen eyesight, a fine ear, and a tenacious memory; and they have all these things for the very simple reason that these are necessary for their survival. Now they are seeking to make themselves heard and to communicate their needs. They have exhausted the sign language, and it is of no use to them in the dark. What should they do in order to speak? Their organs are not yet accustomed to articulating sounds, [117] but they try. Each one makes a word in his own way, which he accompanies with signs, and which we understand in part by intuition. It has been said that all languages must have been monosyllabic in their origin; we see no reason why this should have been so; the first words, perhaps, probably even, were simple articulations. Some nations, like the Chinese, will have kept to this, and composed their words and sentences by uniting monosyllables; but there is no reason to believe that all peoples would have followed this course, and the diversity of languages evidently proves the contrary, especially if we consider the manifest tendency of all of them to retain their primitive structure and organization. But let us return to our Algonquins.

In the beginning they must have had many synonyms, because they all expressed themselves in their own way. All these words must have been received in the language; however, they would have acquired, little by little, less vague meanings, and each would have found its place; if three or four words simultaneously meant *eat, hunger, meat, fruit*, they would have been applied, by tacit agreement, each to a part of the general idea which was: 'I am hungry, give me meat or fruit to eat'. The junction of [118] these words

---

[33] 'Mute, ugly beasts'. Horace, *Satires*, I.3: 100. In this proto-Hobbesian passage, the primeval herd 'fought for their food and shelter with nails and fists, then with clubs, and so on with the weapons which need had later forged, until they found words and names to give meaning to their cries and feelings; then they ceased fighting, founded towns, and laid down laws'.

into more or less syllables would have formed new combinations, by means of which new nuances or new groups of ideas would have been expressed or recalled to mind. All this must have been the work not of one man, but of all at once, each one contributing his share.

The Indians, especially those who are hunters and nomads, do not have a very analytical head. They soon became confused in the formation of their words: receiving their ideas in groups, as nature presents them to us, they wanted to express them at once with all their parts, as they saw them. For example, when they wished to give a name to a certain tree, they did not think of designating it simply by its fruit, or by some other unique feature. Instead they said, *the tree bearing such a fruit, and whose leaves resemble such a thing*,[34] and sought to express all this by a single word. But how could they do this? If they joined all these words together, they would have a new one of enormous length; and their new language, abounding in consonants, was not happily formed for [119] such a linkage. So they took something from each word, and through linking and inserting syllables, or even single sounds from the phrase they had chosen, or rather from the incoherent words which presented it to their minds, they formed a proper name composed of these different parts of ideas; and for those which they could not fit in, ellipsis came to their rescue. They wanted to express too much at once, and with the least number of words possible; they often missed their goal, and made words longer than a sentence would have been; they have words of ten syllables and even more, and monosyllables are very rare in these languages. Out of 3,585 words Zeisberger's Lenape primer offers 74 monosyllables, 419 disyllables, 954 words of three, 974 of four, 766 of five, 241 of six, 111 of seven, 31 of eight, 11 of nine and 3 of ten syllables. It does not seem that this language has even longer words, and we can see that the words exceeding five syllables are not, comparatively, very numerous. Still, the primer we are talking about is far from containing all the words of the language.

Illustrious scholars have thought, as we have already observed, that all languages were monosyllabic in their origin; those of the Indians do not seem to confirm this [120] hypothesis. What seems most probable to us is that languages, like the world, began in chaos, and acquired regularity earlier or later, in one form or another, according to the genius of peoples, their situations or their needs. Those of the Indians of North America have retained much of the

---

[34] [DP:] Does it not seem as if we hear botanists explaining their nomenclatures in Latin? Shouldn't they try using long words like in Algonquin?

chaotic sort[35] which would have presided at their creation. The parts of speech are intermingled in such a way as to suggest that they have not always been subject to the rules which govern them at present, and which, introduced little by little, have only modified, without destroying, the system of word formation which seems to have prevailed from the beginning.

This polysynthetic system is what characterizes the Algonquian languages, as well as all those of America, and necessarily influences their grammatical forms, which differ only [121] in detail. In the fourth chapter of this dissertation we gave examples of this system from the two most distant languages of this continent; we shall now, by means of other examples, show how it operates in those we are discussing here.

Let it not be said that this system is that of all barbarous languages. The Chinese were barbarous in the past, and yet they have followed a quite opposite system. Civilization has not been able to change the primitive organization of their language; it must have been, in its origin, what it was four thousand years ago, and what it still is today.

---

[35] [DP:] The strongest proof that can be given of the mixture of ideas which existed at the time of the formation of these languages is the number of words they have to express the same thing, according to the circumstances which accompany it. There is one verb for 'I want to eat meat' and another for 'I want to eat soup or porridge'; one word for a wound made with a sharp instrument, another for a wound made with a blunt instrument; these languages seldom generalize. See above, chap. III.

3

Franz Boas' 'purely analytical approach' to language classification in the backdrop to American structuralism

Margaret Thomas

3.1 Franz Boas, anthropologist

In 1892, Franz Boas (1858–1942) was struggling to find his footing in the United States as an anthropologist. Born in the city of Minden, then in the Prussian province of Westphalia, to a well-to-do, socially progressive Jewish-German family, Boas first studied geography and physics.[1] He obtained a doctorate in 1881 from Christian-Albrecht University of Kiel for research in psychophysics, specifically, human perception of the colour of sea water. It was a topic which anticipated his life-long interest in the extent to which psychological and situational factors bear on people's experience of apparently objective external phenomena (Stocking 1965). Soon afterward, Boas left for a scientific expedition to Baffin Island, now part of the Canadian territory of Nunavut. He was captivated by the indigenous Inuit people he encountered there (then called 'Eskimo'), and soon afterward discovered his lifework in the study of Native American cultures and languages. After a trip back to Germany, he returned to the United States, determined to make his career in anthropology.

It was difficult for Boas to break into the field, which at that time was carried out more by people in the employ of museums than by university-affiliated academics (Meltzer 2010: 172). He travelled to the Pacific northwest coast of North America to begin what would become a long-sustained connection to

---

[1] Rohner (1969: 309–313) provides a brief chronology of Boas' life, and Andrews (1943) a comprehensive bibliography. The first volume of a projected two-volume biography of Boas, Zumwalt (2019), covers his life, education, and professional relations in detail up to 1906. Herskovits (1953) combines a sketch of Boas' life with a sympathetic interpretation and appraisal of his work. White (1963) is a highly critical analysis of Boas' ethnographic work, which contains useful material about his life gleaned from his writings.

Margaret Thomas, *Franz Boas' 'purely analytical approach' to language classification in the backdrop to American structuralism*. In: *The Limits of Structuralism*. Edited by James McElvenny, Oxford University Press.
© Margaret Thomas (2023). DOI: 10.1093/oso/9780192849045.003.0003

indigenous peoples living there, eking out research funds for multiple short fieldwork trips from the British Committee for the Advancement of Science. He began publishing his work, including data he had gathered on Baffin Island, and studies in physical and cultural anthropology, especially of Native American tribes. Boas also taught for three years at Clark University in Worcester, Massachusetts before resigning in a faculty-wide revolt. Some found him headstrong or difficult to work with (Lowie 1944: 64; Zumwalt 2019: 241). By 1892 Boas was married, the father of two small children, and jobless.

Boas was temporarily rescued by Frederic W. Putnam (1839–1915), curator of the Harvard University-affiliated Peabody Museum of Archaeology and Ethnology. Putnam had been put in charge of organizing an ethnological exhibit for the 1893 World's Columbian Exposition (colloquially known as the Chicago World's Fair), which was timed to mark the 400th anniversary of Christopher Columbus' landing. Putnam made Boas his assistant. The two men worked feverishly to create exhibits that would educate the fair-going public about the status, cultures, and languages of native North Americans. They faced financial obstacles, intense time pressure, delays of all kinds, and an unsupportive administrative infrastructure. In the end, they mounted the exhibit successfully, albeit two months after the general opening of the fair.

Eventually Boas would go on to achieve his career goals. With Putnam's help, he secured positions at New York's American Museum of Natural History and at Columbia University, the latter facilitated by a timely financial donation to the university from Boas' uncle Abraham Jacobi. Although he resigned the museum post a decade later in the wake of a power struggle, he spent more than thirty years as a faculty member at Columbia, where he built up the first academic Department of Anthropology in the United States. Boas served terms as President of the American Anthropological Association, the Linguistic Society of America, and the American Association for the Advancement of Science; he edited the *Journal of American Folklore* and founded the *International Journal of American Linguistics* (which floundered after his death, but then was revived); he influenced a generation of American anthropologists who would disseminate his ideas widely; and he shaped the discipline internationally (Darnell 1998).

Of course, during the frenetic, unsettled, interval when Boas collaborated with Putnam on the Chicago exposition, he could not have foreseen that happy outcome. Yet despite chaotic working conditions, the insecurity of his position at the time, and what he considered inadequate acknowledgement of his professional standing, during his months in Chicago Boas brought to a head a key issue in his orientation to the study of culture, and argued forcefully for his position. That orientation was materialized in the manner in which Boas organized the artefacts he put on display for fair-goers.

Boas' decisions about how to arrange ethnographic materials contrasted with the organization of a competing exhibit of Native American ethnography that was also mounted at the Exposition. The second exhibit had been created under the direction of Washington-based scholars associated with the United States National Museum, the Bureau of American Ethnology, and the Smithsonian Institution, among them Otis T. Mason (1838–1908) and John Wesley Powell (1834–1902), probably the best-known name in Native American ethnography at the time. Half a dozen years before the Chicago exposition, Boas had clashed in print with the Washington group about how to arrange museum collections (Boas 1887a, 1887b, 1887c; Dall 1887; Mason 1887, 1894; Powell 1887). The gist of the conflict is that the Washington-based group characteristically grouped together materials and artefacts for display typologically, that is, by assembling examples of different cultures' methods of (for instance) fishing, or navigation, or treating illness. The collection would then be ordered according to the presumed stage of development from practices and creations of 'savages' to those of 'civilized' peoples—that is, of western Europeans. Boas called this the 'comparative method', and rejected it as a 'vain endeavour to construct a uniform systematic history of the evolution of culture' (1896: 908; 1893a). Instead, Boas favoured a 'historical method' of exhibition, which assembled the products and knowledge of each culture into an integrated display, viewed holistically, and variously related to those of adjacent cultures. In material terms, Boas' approach often meant crafting 'life-group' exhibits of mannequins dressed in the typical attire of a specific group, posed to enact culturally-significant activities in the context of material items they created and used. For the World's Columbian Exposition Boas went further to recruit actual tribal members, who travelled to Chicago, built replicas of their native housing, furnished as was customary to them, and who performed native music and dance for fair-goers.[2]

In this way, the 27 million visitors who attended the Exposition (Hinsley 2016: 239) had the opportunity to view multiple competing representations of Native American cultures, both in the Boasian/historical style and in the Washington/typological or comparative style. Although Boas (1893a) called attention to the contrast between the historical and comparative approaches in a popular-press article introducing ethnology at the Exposition,

---

[2] Bulfinch (2017) provides a modern reading of the convention of subjecting native people to the curiosity of late nineteenth-century fair-goers. Meltzer (2010) gives an account of anthropology at the 1893 Exposition from the perspective of the Washington-based group whom Boas opposed.

public reaction seemed oblivious to the tension between them. Reports from attendees merely commented in passing on the inclusion of 'foreign folk at the fair' and their exotic trappings (Besant 1893: 539; Hawthorne 1893: 570).

3.2 Boasian linguistics

From the vantage point of more than a century later, the difference that so exercised Boas and his Washington-based opponents at the World's Columbian Exposition of 1893 seems at the same time both overblown and more significant than was recognized by the parties involved. On the one hand, it seems overblown because, realistically speaking, there are limited ways to arrange museum specimens, due to inescapable constraints on space, lighting, time, financial resources, and the physical fragility of artefacts. Although the notion that societies necessarily evolve from savagery to Euro-American-style civilization gets little (if any) purchase in the twenty-first century, something can still be gained by comparing the products of one culture with analogous products from another culture. Something different can be gained by viewing cultures as integrated wholes. Granted the strong external constraints on the display of museum artefacts, in actual practice (and to their credit) both Boas and the Washington ethnologists employed both styles of exposition (Jacknis 1985, 2016; Meltzer 2010; cf. Buettner-Janusch 1957). Despite their polarized rhetoric, both sides seem to have behaved reasonably, a fact which undercuts the force of the disagreement.

On the other hand, Boas' promotion of the historical method of museum exhibition is highly salient with respect to his overall intellectual orientation, including to his contributions to American linguistics. In countering Mason's typologically organized exhibits, in which 'classifications … are not founded on the phenomenon, but in the mind of the student' (Boas 1887c: 614), he famously wrote that '[i]n ethnology all is individuality' (Boas 1887b: 589). For Boas the linguist, in language all is individuality, too, in the sense that languages must be examined with full attention to their autonomy, without imposing on them a linguist's presuppositions. In a 1907 letter to a colleague, he labelled this his 'purely analytical' approach; its aim was to describe a language as an individual phenomenon, from the point of view of a native speaker with no knowledge of any other language (Stocking 1974c: 470; see also Boas 1911: 81).

In practice, Boas did admit certain generalities across all languages, due to several factors: mechanical limits on human articulation or on the combination and ordering of linguistic units, or 'the influence of common psychic traits' (Boas 1911: 56–58), a central theme also in his 1920 'The classification of American languages', the text presented here (see Boas 1920: 373). However, he played down the relevance of these factors, in particular by sometimes viewing the latter sceptically. One of Boas' major accomplishments, his editorship of the four-volume *Handbook of American Indian languages* (Boas 1911–1941), provides insight into how he balanced allowing for, and protecting, the individuality of each language against the insight that cross-linguistic generalization makes available. Boas designed the *Handbook* as a collection of comparable sketches of major languages, many written by his students, with some specifying Boas as co-author. In his introduction to the *Handbook*, under a section entitled 'The characteristics of language' (Boas 1911: 15–43), he developed what Voegelin (1952: 439) called 'the Boas plan for the presentation of American Indian languages'. The 'Boas plan' reads more like a loose inventory of properties that Boas reminds analysts to look out for than a strict template for describing a grammar. That is, he listed points a linguist should keep in mind when facing a heretofore unstudied Native American language, without holding authors to a specific descriptive scheme. For instance: Boas (1911: 16) asserts that languages select a limited number of sounds from an unlimited array; they may join concepts together into words, or separate them (1911: 26); stems and affixes may be readily segmentable, or not (1911: 28–29); nouns and verbs may be readily distinguishable, or not (1911: 31–32); nouns may be marked gender, number, case, tense, or not (1911: 36–39).

To prepare readers and contributors to the *Handbook* with an inventory of categories to look out for is not equivalent to imposing a preconceived classificatory framework, a move Boas opposed in principle, both in ethnographic and in linguistic research.[3] Boas would not tolerate the organization of cultures on a developmental scale from 'savage' to 'barbarian' to 'civilized', nor would he tolerate the organization of examples of basketry across multiple Native American tribes from crude to sophisticated. To do so would imply the analyst's commitment to some context-free means of ranking cultures and cultural products relative to each other, a stance that Boas rejected. Likewise, Boas rejected the assumption that languages' morphological properties evolved from 'isolating' to 'agglutinating' to 'inflectional' (1911: 74–75), nor did he accept the claim (made, for example, by du Ponceau in 1838; see Chapter IV of the translation in Chapter 2 of this volume) that Native American languages in general were 'polysynthetic' (Boas 1911: 74–75). Just as each basket must be

---

[3] The point is disputed in Voegelin (1952) versus Stocking (1974c). I agree with Stocking's opinion that Voegelin's reading of Boas' *Introduction* probably lends it a 'more highly structured character than Boas himself had in mind' (Stocking 1974c: 454–455).

understood within the environment of its own creation and use, each linguistic item must be analysed within the environment of the language that employs it. Relying on an expression made famous by Wilhelm von Humboldt (1988 [1836]: 48–54), Boas aimed to classify languages depending 'entirely on the inner form of each language' (Boas 1911: 81).[4] Presumably, that 'inner form' could be arrived at via the Boasian 'purely analytical approach', that is, by inspection of the language from the point of view of a strictly monolingual native speaker, a point of view undeformed by a priori generalizations about other languages, near or far, and without reliance on the apparatus of western European language scholarship.

One lasting impact that Boas had on linguistics in the United States was his development of techniques for collecting ethnological and linguistic data, techniques that provided the basis for his 'purely analytical' approach. A hallmark of Boasian field methods was that they placed the native speaker of the target language at the centre of research. This contrasts with counter-Boasian research programmes that begin with generalizations about the nature of language at large (such as the existence of a 'natural' word order or of markedness hierarchies), or proposals about the specific character of the target language or its family (such as the dominance of polysynthesis in Native American languages). From this starting point, the next step for a counter-Boasian research programme would be to cite language data (typically, lexical items) to demonstrate the scope of generalizations or proposals. William Dwight Whitney (1827–1894), a foundational figure in American linguistics, depicted this approach as one that 'makes the laws and general principles of speech its main subject, and uses particular facts as illustrations' (1875: 315). Some scholars overlaid on the discussion more or less explicit associations across languages, cultures, and races. In contrast, Boas insisted on the mutual independence of languages, cultures, and races, while his method made the output of native speakers its main subject. It began with, and cleaved tightly to, the particular facts of Native American languages.

Boas was by no means the first to conduct fieldwork in American linguistics, since missionary linguists had studied and analysed North American languages on site continuously since the 1600s (Koerner 2004). Likewise, explorers and traders had been gathering language materials directly from native speakers, if in variably formalized ways, ever since Europeans first arrived in North America. In the first half of the 1800s, men like Peter Stephen

---

[4] See Mackert (1993) on Boas' use of Humboldt's term 'inner form', and McElvenny (2019) for Steinthal's role in the transmission of it from Humboldt to Boas.

du Ponceau (1760–1844; see Chapter 2 of this volume) and John Pickering (1777–1846) studied American languages with more scholarly intent, although not always through their own direct experience (Andresen 1990: 92–119). In Boas' day, John Wesley Powell (1834–1292) amassed heterogeneous language data that had been collected by explorers, traders, and missionaries. Powell was only accidentally an anthropologist; he had been a Union Army officer during the US Civil War, and later geologist and explorer of the western part of the country for the Geological Survey. He became the first Director of the Smithsonian Institution's Bureau of Ethnology, later the Bureau of American Ethnology. From that position, and with the support of colleagues who carried out fieldwork at varying levels of professionalization, Powell oversaw publication of a survey of Native American linguistic families (Powell 1891; see Darnell 1998: 69–95). He also created a 'Map of linguistic stocks of American Indians' that would be reproduced frequently and which Boas cites at the beginning of 'The classification of American languages' (Boas 1920: 367).

What Boas added to this stream of work was a distinctive style of collection and analysis of language data. Boasian research required substantial, sustained, face-to-face (usually one-on-one), interaction with members of the culture under study who spoke the group's language fluently. It centred on the oral elicitation of texts, which might be folktales, spontaneous personal narratives, or materials with high cultural value such as myths, poetry, or ritual incantations. Boas insisted on collecting connected texts, not isolated words, on the ground that texts provided rich access to the totality of a language and to the culture of that language (see Boas 1920: 367, with its implied critique of Powell's conventional vocabulary-based approach). The native speaker's role was to dictate the text orally to the linguist, who wrote it down phonetically. Later the linguist and native speaker would walk through the transcribed text, translating it unit by unit by relying on the native speaker's competence in English, or both parties' skill in a shared contact language. From there the linguist segmented and glossed the elicited sounds, words, and syntactic constructions of the language (which Boas called 'grammatical processes') and distilled the patterns of their distribution. Having isolated, say, a word or a construction in the target language, the linguist then consulted with the native speaker to discover the full extent of its permutations and combinatory privileges (Voegelin and Voegelin 1963), and finally arranged them on paper for the reader.

Boas developed these protocols, and trained his students to use them, insisting throughout that 'the writing of a grammar should follow native linguistic habits' (Harrington 1945: 99). The ideal was to produce three documents that comprised the so-called 'Boasian trilogy' (Foley 1999: 470): a dictionary of the target language; a grammar; and a collection of transcribed and glossed texts, wherein individual forms were keyed to their analysis in the accompanying grammar. Boas' *Handbook of American Indian Languages* (1911–1941) demonstrates the output of scholars and students trained to his methods. It comprises twenty sketches of Native American languages, of varying lengths, almost all of which subsume the latter two parts of the Boasian trilogy. Dictionaries were sometimes published separately, but almost every sketch ends with at least one connected text in the target language, meticulously glossed. Moreover, through some combination of Boas' influence on the contributors and his own editorial hand (Voegelin 1952; Stocking 1974c), many contributors adopted a Boasian order of presentation, and recognizably Boasian terminology.

3.3 Boas' 'The classification of American languages' (1920)

Boas' native speaker-centred and text-based field methods, and his 'purely analytical' interpretation of language data formed the empirical basis of his linguistic work. But insisting on the integrity of each language does not mean that he imagined every language to be unique and fully independent of all others. Rather, it signals that he wanted to start the analysis of every language with a clean slate. As he put it in 'The classification of American languages', 'linguistic phenomena cannot be treated as a unit, but manifestations of linguistic activity must be studied each first by itself, then in their relationships to other linguistic phenomena' (Boas 1920: 369).

The title of the essay identifies its central concern. Boas was deeply engaged in determining the genealogical relationships of Native American languages, as a contribution to 'the history of the development of human speech' (Boas 1920: 369).[5] It was a popular preoccupation. For linguists, this work gave them a chance to promote the value of Native American languages, by demonstrating that (for example) Chinook or Algonquian were amenable to the same close analysis that had proven so rewarding in the study of the Indo-European languages—although of course for Boas that meant without assuming that the same analytic categories would hold for Native American as for European languages. For ethnologists, classification of indigenous American languages was

---

[5] Koerner (1990: 115) links Boas' interest in language classification to the influence of German philologist H. Steinthal (1823–1899), a follower of Wilhelm von Humboldt and one of the few scholars of language whom Boas had personally encountered in his student days in Germany. Mackert (1993) analyses where Boas' linguistics departed from that of Steinthal. Solleveld (2019: 468) downplays Boas' classificatory efforts, at least relative to Sapir, calling Boas 'a hoarder, not a taxonomist'.

essential in sorting out the historical relationships among multiple tribes. For the US government, a stable means of classifying Native American peoples would be of high practical value as it struggled to assert its hegemony over the many indigenous groups that inhabited the land now claimed by European immigrants. Towards that end, the federal government funded considerable ethnological and linguistic research, either directly or indirectly.

When Boas came onto the scene, the received classificatory scheme for Native American languages north of Mexico was that established by Powell (1891). Working under the aegis of the Bureau of American Ethnology, Powell had divided Native American languages into fifty-five separate linguistic families. His ethnology was backward-looking relative to that of Boas, in the sense that Powell accepted the then-commonplace view that cultures could be ranked in an evolutionary continuum from 'savagery' to 'barbarism' to 'civilization', with language reflecting cultural level, a view Boas strongly rejected (see Boas 1904: 517–518). (Recall that Powell would become one of Boas' opponents in the Chicago Exhibition controversy, although the two maintained cordial if distant professional relations.) From Boas' point of view, Powell's data were also flawed, for two reasons. First, because Powell had built his classificatory system almost exclusively on the basis of cognate vocabulary items (Powell 1891: 11). Second, because his sources were of variable reliability: some derived from the recollections of explorers or traders, others from notes taken by missionaries who lacked professional training in language study. Boas' article opens with his expression of scepticism about the validity of Powell's classificatory system, on these bases (Boas 1920: 367). Nevertheless, in the 1920 essay as elsewhere, Boas routinely used Powell (1891) as his jumping-off point (e.g. Boas 1911: 82–83, 1917: 3, 1925: 305).[6]

Because classification of Native American languages absorbed so much of Boas' interest, it is surprising that he opened his 1920 essay with an assertion that, after Powell (1891) American linguistics had turned away from matters of classification to focus on studies of individual languages. In fact, the 1920 essay belongs to a sequence of texts by Boas (1894, 1911, 1917, 1920, 1925, 1929, 1938) in which, over time, he worked out what he considered an optimal basis for determining the relationships of languages. Certainly, studies of individual languages did multiply in the early 1900s, in large part due to the industry of Boas and his students (see Boas 1932). But Boas' own publication record documents his continued interest in classification, as do the publications of his

---

[6] Stocking (1974c: 456) considers Boas' research to have been essentially Powellian in scope and methodology until 1890, when Boas started working on Chinook.

students such as Dixon and Kroeber (1903), Sapir (1915), and Radin (1919). Perhaps Boas' assertion that after Powell 'students of American languages have paid more attention to a better understanding and a more thorough knowledge of the single languages than to classification' (Boas 1920: 367) represents less the actual state of the field in 1920 than it does Boas' aspirations for its future direction.

To summarize the content of Boas (1920), the text explores competing rationales for the observed differences and similarities across Native American languages. It begins with a polite dismissal of Powell (1891), then moves on to discuss rival explanations for the relatedness of languages. Boas gives little attention to the possibility of parallel but independent innovation. The two major competitors are genealogical relatedness and diffusion, that is, borrowing of linguistic features from one language to another. He criticizes some of his former students for their readiness to conclude that the presence of shared vocabulary items implies genetic relatedness (Boas 1920: 367), and finds fault in his own earlier acceptance of morphological parallels as proof of the same (1920: 367–368). By 1920, Boas was conservative about claims for hypothesized genetic relatedness (1920: 367–369, 374–375), on the grounds that without historical data that capture earlier forms of the languages in question—data that would have to be reconstructed for Native American languages that lacked native traditions of writing—we cannot determine family relationships with any confidence. Rather, he illustrates examples of the diffusion of sounds, grammar (under which Boas subsumed morphology), and words (1920: 369–370). While conceding difficulties to the diffusionist stance (1920: 373), Boas leans away from genetic relatedness towards the presumption that languages in contact influence each other more than is generally recognized. He ends by calling for closer study of both similarities and differences across Native American languages (1920: 375–376).

Haas (1976: 67) characterizes the 1920 essay overall as '[Boas'] programmatic statement'. Along the way, Boas displays many of the hallmarks of his linguistics, including an emphasis on the individuality of each language. In the course of his exploration of evidence for diffusion (Boas 1920: 369–370), he stresses the heterogeneous morphological complexion of Native American languages, citing the fact that some employ reduplication extensively, others not at all. Likewise, incorporation is very developed in some languages while in others it is either present only in a modified form, or absent entirely. The same goes for case phenomena. Boas (1920: 371) points out that certain Native American languages disrupt the western grammatical tradition that distinguishes affixes (a closed class of words) from stems (an open class, the realization of which may be modified in construction with an affix; see also Boas 1911: 33–35). In Athapascan, Tlingit, Kwak'wala ('Kwakiutl'), and Sioux, the classic affix/stem distinction does not fully hold, since 'verbal ideas are expressed by different stems according to the form of the object in regard to which the verb predicates', particularly in the case of verbs of motion or existence. To quote an assertion that appears throughout Boas' writing, we 'cannot say that the occurrence of the same phenomenon is always due to the same causes' (1896: 904; see also 1887a: 485; 1887b: 589).

Boas (1920: 371) closes his catalogue of morphological variation across Native American languages by adding that it is an empirical question whether instances of inter-tribal diffusion (of features such as reduplication, incorporation, or inflection of a verb according to the physical shape of its object) coincide with each other. He takes the position that one cannot expect convergence of (what we might now call) phonetic, lexical, or morphological isoglosses—an observation consistent with Boas' conception of the individuality of each language's 'inner form'.

It is worthwhile reviewing the 1920 essay as part of a panorama of Boas' writings about classification of Native American languages. Boas (1920: 367–368) retreats from his own unidentified work 'as early as 1893' that interpreted morphological similarities shared across Pacific northwest languages as due to genetic relatedness. The reference is to a paper he read at the Congress of Anthropology held in Chicago on 28 August 1893 in conjunction with the World's Columbian Exhibition, 'Classification of the languages of the North Pacific coast', published as Boas (1894; see Holmes 1893: 429–430). In this text, Boas anticipates a counter-Powellian theme of the 1920 paper, namely that the classification of languages must go beyond comparison of cognate vocabulary items to take into account structural properties as well (Boas 1894: 346). However, in 1894 he invested morphological similarities with more significance for genealogical traceability than he would later allow. In fact, the 1894 paper asserts, on morphological grounds, the genetic relatedness of languages which modern scholarship now rejects. For instance, Boas wrote that 'structural resemblance must be considered final proof of a historical connection between [Tlingit and Haida]' (1894: 342). Tlingit is now identified as a member of the Na-Dene family, and Haida as an isolate. On similar grounds, Boas wrote that 'there must be a common source from which [Kwak'wala ("Kwakiutl"), Chemakum, and Salish] have sprung' (1894: 343). Kwak'wala is now treated as part of the Wakashan family and Chemakum of the Chimakuan family, with both fully independent of the Salish family.

Two years later, in an 1896 article in *Science*, Boas played out a similar argument, somewhat less boldly and in ethnology rather than linguistics. He weighed the validity of diverse explanations for material similarities across cultures: genetic relatedness; shared geography or environment; or 'the uniform working of the human mind' (Boas 1896: 901). He noted the limits of these explanations, and promoted a 'historical method' (1896: 908), which would study cultural phenomena in the context of the practices of neighbouring groups. Historical analysis might attribute similarities to environmental conditions, to universal psychological factors, or to inter-tribal diffusion. Boas emphasized that 'careful and slow detailed study' (1896: 906) is required, and that anthropologists must recognize that similar effects are not necessarily due to similar causes—a motif in Boas' writing in ethnology, as in linguistics.

Returning to the chronology of Boas' publications about language classification, the next relevant text is a passage in Boas' most-cited work, his Introduction to the *Handbook of American Indian Languages* (1911: 50–58). Here he gives an even-handed exposition of explanations for shared characteristics by genetic relatedness versus by diffusion, offering examples of linguistic phenomena that each seems able to adequately explain, as well as counter-examples where each of those explanations fail. Boas also debunks two proposed explanatory factors which he considers implausible, namely, that similarities of environment (climate, terrain) lead to similarities of language, and the influence of common psychological traits. Overall, in 1911 Boas seems uncommitted to one explanation over another.

Boas (1917) is the editor's introduction to the first issue of the *International Journal of American Linguistics*. His comments about classification express caution about how much weight to put on cross-linguistic phonetic or morphological parallels. He offered that 'attempts to classify languages from these points of view do not lead to very satisfactory results' (1917: 4). But by the time of his 1920 article, his confidence seems to have increased. In the text, he specifically asserts that languages whose speakers live in proximity to each other are very likely to share phonetic properties as a result of the transculturation of women from one group to another, by marriage or abduction and enslavement (Boas 1920: 371–372; see also Boas 1925: 310). Similarity of words and classes of words might be due to cultural or social phenomena which had passed from tribe to tribe (which, in other work, he attributed in part to shared material circumstances; Boas 1920: 372, 374). Although he conceded that the spread of morphological traits is harder to explain than the spread of lexical items, Boas (1920: 373–375) cites many examples. A 1924 conference paper, published as Boas (1925), seems to step backwards in emphasizing phonetic, lexical, and even syntactic diffusion, while evincing doubt about the transmission of morphological features across language (1925: 310). In 1929, Boas returned in an essay to multiplying examples of morphological diffusion, and writing even more confidently that 'It seems to me to be almost impossible to explain [morphosyntactic similarities] without assuming the diffusion of grammatical processes over contiguous areas' (Boas 1929: 6). He then reprised his theme that similar phenomena may arise from different causes, ending with 'we have to recognize that many of the languages have multiple roots' (1929: 7). Boas (1938: 134–139), written as part of an introductory textbook in anthropology, makes these same points. He would probably have been gratified to see that, a century after he wrote the article, accounting for shared morphological features by balancing genealogical factors against diffusion is still a topic of lively discussion (Gardani et al. 2015).

3.4 Boasian linguistics in retrospect

If the 1920 essay provides a microcosm of some of Boas' most characteristic linguistic preoccupations, it likewise illustrates where his work has met criticism. Wax (1956: 64) expressed scepticism of Boas' 'antitheoretical position'; cited one of Boas' own students as concerned that his reluctance to generalize amounted to an 'incapacity for synthesis'; and concluded that Boas produced neither satisfying history nor valid science. While White (1963) focused on Boas' ethnography rather than his linguistics, White's conclusions seemed to agree with those of Wax: Boas' 'unwillingness to generalize tended to oppose the development of a science of culture' (White 1963: 65). White also raised in passing other points of dissatisfaction, for example, that granted the weight Boas invested in diffusion, how did he determine that a linguistic feature diffused from language X to language Y, rather than vice-versa (1963: 39–43)? Moreover, White initiated what has become a large literature debating the validity of Boas' deepest dive into Native American culture and language, his work on the Kwakwaka'wakw ('Kwakiutl') tribe, on the grounds that Boas' primary informant, George Hunt (1854–1933), was not a native speaker of their language, and that Hunt identified with the group only through marriage (White 1963: 30–34; Cannizzo 1983; Jacknis 1991; Berman 1994, 1996; Briggs and Bauman 1999; Wilner 2015).[7] White (1963: 33, 64, 67) extended a

---

[7] White (1963: 30–34, 55) further argues that Boas illegitimately assumes credit for work actually carried out by Hunt. Briggs and Bauman (1999: 519) criticize Boas as having shaped the materials he collected in ways that made him 'complicit in naturalizing white control of Native American

similar critique regarding Boas' main informant for Tsimshian, Henry W. Tate (ca. 1860–1914).

What these various critiques all acknowledge, and variously attempt to destabilize, is Boas' vast and well-recognized influence on the development of American anthropology and linguistics. Two linguists who followed him in the study of indigenous American languages stand out as witnesses to that influence, although neither followed Boas' footsteps uncritically. His student Edward Sapir (1884–1939) adopted Boasian methods, eliciting connected texts directly from native speakers and then building an analysis out of those texts. Like Boas, Sapir avoided imposing on Native American language data either the categories of western European language science, or preconceived notions about the general traits of 'Indian' languages. Sapir shared Boas' interest in how culture, including language, bears on perception, experience, and 'world view' (Koerner 2002)—an interest which Boas arguably inherited from Steinthal, and Steinthal from Humboldt (and Humboldt from Johann Gottfried Herder [1774–1803], making allowance for the evolution of the idea and for shifts of emphasis from generation to generation; Koerner 1990). Sapir, however, had a flair for theory and integrated speakers' subjectivity into his linguistics more thoroughly than did Boas in, for example, his famous discussion of 'the psychological reality of the phoneme' (Sapir 1933). Sapir passed on that orientation to his student Benjamin Lee Whorf (1897–1941), whose name is now most frequently identified with the associated notion of linguistic relativity. Sapir also looked deeply into the texts that he elicited to probe the subjectivity of his individual native-speaker partners within their cultural worlds. In this, Sapir read more closely between the lines of Boasian collected texts than did Boas himself (Darnell 1990).

In other ways, too, Sapir parted ways from Boas. He produced more sophisticated linguistic analyses than those of his teacher, and he was more daring in his classification of languages into families, reducing Powell's fifty-five families down to six. In the 'Classification' essay, Boas (1920: 367, 375) evinces scepticism of Sapir's claims about genetic relationships between, for example, Haida and Tlingit. Countering Boas' evaluation, Sapir (1921: 205) protested that '[t]he theory of "borrowing" seems totally inadequate to explain those fundamental features ... that have been pointed out in common' between exactly

communities'. The essays in Blackhawk and Wilner (2018) bring to centre stage indigenous peoples' perspectives on Boas and his 'circle', and in doing so raise many important issues. An additional, less disfiguring, shortcoming is that by the standards of modern scholarship Boas was 'notoriously sparse in his acknowledgement of intellectual debt' (Bunzl 1996: 63; see also Darnell 1988: 31)—and as Lowie (1944: 63) put it, he was 'curiously indifferent to the comfort of the reader'. In the version of Boas (1920) that appears in this volume, I have tried to redress some of these latter faults in footnotes.

those two languages. Swadesh (1951: 1) labels Boas' and Sapir's different attributions of shared features among Native American languages to diffusion versus common origin as 'the classic controversy'.

A second influential follower of Boas, Leonard Bloomfield (1887–1949), was never his direct student. But he supported and developed Boas' pursuit of a 'purely analytical' descriptive approach where 'philosophical prepossessions were only a hindrance' (Bloomfield 1933: 19), and he appreciated those parts of Boas' work where a natural-scientific mindset prevailed. Like Boas and Sapir, Bloomfield elicited, glossed, and analysed connected texts from native speakers, then assiduously worked over the corpus to discover its phonetic, phonological, lexical, and grammatical features—with more elaborate attention paid to sounds than to words or syntax. He assumed the integrity of each language, and took its description as the starting point for study. In fact, Bloomfield's fieldwork seemed to place the native speaker in a maximally central position, in that he was stricter in immersing himself in the target language than either Boas or Sapir. Bloomfield also resisted the temptation to fill out a paradigm by asking a native speaker to produce any missing forms. He preferred instead to wait for the form to come up spontaneously (Voegelin 1959: 114).

On the other hand, Bloomfield considered Boas' and Sapir's explorations of the interaction of language, culture, and 'world view' to be external to the kind of empirical, 'mechanistic' science of language that he was committed to building (e.g. Bloomfield 1926). From the early 1920s, Bloomfield abandoned his endorsement of German experimental psychologist Wilhelm Wundt (1832–1920) to adopt an anti-mentalistic stance, because, in Bloomfield's view, a truly scientific, autonomous, discipline of linguistics could not traffic in immaterial cognitive phenomena such as consciousness or thought. This disposition was contrary to Boas' easy acceptance of 'the unconscious character of linguistic phenomena' which, to Boas, assured the spontaneous regularity of (for example) native speakers' differential treatment of objects according grammatical gender or animacy (Boas 1911: 67–73). Moreover, Bloomfield valued economy and rigorous formality in descriptive style to an extent that exceeded the standards of either Boas or Sapir. He contributed little to the controversy about diffusion versus genetic relatedness, perhaps because he viewed the matter as drifting too far from the observable facts of language (Haas 1976: 65). Some of what would later be called 'post-Bloomfieldian' linguistics departs from Bloomfield's own work, but it carried forward certain points where Bloomfield's ideas differ most from those of Boas, notably, Bloomfield's pursuit of rigour and economy in descriptive statements.

Different as Sapir and Bloomfield were, they both owed a great deal to Boas. They both also played important roles in what came to be called 'American structuralism', an approach that dominated linguistics in the United States until the middle of the twentieth century (Hymes and Fought 1981; Thomas 2019). American structuralism includes (but is not exhaustively identified with) post-Bloomfieldian linguistics, and overlaps with, but still is distinct from, the sub-varieties of European structuralism associated with Ferdinand de Saussure (1857–1913). American structuralism emphasized the scientific study of language as an autonomous discipline—autonomous from other disciplines, including philology and literary criticism, and autonomous from study of the historical development of individual languages. Some, but not all, American structuralists preferred to define linguistic categories by examining their distribution rather than by referring to shared elements of meaning. Thus, an English noun is a form-class which typically may be inflected for plurality, and may appear as a subject or object (Hockett 1958: 225–226), rather than a word that labels a person, place, or thing. American structuralists carried out close analyses of the patterns that make up the grammar of a language, especially in morphophonology. They also downplayed cross-linguistic generalizing, and avoided attributing structural properties of a language to its speakers' purported psychological or cultural habits (much less, speakers' ethnic or racial identities). Some of these features of American structuralism reflect the influence of Boas. It is not surprising that Boas' work contributed to American structuralism, granted his influence on Sapir and Bloomfield, among others. From the perspective of the twenty-first century, however, Boas himself cannot be considered a 'structuralist', American or otherwise, for several reasons.

First, insofar as 'structuralism' (in linguistics) labels a complex of ideas about language associated with Saussure, there is an obvious chronological problem. The core exposition of Saussurean structuralism, Saussure's *Cours*, was not published until 1916, which, as Falk (2004) points out, was well after Boas had already established the major pillars of his approach to language. Bloomfield published an approving review of the *Cours* in 1924, but neither Bloomfield nor his readers seemed to have considered it a turning point in the history of linguistics. The conventional date for the arrival of Saussurean structuralism in the United States is 1941, when it began to be propagated, in idiosyncratic form, by the Russian and Prague School scholar Roman Jakobson (1896–1982) after he immigrated to New York to escape Nazi persecution. In most accounts, Jakobson met with a very reserved reception (Murray 1994: 215–219), with Boas being one of the few who welcomed him warmly and helped him get settled professionally (Jakobson 1944, 1979). However, the interval during which the two men knew each other was short and came very late in Boas' career: Jakobson began a series of lectures on Saussure at the wartime École Libre des Hautes Études in New York beginning in 1942; Boas died in December of that year.

Second, some core aspects of structuralism cannot be located in Boasian linguistics. For example, although Boas searched for and distilled patterns of distribution of the linguistic units and 'grammatical processes' in the languages he studied, he did not fully conceive of language as a system of interlocking parts in which everything holds together (Stocking 1974b: 8, 1974c). In his multiple studies of Kwak'wala ('Kwakiutl'), Chinook, or Tsimshian, Boas examined his elicited data in order to isolate each language's minimal sound units, and he often pointed out differences in the inventory of sounds in one language versus another. But he did not look for sound correspondences, that is, for patterned distributions of sounds in the phonology of Native American languages, the modern gold standard for genetic relationships (Campbell and Poser 2008: 172–176). Notice that in the 'Classification' essay, Boas (1920: 369) describes 'the extraordinary development of the series of k sounds and of laterals (l sounds)' among various Pacific northwest coastal languages. He does so without attempting to contextualize the distribution of /k/ or of /l/ as members of specific subsets within the tissue of phonological systems of Pacific northwest coastal languages. As Hymes (1961: 90) put it, 'Boas did not develop or use the structural concept of the phoneme, which implies interferences from the internal relations of a system more than interferences from discrete pieces of reality. Boasian grammars itemize, they do not structure'. Likewise, others of Saussure's trademark notions are not readily recognizable in Boas' work: 'value'; *langue* versus *parole*; the claim that the negative relation of difference is the critical defining feature among linguistic units (Joseph 2002, 2012: 642–648; Normand 2004).[8]

On the other hand, some tenets of structuralism do seem to emerge in Boas' writings. But—to exploit terms Boas uses in a different context—they are probably best understood as independent developments, due neither to diffusion nor to a genealogical relationship of ideas. A case in point is Saussure's important separation of diachrony from synchrony (Falk 2004: 109–110). Boas took the autonomy of diachrony and synchrony for granted, as a facet of his 'purely analytical approach', insofar as that approach records a monolingual native speaker's knowledge of the target language in the absence of comparison to

---

[8] Jakobson (1944) leaves a different impression. He reviews Boas' work with characteristic verve, and finds much in it that coincides with Jakobson's own idiosyncratic take on Saussure.

any other language, or to any other developmental stage of the same language. As Boas (1911: 82) wrote: 'Although, therefore, an analytical grammar cannot lay claim to present a history of the development of grammatical categories, it is valuable as a presentation of the present state of grammatical development in each linguistic group'. Bloomfield takes the same stance in the last pages of chapter 1 of his handbook *Language*, as the endpoint of a speed-trip through the history of linguistics. Without mentioning either Boas or Saussure by name, Bloomfield asserts that the descriptive (in Boas' terms 'purely analytical') linguistics that he will champion is independent of, but fundamental to, historical linguistics: 'All historical study of language is based upon comparison of two or more sets of descriptive data' (Bloomfield 1933: 19). The distinction between synchronic and diachronic linguistics is considered a cornerstone of Saussurean linguistics. It was foundational to American structuralism as well. But that does not make Boas a structuralist.

Saussure's famous doctrine of the arbitrary relationship holding between the signifier and the signified presents an interesting case in considering Boas' relationship to structuralism. The idea is usually developed as a claim about the relationship of an acoustic image (word) to a particular concept (its meaning). In that sense, Boas neither comments on nor contradicts the assertion that their relationship is arbitrary. But he has a lot to say about the arbitrariness of the relationships of language, culture, and race. Boas' work overall stands as a challenge to the received understanding that associated particular languages to particular cultures, and even to the race of speakers of those languages. The point appears again and again in his writings, perhaps most developed in Boas (1911: 5–14; and reiterated in particular in a paper written for a German readership, Boas 1925: 306), where he insisted that language, culture, and race are independent phenomena. Although he does not anticipate Saussure's principle of arbitrariness, Boas' assertion of the individuality of every language is compatible with the structuralist doctrine of the arbitrariness of the linguistic form, because to approach every language without preconceptions requires the analyst to abandon any expectations of predictable, necessary links between language and culture, and, Boas maintained, also abandon any notion of necessary links across race, language, and culture. Some Native American languages boasted of reduplication, some of incorporation, some of both, some of neither; there was no meaningful connection between the distribution of those traits and the culture and race of their speakers.

Nevertheless, in Boas' refusal to view some languages as more or less evolved as others, his insistence on the integrity of every language within which '… all is individuality', and his close study of the features of Native American languages, Boas championed ideas basic to American structuralism, and anticipated some of its most characteristic preoccupations. To quote Hymes again, Boas' legacy was in 'clearing the way for, but not quite occupying the ground of, his structurally-minded successors' (Hymes 1961: 90).

The classification of American languages

Franz Boas (1920)

[367] Ever since Major Powell completed his classification of American languages, which was published in the seventh volume of the Annual Reports of the Bureau of (American) Ethnology, and a revised edition of which is contained in the first volume of the *Handbook of North American Indians*, students of American languages have paid more attention to a better understanding and a more thorough knowledge of the single languages than to classification. Much of the material on which Major Powell's work is based is exceedingly scanty, and it is obvious that more accurate studies will show relationships between linguistic stocks which at the time could not be safely inferred. The classification is largely based on vocabularies. Many of these were contained in old literature and are very inadequate. Others were hastily collected in accordance with the exigencies of the situation, and neither Major Powell nor any of his collaborators, like Albert S. Gatschet and James Owen Dorsey, would have claimed that their classification and the map of distribution of languages could be considered as final.[1]

Of late years, largely through the influence of Dr. Edward Sapir, the attempts have been revived to compare, on the basis of vocabularies, languages which apparently are very distinct, and Drs. Sapir, Kroeber, Dixon, and particularly Radin, have attempted to prove far-reaching relationships.[2]

---

[1] Gatschet (1832–1907) worked under John Wesley Powell at the Bureau of American Ethnology in Washington DC, studying the language of the Klamath people on the Oregon/California border. Dorsey (1848–1895) was a missionary who collected Siouan language data. The map that Boas refers to here is evidently one that Powell prepared to show the distribution of language families in North America, as discussed in Powell (1891: 25–30). That map appears neither in the 1891 text nor in the 1966 reprint, but is appended to the end of Hodge (1912). It can be examined online, in full colour, through the United States Library of Congress website, at (<https://www.loc.gov/item/2001620496/>, accessed 13 October 2022).

[2] Sapir, Kroeber, Dixon, and Radin were direct students of Boas, all deeply influenced by him even as they sometimes resisted or rebelled against his influence (Darnell 1998). All of them had extensive fieldwork experience, and all contributed to debate about genetic relationships among Native American languages. Edward Sapir (1884–1939) is usually identified as Boas' most linguistically talented student; he became a major figure in the development of linguistics in early twentieth-century America. Sapir (1915) may be an example of what Boas had in mind as '[attempts] to prove far-reaching relationships'. Alfred Louis Kroeber (1876–1960) led the institutionalization of anthropology at the University of California at Berkeley, and stimulated study of northwest Pacific languages. Roland Burrage Dixon

Since for many years I have taken the position that comparison between American languages should proceed from the study of fairly closely related dialects towards the study of more diverse forms, it seems desirable to state briefly the theoretical points of view upon which my own attitude has been and is still based.[3] As early as 1893 I pointed out that the study of the grammar of American languages has demonstrated the occurrence of a number of [368] striking morphological similarities between neighboring stocks which, however, are not accompanied by appreciable similarities in vocabulary.[4] At that time I was inclined to consider these similarities as a proof of relationship of the same order as that of languages belonging, for instance, to the Indo-European family. While further studies, particularly in California, have shown that we may generalize the observations which I made based on the languages of the North Pacific coast, I doubt whether the interpretation given at that time is tenable.[5]

When we consider the history of human languages as it is revealed by their present distribution and by what little we know about their history during the last few thousand years, it appears fairly clearly that the present wide distribution of a few linguistic stocks is a late phenomenon, and that in earlier times the area occupied by each linguistic family was small. It seems reasonable to suppose that the number of languages that have disappeared is very large. Taking our American conditions as an example, we may observe at the present time that many languages are spoken by small communities, and while there is no proof of the recent development of any new very divergent language, there are numerous proofs showing the extinction of some languages and the gradual extension of others. As the area occupied by the Indo-European family has gradually extended and as foreign languages have become extinct owing to its expansion, so we find that Chinese has gradually expanded its area. In

---

(1875–1934) took his PhD in Anthropology at Harvard under Boas' early-career patron Frederic W. Putnam, but commuted to New York to study with Boas at Columbia in 1898–1899 (Bernstein 1993). Dixon later participated in the Jesup North Pacific Expedition that Boas led. Working with Kroeber, he proposed a classification of all Californian languages into four groups (Dixon and Kroeber 1903). Paul Radin (1833–1959) studied under Boas at Columbia, completing a dissertation on Ho-Chąąnk ('Winnebago'). In singling out Radin here, Boas probably had Radin (1919) in mind.

[3] On the value of studying dialects, see Boas (1917: 5).

[4] Boas refers here to a paper he read at the Congress of Anthropology held in Chicago on 28 August 1893, published as Boas (1894). See the introductory essay in this chapter for commentary.

[5] With this statement, Boas retreats from his earlier investment in the significance of morphological resemblances across languages with regard to establishing genetic relatedness. Later, Boas (1929) goes further, arguing that similarity of morphological structures between two languages in contact, X and Y, most likely derive from diffusion, not from a genetic relationship between X and Y. He provides many examples, and closes by citing Karl Richard Lepsius, Georg von der Gabelentz, Eduard Prokosch, and Hugo Schuchardt as support for the existence of 'mixed' languages, arrayed across a gradient from less to more borrowing.

Siberia, Turkish and other native languages have superseded the ancient local languages. In Africa the large expansion of Bantu is rather recent. Arabic is superseding the native speech in North Africa. In America the expansion of Algonquin speech has been continuing during the historic period, and several of the isolated languages of the Southeast have been superseded by Creek and related languages.[6] I have discussed this question in another place and have explained my view that probably at a very early time the diversity of languages among people of the same physical type was much greater than it is now.[7] I do not mean to imply by this that all the languages must have developed entirely independently, but rather [369] that, if there was an ancient common source of several modern languages, they have become so much differentiated, that without historical knowledge of their growth, the attempts to prove their interrelation cannot succeed.[8]

It should be borne in mind that the problem of the study of languages is not one of classification but that our task is to trace the history of the development of human speech. Therefore, classification is only a means to an end. Our aim is to unravel the history of the growth of human language, and, if possible, to discover its underlying psychological and physiological causes. From this point of view, the linguistic phenomena cannot be treated as a unit, but the manifestations of linguistic activity must be studied first each by itself, then in their relations to other linguistic phenomena.[9]

The three fundamental aspects of human speech are phonetics, grammar, and vocabulary. When we turn to their consideration separately, we find, at least in America, a curious condition. The study of phonetics indicates that certain features have a limited and well-defined distribution which, on the

---

[6] Boas (1925: 306, 1938: 139–141) reiterates the point about the expansion of the range of some languages at the expense of others, citing the same examples. Whatever expansion of Algonquian and Creek Boas perceived in 1920 has not been sustained into the twenty-first century: with the exception of Massachusett/Wampanoag, which is being brought back into use, Eastern Algonquian languages are extinct or nearly so. Among Central Algonquian languages, only Cree and Ojibwe survive and are undergoing revitalization. For Plains Algonquian languages, Arapaho and Cheyenne alone remain; both are classified as moribund. Muscogee ('Creek') now has only about 5,000 speakers. (Data from Ethnologue, <https://www.ethnologue.com/>, accessed 16 February 2020).

[7] The reference may be to Boas (1911: 11–14).

[8] Relative to his peers, and some of his students, Boas set very high standards for postulating genetic relationships. Meeting that standard is of course harder where data from older versions of the languages in question are unavailable—as in the case of North American indigenous languages, none of which developed orthographic traditions in the pre-Columbian period.

[9] Stocking (1974b) discusses the tension between the various influences on Boas' intellectual development, specifically, his commitment to 'the historicist spirit of romantic idealism' (8–9), and his scientific training in 'the tradition of atomistic analysis of elements and of mechanical causal determinism' (11). In this passage, Boas brings both these commitments into play, by asserting that the ultimate goal of linguistic research is to arrive at a holistic understanding of human language, while also declaring that the path toward that goal lies in close study of the features of individual languages, without assuming that those features will necessarily converge across languages.

whole, is continuous. To give an example: the extraordinary development of the series of *k* sounds and of laterals (*l* sounds) is common to the most diverse languages of the North Pacific coast, while in California and east of the Rocky mountains this characteristic feature disappears. In a similar way nasalization of vowels is absent in the northwest part of America, but it is very strongly developed on the central and eastern plains. The labialization of *k* sounds following an *o* or *u* is widely spread in the extreme Northwest, and infrequent outside of that territory.[10] The study of the phonetics of America is not sufficiently developed to describe in detail areas of distribution of characteristic sounds or sound groups, but it may safely be stated from what we know, that similar phonetic traits often belong to languages which are morphologically entirely distinct; and that on the other hand, very great phonetic differences develop in the same linguistic stock.

The study of the morphology of American languages illustrates also definite areas of characterization. It is, for instance, most [370] striking that reduplication as a morphological process occurs extensively on the Great Plains and in the Eastern Woodlands, as well as in that part of the Pacific coast south of the boundary between British Columbia and Alaska. Among the great families of the north it is entirely unknown.[11] Incorporation, which in earlier times was considered as one of the most characteristic traits of American languages, is also confined to certain definite groups. It is characteristically developed in the Shoshoni group, Pawnee, Kutenai, and Iroquois, while north of this region it is either absent in its characteristic form, or only weakly developed.[12] The use of instrumentals, which indicate the manner of action as performed with parts of the body, or by other instruments, shows also on the whole a continuous distribution. It is a fundamental trait of Kutenai, Shoshoni, and Sioux, and in all of them it is expressed in a similar manner.[13] The use of true cases and of locative and similar noun forms occurs among the Shoshoni and some of their neighbors, while in other regions it is rather rare.[14] Of even greater importance is

---

[10] Boas (1894: 339–340) provides additional examples of areal distribution of phonetic features across genetically unrelated North American languages.

[11] Boas (1925: 308, 1929: 5–6) expands on the discontinuous distribution of reduplication.

[12] Boas (1911: 74–75) develops the point. Modern scholarship agrees with Boas in classifying all four languages or language families he mentions here as genetically independent, notwithstanding their shared trait of incorporation. Note Boas' reference to 'earlier times' when incorporation was considered a distinctive feature of Native American languages in general. Whitney (1867: 348–349) illustrates this stance, as does Brinton (1886), who cites Steinthal (1860) as claiming that incorporation is characteristic of Native American languages overall.

[13] Boas, and modern scholarship as well, assign Kutenai, Shoshoni, and Sioux to separate stocks. For discussion of instrumental constructions, see Boas (1900, 1926) and Boas and Deloria (1939: 45–52).

[14] Boas' claim needs to be interpreted carefully. Dixon and Kroeber (1903: 12) surveyed languages over a larger area than where Boas worked, and concluded that the 'material' cases such as locative and

the differentiation between nominal and verbal concepts, and between neutral and active verbs, the distribution of which is somewhat irregular.[15]

Although our knowledge of these phenomena is not by any means adequate, it appears fairly clear that, when the various features are studied in detail, the areas of their distribution do not coincide.

The study of the vocabulary presents similar conditions. It would seem that the number of loan words in American languages is not as great as in European languages. At least, it is difficult to recognize loan words in large numbers.[16] It is, however, striking that the word categories which appear in neighboring languages are sometimes quite similar. This appears, for instance, in the case of terms of relationship. The remarkable extent to which the use of reciprocal terms of relationship is found on the western plateaus, is a characteristic example.[17] It is intelligible that nomenclature and cultural states are closely related, and, therefore, it seems plausible that similarities in underlying categories of vocabularies will occur where cultural conditions are the same or nearly the same.

[371] This remark has no direct bearing upon the stems that underlie word formation. To a certain extent they are dependent upon morphological characteristics, at least in so far that non-existent grammatical categories must be

---

instrumental 'are a prominent feature of Californian languages. It appears that they are absent from only three stocks, namely, the Chumash and Salinan in the southwest [and Yana]'. Boas himself mentions in passing locative constructions in Kwak'wala ('Kwakiutl'), Salish, and Chemakum (Boas 1899 in Stocking 1974a: 90). Regarding cases with 'formal significance' (objective, 'subjective', genitive—presumably Boas' 'true cases'), Dixon and Kroeber (1903: 12) report that 'out of twenty-two stocks in California, twelve or thirteen have at least one such case'. The exceptional, 'true'-caseless, areas, include the northwestern region where Boas' attention was concentrated. Regarding Shoshoni, Kroeber (1909: 270) mentions that Bannock (which, along with Shoshoni, is now subsumed within the Numic branch of Uto-Aztecan) does not mark objective case, but he does mention the occurrence of locative case (276). For a modern perspective on these data, *The World Atlas of Language Structures Online* indicates that among the languages Boas worked with, Kutenai, Haida, and Tsimshian all lack case (<https://wals.info/feature/49A#4/49.72/265.95>, accessed 20 February 2020). Shoshoni is not included in the *WALS* database. Boas' statement about the rarity of case might be reconciled with Dixon and Kroeber's findings if one interprets Boas to be claiming here that what is rare is the co-occurrence of 'true cases' with 'material cases': that is to say, that languages that host both objective/subjective AND locative/instrumental cases are rare.

[15] Thalbitzer (1911: 1006–1007; see also 1057–1059), in a grammatical sketch Boas solicited for volume 1 of the *Handbook of American Indian languages* (Boas 1911–1941), he characterizes the demarcation of parts of speech in Inuit ('Eskimo') as tenuous. For neutral versus active verbs, see Boas (1911: 76).

[16] A sparsity of loanwords in Native American languages, at least relative to their occurrence in European languages, does not seem to be a theme in Boas' writings. Nevertheless, Boas (1938: 136–137) gives several examples, and Boas (1911: 47; 50) remarks on loanwords from English that have been accepted into Native American languages.

[17] Boas (1938: 131, 141) returns to the point without identifying specific languages. On similarities of kinship organization in Tlingit, Haida, Tsimshian, and Athapascan—all unrelated—see Boas (1924: 324). Note, however, that these languages were all spoken in the Pacific northwest area, not the 'western plateaus'.

supplied in other ways. When, for instance, some languages, like the Eskimo, lack those adverbial elements which correspond to our prepositions (in, out of, up, down, etc.), these must be supplied by special verbs which do not need to exist in languages that abound in locative verbal elements.[18] On the whole, a certain correlation may be observed between the lexicographical and morphological aspects of a language. The more frequently 'material' concepts (in Steinthal's sense) are expressed by morphological devices, the more generalized are, on the whole, the word stems, and words are generally formed by limitation of these stems.[19] When we find similar structure, we find, therefore, also a tendency towards the development of similar categories of stems. There are, however, others that are not so determined. It is, for instance, characteristic of many American languages that verbal ideas are expressed by different stems according to the form of the object in regard to which the verb predicates. This feature occurs particularly in verbs of existence and of motion, so that existence or motion of round, long, flat, etc., objects, are differentiated. This feature is prominent, among others, in Athapascan, Tlingit, Kwakiutl, and Sioux.[20]

While I am not inclined to state categorically that the areas of distribution of phonetic phenomena, of morphological characteristics, and of groups based on similarities in vocabularies are absolutely distinct, I believe this question must be answered empirically before we can undertake to solve the general problem of the history of modern American languages. If it should prove true, as I believe it will, that all these different areas do not coincide, then the conclusion seems inevitable that the different languages must have exerted a far-reaching influence upon one another. If this point of view is correct, then we have to ask ourselves in how far the phenomena of acculturation extend also over the domain of languages.[21]

---

[18] Thalbitzer (1911: 1015–1021) illustrates this trait in several dialects of Inuit ('Eskimo'). See also Boas (1912: 758).

[19] German philologist H. Steinthal (1823–1899) was an important influence on Boas (Bunzl 1996: 67–69; cf. Mackert 1993). For the point that Boas makes here, about 'material' morphology joined to generalized word stems, see Steinthal (1860: 317–318) and McElvenny (2016). For examples in Inuit ('Eskimo'), see Boas (1912: 758).

[20] All four represent distinct language families, in 1920 as today. For examples of 'classifying suffixes' in Kwak'wala ('Kwakiutl'), see Boas (1900: 720); for Dakota, see Boas (1938: 130). For examples of languages (Sioux, Haida) that combine verbal stems with very general meanings (e.g. 'sever') with elements that specify information about instrument or manner ('sever by pressure', i.e. 'to break'), see Boas (1938: 129) and Mackert (1993: 339).

[21] Boas (1917: 2–5) anticipated the point that the grouping of Native American languages according to similarities of phonetic, morphological, and lexical features do not necessarily coincide, and that this fact poses a challenge to their classification. He reiterated and expanded on the issue in Boas (1929).

Considering the conditions of life in primitive society, it is [372] intelligible how the phonetics of one language may influence those of another one. Many of the American tribes are very small and intertribal marriages are, comparatively speaking, frequent, either owing to peaceful intercourse, or to the abduction and enslavement of women after warlike raids. There must always have been a considerable number of alien women in each tribe who acquired the foreign language late in life and who, therefore, transmitted the foreign pronunciation to their children.[22] It is true that we cannot give definite observations which prove the occurrence of this phenomenon, but it can hardly be doubted that these processes were operative in all those cases where the number of alien women was considerable in proportion to the number of native women. The objective study of languages also shows that phonetic influences do spread from one people to another. The most characteristic example probably is that of the southern Bantu who have adopted the clicks of the Bushmen and Hottentots, notwithstanding the hostility that prevails between these groups.[23]

It is not so easy to understand the development of similar categories of words in neighboring languages. It is undoubtedly true that forms of social and political organization, as well as religious life, have become alike among neighboring tribes owing to a process of acculturation. The similarity in forms of life creates the necessity of developing terms expressing these forms, and will thus bring about indirectly similarity in those ideas that are expressed by words. When we apply this assumption to such concepts as terms of relationship, in which we remain in doubt as to whether the term creates the feeling accompanying the subsummation of an individual under a category, or whether the feeling creates the term, it seems difficult to understand the psychological process that led to the similarity of classification, although the facts of distribution make it perfectly clear that the similarities are due to diffusion. This difficulty is still greater when we deal with the fundamental concepts contained in the ancient stems that underly the modern words. How, for instance, should the habit of mind to classify all motion according to form spread from one language to another?[24]

[373] Equally difficult to understand is the spread of morphological traits from one language to another. Nevertheless, I am very much inclined to believe that such transfers do occur, and I even consider it possible that they may

---

[22] This returns a point raised in Boas (1917: 3).
[23] Boas adverts to this same example in Boas (1911: 45).
[24] Boas (1931: 164) illustrates this feature in an analysis of Kwak'wala ('Kwakiutl') vocabulary: 'verbs of position and handling are diversified [in regard to the form of the object acted upon]'.

modify fundamental structural characteristics. An example of this kind is the intrusion of nominal cases into the upper Chinook dialects, presumably due to Sahaptin influence.[25] I believe that the peculiar development of the second third person in Kutenai which is so characteristic of Algonquin, is also due to a contact phenomenon, because we find hardly anywhere else a similar development of this tendency.[26] Still another case of peculiar parallelism is found among the Eskimo and Chukchi. Notwithstanding the fundamental differences between the two languages, the modern development of the verb with its numerous semi-participial forms, shows a peculiar parallelism.[27] The traits in question are entirely absent in neighboring languages, and for this reason it is difficult to abstain from the conclusion that these similarities must be due to historical reasons.

The distribution of these phenomena the world over is so irregular, that it would be entirely unwarranted to claim, that all similarities of phonetics, classification of concepts, or of morphology, must be due to borrowing. On the contrary, their distribution shows that they must be considered as due to psychological causes such as the unavoidable necessity of classification of experience in speech, which can lead to a limited number of categories only, or the physiological possibilities of articulation, that also limit the range of possible sounds which are sufficiently distinct to the ear for clear understanding.[28]

To give a few examples: it would hardly be possible to claim that the numerous instrumental prefixes of the Haida and those of Shoshoni, Kutenai, and Sioux, are historically related.[29] It is true that Shoshoni, Kutenai, and Sioux form a continuous group to which might be added many of the Californian languages. Considering the continuity of this area and the absence of analogous

---

[25] Boas (1910: 573) notes that 'Certain locative affixes which express the syntactic relationships of nouns occur in [Upper Chinook] but these seem to have been borrowed from Sahaptin'. Interestingly, in a sketch of Lower—not Upper—Chinook, Boas (1893b: 59) notes the absence of case.

[26] Boas (1926: 93–96) depicts the distinction between two third-person markers in Kutenai, absolute and obviative. Where a subject and direct object are both in the third person, an object or indirect object takes the obviative form. Likewise, when third person subjects appear, locatives and temporals appear with obviate marking; so do direct objects in construction with possessive pronouns. See Boas (1929: 4). Boas (1917: 6) adverts to an additional trait shared by Kutenai and Algonquin, namely that distinguishing between subordination and coordination presents a steep challenge to linguistic analysis.

[27] Boas (1929: 5–6) catalogues a number of grammatical features that Eskimo and Chukchi share, although they are unrelated genetically.

[28] Boas (1896) is an early exposition of what he sees as the factors that bear on the distribution of ethnological and linguistic phenomena. In particular, against the 'comparative' method—the presumption that the presence of shared features of languages X and Y necessarily indicate the genetic relatedness of X and Y—he juxtaposes the 'historical method', which admits the effects of environmental, psychological, and 'historical' factors (905). In this context, the word 'historical' means 'relating to the history of interactions between speakers of X and speakers of Y'.

[29] See footnote 15 above.

forms outside, I am strongly inclined to believe that some historical reason must have led to their peculiar development, but it would be difficult to connect historically the Haida with this district.[30] [374] In the same way, it would be rash to associate the strong development of glottalized sounds in Chili with the analogous sounds on the Northwest Coast of America;[31] the distinction between neutral and active verbs among the Maya, Sioux, and Tlingit;[32] or the occurrence of three genders in Indo-European and in Chinook.[33]

Our experience in Indo-European and Semitic shows clearly that extended borrowing of words may occur and that borrowed words may undergo such changes that their origin can be understood only by historical study.[34] That similar phenomena have occurred in American languages is indicated by the distribution of such words as names of animals and of plants which are in some cases borrowed. Other classes of nominal concepts are not so subject to borrowing on account of the extensive use in many American languages of descriptive terms. Nevertheless, in mixed settlements considerable numbers of borrowed words may be found. An example of this kind is presented by the Comox of Vancouver island who speak a Salish language with a strong admixture of Kwakiutl words, or by the Bellacoola, another Salish people, who have borrowed many Kwakiutl and Athapascan terms.[35] There is no particular difficulty in understanding the process which leads to the borrowing of words. Intertribal contact must act in this respect in a similar way as international contact does in modern times.[36]

---

[30] For Haida instrumental prefixes, see Swanton (1911b: 218–227). To be clear, Boas' claim here is that instrumental marking in Shoshoni, Kutenai, and Sioux may be due to diffusion across these languages which once were spoken over the modern states of Nevada to the Dakotas to the Montana/British Columbia border. However, instrumental marking appearing in Haida cannot reasonably be attributed to borrowing, granted that the homeland of its speakers is the Haida Gwaii archipelago off the western coast of central British Columbia.

[31] Boas (1917: 3) adverts to glottalized sounds as an example of a widespread phonetic feature among Native American languages, the distribution of which does not coincide with morphological grouping. *The World Atlas of Language Structures Online* (<https://wals.info/feature/7A#2/19.3/152.9>, accessed 25 February 2020) documents a cluster of languages with varied glottalized consonants in the Pacific Northwest, and two languages centred in southern Chile, Qawasqar, and Selknam.

[32] For neutral versus active verbs in Siouan languages, see Swanton and Boas (1911: 910–911, 914–915); for Tlingit, see Swanton (1911a: 217).

[33] Masculine, feminine, and neuter genders are well-known in Indo-European languages, e.g., in German, Slavic, and Greek. Boas (1910: 597–605) analyses masculine, feminine, and neuter gender in Chinook.

[34] Boas (1938: 136) makes the same point, sending readers to Bloomfield (1933) for more on the topic.

[35] Recall that the Salish family (of which Nuxalk ['Bellacoola'] and Comox are members) is genetically unrelated from both the Athapascan and Waskashan (subsuming Kwak'wala ['Kwakiutl']) families.

[36] Whitney (1898: 115–120) probably represents the received understanding of lexical borrowing at the beginning of Boas' career. Whitney (1881: 18) is sceptical that borrowing of 'structural elements' not already instantiated in the receiving language can be borrowed, including grammatical distinctions,

If these observations regarding the influence of acculturation upon language should be correct, then the whole history of American languages must not be treated on the assumption that all languages which show similarities must be considered as branches of the same linguistic family. We should rather find a phenomenon which is parallel to the features characteristic of other ethnological phenomena—namely, a development from diverse sources which are gradually worked into a single cultural unit. We should have to reckon with the tendency of languages to absorb so many foreign traits, that we can no longer speak of a single origin, and that it would be arbitrary whether we associate a language with one or the other of the contributing stocks. In other words, the whole theory of an 'Ursprache' for every group of modern languages, [375] must be held in abeyance until we can prove that these languages go back to a single stock and that they have not originated, to a large extent, by the process of acculturation.

From this point of view I should not be inclined to claim, for instance, that Tlingit and Athapascan are members of the same linguistic family. There is not the slightest doubt that the morphology of the two groups shows the most far-reaching similarities. Since, furthermore, the two languages are contiguous, the inference is inevitable that these similarities must be due to historical causes. It is, however, another question whether we are to infer immediately that these differences are due to the fact that in very early times the two groups had a common 'Ursprache'.[37] The vocabularies of Tlingit and Athapascan are fundamentally distinct, and it does not seem to me that Dr. Sapir has proved his case of relationship between the two languages by the comparison of a limited number of words that show slight phonetic similarities.[38] The question would remain to be answered, why there should be such fundamental dissimilarities between by far the larger number of words, and the question should still be asked how these dissimilarities are to be explained.

It is true enough that in a comparison of modern Indo-European languages, without any knowledge of their previous history, it might be very difficult

---

word order, or tense, person, or number marking. In contrast, Boas (1920: 373) cites instances of what he considers to be the kind of borrowing that Whitney doubts.

[37] Boas' student Kroeber (1913) supported and developed the point, arguing that territorial continuity and contiguity must be considered as factors in determining genetic relationships, alongside lexical and formal resemblances.

[38] Sapir (1915) argues extensively for the morphological relatedness of Athapaskan, Tlingit, and Haida as part of his conjectured Na-Dene language family. He concedes that supporting lexical evidence is weaker, but goes on to reconstruct some 300 stems and grammatical elements for Na-Dene. Boas was unconvinced. However, Boas (1907) seemed more optimistic about connecting Tlingit and Athapascan genetically in a letter to Swanton in response to a draft of what would become Swanton (1911a). Stocking (1974a: 180–181) reprints the letter.

to prove relationship—let us say, between Armenian and English—and we might be compelled to adopt a similar conclusion as the one suggested here. Partially this inference would be correct, because our modern Indo-European languages contain much material that is not Indo-European by origin. The fundamental question is whether this material may become so extensive and influence the morphology so deeply that the inclusion of a language in one group or another might become arbitrary. I think it is well worth considering whether the similarities between Finnish and Indo-European, to which Sweet has called attention, may not be due to such a process of acculturation.[39]

To sum up, it seems to my mind that a critical attitude towards our problem makes it necessary to approach our task from three points of view. Firstly, we must study the differentiation of dialects [376] like those of the Sioux, Muskoki, Algonquin, Shoshoni, Salish, and Athapascan. Secondly, we must make a detailed study of the distribution of phonetic, grammatical, and lexicographical phenomena, the latter including also particularly the principles on which the grouping of concepts is based. Finally, our study ought to be directed not only to an investigation of the similarities of languages, but equally intensively towards their dissimilarities. Only on this basis can we hope to solve the general historical problem.

COLUMBIA UNIVERSITY,
NEW YORK CITY

---

[39] Sweet (1900: 117–126) traces the contact-induced influence of Indo-European on Finnish.

4
Georg von der Gabelentz's typology
Humboldtian linguistics on the threshold of structuralism

James McElvenny*

4.1 Introduction

The German sinologist and general linguist Georg von der Gabelentz (1840–1893) is a favourite figure among those who would seek to extend the temporal and conceptual limits of structuralism. Gabelentz was indisputably a creature of the nineteenth century—he lived his whole life within that century's chronological and intellectual confines—but, as later linguists and historians of the field have observed, he seemingly anticipated many concerns current in the structuralist era of the twentieth century. Eugenio Coseriu (1967) famously went so far as to identify what he saw as specific terminological and textual parallels between the *Cours de linguistique générale* (*Course in general linguistics*; 1922 [1916]) of Ferdinand de Saussure (1857–1913), generally considered the founding scripture of structuralism, and Gabelentz' (2016 [[1]1891,[2]1901]) magnum opus, *Die Sprachwissenschaft* (*The Science of Language* or *Linguistics*). Coseriu undoubtedly read too much into Gabelentz' writings (cf. Koerner 1978 [1974]; 2008), but the intuition that Gabelentz was in some sense ahead of his time was not misguided.

We do not want to fall into the teleological trap of assuming that Gabelentz was a 'forerunner' of structuralism, that he had already taken the first steps down a path along which other linguists would inevitably follow. We can, however, profitably examine Gabelentz' status as a transitional figure who, in his endeavour to rejuvenate old ideas, arrived at positions similar to those representative of the structuralist revolution. This is nowhere more apparent than in Gabelentz' proposal for a 'typology' of languages, which he first set out under this name in his posthumous 1894 essay 'Typologie der Sprachen,

---

* Funded by the German Research Foundation (DFG) – Project ID 262513311 – CRC 1187 'Media of Cooperation'.

James McElvenny, *Georg von der Gabelentz's typology*. In: *The Limits of Structuralism*. Edited by James McElvenny, Oxford University Press. © James McElvenny (2023). DOI: 10.1093/oso/9780192849045.003.0004

eine neue Aufgabe der Linguistik', translated here into English as 'Typology of languages—a new task of linguistics'.[1]

Gabelentz' essay represents the first time that the term 'typology' was used in print in a specifically linguistic sense,[2] and the project Gabelentz envisaged sounds very much like linguistic typology as later practised in the second half of the twentieth century. In his classic historiographic study of Gabelentz' typology project, Frans Plank (1991: 421–422) highlighted a vogue among typologists of his day for citing a passage in the second edition of Gabelentz' *Sprachwissenschaft* that is essentially a condensation of the key points in the typology essay:

> Every language is a system, all of whose parts hang together and work together organically. We have an inkling that none of these parts could be missing or be different without changing the whole. But it also seems as if certain traits were more important than others in the physiognomy of languages. It would be necessary to uncover these traits, and then we would have to investigate what other peculiarities co-occur with them regularly. I am thinking of peculiarities of word and sentence structure, the preference for or neglect of certain grammatical categories. I can, I must assume that all of these interact with the phonetic properties of the language in some way. The induction that I demand here may be frightfully difficult; and if and in so far as it were to succeed, it will require incisive philosophical reflection in order to discern the rules, the active forces behind the regularities. But what an achievement it would be if we could take a language and say to its face: You have this feature, therefore you have the following properties and such and such total character! If we could—as bold botanists have tried—reconstruct the lime tree from the lime leaf. If I may be permitted to christen an unborn child, I would choose the name *typology*. Here I perceive a task for general linguistics, which it could already attempt with the means available to it today. It would bear fruits that

---

[1] This is the only complete translation of Gabelentz' essay into English to date. The essay has, however, recently been rendered into French in two separate translations, undertaken independently of one another: François (2017: 365–369) and Samain (2020).

[2] In Gabelentz' 1894 essay the term 'typology' (*Typologie*) is in fact consistently printed as *Hypologie*, including in the title of the essay. This is almost certainly a typographic error that was left standing because Gabelentz died before he was able to correct the printer's proofs. The 1901 second edition of Gabelentz' *Sprachwissenschaft* contains new passages that convey the core points of Gabelentz' project as outlined in the essay and here the term appears as *Typologie* (see Gabelentz 2016 [^{1}1891,^{2}1901]: 507, 510). The second edition of *Die Sprachwissenschaft* appeared almost ten years after Gabelentz' death and was revised posthumously by his nephew, the linguist Albrecht von der Schulenburg (1865–1902). There has been some debate about whether Schulenburg's revisions truly reflect Gabelentz' intentions; we side here with Plank (1991) and consider Schulenburg's revisions to be a faithful rendering of Gabelentz' ideas. The fact that there was so much confusion surrounding Gabelentz' use of the term *Typologie* in the 1894 essay attests to the novelty of the term among linguists.

in comparison to those of historical-comparative linguistic research are no less ripe and probably deliver deeper insights. What we up until now have said about the mental relatedness between languages, related traits in languages from different genealogical lineages, this will take on tangible form, it will be represented in definite numerical formulas; and then speculative thinking will take up these formulas in order to turn the empirical observations into necessary connections.

(Gabelentz 2016 [[1]1891,[2]1901]: 507)

On this passage, Plank (1991: 421) commented, 'It would be difficult to formulate the research programme of linguistic typology more succinctly'. This seemingly prescient passage is all the more remarkable because it sounds so out of tune with much of mainstream linguistic scholarship of the time in which it was written. Linguistics in the last decades of the nineteenth century was dominated by the Neogrammarian school, who had a (not entirely deserved) reputation for being obsessed with problems of historical sound change as a basis for postulating genealogical relations between languages, and for restricting their efforts almost exclusively to the Indo-European family.

As Professor of East Asian Languages at the Neogrammarian stronghold of the University of Leipzig from 1878 to 1889, Gabelentz shared an institutional home with several leading Neogrammarians at a time when the movement was at its height (on Gabelentz' biography, see Vogel and McElvenny 2019; McElvenny 2017a). But Gabelentz was a critic of the Neogrammarians. He wanted a linguistics that embraced all the languages of the world: Chinese and other classical non-Indo-European languages, of course, but also all the traditionally unwritten languages that in this era were being documented by European missionaries and colonial officials. Gabelentz did not want to lose sight of the big picture, the grand questions of 'general linguistics' as they had been conceived by such figures as Wilhelm von Humboldt (1767–1835) and his followers earlier in the nineteenth century (cf. Elffers 2012). In *Die Sprachwissenschaft*, Gabelentz wrote:

Most of us linguists have limited [our] work to the investigation of one or another language family, and the genealogical-historical school [represented at this time chiefly by the Neogrammarians—JMc] has shown such amazing progress that they deserve a certain degree of self-satisfaction. It seemed reasonable to say: Progress in linguistics occurs only in this school. Others might call themselves philologists, language philosophers, or even language experts or polyglots, or whatever they like, but they shouldn't claim to be linguists and what they do to be linguistics. But whoever says this confuses the little field that they plough with the commons of a large community, or if I may put it in terms of a common Chinese saying, passes judgement like someone who sits at the bottom of a well and says the sky is small.

(Gabelentz 2016 [¹1891,²1901]: 12)

For their part, the Neogrammarians and their supporters, inasmuch as they paid any attention to Gabelentz, generally saw his work as the last gasp of a tradition that had been largely superseded by their own scientific advances. On the posthumous second edition of Gabelentz' *Sprachwissenschaft*, the Neogrammarian sympathizer Ludwig Sütterlin (1863–1934) wrote: 'Gabelentz' book seems to us like a remnant of a former time: with him dies a point of view that in the end was established by Wilhelm von Humboldt' (1904: 319).

In the following sections, we will explore some of the main aspects of Gabelentz' thought as contained in his proposal for typology and see how his ideas could appear outmoded to his Neogrammarian contemporaries but prophetic to linguists in later generations. The first idea, which we look at in section 4.2, is the conception of language as a system, perhaps the defining tenet of structuralism, which in Gabelentz' thought was anchored in the nineteenth-century metaphor of language as an 'organism', a key notion of the Humboldtians. In section 4.3, we then turn to Gabelentz' appeal to 'definite numerical formulas' and statistical methods in capturing language structures, an endeavour very much in the spirit of scientific thinking in Gabelentz' time but which had only a marginal place in linguistics. Finally, in section 4.4, we conclude by tracing the lineage of linguistic typology in the twentieth century which, although it has points of contact with Gabelentz, was largely an independent development.

4.2 Language systems, language organisms, and Humboldtian typology

'Every language is a system, all of whose parts hang together and work together organically', so begins the typology passage in the second edition of Gabelentz' *Sprachwissenschaft* (2016 [¹1891,²1901]: 507; cf. ibid.: 18, 511–512). This statement has a clear antecedent in the typology essay, where Gabelentz (1894a: 4) writes: '[Languages] are free organic structures, and because they are, and inasmuch as they are, all of their parts stand together in a necessary configuration'. These twin statements may remind us of a central slogan of later structuralism, namely that 'each language forms a system where everything holds together' (often quoted in the original French: 'chaque langue forme un système où tout se tient'), which first appeared in print in the 1903 *Introduction à l'étude comparative des langues indo-européennes* (*Introduction to the comparative study of Indo-European languages*) of French structuralist Antoine Meillet (1866–1936; 1903: x, 159, 407).[3]

In putting this proposition forward, Meillet (1903: 407) felt he was stating a commonplace that 'it has been impossible to ignore' since the 1879 *Mémoire sur le système primitif des voyelles dans les langues indo-européennes* (*On the original vowel system in the Indo-European languages*) of his teacher Saussure. Even though Meillet attributed this insight to the previous generation, the conception of languages as self-contained, internally coherent systems is traditionally considered one of the key innovations of the structuralist revolution, which overcame the allegedly 'atomistic' attitude of the Neogrammarians (see, for example, Jakobson 1932: 247; Cassirer 1945; Trnka et al. 1964 [1958]). The Neogrammarians themselves did not necessarily see any great contrast between Saussure's system-oriented approach and their own work. Indeed, when his *Mémoire* was published, Saussure faced accusations of plagiarism spread through a whispering campaign: several of Saussure's Neogrammarian teachers felt that the data and methods in the *Mémoire* drew on their existing reconstructions of Proto-Indo-European without sufficient acknowledgement (see Joseph 2012: 242–247).

But whatever particular methodological advances may have been made by the Neogrammarians or the first structuralists, and despite whatever polemical contrasts some schools may have tried to set up against their predecessors, the conception of languages as systems was part of the common background to much of linguistic scholarship in the nineteenth century (see Kohrt and Kucharczik 2001). The structuralist reformulation of these ideas in the twentieth century is therefore not so much a revolutionary break with the past as a continuation and further development. The continuities are in part obscured by differences in terminology. In nineteenth-century scholarship, it was common to talk about the 'organisms' of languages. Gabelentz partakes in this usage when he describes languages as 'free *organic* structures'. Saussure, for that matter, also used 'organism' (*organisme*) and 'system' (*système*) as synonyms in the *Cours de linguistique générale* (e.g. Saussure 1922 [1916]: 40–42).

---

[3] On Meillet's status as a pioneering structuralist and his concept of 'grammaticalization', see Chapter 5 of this volume.

We must note that this usage of 'organism' was for most scholars strictly metaphorical. The intention was to draw an analogy between the nature of both languages and living things as organized wholes, and not to imply that languages are literally biological organisms. There were, however, leading linguists, acting under the influence of materialist metaphysics, who did conflate the linguistic and the biological, the most famous case being August Schleicher (1821–1868; see McElvenny 2018b). But many linguists—including Gabelentz (2016 [[1]1891,[2]1901]: 18) and Saussure (1922 [1916]: 18–19)—maintained their metaphorical usage of 'organism' while explicitly rejecting the literal biological interpretation.

The organism metaphor was a prominent feature of the Humboldtian tradition in which we can situate Gabelentz' work. Humboldt himself frequently spoke of the 'organisms' of languages (see Di Cesare in Humboldt 1998 [1836]: 57–66), by which he meant: 'There is nothing individual in language, every one of its elements shows itself only as part of a whole' (Humboldt 1905 [1820]: 14–15). This understanding of the structured nature of languages was combined in Humboldt's writings with the idea that language is the 'forming organ of thought' (Humboldt 1998 [1836]: 180). For Humboldt, language is not merely a passive medium of expression; rather, there is a dialectic relationship between thought and language in which each actively shapes the other. In order to discern the connections between the two, argued Humboldt, we need, on the one hand, to make comprehensive descriptions of the organisms of individual languages and, on the other, to compare analogous structures across languages (see Trabant 1986, 2012: ch. 8; McNeely 2020). Taking their cue from Humboldt's writings, numerous nineteenth-century language scholars pursued this dual programme of grammatical description of individual languages and cross-linguistic comparison of specific grammatical categories (see McElvenny 2017b). Gabelentz (2016 [[1]1891,[2]1901]: 409) considered his research to be a contribution to this programme and acknowledged Humboldt as its initiator.

But the respective writings of Humboldt and Gabelentz are separated by several decades, in which many differing interpretations and applications of Humboldt's ideas were made, and this intervening work inevitably mediated Gabelentz' understanding of Humboldt. One of the most prominent Humboldt interpreters was H. Steinthal (1823–1899), whose linguistic scholarship was part of his broader project of *Völkerpsychologie* (literally 'psychology of peoples' or 'ethnopsychology'), developed in collaboration with Moritz Lazarus (1824–1903). *Völkerpsychologie* aimed to characterize the *Volksgeist* or 'national mind' of each people through research into their history, culture, and, above all, language (see Klautke 2013; Trautmann-Waller 2006). Steinthal's grammar-writing (e.g. Steinthal 1867) and efforts at typological language classification (e.g. Steinthal 1860) followed the two tracks laid down by Humboldt. While Gabelentz was not uncritical of Steinthal's linguistics (see McElvenny 2017b: 6–12), there was a clear alignment between the two in their goals and methods, all anchored in a common appeal to Humboldt. In *Die Sprachwissenschaft*, Gabelentz summarized the ultimate goal of Humboldtian 'general linguistics' as follows:

> The goal to which general linguistics must aspire can be no other than to establish the mutual relations between national character and language. Here the mental and temperamental kind, the living conditions, the level of civilization of peoples and families of peoples—there the phenomena, the forces and achievements of their languages. And, between these two, equations that say: the more so on this side, the more or less so on the other.
>
> (Gabelentz 2016 [^{1}1891,^{2}1901]: 502)

In the typology essay, this goal is restated, and the mutual dependence of linguistic, ethnographic, and historical research is foregrounded.

> Working out the connection [between the typical traits, the ruling tendencies in languages] is the ... highest task. And here linguistics will once again turn to ethnology and history; it will reach out from them and also towards them—it is the construction of a tunnel, undertaken simultaneously from both sides of the mountain. From one side will be explained: this is the character of the language, therefore this is the character of the national mind. From the other side will be concluded: these are the constant living conditions, these are the historical experiences, these the habits and cultural achievements of the nation, so its mental kind must be like this.[4]
>
> (Gabelentz 1894a: 7)

Exactly how Gabelentz imagined this endeavour would proceed in practice can be found in *Die Sprachwissenschaft*, in a section devoted to

---

[4] Gabelentz' formulation here echoes the words of Karl Wilhelm Ludwig Heyse (1797–1855), an associate of Humboldt and teacher to Steinthal. In his 1856 *System der Sprachwissenschaft*, edited and published posthumously by Steinthal, Heyse (1856: 231) similarly saw the 'highest task' of the comparative study of language from a philosophical perspective to be a 'classification of languages according to their inner character, their essential properties', a task he undergirded with a reference to Humboldt. Plank (1991: 445–447) highlights several other similarities between passages in Heyse's book and Gabelentz' writings.

Sprachwürderung or the 'appraisal of languages' (Gabelentz 2016 [¹1891,²1901]: 409–502). Here Gabelentz identified structural features supposedly characteristic of various languages and sought to explain these through aspects of the physical and mental life of their speakers. For example, Gabelentz (2016 [¹1891,²1901]: 434–438) drew parallels between the structural features of 'Malay languages' (Gabelentz' category more or less corresponds to what we would today call the Malayo-Polynesian subgroup of Austronesian) and 'Semitic languages'. In both groups, so he claimed, verb–subject word order predominates, and this is an expression of 'lively sensuality', since first the speaker names the sensory impression they have received and then they name the cause of that impression. This sensuality is in turn supposed to be evidence of receptivity and egotism, which explains the ease with which both Malays and Semites assimilate foreign thinking and other cultural material and make it their own, as well as their desire to travel and settle in new lands. It is these qualities that make Malays and Semites such successful merchants and students, but also 'robbers and thieves'.

But if, on the other hand, we compare Malays and Ural-Altaic peoples, two groups that are supposedly both of 'mongoloid type' in terms of their physical characteristics (Gabelentz 2016 [¹1891,²1901]: 438), then we can observe the effect of living conditions on linguistic structure. The homeland of the Ural-Altaic peoples is in the steppes of northern and central Asia, an environment with harsh living conditions that forces a nomadic lifestyle on its inhabitants. 'In such a school of life', writes Gabelentz (Gabelentz 2016 [¹1891,²1901]: 440), 'man is not raised to spirited initiative, but instead to a sustainable goal-conscious energy'. By contrast, the 'abundant tropical world' of the Malays stimulates their sensuality and the view of the far sea awakens the longing of these excitable people for travel and adventure: 'The herdsman [i.e. Ural-Altaic person] yields to the forces of nature, the seaman [i.e. Malay] takes up the struggle against them; the former is pressured by hardship, the latter is attracted by danger' (Gabelentz 2016 [¹1891,²1901]: 440). This environmentally conditioned difference in temperament is then manifested in their languages in various ways. Just one example Gabelentz (Gabelentz 2016 [¹1891,²1901]: 441–443) offers is the way in which the plodding Ural-Altaic speaker builds up their speech piece by piece: cause before phenomenon, subject first in the sentence; adnominal and adverbial attributes carefully placed before their heads. The sensual Malay is the opposite: verb first, other parts of the sentence later; heads first, followed by attributes.

To our modern eyes, Gabelentz' characterizations of alleged national mentalities and lifestyles would seem to rely on crude, racist stereotypes, while the connections he draws between these and linguistic features have the dubious quality of just-so stories. Of these examples, Gabelentz (1894a: 1) said himself that he was 'working at a less fine-grained level, ... sticking to the most tangible details'; his hope was that his proposal for typology would bring rigour to this enterprise. But we may legitimately ask if the entire project was simply misconceived. Certainly his Neogrammarian contemporaries were quite critical of such talk of national minds and temperament. In his 1880 *Principien der Sprachgeschichte* (*Principles of Language History*),[5] a book often referred to as the 'Neogrammarian Bible', Hermann Paul (1846–1821) refuted at length the notion of a national mind as propounded by Lazarus and Steinthal. He praised Steinthal's psycholinguistic analyses with respect to individual speakers, and even emulated Steinthal in this area, but the idea of the superordinate mind of the nation that lay at the heart of *Völkerpsychologie* and allied approaches he rejected as metaphysical extravagance (cf. Klautke 2013: 30–32). Paul's sober realism allowed him only to recognize individuals who interact with one another.

By the turn of the twentieth century, *Völkerpsychologie* had become associated with Wilhelm Wundt (1832–1920), a professor of philosophy at the University of Leipzig and a founding figure of experimental psychology. Wundt had long since adopted the term *Völkerpsychologie* from Lazarus and Steinthal and reconfigured it to suit his own theoretical purposes. From 1900 to 1920, he published a grand, ten-volume survey of *Völkerpsychologie* as he understood it, of which the first volume dealt with language. In harmony with the spirit of the times, and in keeping with his role as a pioneering experimentalist, Wundt was wary of the metaphysical implications of positing a national mind. Nevertheless, he insisted that it is possible to scientifically investigate a *Volksseele* or 'national soul', a shared mentality of the people manifested in its language and other cultural products (see Wundt 1900: 7–18). Paul felt that Wundt was stricken by more or less the same metaphysical confusion as Lazarus and Steinthal before him and, in the 1909 fourth edition of his *Prinzipien*, extended his critique to Wundt's version of *Völkerpsychologie*. Other Neogrammarians and their supporters, such as Berthold Delbrück (1842–1922; 1901) and Ludwig Sütterlin (1902), essentially joined Paul in this critique of Wundt's *Völkerpsychologie*, even if they were less direct. Delbrück and Sütterlin preferred simply to ignore Wundt's claims about the national soul and discussed exclusively his individual psychology (cf. Klautke 2013: 70–71).

[5] In the first edition of 1880, the title of Paul's book was spelt *Principien der Sprachgeschichte*. Following an orthography reform, the title became *Prinzipien der Sprachgeschichte* from the 1898 third edition onwards.

In this environment, it is easy to see how Gabelentz' Neo-Humboldtian general linguistics, with typology as a core component, might seem like a 'remnant of a former time', as we saw Sütterlin (1904: 319) comment in section 4.1. In its ultimate aims, Gabelentz' project represented a revival of ideas that had long been unfashionable among linguists. In its emphasis on the internal coherence of language systems, however, it picked up on a theme that was becoming increasingly important in linguistic scholarship, and whose importance would only reach a crescendo in the structuralist era.

4.3 Surveys and statistics

While the conceptual foundations of Gabelentz' typology project may have harked back to an earlier age, the methods on which it was built were inspired by some of the latest advances across the human and natural sciences. In order to capture, characterize, and compare the organic structures of the world's languages, Gabelentz looked to contemporary developments in statistics.

In the typology essay, Gabelentz (1894a: 5) points out that many grammatical traits seem to form clusters across diverse languages, and that often these clusters cannot be attributed to a common genetic inheritance or to areal diffusion, the two explanatory factors to which nineteenth-century linguists would classically appeal. As an example of the kind of phenomena he has in mind, Gabelentz (1894a: 5) cites the fact that many languages with ergative-absolutive case marking also tend to put their genitive modifiers before the head noun and adjectival modifiers after the head. This alignment of features can be found in such far-flung languages as Basque, Tibetan, and Greenlandic. Conversely, languages known to be genealogically related frequently differ significantly from one another in their grammatical traits. Here he mentions how three language families—the 'Indo-Chinese' family (which more or less corresponds to our present-day Sino-Tibetan), Munda languages of India (which Gabelentz calls *kolarisch*), and Malay—which are characteristically polysyllabic and agglutinative have members that are isolating. The deep agreement in linguistic structure in the absence of the traditional explanatory factors and disagreement in languages that ought to be similar suggest some other necessary connection between these traits.

It is at this point that Gabelentz' notion of languages as 'free organic structures' comes into its own. He wants to quantify the distribution of traits across the world's languages in order to determine whether the apparent clusters they form represent statistically significant relationships:

Expressed statistically: *A* goes with *B* in ¾ of cases—*B* with *A* in perhaps ⅗ or ½ of cases; the co-occurrence is not necessary, but it is more frequent than we would want to attribute to chance alone. We may suppose that we are on the trail of two sympathetic nerves, which do not work together completely regularly, and now we would like to know the place where and how they are connected as well as the reason why this connection is sometimes disturbed.

(Gabelentz 1894a: 5)

Gabelentz (1894a: 6) goes on to sketch a programme for collecting the required data and compiling the statistics. First of all, he suggests establishing a commission to administer a questionnaire covering all possible grammatical properties in the world's languages. Questionnaires had long been a favourite means of data collection in linguistics and other sciences. In Gabelentz' time, Georg Wenker's (1852–1911) *Sprachatlas des Deutschen Reiches* (*Language Atlas of the German Empire*) was built upon a questionnaire-based survey of German dialects. While the project had been started on Wenker's private initiative, from 1879 it enjoyed the official patronage of the Prussian Ministry of Culture (see Knoop et al. 1982). Other official and semi-official language and dialect surveys conducted in this era include George Grierson's (1851–1941) *Linguistic Survey of India* (see Majeed 2018)—begun in 1894 after many years of lobbying the British colonial government for support—which relied on written questionnaires filled out by local officials; and Jules Gilliéron's (1854–1926) *Atlas linguistique de la France* (*Linguistic Atlas of France*), begun in 1897, which employed a single trained fieldworker, Edmond Edmont (1849–1926), to complete the questionnaires.

Gabelentz himself already had some experience with government sponsorship for questionnaire-based linguistic survey work: the Colonial Department of the German Foreign Office commissioned him to write the *Handbuch zur Aufnahme fremder Sprachen* (*Handbook for Recording Foreign Languages*; Gabelentz 1892; see Kürschner 2009), a guide to collecting basic vocabularies and grammatical information about languages in the field. This handbook followed in a well-established tradition of guides to scientific observation produced under the auspices of European governments (e.g. Herschel 2011 [1849]; Neumeyer 1875). These guides were issued to members of the navy, merchant marine, and other travellers to foreign lands and contained instructions on collecting accurate scientific data relating to climate, geology, flora and fauna, and the languages and cultures of foreign peoples.

The second stage in Gabelentz' survey programme is to process the data collected by applying what he called the 'statistics of conjunctures', an approach that would provide a 'mechanical' means of capturing an ironclad scientific image of the structure of the world's languages:

> The second step is purely mechanical, the statistics of conjunctures, which I briefly demonstrated above. Through this technique we will arrive in an irreproachably exact way at the knowledge of truly typical traits. What we have long suspected, what I myself have tried to show in isolated examples in my book [*Die Sprachwissenschaft*]: those predominating tendencies that manifest themselves in the most diverse facets of the life of language, they will now really be calibrated according to their content and value—in numbers, as if they were weights and measures. The ground would now be cleared for a truly valuable calculation of probability: from a dozen known properties of a language we would be able to conclude with certainty a hundred others; the typical traits, the ruling tendencies would lie clear before our eyes.
> (Gabelentz 1894a: 6–7)

The 'typical traits' and 'ruling tendencies' identified through these means can then be addressed by the 'third, highest task' of general linguistics, which involves moving from observing a mere 'co-occurrence' to establishing a true 'connection' that rests on the mentality, lifestyle, and living conditions of the speakers of each language (Gabelentz 1894a: 7).

As master of the art of intuiting typical traits, Gabelentz named the French pioneer of comparative anatomy and palaeontology Georges Cuvier (1769–1832), 'who in his mind reconstructed from a single bone the whole animal' (Gabelentz 1894a: 4). Cuvier (1812: 58) famously spoke of the 'correlation of forms in organized beings', the dependencies between parts in the anatomy of organisms. This 'correlation of forms' allows the palaeontologist to reconstruct an organism from fragmentary fossil evidence: from one partial imprint they can infer the likely structure of the entire creature. Cuvier described biological organisms in much the same terms as those later used by nineteenth-century language scholars to characterize linguistic 'organisms':

> Every organized being forms an ensemble, a unique and closed system, all of whose parts are in mutual correspondence and contribute to the same final action through a reciprocal reaction. None of these parts can change without changing the others as well; and consequently each of the them, taken separately, indicates and gives the others.
> (Cuvier 1812: xlv)

As Plank (1991: 433–436) observes, invoking Cuvier had become a commonplace in linguistic scholarship by Gabelentz' time, and Gabelentz was probably just continuing this practice without having any direct or intimate knowledge of Cuvier's work or comparative anatomy more generally. In particular, Plank (1991: 435–436) points out that Gabelentz' colleague Friedrich Techmer (1843–1891) quoted this passage from Cuvier at length in support of his 'palaeontology of phonetics' (Techmer 1880: 60–61). Following the model of Cuvier, Techmer envisaged the possibility of reconstructing the sound systems of ancient languages:

> Admittedly, phonetic palaeontology is not yet as advanced as its equivalent in the natural sciences. But we are already learning more and more to recognize a harmonic structure in the sound system of naturally developed languages and to determine the 'musical key' of the whole; and it may be hoped that we may be able to *find unknown sounds* missing in each dead language, like x, y, z ... from equations, when all that is given is the necessary number of quantities and equations, that is [a sufficient number of] sounds and their relations.
>
> (Techmer 1880: 61)

The reconstruction of ancient sound systems on partial evidence, including hypothesizing the existence of unattested sounds, was one of the major breakthroughs made in these years by the Neogrammarians and those in their orbit. This is the project in which Saussure was engaged in his *Mémoire*, which we discussed in section 4.2.

Techmer (1880: 60) hoped specifically for more research that would deliver a 'thorough statistics of the relative occurrence of sounds within the same language' as an aid to formulating his equations, and cited several examples of existing studies in this vein (see Techmer 1880: 174–175, note 12). However, these studies were not concerned with structural dependencies between sounds within languages but rather just with their relative frequencies of occurrence.[6] This can be seen, for example, in the contributions of American linguist William Dwight Whitney (1827–1894) cited by Techmer. Whitney

---

[6] Heyse (1856: 238), also cited by Techmer (1880: 174–175, note 12) here, used some of the frequency counts Techmer mentioned to offer opinions on the character of various languages in a style that might remind us of Gabelentz' later work. For example, Heyse (1856: 238) said that the 'retention of full original vowels' in Latin gives the language a 'full, powerful sound, which expresses a calm seriousness, solemn dignity', while Ancient Greek has a 'lighter flow, greater flexibility ... in harmony with the greater liveliness, flexibility, multifaceted education and the predominant talkativeness of the Greek national character'.

introduced what we might describe as a variationist perspective on sound change: he was conscious of the fact that there is always diversity in the speech community, that speakers will produce slightly different forms and sounds. Sound change as studied in classical historical-comparative linguistics, he argued, occurs when some sounds come to be used more frequently and others less so. In order to gather empirical data in support of this hypothesis, Whitney tabulated the frequencies of sounds in corpora of various Indo-European languages, from Sanskrit to historical varieties of Germanic, to Modern English (see, e.g. Whitney 1874).

From his frequency tables, Whitney was able to identify 'tendencies' in the diachronic development of sounds, such as the tendency in the history of Indo-European languages to gradually reduce the openness of vowels (Whitney 1874: 205–207). This tendency was supposedly a manifestation of a more general 'tendency to economy' in language that Whitney saw driving all diachronic change. Speakers constantly seek to expend the minimal amount of effort in expressing themselves, and this leads to the gradual reduction of linguistic forms, but also to the renewal of grammar: as collocations and compounds are reduced, they are compacted into new affixes and inflections (see Whitney 1875: 53; cf. McElvenny 2020). In the case of Indo-European vowel sounds, articulating closed vowels in preference to open vowels represents a reduction in effort because the speaker does not have to open their mouth as wide. Whitney's statistical treatment of sound change is 'atomistic', in that it considers only the relative frequency of specific sounds diachronically rather than the relations between sounds in the synchronic system of a language. In addition, in seeking an explanation for the observed changes, Whitney did not appeal to the inherent properties of the linguistic system, but rather to external factors, namely articulatory effort expended by the speaker. Nevertheless, Techmer saw data of this kind as a necessary input for his structural equations.

Another important source for Gabelentz highlighted by Plank (1991: 438–455) is the work of the French polymath Raoul de la Grasserie (1839–1914), in particular Grasserie's study 'De la classification des langues' ('On the classification of languages'; Grasserie 1889–1890).[7] In this text, Grasserie

---

[7] Grasserie's 'De la classification des langues' was published in two instalments in the *Internationale Zeitschrift für allgemeine Sprachwissenschaft* (*International Journal for General Linguistic*). Techmer was the founder and editor of this journal, and Gabelentz a member of the editorial board. In *Die Sprachwissenschaft*, Gabelenz (2016 [[1]1891,[2]1901]: 508) also cited Grasserie's (1882-1914) *Études de grammaire comparée* (*Studies of comparative grammar*), a series of monographs on the cross-linguistic comparison of grammatical categories, which Grasserie was still actively publishing at the time Gabelentz was writing.

(1890: 297) looked to the example of botany and zoology in developing 'natural' classifications of organisms based around the principle of the 'subordination of characters' (cf. Greenberg 1974: 43–44). A key principle of Cuvier's comparative anatomy, the subordination of characters is the notion that certain 'dominant' characteristics are decisive in determining the 'type' of an organism, while other characteristics are merely dependent on the dominant ones. Gabelentz (1894a: 4) invokes a version of this principle shortly before mentioning Cuvier when he says, 'It also makes sense that certain traits in the physiognomy of languages, above all lexical, stylistic and syntactic features, are especially characteristic'. In the typology passage of the second edition of *Die Sprachwissenschaft* we can also read: 'But it also seems as if certain traits are more important than others in the physiognomy of languages' (Gabelentz 2016 [[1]1891,[2]1901]: 507).

Although these antecedents within linguistics undoubtedly played a central role in shaping Gabelentz' typological ideas, it is quite likely that Gabelentz also derived inspiration from contemporary developments outside his own field. We may point in particular to the statistical notion of 'correlation' introduced in the late 1880s by Francis Galton (1822–1911). Galton's correlation describes situations in which it is possible to find two variables in a set of data whose values co-vary in a regular way (see Galton 1888–1889; Porter 1986: 286–296). This relationship can be used to predict the value of one variable from the other and, more importantly, may be a sign of an underlying cause that determines the values of both. In examining putative underlying causes among correlations in social and cultural data, Galton highlighted the difficulty of distinguishing features that are structurally interdependent from clusters of properties inherited or diffused from a common source. In his exchange with the anthropologist Edward Burnett Tylor (1832–1917), Galton famously pointed out that many of the apparent inherent structural correlations Tylor observed across kinship systems from around the world could very well be merely clusters of features that have been inherited or diffused widely (see the discussion in Tylor 1889: 270–272). The difficulty of teasing out system-internal and external factors like these has come to be known as 'Galton's problem'.

Gabelentz' 'statistics of conjunctures' sounds very much like correlation as conceived by Galton: Gabelentz similarly aims to quantify structural traits in languages and state in probabilistic terms the conditions of their co-occurrence, all the while eliminating external confounding factors. Gabelentz and Galton also share in a similar intellectual heritage: Galton adopted the term 'correlation' because of its existing use in research on inheritance in biology, a usage that ultimately goes back to Cuvier's comparative anatomy, as we saw earlier in this section (see also Galton 1888–1889: 135; Porter 1986: 290). Galton's original motivation for engaging with statistical questions was in fact his interest in biological heritability. As the founder of eugenics, Galton was in search of methods for tracing the transmission of desirable traits from generation to generation.

Galton's statistically ramified notion of correlation enjoyed a wide reception in the scientific community and was publicized in various generalist and specialist venues. Gabelentz would almost certainly have been aware of these developments. Quite apart from the widescale reception of Galton's ideas, Gabelentz had a background in statistics: as a university student, he had majored in public administration (*Kameralistik*), a discipline that made extensive use of statistical methods for modelling social and economic phenomena (see Vogel and McElvenny 2019: 18). Indeed, the origins of statistics as a field lie in efforts to collect and process mass data to aid in the administration of the state.

Above all, however, the programme Gabelentz sketches in his typology essay resembles approaches in physical anthropology, a major branch of the human sciences in the nineteenth century. The overarching goal of physical anthropology was to identify the distinctive characteristics of human 'races' by measuring various features of the human body—such as skull shape or colour of the skin, hair, and eyes—in different populations around the world and calculating from these data average values defining different human 'types'. There are indications in Gabelentz' writings that the analogy with physical anthropology was uppermost in his mind. For example, he habitually refers to the 'physiognomy' and 'physiognomic traits' of languages (Gabelentz 1894a; 2016 [^{1}1891,^{2}1901]: 507). While the term 'physiognomy' and its derivatives were often used in an extended, metaphorical sense in Gabelentz' day, in its literal meaning the term refers to the facial or other physical features of a person that may reveal both their individual and 'racial' character.[8] Like linguists, physical anthropologists were already engaged in widescale state-sponsored surveys, such as the German Anthropological Society's survey of school children in Germany, co-ordinated by Rudolf Virchow (1821–1901) with the support of the Prussian Ministry of Culture, which sought to identify the 'racial' composition of the German population (see Virchow 1886). Instructions on taking body measurements were also a standard part of government-issued guides to

---

[8] For a discussion of Humboldt's rather critical stance towards earlier, eighteenth-century versions of physiognomy, see Friedrich (2000).

scientific observation for travellers. The prevailing practice of physical anthropologists therefore provides a model of survey and statistics in service of characterization and comparison that Gabelentz may have sought to imitate in his proposal for typology.

These potential influences on Gabelentz from outside disciplinary linguistics should not be underestimated, especially when we consider Gabelentz' advocacy for statistical methods. Towards the end of the nineteenth century, statistical insights were increasingly informing the epistemology of the human and natural sciences, with a probabilistic conception of scientific laws becoming widespread (see Porter 1986: ch. 7), but linguistics remained largely impervious to these developments. Linguists were for the most part caught up in controversies surrounding the Neogrammarians' espousal of 'exceptionless' sound laws and the more idiographic inclinations of their critics. Wilhelm Wundt attempted to introduce a probabilistic perspective into these debates when he described the Neogrammarians' claims for the 'exceptionless' nature of sound laws as polemical overstatement for 'generally valid' (see Formigari 2018). Wundt (e.g. 1886, 1908 [1883]: 124–145) recognized a hierarchy of laws based on the scope of their validity: the more generally applicable a law, the fewer the factors that can interfere with its operation and cause apparent exceptions. The level of generality of a law, and therefore its place in the hierarchy, is to be determined by statistical investigation of the phenomena in which the law is manifested (Wundt 1908 [1883]: 138).

Gabelentz (1893; 1894b) himself, shortly before his death, made an ill-fated foray into the application of statistical methods to historical-comparative research. In an effort to prove a putative genealogical link between Basque and Berber, he drew up tables of probable sound correspondences between languages and dialects in these groups.[9] Sound correspondences in Basque and Berber are not absolute, as they are in Indo-European, argued Gabelentz, because these are languages 'at a lower cultural level' and as such allow a much greater variation in pronunciation (Gabelentz 1893: 606). A probabilistic proof should therefore suffice to identify cognates. Once again we see Gabelentz' work degenerate into crude generalizations and prejudice.

Gabelentz' attempted contribution to historical-comparative linguistics was largely ignored, and even those few contemporaries who did engage with it were unimpressed. Hugo Schuchardt (1842–1927)—a vociferous opponent of the Neogrammarians who might have otherwise been sympathetic

---

[9] Most present-day linguists do not recognize a genealogical link between Basque and Berber: Basque is generally taken to be an isolate language and Berber a subgroup within the Afro-Asiatic family.

to Gabelentz' aim of effecting methodological renewal—rejected this work as incurably dilettantish, criticizing Gabelentz for his apparent ignorance of the grammatical principles of the languages studied, his cavalier treatment of the linguistic data and his general laxness of method (see Schuchardt 1893; Hurch and Purgay 2019; McElvenny 2019: 48–55).

The use of statistical methods as a means of structural analysis only gained a foothold in linguistics around the 1930s, well into the structuralist era. The best known work of this kind would have to be that of George Zipf (1902–1950), who quantified various aspects of languages and postulated lawlike relationships between the variables he identified. For example, Zipf (1965 [1935]) observed an inverse relation between degree of inflection in a language and the fixedness of its word order; that is, the more highly inflected a language is, the more flexibility it typically permits in the ordering of words in the sentence (Zipf 1965 [1935]: 245–251). But the focus of Zipf's research lay on the interaction between individual structural features in languages and external factors of usage, such as his demonstration that the length of words co-varies regularly with their frequency of occurrence: the more frequent a word, the shorter it will be (Zipf 1965 [1935]: ch. 2).

Even when discussing relationships between structural features, Zipf's preferred mode of explanation was functional: for Zipf, as for Whitney, the guiding imperative in communication, as in all human activity, was to minimize the effort expended, as is brought out succinctly in the title of his 1949 monograph *Human Behavior and the Principle of Least Effort*. In the case of the relation between inflection and word order, Zipf (1965 [1935]: 246) argued that information about the role of words in the sentence can be expressed either by the morphological means of inflection or the syntactic means of word order, or this information can be distributed across these two domains of the grammar. The relationship between inflection and word order is therefore not so much an inherent property of the linguistic system as it is a response to functional pressures. Zipf's linguistic statistics should perhaps be seen more as a recapitulation of the approach pursued earlier by Whitney than an attempt at a true analysis of the internal coherence of language systems.

At the time Gabelentz formulated his typology project, statistical methods were being adopted widely in many fields and were reshaping the epistemological outlook of the human and natural sciences. Although there had been attempts to apply statistical methods to language data, and there were isolated statements about the desirability of extending these methods to describing aspects of linguistic systems, the mainstream of the discipline continued to think and talk in absolute terms. The application of statistics to capturing structural properties of languages and their interrelations was pursued only in the twentieth century, some time into the structuralist era. But this work was still not directed towards Gabelentz' aim of characterizing language systems.

4.4 Typology in the twentieth century

A recognized subfield of linguistics with the name 'typology' and bearing many of the features envisaged by Gabelentz finally emerged in the mid-twentieth century. Here for the first time we see the combination of linguistic surveys supported by statistical methods with a focus on the interactions between mutually dependent features within language systems. What we do not see, however, are the dubious appeals to speakers' mentality and lifestyles that formed the ultimate foundation of Gabelentz' project. The typology of the mid-twentieth century is epitomized by the work of Joseph Greenberg (1915–2001).

In some of his earliest typological writings, Greenberg (1963) surveyed features in diverse languages from around the world in order to arrive at a series of 'universals' of language structure, most of which he stated in implicational and probabilistic terms. An implicational universal is a claim of the form that if a language has one feature, it will most likely—and perhaps even necessarily— have some other feature. For example, Greenberg (1963: 73–113) examined the correlations between the order of grammatical functions in the sentence, whether a language has prepositions or postpositions, and whether an adjective normally precedes or follows its head noun. From his survey, he arrived at such statements of universals as 'languages with dominant VSO [verb-subject-object] order are always prepositional' and '[w]ith overwhelmingly greater than chance frequency, languages with normal SOV order are postpositional'. There is an unmistakable commonality in spirit between Greenberg's implicational universals and Gabelentz' statistical regularities revealing 'sympathetic nerves' in languages, which we examined in section 4.3.

But Greenberg merely states the structural relations and universals he identifies; he does not proceed on to Gabelentz' 'third, highest task' of trying to account for these phenomena in terms of ethnology or ethnopsychology. As Greenberg (1974: 48) pointed out himself, his typological efforts followed on from the school of anthropological linguistics that formed in the early twentieth century around Franz Boas (1858–1942) at Columbia University in New York. Boas, a German by birth who had received his entire education in that country, had strong links to the Humboldtian tradition of linguistic scholarship, in particular as it was developed and propagated by Steinthal (see Bunzl 1996; Trautmann-Waller 2006: 289–295). But in the Boasian school, the goal of setting up connections between language, psychology, and 'race' was incompatible with the increasing commitment to cultural relativism.

A common motif in much nineteenth-century thought was an evolutionist conception of civilization, centred around the idea that there is a unidirectional development in human culture through distinct stages, culminating in nineteenth-century European man. But there were always dissenting voices: many nineteenth-century scholars—including Humboldt, Steinthal, and his like-minded colleagues—began fitfully to develop a pluralistic conception of culture. Each culture was taken to be unique in its own way and not merely part of a deterministic evolutionary scheme (see Kalmar 1987; Joseph 1999; Rousseau and Thouard 1999). Even Gabelentz—despite making reference to 'lower levels of culture', as we saw in section 4.3—objected to the notion that there is a single path of development in the history of human language (see McElvenny 2016, 2017b: 13–14). Around the turn of the twentieth century, Boas sharpened this incipient critique even further, rejecting any assumption of a ladder of cultural and linguistic evolution. This became the official position of his school (see Darnell 1998: ch. 14).[10]

The new Boasian position is reflected clearly in the linguistic typology of his student Edward Sapir (1884–1939), which Greenberg acknowledged as a direct inspiration for his own work. In his 1921 book *Language*, Sapir (1921: ch. 6) offered a fine-grained analysis of various structural features across diverse languages and used these to put forward a preliminary overview of common language types. However, Sapir denied that these types somehow pinpointed the essential nature of these languages; on the contrary, he observed that language types are highly mutable diachronically (Sapir 1921: 154–156). Elsewhere in his book, Sapir expressed great scepticism about drawing direct links between linguistic structures and the mentality and culture of speakers. Sapir (1921: 230) admitted that there are often 'coincidences' of 'language, race, and culture', but that these are not because of an 'inherent psychological relation between language, race, and culture', but rather due to a 'readily intelligible historical association'. The Boasians' rising commitment to relativism and breakdown of racial essentialism effectively rendered questions of links between ethnography and linguistic typology moot. In light of this attitude, we can see why Greenberg would stop after completing the descriptive task and not seek 'deeper' ethnographically motivated explanations, as Gabelentz and the earlier Humboldtians had done.

---

[10] On Boas' innovations in linguistics and ethnography, see Chapter 2 of this volume.

Although Greenberg and Gabelentz in some respects shared an intellectual lineage through the Humboldtian tradition, Greenberg would seem to have developed his typology without any knowledge of Gabelentz' writings in this area. In his very well-informed historiographic treatment of the field, Greenberg (1974) makes no mention of Gabelentz' typology essay or the appearance of the term in the second edition of *Die Sprachwissenschaft*.[11] Greenberg (1974: 13) dates the first use of the term 'typology' in a specifically linguistic sense to 'around 1928' in the work of the Prague School, one of the cradles of classical structuralism (on the history of the Prague school, see Toman 1995). It was adherents of this school, argues Greenberg (1974: 45–47), who began to pose questions about universal patterns in structural dependencies within phonological and morphological systems across languages.

Gabelentz' proposals for a 'typology' of languages in his 1894 paper and in the revised 1901 second edition of *Die Sprachwissenschaft* seem to provide a tantalizing glimpse of the direction linguistic scholarship was about to take. But we should perhaps treat Gabelentz as a representative—and an obscure representative at that—of broader currents in disciplinary linguistics, rather than as a lone genius who anticipated key breakthroughs of the structuralist revolution. In his conception of languages as 'free organic structures', he merely continued a theme common in Humboldtian scholarship that was later refurbished by others to become a central tenet of structuralism. Other Humboldtian themes he perpetuated, such as seeking connections between linguistic structures and the putative mentality and living conditions of speakers, did not experience a revival but were abandoned out of embarrassment at their association with chauvinist ethnography. The most innovative aspect of Gabelentz' typology project, inspired by contemporary advances that mostly took place outside linguistics, was his suggestion of applying statistical methods to capturing the 'physiognomic traits' of languages. But this is an undertaking that Gabelentz never realized himself and which was not taken up in his immediate environment. Statistically based linguistic typology appeared only half a century after Gabelentz' death and was more or less an independent invention.

---

[11] Greenberg (1974: 40) does mention Gabelentz, but only in connection with his work on Chinese, which exploded some of the more rudimentary nineteenth-century schemes of morphological language classification. These schemes, the prime example of which is perhaps that put forward by Schleicher (1859, 1860: 33–71), generally imagined a progressive development from isolating to agglutinating and, finally, inflecting morphology as languages climb up the evolutionary ladder (see Morpurgo Davies 1998: 213–215; cf. McElvenny 2021: 4–6). Gabelentz' work on Chinese helped to show up such classifications as excessively simplistic: not only is it reductive to classify languages according to a single property, but there is evidence that Chinese previously exhibited inflection and in fact represents a counterexample to the supposed direction of morphological evolution.

Typology of langugaes—a new task of linguistics

Georg von der Gabelentz (1894)
Translated by James McElvenny

If linguistics is to answer the question of where the diversity in human language structure comes from, then the first thing that it will do, and which it has already been doing for some time, is this: it selects the most striking structural types—structural styles—and analyses, characterizes them. It explains the meaning of every peculiarity noticed according to the principle of *idem per idem*[1]—that is, it translates the linguistic phenomena back into the psychological, and in this way attains overviews of races and nations and tests the validity of these overviews against what is known from ethnology and history. This method would contain the greatest guarantee of certainty if it did not have to reckon with so many disturbing forces, which so often escape all observation and exact consideration. No one has made keener and deeper use of this method than Byrne (*Principles of the Structure of Language*).[2] But in my opinion he has paid too little attention to the disturbing factors, set the unknown values in his equations to zero, and at times he works with concepts that are too loose. Such a thinker is particularly susceptible to all these dangers. I hoped to be able to avoid them in my *Sprachwissenschaft* by working at a less fine-grained level, by sticking to the most tangible details: on the side of languages, to some of their most conspicuous physiognomic traits and, on the side of nations and races, to the broadest masses and to those who have presumably been subject to the same living conditions for the longest time and so have developed certain one-sided mental and temperamental dispositions to

---

[1] *Idem per idem* is generally known as the name of a logical fallacy involving a circular explanation (see Willems 2019: 117). Here, however, Gabelentz uses *idem per idem* to refer to the doublesidedness of the linguistic sign.

[2] James Byrne (1820–1897) was an Irish clergyman and linguistic scholar. Gabelentz is referring here to Byrne's 1885 *General Principles of the Structure of Language*, 2 vols. Gabelentz cites Byrne also in *Die Sprachwissenschaft* (2016 [^{1}1891,^{2}1901]: 450–451 et passim). See Plank (1991) for discussion of Gabelentz' reading of Byrne.

the greatest degree. It was only ever an attempt, but I still believe today that I did not go far [2] enough rather than too far. I knew from the beginning that there were a lot of details to add; a substantial book could have been made out of the one chapter in my *Sprachwissenschaft*,[3] but not an exhaustive one like that which Byrne sought to deliver.

Was the path taken really the only one that is passable? And if it is not: are there no others that are just as certain, perhaps even more certain?

The forces through which languages are shaped are of two kinds, according to their origin: native and foreign. Under the native forces I understand all those and only those that are rooted in the language community itself, in the nation. I know that many would like to further distinguish here between inherited disposition and the upbringing in which the native soil itself plays the role of teacher, but these can rarely be separated from one another.

Nevertheless, this issue still deserves consideration, since mass migrations occur frequently in human history. Here we would have a disturbing factor, which in addition will in most cases be uncontrollable and prehistoric in origin. But I do not want to overestimate the influence of this factor, since in nations and languages the distance between the inherited dispositions and the new tasks of life—insofar as these tasks can be fulfilled by the dispositions—seems to balance out in not too long a time. Both the nation and language would have to be in bad shape if they did not contain hidden forces in themselves that only await stimulation in order to awake from their slumber. But in both nation and language fully developed forces can also fall asleep if they have not had the opportunity to be exercised for a long time. We know of language families of very uniform type and then others with an astounding diversity of structural forms, and in both cases we believe we can discern the reason for this. Running parallel to the unity or diversity in human language structure is, on the ethnological-historical side, the essential similarity or difference of a nation's living conditions. The ancient languages are not always the best witnesses here, and that kind of research which drills down to the proto-languages does not bring the most usable material to the surface. This research may try to reconstruct an image of the proto-nation from the proto-language, but it would simply go around in circles if [3] it were to seek to elucidate the proto-language on the basis of the proto-nation. On the other hand, this approach is correct when it measures the racial disposition against the proto-language: the racial

---

[3] Gabelentz is referring to his chapter on the 'appraisal of languages' (*Sprachwürderung*; Gabelentz 2016 [[1]1891,[2]1901]: 409–502). See section 4.2 of the introductory essay above.

disposition has developed in different directions in the individual nations and yet it has done so through basically the same pushing and pulling forces. But even this may be limited; the common characteristics of a family are perhaps only significant when they have been retained in living form. When Latin gives up the Indo-European vowel grades except for a few scanty remnants, when its daughters lose their case endings, and when Modern Persian and, in strangely different ways, the Slavic languages have altered the old accent system, when in the Indo-Chinese family polysyllabic and monosyllabic languages,[4] isolation, agglutination and inflection, and the most diverse forms of sentence structure have been developed, then we know that on this point the linguistic and racial kind has shown itself to be flexible. We may then ask further what has caused this flexibility, and if history does not answer this question, if it does not reveal how much is to be attributed to the new homeland or to the disturbing or encouraging influences of the neighbouring nations, then we have at least gained negative knowledge.

Since our science, above all thanks to Hugo Schuchardt and Lucien Adam, has turned its attention to those new-born mixed languages, we can also make use of language mixtures for our purposes.[5] Of course, least suited to our purposes are those deformed products of international business communication in which no nation has made itself mentally at home or lived its mental life to the full. I must exclude from my research whole groups of languages that seem to me suspicious in this respect, such as those of the Melanesians, those of the Gold Coast of Africa, and others. But we also know that this was the beginning of some languages that today count among the best. Here the bastard was made legitimate through subsequent marriage, and in and with the new nation grew a new language. And so we have once again that which is important to us: free structures that have grown on native ground.

Consequently, the material we have for undertaking our research is actually richer and more reliable than it appeared at first sight. The languages of civilized nations, however, with their power developing in all directions, are less suitable objects of research [4] than the languages of lower races, with a one-sided upbringing and disposition.—That's enough for initial orientation.

---

[4] Gabelentz' 'Indo-Chinese family' corresponds more or less to present-day Sino-Tibetan, although the inclusion of Thai and other Kra-Dai languages in this family is at best controversial today. See also Gabelentz (1881: 4–5) and Gabelentz (2016 [^{1}1891, ^{2}1901]: 270, 449 et passim) for indications of where he drew the boundaries of the Indo-Chinese language family.

[5] Hugo Schuchardt (1842–1927) and Lucien Adam (1833–1918) are two linguists, principally active in the late nineteenth century, who made pioneering contributions to the study of Creole languages (see Moreira de Sousa, Mücke, and Krämer 2019).

If I disregard those foreign disturbing influences—as long as they remain foreign and a source of disturbance—and disregard as well those languages in which I suspect such influences, then I may say the following of the languages left over: they are free organic structures, and because they are, and inasmuch as they are, all of their parts stand together in a necessary connection. This makes sense a priori, and cannot be otherwise, and yet a lot is said by it. From the same mental disposition, the same historical conditions emerges everything that a language is and has: its phonology as much as the formation of its words, its sentence structure and the national style, the grammar and the vocabulary.

We may put this forward as a thesis and be sure of general agreement. It also makes sense that certain traits in the physiognomy of languages, above all lexical, stylistic and syntactic features, are especially characteristic. If we go further, if we want to imitate the gypsy fortune teller, who sees in the palm of the hand the whole person, or Cuvier,[6] who in his mind reconstructed from a single bone the whole animal—if we measure the theory against the facts, then it soon seems as if we had only the sad choice between either immediately declaring bankruptcy or artificially inflating the value of our stocks through trickery until bankruptcy results by itself.

But we cannot renounce a necessary idea that must ultimately be correct simply because the first attempt to realize it was unsuccessful. We must clothe the idea in a controllable form, and no form is more controllable than the statistical. It is here that I would like to see the work begin. If above I spoke of cases where languages of one and the same family have taken on a very different character, then I would now like to turn my attention to those other cases, where languages of different stocks have similar traits that reveal an elective affinity. In this way, I was able in my *Sprachwissenschaft* to compare the Malay languages with the Semitic languages in terms of their syntax—I could have also mentioned some correspondences between them in word formation and morphology.[7] That neighbouring peoples of different stocks often share features in their phonologies [5] has been observed frequently, and even by me, and may be amenable to explanation. But it seems rather mystical that in China and in the Trans-Gangetic Peninsula three otherwise polysyllabic and agglutinating language families, Indo-Chinese, Munda and Malay, have monosyllabic-isolating members, while Chinese, Burmese and Siamese with its group manifest such a fundamentally different mental character from other

---

[6] Georges Cuvier (1769–1832) was a founding figure of palaeontology and comparative anatomy. See section 4.3 above.
[7] See Gabelentz (2016 [^{1}1891, ^{2}1901]: 434–438) and section 4.2 above.

languages in the Indo-Chinese family. And Siamese, for its part, is so similar to the unrelated Annamite that it is as if the same building plan were here carried out in granite and there in sandstone.[8]

Hardly less astonishing is another phenomenon that can be observed, when two physiognomic traits that seem to have absolutely nothing to do with each other re-appear together at different places in the world of languages. Let me offer the most compelling example of this kind that I know. The Basque language in Europe, Tibetan in Asia, Greenlandic and its relatives in America and the languages of black Aboriginal people in Australia are different enough from one another in their grammatical structure. But the first three have in common two otherwise rare traits: first of all, instead of a subject and object case, they have an active-instrumental and a neutral-passive case, so that—to put it in our terms—the object of an active (i.e. transitive) verb and the subject of a neutral (intransitive) verb on the one hand and the subject and the instrument of an active (transitive) verb on the other always appear in the same case.[9] Secondly, they all distinguish sharply between the two kinds of adnominal attribute in that they put the genitive before its head and the adjective after the head. Expressed statistically: *A* goes with *B* in ¾ of cases—*B* with *A* in perhaps ⅗ or ½ of cases; the co-occurrence is not necessary, but it is more frequent than we would want to attribute to chance alone. We may suppose that we are on the trail of two sympathetic nerves, which do not work together completely regularly, and now we would like to know the place where and how they are connected as well as the reason why this connection is sometimes disturbed.

We should probably be prepared for such occasional disturbances everywhere, and certainly for numerous formulas that say: the phenomenon *A* appears with such and such a [6] probability with *B*, *C*, *D*, etc, but rarely with *E*, never with *F*. And these are the statistics that I am looking for. The question arises: can this already be achieved? and what is achieved by it?

That this can be achieved with the means available to us today is something that I can safely guarantee. Drafting the plan should not be too difficult at all, and there is a rich supply of literary aids; the only effort required is to pick them out. The study of languages conquers one province after another,

---

[8] Here as elsewhere in the translation we have more or less retained Gabelentz' antiquated geographical, linguistic and ethnographic terminology. The 'Trans-Gangetic Peninsula' corresponds to what we would now call continental South-East Asia, 'Siamese' is Thai, and 'Annamite' is Vietnamese. On the 'Indo-Chinese family', see note 4 above. Here we have translated Gabelentz' 'der kolarische [Sprachstamm]' as 'Munda'.

[9] Gabelentz is describing what would today be called 'ergativity'. See Dixon (1994) for a modern description of this grammatical phenomenon and Stockigt (2015) for a historiographic exploration of this concept. The glosses 'transitive' and 'intransitive' have been inserted directly in the text of the translation to make Gabelentz' description easier for the modern reader to follow.

and marks its rule through ever more competent textbooks. Indeed, the edifice must be erected on a broad base; every important type must be exhibited to its best advantage, and for every language a well legitimated representative must be available for questioning. Little would be achieved in this respect with schematic-mechanical extracts from random—at times even mediocre—grammars. But as large a number as possible of the most diverse languages must be represented, more than a single person can command. This work requires a commission, and the commission requires a programme that covers the smallest details, and this programme requires more self-effacing obedience than we can expect from most scholars. But such difficulties are to be overcome.

Under this programme I imagine a kind of questionnaire that exhaustively surveys category by category all grammatical possibilities, so that every question can be answered with either 'yes' or 'no'. Posing such questions is difficult for the questioner, and it is sometimes also difficult for the respondent to answer, but neither of the two is being asked for the impossible.

The second step is purely mechanical, the statistics of conjunctures, which I briefly demonstrated above. Through this technique we will arrive in an irreproachably exact way at the knowledge of truly typical traits. What we have long suspected, what I myself have tried to show in isolated examples in my book: those predominating tendencies that manifest themselves in the most diverse facets of the life of language, they will now really be calibrated according to their content and value—in numbers, as if they were weights and measures. [7] The ground would now be cleared for a truly valuable calculation of probability: from a dozen known properties of a language we would be able to conclude with certainty a hundred others; the typical traits, the ruling tendencies would lie clear before our eyes.

Clear but still raw, as long as we can only speak of a co-occurrence and not of a connection. Working out the connection is the third, highest task. And here linguistics will once again turn to ethnology and history; it will reach out from them and also towards them—it is the construction of a tunnel, undertaken simultaneously from both sides of the mountain.[10] From one side will be explained: this is the character of the language, therefore this is the character of the national mind. From the other side will be concluded: these are the constant living conditions, these are the historical experiences, these the

---

[10] The metaphor of building a tunnel from two sides of a mountain had famously been used by the physiologist Ewald Hering (1834–1918) to describe the relationship between physiological and psychological approaches to research into perception (Hering 1878: 106). See Ash (1995: 52–60) for discussion of the historical context.

habits and cultural achievements of the nation, so its mental kind must be like this. Here the picks from the other side become audible, unless we have literally dug ourselves into an untenable position. Once again that subjectivity of which general linguistics and its representatives is so often accused may manifest itself. But how far it is pushed back, how far the most objective data that we could demand, data that can be determined in calculable numbers, now reaches! If the work were only to progress so far, only to the point of incontestable statistics, then general linguistics would no longer need to envy the solid foundations of historical-comparative research. And if the work gets further, then we may see realized at the beginning of the twentieth century what the beginning of the nineteenth vainly tried to work out through speculation: a truly general grammar, completely philosophical and yet completely inductive.

Berlin. Georg von der Gabelentz.

> *This article had been typeset and was to be sent to its author for proofreading when the sad news of his passing arrived. Dr. Hans Georg Conon von der Gabelentz, member of the academy and professor at the University of Berlin, died on the 10th of December 1893.*
>
> —*The Editor*

5
Grammaticalization and the sentimental evolution of Antoine Meillet

John E. Joseph

5.1 Introduction

Antoine Meillet (1866–1936) was the most important linguist of the first half of the twentieth century in France, while his students would dominate the second half. He was born in his mother's family home in Moulins in central France, and grew up in the still smaller town of Châteaumeillant, about 100 kilometres to the west, where his father was appointed notary. When he was eleven his mother died, and his father moved back to Moulins so that his sons could attend its lycée (now the Lycée Antoine Meillet). In 1884 Antoine went to Paris to further his studies, first at the renowned Lycée Louis-le-Grand, then the following year at the Sorbonne. There he was especially inspired by the courses in Gothic and Old High German given by Ferdinand de Saussure (1857–1913), from whose teaching Meillet absorbed the principles of what would later come to be known as structural linguistics, in the wake of the posthumous publication of Saussure's *Cours de linguistique générale* (1922 [1916]).

For the rest of his life Meillet credited Saussure with the outlook on language that characterized his own work and that of two generations of linguists for whom Meillet was the *grand maître*, including Joseph Vendryès (1875–1960), Robert Gauthiot (1876–1916), Marcel Cohen (1884–1974), Georges Dumézil (1898–1966), Lucien Tesnière (1893–1954), Émile Benveniste (1902–1976), and André Martinet (1908-1999) (for an overview see Chevalier and Encrevé 2006). In all of their writings one finds an approach to linguistic problems from the point of view of the whole system, either synchronic or diachronic. A defining characteristic of Meillet's linguistic analyses was to focus on those elements that appear strange or surprising in the perspective of the language system as a whole, and to delve into them as a key to a deeper understanding of the system and its operation (for more on Meillet, see Bergounioux et al. 2006).

John E. Joseph, *Grammaticalization and the sentimental evolution of Antoine Meillet*. In: *The Limits of Structuralism*, Edited by James McElvenny, Oxford University Press. © John E. Joseph (2023).
DOI: 10.1093/oso/9780192849045.003.0005

Starting in 1910, Meillet contributed a series of articles to *Scientia*, an Italian journal which he described as being aimed at 'a wide but scientifically curious audience', and not 'specifically destined for scholars specializing in linguistics' (Meillet 1921: vii). His 1912 article 'L'évolution des formes grammaticales' (The evolution of grammatical forms) was one of these, and, as it turned out, it would have an enduring influence on linguistics through its introduction of the term and concept *grammaticalisation* (see Hopper and Traugott 2003, Smith et al. 2015).

The idea that, in the history of a particular language or language family, certain bound inflectional morphemes had at an earlier stage been separate words was far from new.[1] To take one familiar example, the future endings of Romance verbs coincided too closely with the present tense of *habere* 'to have' for it to be a coincidence; and at least since Nebrija's Spanish grammar of 1492 the idea was in print that Latin 'synthetic' futures such as *amabo* 'I shall love' had been replaced by new 'analytic' futures such as French *aimerai*, originally *aimer-ai* 'I have to love' (see E[lliott] 1892). The new insight offered by Meillet was that a range of seemingly diverse changes might be categorized together as being of this nature, and as constituting a single process occurring regularly and gradually across unrelated or distantly related languages.

5.2 Meillet's evolving approach to language

The 1912 article marks a significant mid-point in Meillet's evolution as a linguist. The previous decade had seen him appointed to a chair in the Collège de France, succeeding Michel Bréal (1832–1915). In the same period he was establishing his broader intellectual credentials as the principal linguist attached to the Durkheimian school of sociology and its journal *L'année sociologique*. The year 1903 had been the high water mark of the much publicized debate between Émile Durkheim (1858–1917) and Gabriel de Tarde (1843–1904) over the place of psychology within sociological research, and over what forms that psychology could and could not take. Durkheim and his associates won by default with Tarde's death in 1904.[2]

---

[1] McElvenny (2020) discusses some of the nineteenth-century background to Meillet's concept, particularly the version of agglutination theory found in the work of Georg von der Gabelentz (1840–1893). Despite overlaps and parallels, it is worth noting that Meillet (1912) does not refer to agglutination, perhaps in order to make clear that grammaticalization as he conceives it covers a much wider range of phenomena.

[2] For more on the debate, including the video of a 2007 re-enactment featuring Bruno Latour as Tarde and Bruno Karsenti as Durkheim, see http://www.bruno-latour.fr/node/354.html, last accessed 14.10.2022.

In these years Meillet took pains to stay in line with Durkheimian methodology, most strikingly in 'Comment les mots changent de sens' (How words change meaning), in the volume of *L'année sociologique* for 1905/6.³ It contains his clearest statements about why language fits the definition of a 'social fact' as Durkheim described it. Meillet presents as the driving force in historical change the movement from specialist dialects or argots, such as those of farmers or sailors, to the general language, identifying this as essentially a social change. He gives examples of what he will later call grammaticalization, such as Latin *homo* giving the French impersonal *on*, but says here that '[t]hese cases where the essential agent of change is the grammatical form are of a rather rare sort' (Meillet 1905/6: 10).

Meillet never ceased to proclaim the social nature of language, but by 1912 his focus had begun to shift away from sociological method, perhaps because he thought he had laid out what was needed in that regard. His perception of the rarity of grammaticalization changed as well. In the 1912 article it has come to occupy centre stage, displacing that movement of forms between social dialects which had been his focus in 1905/6.

5.3 How grammaticalization works: the loss of autonomy

The 1912 article's two instances of the term *grammaticalisation* occur in its opening section and closing paragraph. Both are in scare quotes, which indicates their novelty, but without any other comment, suggesting that Meillet regarded them as being self-explanatory.

The article opens by saying that two processes produce grammatical forms. The first is analogy. Meillet explains how analogy was the only explanation for exceptions to sound laws allowed by the Neogrammarians. Their single-mindedness, he suggests, was responsible for the lack of attention over the previous four decades to the second process, which he identifies as 'the passage of autonomous words to the role of grammatical agents', in other words, grammaticalization.

He gives the example of French *suis* 'am'. It is, he says, autonomous in *je suis celui qui suis* (I am that I am), and still retains a certain autonomy in *je suis chez moi* (I am at home). But it 'has almost ceased to be anything other than a grammatical element in *je suis malade* (I am sick), *je suis maudit* (I am accursed), and is only a grammatical element in *je suis parti* (I've departed),

---

³ Confusingly, the issue's cover says 'Neuvième année, 1904–5', followed by the publication date 1906; but the internal pages of the issue say '*L'année sociologique*, 1905–6'.

je suis allé (I've gone), *je me suis promené* (I've taken a walk)'. Intriguing are the things Meillet leaves tacit. Is it the first or second *suis* he is pointing to in the Biblical *je suis celui qui suis* (Exodus 3:14), or both? What about the clitic subject pronoun *je*, which from today's perspective seems like a more clear-cut case of grammaticalization than *suis*? His choice of words—'still retains', 'ceased to be'—clearly implies that originally autonomous elements have over time lost their autonomy and become 'merely' grammatical.

But what this autonomy consists of is not so clear. What precisely is the difference between the *am* of 'I am at home' and the *am* of 'I am sick' (there is no reason to expect any French–English contrast on this)? Is it that the adjective 'sick' modifies the subject, but the locative 'at home' modifies the verb—so that I could say 'I eat/work/sleep/etc. at home', whereas 'I eat/work/sleep/etc. sick' would be strange utterances? This is no more than a guess; Meillet relies on the intuition of his non-specialist readers to recognize the truth of what he asserts.

What is clear is that the concept of grammaticalization as first used by Meillet meant loss of self-governance, becoming dependent on another element. The dependence is clearly syntactic in the examples such as *je suis parti*, where *suis* has become an auxiliary, but it seems to be partly semantic as well. Some of his later examples will be more plainly semantic, as when he says that *petits* in *les petits enfants* 'the little children' has grammaticalized into an 'accessory word' (*mot accessoire*), since, after all, all *enfants* are *petits* (Meillet 1912: 388 [1921: 134]). Still other examples show the phonological weakening that often happens in parallel with grammaticalization.

5.4 The link to Saussure's 'relative motivation'

When Meillet argues that grammaticalization is a more important process than analogy because it 'transforms the whole of the system', we see him thinking in a diachronic rather than a historical way, to invoke a distinction introduced by Saussure (see Joseph 2012: 383, 551–552). Grammaticalization as Meillet describes it in 1912 has some points in common with what Saussure taught the year before in some of his final lectures on general linguistics in Geneva. Discussing limits on the arbitrariness of linguistic signs, Saussure noted that the evolution from Latin to French saw 'an enormous displacement in the direction of the unmotivated' (Saussure and Constantin 2005: 233; cf. Saussure 1922 [1916]: 184). For example, 'friend' and 'enemy' in Latin were the transparently related *amicus* and *inimicus*; but the French counterparts *ami* and *ennemi* are not perceived as related by French speakers. *Ennemi* 'has reverted to absolute arbitrariness' (Saussure 1922 [1916]: 184).

This is not far from the example Meillet gives of Proto-Germanic *hiu tagu* 'this day' grammaticalizing to become Old High German *hiutu* and Modern German *heute* 'today'. English *today* is itself an example of this type, which again not everyone today would classify as grammaticalization, since its result is a lexical rather than a grammatical form, although for Meillet these are core examples. When Saussure says in 1911 that '[a]ll the movement that evolution represents for the language can be summarized in a back-and-forth between how much is perfectly unmotivated and relatively motivated' (Saussure and Constantin 2005: 232–233), he again seems to anticipate Meillet's position that grammaticalization is the more important of the two processes of change because of its effect on the entire system.[4] Meillet did not attend Saussure's Geneva lectures, but as detailed in Joseph (2010, 2012: 318–327), the basic outlines of Saussure's teaching on general linguistics were already in place in the courses he gave in Paris on Germanic linguistics and occasionally other subjects from 1881 to 1891, when Meillet (starting in 1887) was his student.

From about 1920 Meillet will go further still, in a shift likely prompted by his reading of Saussure's *Cours de linguistique générale* (1922 [1916]). Here Saussure said that English gives a much more prominent place to the unmotivated than German does, since German indicates grammatical relations through the inflections on nouns and verbs, whereas English does it through position and the use of auxiliaries and prepositions. In this sense, German is more 'grammatical' and inclined towards the motivated, while English is more 'lexical' and inclined towards the radically arbitrary.

> These are like two poles between which the whole system moves, two opposed currents which share the movement of the language: the tendency to use the lexicological instrument, the unmotivated sign, and the preference accorded to the grammatical instrument, that is to say, the rule of construction. ... The ultra-lexicological is typified by Chinese, whereas Indo-European and Sanskrit are specimens of the ultra-grammatical.
> (Saussure 1922 [1916]: 183; cf. Saussure and Constantin 2005: 234)

---

[4] Bat-Zeev Shyldkrot (2008) explores other aspects of the Saussurean background to Meillet's concept of grammaticalization.

5.5 The co-evolution of language and mentality

This becomes a leading idea in Meillet's later thought. In a coda dated 5 May 1920 which he added to his 1909 paper 'Sur la disparition des formes simples du prétérit' (On the disappearance of the simple forms of the preterite) for its republication in his 1921 collection of papers, he says that

> [t]he essential feature of the morphological structure of Indo-European, and still of Latin, is that the word does not exist independently of the grammatical form: there is no word meaning 'horse', there is a nominative singular *equus*, a genitive singular *equi*, an accusative plural *equos*, etc. and no element signifying 'horse' can be isolated independently of the endings. On the contrary, in the modern type represented by English and, a bit less well by French, the word tends to exist independently of any 'morpheme': whatever role it plays in the sentence, in English one says *dog* and in French *chien*, where Latin had a series of forms depending on the cases.
>
> (Meillet 1921: 156–157)

Soon he will depart quite dramatically from Durkheim and develop ideas about the psychological development of the Indo-European peoples from an early 'concrete' stage to a more advanced 'abstract' stage. In his paper on 'Le caractère concret du mot' (The concrete nature of the word), presented to the Société de Psychologie in 1922 and published in the *Journal de Psychologie* the following year, Meillet wrote that 'a Roman was not capable of naming "the wolf in itself". ... The universal tendency of language, in the course of civilization, has been to give the noun a character more and more independent of all its particular uses' (1936 [1923]: 11–13). In the discussion following the paper, Meillet insisted that the development of languages must go from the concrete towards the abstract, and that, in consequence, '[t]he mentality of an Indo-European differs completely from a modern' (1936 [1923]: 17; see further Joseph 2014).

Either Meillet presented very different visions of linguistic evolution to audiences of sociologists and psychologists, or his own mentality was evolving. Or perhaps both. In any case, at the mid-career point of 1912, grammaticalization too appeared to him very clearly as a move from the concrete to the abstract. But the meaning of these two terms is notoriously slippery, over both long and short stretches of time (see Joseph 2018: 201–232). In 1912 concreteness seems to equate for Meillet with *precision* of meaning and the *force* with which the speaker wants to emphasize it. This idea of force connects with the tendency of words, as they grammaticalize, to be reduced phonologically; and to the link which Meillet makes between phrases becoming clichés, 'habitual' collocations, on their way to grammaticalization. He points out that syntactically significant word order too is the result of the same process. Describing how, in the English sentence *Peter hits Paul* or the French *Pierre bat Paul*, as opposed to *Paul hits Peter* or *Paul bat Pierre*, word order has taken on the character of a morpheme, Meillet has recourse to the term *grammaticalisation* for the second and final time.

It seems in the end that it is the back-and-forth between, on the one hand, the urge towards forceful, original expression, and on the other, habit, plus the fact that only so many 'original' collocations are available, that pushes the process of grammaticalization as Meillet saw it in 1912.

5.6 The link to Bally's stylistics

It is significant that Meillet ends the 1921 reprinting of the article with a footnote directing the reader to work on stylistics by Charles Bally (1865–1947) and Leo Spitzer (1887–1960), concerning the role of *sentiment* 'feeling' in the creation of grammatical forms (Bally 1905; 1909; 1913; Spitzer 1918). McElvenny (2020) has made a link here to aesthetics, another concept which was undergoing a long-term semantic shift. Bally, a classicist, used it in its etymological sense, which involves feeling of any sort, but this was being superseded by the more specialized sense of *artistic* feeling (outside science, that is: consider that no 'anaesthetic' numbs one's musical taste).[5] Bally's stylistics was aimed at a language's aesthetic side in the etymological sense of the affective resources of everyday language, and he explicitly distanced it from literary creation and the style of individual writers or speakers (see Joseph 2022a). The book by Spitzer which Meillet cites is also focused on languages, although Spitzer's detailed philologically based studies draw far more on literary writers than Bally ever does.

A key distinction here is where stylistics is positioned with regard to *langue* and *parole*. Bally's stylistics is concerned with *langue*, and the examples he gives (which by all evidence come from his own introspection) serve as illustrations of it. Spitzer is after the back-and-forth shaping of *langue* by *parole* and vice-versa, including the aesthetic effects visible in the *parole* of literary

---

[5] To narrow the time frame of the change: for Immanuel Kant (1724–1804), aesthetics covered all sensory perception. Its current meaning, restricted to art and beauty, dates from the first half of the nineteenth century, and only then did the term come to be applied to earlier work such as Edmund Burke's (1729–1797) on the sublime. The linguistic dimension of aesthetic analysis was underscored early on, notably by Samuel Taylor Coleridge (1772–1834), and also by Adolphe Pictet (1799–1875), mentor to the young Ferdinand de Saussure and author of a book entitled *Du beau* (see Joseph 2012: 217–219). Pictet conceived his aesthetics essentially as a semantic enquiry into the meaning of *beauty*.

writers. If there had existed more studies that, like Bally's, focused on everyday spoken language rather than literary writings, Meillet might well have cited them in preference to Spitzer, who because of his refusal to disavow the literary dimension would never get more than grudging respect from the linguistics establishment, and sometimes outright hostility.[6]

Despite Bally's demurrals, readers in his time and in ours assume that the *stylistique* of his titles is aesthetic in the literary sense, and McElvenny rightly points out how in more recent linguistics any aesthetic heritage in earlier work has been swept under the rug. The idea of expression, which in the Romantic period vied with representation and communication to be the fundamental purpose of language, has been gradually mechanized—taken out of the wilful control of the human Subject, and turned into a set of formal devices that are part of the language system. In other words, expression itself was grammaticalized.

McElvenny recognizes that Meillet's position was not deeply aesthetic, but part of a 'secret history of grammaticalization' that is recoverable in part from the added references of 1921, in part from overlap between Meillet's descriptions of the process and earlier views on expressive language by Gabelentz, who also invoked the aesthetic dimension, in its usual modern sense of individual style. I suggested above that expression itself is grammaticalized when it shifts from being an independent function of language to a mere set of linguistic devices. That is tantamount, in reverse direction, to Saussure's contention that changes in *langue* originate in *parole*. Many more innovations are introduced in *parole* than end up getting the social sanction required to make them part of the *langue*, or more precisely, of a new *état de langue*, since for Saussure any change in the *langue*, a system of values generated by the differences amongst elements, produces a new *langue*. Expression belongs to *parole*, being about how individual speakers make use of the socially shared language system so as to give a distinctive voice to the texts they produce. If the structures which they innovate for doing so come to be socially shared, they enter into the *langue*, by definition. Meillet puts this in terms of their losing their distinctive expressivity and becoming 'habitual'. Taylor (1981: 30–31) finds that Bally as well sees conventionalization as key to an element's changing status as affective or 'conceptual' (Bally's term was *intellectuel*), although not in the unidirectional way which grammaticalization represents.

---

[6] This was particularly the case after his emigration to the USA in the 1930s, and came to a head in his polemics with Leonard Bloomfield (1887–1949) (Bloomfield 1944; Spitzer 1944).

5.7 Parallels with Saussure (1912)

We have seen how Saussure's lectures of 1911 on the lexical and grammatical poles in a language relate to Meillet (1912). In the final publication of his lifetime, Saussure (1922 [1912]) proposes an Indo-European development which, although it does not refer explicitly to the sort of affective elements that Bally was concerned with, can be read as implying affectivity. The paper starts from Saussure's identification of a previously undetected set of adjectives in the Indo-European languages which have three things in common:

— a shared feature of sound which is relatively rare in occurrence, namely a diphthong with the vowel /a/,
— a shared isolation within the language system, each of the adjectives being attached 'neither to a strong verb nor to any etymological family', hence stranded on the associative axis, and
— a shared feature of meaning: all of them have to do with some 'infirmity', or a deviation from the 'right' or 'straight'.

Saussure includes as diphthongs not just vowel + /u/ or /i/, but vowel + any sonant (/i u r l n m/). So the set of adjectives in question in the 1912 paper (Saussure gives around thirty examples each in Latin and Greek, plus a few in other Indo-European languages) are ones containing /ai/ (including Latin *caecus* /kaikus/ 'blind' of the paper's title), /au/ (e.g. *claudus* 'limping'), /ar/ (*parvus* 'puny'), /al/ (*valgus* 'wobbly'), /an/ (*pandus* 'crooked') or /am/ (Greek γαμψός *gampsós* 'bent').

Their meanings place these words, putatively, in Bally's category of affective elements (see Joseph 2023b). Saussure suggests that these words were bound together by a shared semantic feature which speakers either were never aware of or eventually forgot. They were bleached away, like the semantic content of grammaticalized forms. He imagines

> a time when there existed perhaps only four or five adjectives of 'infirmity' with the diphthongs *ai, au, an*, etc. Around this nucleus furnished by chance, ever more numerous formations will have come to fix themselves, where a certain community of ideas favoured diphthongs with *a*. It would thus involve a fact of lexical analogy ...
>
> (Saussure 1922 [1912]: 599; my translation)

For Saussure, the key question in language change is not: Why are new forms introduced? Changes in the phonetic realization of phonemes happen constantly in the *parole* of speakers of the language. New forms are introduced, only a tiny proportion of which will find the social sanction that will make them part of *langue* (in a new *état de langue*). The real question is: Why are certain forms sanctioned and not others? (see Saussure 1997: 47). The scenario that Saussure is positing for the Latin adjectives is that a few of them happened to get realized in *parole* with /a/ diphthongs, and then the diphthongs with /a/ got 'favoured' for words sharing the general idea of infirmity. This analogical formation then affected the competition amongst innovative forms that occurs within *parole*.

If it is less than perfectly obvious that grammaticalization involves a move from *parole* to *langue*, this is partly due to Meillet's order of presentation. He starts from the semantic, giving examples of a single word, *suis* 'am', which undergoes no change of form, just a loss of meaning, or rather, as discussed above, a cleavage into cases where it has its original copulative meaning, and other cases where it no longer does. More precisely: a continuum, from complete semantic meaningfulness, to two degrees of semi-meaningfulness, to no meaning apart from its grammatical significance. But there is no continuum in the Saussurean dichotomy; and in any case, *suis* in its full copulative sense, as the first-person singular of *être* 'to be', is as much a part of the French *langue* as is its auxiliary *Doppelgänger*. Or is it? There is an undercurrent here of an ancient perception of grammar being more 'natural' and fundamental than lexicon, which is treated as relatively superficial and artificial, or whatever the opposite of the natural is taken to be in a given period (see Joseph 1995, 2000).

This undertow pulls at Meillet when he comments that his very first example, *je suis celui qui suis* 'I am that I am', where *suis* is a fully 'autonomous word', is 'moreover very artificial'. The immediate sense in which it is artificial is that it is not a sentence one would expect to hear produced by the average speaker of French, or indeed by any speaker of French who is not quoting the Bible passage. But what is especially intriguing is his saying that this opening example he has chosen is *du reste*—'moreover', 'besides', 'what is more'—very artificial. He is neither apologizing for the artificiality nor pretending it is not there. The artificiality is a sort of addition to the autonomous character of the word, not in contrast with that character, perhaps in harmony with it.

5.8 The politics of grammar ...

Meillet does not overtly express discomfort with elements lying outside the norm, escaping safe containment within the grammatical apparatus. But neither does he hint at any example of moves in the opposite direction, what would later be called 'degrammaticalization' (see section 5.9 below), where a grammatical element becomes an autonomous word. If from his silence I infer a certain satisfaction with the process, I may be reading that into Meillet's article from my own experience of latter-day linguists, for whom the enduring appeal of grammaticalization lies partly in its reassuring resonance with the faith that what is free for individuals to choose—and therefore beyond the linguist's control—is always liable to be sapped of its semantic strength, leaving it vulnerable to capture and incorporation by the system, the language, and brought within the linguist's purview.

Another aspect of McElvenny's secret aesthetic side to Meillet's treatment of grammaticalization is hidden in plain sight. Amongst its key words recurring early on (Meillet 1912: 385) are *autonome* 'autonomous' and *autonomie* 'autonomy', the literal meaning of which is the political one of being self-governing. In grammar, some elements are said to 'govern' other elements; in inflecting languages this metaphor—which linguists do not think of as metaphorical—is used to explain the case endings of nouns when they are the objects of verbs and prepositions, for example. The verbs and prepositions govern their objects, and sometimes the choice of preposition is governed by the verb. In other words, it is the verb that does the choosing, not the speaker. Therein lies the 'politics' of grammatical governance and autonomy.[7]

While putting the 'autonomous word' at the very heart of the definition of grammaticalization, Meillet questions the legitimacy of the dyad 'synthetic and analytic languages', a terminological variant on the distinction we saw Saussure lay out above as grammatical versus lexicological. Meillet's attack is on the terms rather than the concept: the term 'analytic' implies that the motivation for the use of autonomous elements in a compound form is to 'analyse' what is left unanalysed in the case of a synthetic form. 'It is not in order to analyse that compound forms are used', he says, 'it is for purposes of expression'. Not, in other words, about the representational function of language, at least not for its own sake. He relates it to what is 'habitual', as opposed to what serves for 'forceful' expression. 'Analysis and synthesis', he insists, 'are logical terms which are entirely misleading about the real processes'; for 'this is not a matter of logic, but of a feeling to be rendered and of an action to be exerted on an interlocutor'.[8] A matter, in other words, of expression, together

---

[7] Kant's application of 'autonomy' in the context of free will and self-governing reason lends philosophical overtones to Meillet's metaphor that are inseparable from the political ones. In the one instance in this article where Meillet describes grammaticalization as a change from autonomous word to grammatical 'agent', he clearly does not mean 'agent' in the philosophical sense of a wilful subject (which would be autonomous, following Kant), but refers rather to its non-technical use to denote someone who acts on behalf of someone else. But when, as noted in section 5.2 above, Meillet (1905/6) speaks of grammatical form being the 'essential agent of change' in a case of grammaticalization (*homo* → *on*), he does seem to imply that the language system is driving the change.

[8] As logical terms, synthesis and analysis lead back once more to Kant, for whom a statement about *A* and *B* is analytic if all the terms of *B*, the predicate, are already contained in *A* ('All bodies are extended', where it is impossible to imagine a body without extension), and synthetic if *B* introduces a term not

with communication, conceived of in what might fifty years later have been called performative terms.

This can be read as a late trace of Meillet's allegiance to Durkheim, fighting a logic-based psychology with the aid of weapons from the sociological arsenal of actions and habits.[9] At the same time, the political metaphor of autonomy foreshadows the next phase of Meillet's linguistic development, when he fashions himself into the linguistic guru of the 'new Europe' in the wake of the First World War. Meillet (1928 [1918]) foresees that not all European languages are going to survive the changes under way. Which survive will be determined by a sort of natural selection in the environment created by the rise of civilization on a continent thrust into modernity with the sweeping away of the old order.

> Small national languages are a step by which uncultivated peoples pass on the way to approaching universal civilization.
>
> But the multiplicity of small languages currently in use in Europe, already inconvenient, is preparing crises that will be difficult to resolve, because it goes against the general tendency of civilization.
>
> (Meillet 1928 [1918]: 244; my translation)

Hungarian, for example, he thought condemned to disappear, given its relatively small number of speakers, its isolation vis-à-vis the languages surrounding it geographically, its 'complicated structure' and its being the vehicle of what Meillet did not consider to be 'an original civilization' (Perrot 2009: 11).[10] There is a striking homology between how Meillet saw the semantic weakening and loss of autonomy of grammaticalized elements, and the fate of whole languages if they lack those things that he believed give a language force. The

---

already contained in *A* ('all bodies are heavy', where it is possible to imagine a weightless body). Meillet however was no Kantian, whether or not Sériot (2014: 17) is right about Meillet's (1921: viii) statement that '[e]ach century's grammar corresponds to its philosophy' being a paraphrase of Kant's 'a given period's metaphysics bears the marks of its physics'. Meillet goes on to equate logic with mediaeval philosophy, and sees *grammaire générale* as its continuation; whereas the nineteenth century, 'in extending to psychic and social facts the method of observation of facts in use in the physical and natural sciences since the Renaissance, has led to the grammar of each language being presented as a totality of facts', at which point he gestures towards Saussure (1922 [1916]). The word *sentiment* 'feeling' occurs one further time in the article, when Meillet (1921: 136; below, p. 129) says that when speaking of a *pied de lampe* we think of neither a foot nor a lamp but may have some vague feeling of them.

[9] See Joseph (2020: 116–117) on *habitude* and *habitus* in the work of Durkheim and his nephew and protégé Marcel Mauss (1872–1950).

[10] Joseph (2022b) discusses how these views of Meillet's were rejected in Hungary, including by his student and protégé Aurélien Sauvageot (1897–1988), whom Meillet had sent to Budapest to learn Hungarian, and who became France's premier specialist in Finno-Ugric languages, as Meillet had intended him to be. In a book published posthumously, Sauvageot (1992: 160) wrote that '[i]f a language succumbs, it is because it failed in its expressive task'.

general tendency of civilization to which he refers is a centripetal one, linguistically and culturally—and where linguistic diversity is concerned, subsequent history has borne him out in general, even if not on all the particulars. As for national civilizations, he lived long enough to hear Quislings in his own country denounce French civilization as decadent, with its hope for renewal lying with Fascism, although he was dead before the German takeover in 1940 which took that argument as one of its justifications.

5.9 ... and the politics of linguistics

Another homology is that between the grammaticalization process and the development of linguistics itself. I have mentioned how a part of the enduring appeal of grammaticalization for linguists may be its implication that today's *parole* is tomorrow's *langue*. Without denying the importance of the linguistics of *parole*, which Saussure had planned to develop prior to his unexpected death, and which some later text-focused linguists can be said to have undertaken, one can assert without fear of contradiction that, for mainstream linguistics, *langue* is its comfort zone. Indeed the great challenge for a linguistics of *parole* would be not to turn everything into *langue*, to systemize everything it meets, to the point that all of individual production only *appears* to be individual creation. Look hard enough and you will discover the hidden pulleys which make the puppet dance. The core work of linguists is, for the most part, to grammaticalize, to expose the sham of autonomy by formulating the hidden dependences and governances.

Lest the homology suggested here seem forced, consider the history of 'degrammaticalization', a term proposed by Lehmann (2015 [1982]) for a hypothetical process which he argued could not occur. This was during a period when 'natural morphology' was in vogue, and the idea was that grammaticalization was a natural process which it would be unnatural to think might be contravened. Indeed the present-day prominence of grammaticalization within historical linguistics is a continuation of the interest in it that arose in this context. By the late 1970s it was being routinely stated by linguists that grammaticalization is unidirectional, and cannot be reversed.[11] When various linguists suggested counterexamples, culminating with Norde (2009), the knee-jerk reaction of many linguists was to find a means of rejecting them as not *really* counter-examples; Lehmann (2015 [1982]: 192–194) is a case in

---

[11] Lehmann (2015 [1982]: 18) cites as examples Givón (1975: 96), Langacker (1977: 103–104), and Vincent (1980: 56–60).

point, maintaining very reasonably that he intended degrammaticalization as an empirical hypothesis, and that therefore attempts to falsify it strengthen its scientific credentials. He makes clear, though, that, in his view, it has not been thoroughly falsified. That this is his honest belief does not disarm it as a strategy for maintaining fundamental faith in unidirectionality, hence in the ultimate autonomy of the grammatical system and its potential for absorbing independent elements.

Structuralism in particular has undergone decades of accusations of being opposed to the Subject, that autonomous ideal who says Cogito ergo sum/I think therefore I am/je pense donc ... *je suis*, Meillet's premier example of grammaticalization. The Cartesian assertion would have seemed a more obvious choice for Meillet than the Biblical one, and no less familiar to the wide audience he envisaged. But *je suis celui qui suis* was, *du reste*, very artificial, making it strangely preferable. It is true that many structural linguists have chipped away at the ideal of the Subject, even when trying to make a place for it, as Saussure did by positing *parole* as the sphere of the individual. But this is not peculiar to structuralism. All of linguistics has always been dedicated to establishing the existence of invariants, and in the process marginalizing and swallowing up variation in all its vast messiness, denying and erasing any claim an element might have to autonomy.[12] Grammaticalization is an allegory of what linguistics itself has always been about.

---

[12] This applies even—indeed, especially—to 'variationist' sociolinguistics, the attempt to find social meaning for variations which appear to elude explanation within the linguistic system as traditionally conceived.

The evolution of grammatical forms

Antoine Meillet (1912)
Translated by John E. Joseph

The processes through which grammatical forms are constituted are two in number; both are well known, even by people who have never studied linguistics, and everyone has had occasion, if not to focus on them, at least to observe them in passing.[1]

One of these processes is analogy; it consists of making a form on the model of another; take the French examples *nous finissons* 'we finish', *vous finissez* 'you finish', *ils finissent* 'they finish'; *nous rendons* 'we render', *vous rendez* 'you render', *ils rendent* 'they render'; *nous lisons* 'we read', *vous lisez* 'you read', *ils lisent* 'they read'; based on *nous disons* 'we say', *ils disent* 'they say', the child who is learning to speak is led to form *vous disez* (rather than standard French *vous dites* 'you speak') without ever having heard such a form: this is what is called an *analogical* form. All the regular forms of the language can be qualified as analogical; for they are made on existing models, and it is by virtue of the grammatical system of the language that they are recreated, each time someone needs them. But usually these regular forms are also those which one has had the occasion to observe and, except in the case of new or rare words, the form obtained by the functioning of the grammatical system most often reproduces a form already heard and enregistered in the memory. Tradition is in agreement with the needs of the system. But it sometimes happens, as in the case cited, that tradition and system are not in agreement, and that, given the state of the language at a given moment, there are several possible forms; then analogy produces new forms, independent of tradition. And it is in these cases that *analogical forms* are usually spoken of; it would be more correct to say: *analogical innovations*.[2]

---

[1] It seems odd to open an article introducing a novel linguistic concept by declaring that it is well known to everyone. But this falls out from Meillet's Durkheimian concept of *langue* as a 'social fact'. Linguists may have extraordinary diachronic knowledge, but knowledge of the synchronic system is shared by all speakers.

[2] Another curious statement: both innovation and form are 'correct' here, but perhaps Meillet considered innovation more precise.

[385] The other process consists of the passage from an autonomous word to the role of grammatical element. For example *suis* 'am' is an autonomous word in the sentence, admittedly very artificial, *je suis celui qui suis* 'I am that I am',[3] and it still has a certain autonomy in a sentence such as: *je suis chez moi* 'I am at home'; but it is almost no more than a grammatical element in: *je suis malade* 'I'm ill', *je suis maudit* 'I'm accursed',[4] and it is absolutely just a grammatical element in: *je suis parti* 'I('ve) left', *je suis allé* 'I've gone/I went', *je me suis promené* 'I('ve) walked', where no one thinks nor could think of the proper value of *suis*, and where what is improperly called the auxiliary is only part of a complex grammatical form expressing the past.[5] It is however clear—and the history of the language makes this evident—that *suis* in *je me suis promené* is the same word as in *je suis ici* 'I am here'; but it has become a constituent part of a grammatical form.

These two processes, the analogical innovation and the attribution of a grammatical nature to a formerly autonomous word, are the only ones through which new grammatical forms are constituted. The details can be complicated in each particular case; but the general principles are always the same.

Since the beginning of systematic comparative grammar, we have been led to attribute more importance sometimes to the one and sometimes to the other of the two processes. The founder of the comparative grammar of the Indo-European languages, Franz Bopp, believed that examining the most ancient types of each idiom would enable him to return to forms that were in a sense primitive, susceptible to being analysed into the elements which composed them; for him, a word such as Sanskrit *émi*, Greek *eimi*, Lithuanian *eimi*, analysed themselves naturally into a word *ai* 'go', and a word *mi* 'me'.[6] But, for each analysis like this one, which is plausible—although naturally unprovable—Bopp was led to propose a hundred others which were either very dubious or totally inadmissible. After some fifty years of fruitless efforts in this genre, it was understood that the ultimate origin of grammatical forms is beyond our

---

[3] This is what God says to Moses in Exodus 3:14. Meillet does not indicate whether in calling *suis* autonomous here he means both instances of it; one might have thought that he considered the second more autonomous than the first, since it signifies pure existence, rather than just being a copula, and moreover does not have a subject pronoun cliticized onto it.

[4] Why Meillet considers *suis* to have more autonomy in *je suis chez moi* than in *je suis malade* may have to do with the grammatical analysis of the sentences: *chez moi* is a locative prepositional phrase which modifies the verb, whereas *malade* and *maudit* are adjectives which modify the subject, *je*, with *suis* in a purely copulative role (see section 5.3 above).

[5] 'Improperly' presumably because auxiliary suggests that *suis* somehow 'helps' the verb *aller* or *promener*, or at least 'adds' something to it.

[6] See, e.g., Bopp (1839: 67–68). Franz Bopp (1791–1867) is credited with inaugurating the 'agglutination' theory that occupied a prominent place in nineteenth-century linguistics (see section 5.1 above).

grasp. All known languages only appear at a more or less later date, most of them only in the modern period, and all in complete forms, which presuppose a long prior development; the languages of less civilized peoples often have delicate structures; [386] they do not have behind them a less long history than do the languages of more civilized peoples.[7] No idiom, whatever it be, gives on whatever scale the idea of what a 'primitive' language can have been,[8] whence it follows that no empirical data permit us to address, let alone resolve, the problem of the initial origin of grammatical forms. Linguists study the transformations of grammatical systems; they are not concerned with the creation of these systems. No doubt when a word passes to the role of a grammatical form, it can be said that, in a certain sense, a form has been *created*, but this creation takes place inside a language which already offers a complete grammatical organization, and this creation does not give us an idea of what can have happened in a time when there existed no beginning of a grammatical organization. Nevertheless we can maintain that, analogy being by definition excluded from the initial origin of forms, the only process which remains is the progressive attribution of a grammatical role to autonomous words or to ways of grouping words. In this sense, Bopp was obviously right; but his illusion was to think that, with the late data we possess, we can so much as glimpse how the forms existing in known languages, through either historical data or comparative processes, first acquired the values they possess.

By renouncing efforts to determine the initial origin of forms and proposing only to follow their development, linguists have been led to concentrate above all on the study of analogical innovations:[9] for, given an already constituted system which transforms bit by bit, analogy is the main agent which ceaselessly modifies the details, and sometimes even the general structure of the system. The linguistic movement which began around 1870 and that has often been labelled as the 'Neogrammarian' movement is entirely dominated by two

---

[7] When Meillet says languages 'appear', he is speaking of their first written traces. Hence it is somewhat confusing when he says that all languages have the same length of 'history' behind them, since he means what is usually called pre-history. His patronizing reference to more and less civilized peoples rather spoils the linguistic egalitarianism he is asserting; and unfortunately such references are not uncommon in Meillet's work. Meillet (1928 [1918]) considers the 'languages of civilization' to be few in number, including in Europe only French, German, English, and Russian (see section 5.8 above).

[8] 'Primitive' here signifies 'historically first'. Meillet puts it in scare quotes probably to deny any possibility of knowing what the first stages of a language were. One would like to think that he is also distancing himself from any characterization of those early stages as 'primitive' in the negative sense which that adjective had begun to acquire, but it is not clear that this is so.

[9] A contentious affirmation: the period is thought of mainly in terms of its concern for establishing 'sound laws' which were exceptionless, following the Neogrammarian order which the next sentence will discuss, and for which analogy was a sort of escape hatch for dealing with apparent exceptions. They would not qualify as exceptions were they not relatively rare—as indeed Meillet characterized them in his 1905/6 article discussed in section 5.2 above.

ideas: the constancy of the correspondences between phonemes of a single language at two successive dates, which are known by the name of 'phonetic laws', and the importance attributed to analogical innovations. When starting in 1878 Brugmann and Osthoff published a set of studies conceived following the new ideas, they called it *Morphologische Untersuchungen* (Morphological research), and analogy took up most of the pages. Hermann Paul's *Prinzipien der Sprachgeschichte* (Principles of linguistic history), which presented the principles of the new school, is essentially a theory of analogy. And when the late Victor Henry wanted to disseminate the ideas of the 'Neogrammarians' in France, he began with a study of *Analogie*.[10]

Though never lost from sight, the other process of innovation, the passage of autonomous words to the role of grammatical agents, has been much less studied over the last forty years. Now we are starting to concentrate on them once again. The importance of this is in fact decisive. Whereas analogy can renovate the detail of forms, but usually leaves intact the existing overall plan of the system, the 'grammaticalization' of certain words creates new forms, introduces categories which previously had no linguistic expression, transforms the system as a whole. Innovations of this type result, moreover, as do analogical innovations, from the use which is made of the language; it is an immediate and natural consequence of its use.[11]

***

A sentence essentially consists of an affirmation; it normally includes a subject, which is to say a word indicating about whom or what something is affirmed, and a predicate, which is to say a word indicating what is affirmed. The subject can be unexpressed, if known to the interlocutors; this is what normally happens with the imperative, a form which, by definition, is addressed to an interlocutor: *viens, venez* 'come' have no need of a subject; it is only if the interlocutor is not sufficiently designated by the situation that the person interpellated is called out: *viens, Pierre*. If someone is expected, one can say in Russian: *pridët* 'he is going to come' or, in Latin, *uenit* 'he is coming' without having to further designate the person, who is known by virtue of the situation or an earlier sentence. Or else, especially in the Indo-European languages, the form of the verb can suffice to designate the person: Russian *pridu* 'I am going to come', Latin *uenio* 'I am coming'. Apart from particular cases of this sort, a

---

[10] Osthoff and Brugmann (1878); Paul (1880); Henry (1883).
[11] This is an affirmation of Saussure's teaching that language change begins in *parole*.

sentence is composed essentially of a subject and a predicate, where the predicate can be a noun as in Russian *dom nov* 'the house is new', or a verb as [388] in Russian *Pëtr pridët* 'Peter is going to arrive'. These words are the principal words of the sentence. A sentence can include other principal words, thus a complement in a sentence such as, in Latin, *aedifico domum* 'I am building a house'; or *eo Romam* 'I am going to Rome', or *venio Roma* 'I come from Rome', or *habito Romae* 'I live in Rome'. The principal words are those which indicate the essential ideas for which the sentence is made.

But sentences are not made solely with principal words. In most cases other words are needed which determine, which specify the value of these principal words. Take a sentence such as: *laissez venir à moi les petits enfants* 'let the little children come to me'.[12] French orthography divides it into seven different words. Without dwelling on *à moi* 'to me', where *à* is hardly more than a grammatical element, nor provisionally on the article *les* 'the' which is also a sort of grammatical tool, we have here two words each of which is grouped with another: *laissez* 'let' and *petits* 'little'. Each of these words has its own meaning; but this meaning takes its value in the sentence only by its grouping with the neighbouring word. *Laissez* 'let' can be a principal word, in *laissez cela* 'leave that' for example; but here *laisser venir* 'let come' forms a set, where *laissez* is, to some degree, an auxiliary.[13] *Petit* 'little' has its own value, and, even, so far as an adjective can be one, the principal word, for example if someone says: *apportez le petit paquet* 'bring the little packet (and not the big packet next to it)'; but here *petits* only indicates an accessory quality of *enfants* 'children'. So, besides the principal words, there are *accessory* words. A word which is principal in one sentence is accessory in another; *venir* is accessory in the exclamative sentence: *il vient me dire cela!* 'he up and says that to me!'. And there are all the intermediate degrees between principal words and accessory words; *laissez* in the sentence cited is less an accessory word than is *faire* in *faites le venir* 'have him come'. But, in any given sentence, it is important to mark a clear distinction between the principal words and words which are more or less accessory.

Now, from the fact that a word is accessory, two kinds of alterations result, those which affect meaning, and others which affect pronunciation.

---

[12] Luke 18:16, Matthew 19:14, in both of which the Greek has just τὰ παιδία (*ta paidia*) 'the children'. Hence the French *petits* and English *little* cannot be ascribed to literal translation.

[13] DeLancey (2004: 1590) notes that the words 'to some degree' show how Meillet conceives of grammaticalization as 'a gradual process rather than a sudden categorial shift'. This is correct, although DeLancey's wording suggests that it is a process which will always eventually reach an end point of full grammaticalization—or indeed of disappearance, according to Hopper and Traugott's (2003) 'cline of grammaticality'—whereas Meillet's example indicates a stabilized continuum.

Each time a linguistic element is used, its expressive value diminishes and the repetition of it becomes easier. A word is neither understood nor uttered twice with exactly [389] the same intensity of value. This is the ordinary effect of habit. A new word is vividly striking the first time one hears it; as soon as it is repeated, it loses some of its force, and soon it is no stronger than an element that has been current for a long time. This is even more true of a group of words: most people speak and especially write by means of ready-made formulas, of 'clichés'; hence two usual words appear almost new if they are paired for the first time or if, at least, they are paired when they are not ordinarily paired; Horace pointed out long ago the force of a new alliance of words, a *iunctura noua* 'new juncture'; he illustrated it with many examples. Orators and writers who take care with style, which is to say with expression, make an effort above all to combine words in a way that is not banal and that consequently can make an impression on the hearer or reader. And if, at the end of several decades of literary use, a language is in general worn out by literature, if all the writers in all the great languages of Europe are now almost reduced to writing in either a banal or an artificial manner, this is no doubt largely because the number of alliances of new words which are practically possible in a given idiom is limited.

If then a grouping of words becomes frequent, if it is often repeated, it ceases to be expressive, and is reproduced more and more automatically by speakers. There was a time when *je laisse venir* 'I let come' constituted two genuinely distinct words and when *laisser* 'leave' had its full semantic value in an expression of this type.[14] But people got into the habit of grouping *laisser* with an infinitive, and the result was a rapid weakening of this word which lost its proper meaning, to become a sort of auxiliary of a principal word. Nevertheless *laisser* has not yet passed to the role of grammatical element because that phrase is used to express a very special and still concrete notion, and because *laisser* retains a clear autonomy of meaning and of form.

When a word is grouped with another in a way that tends to become fixed in certain cases, the result is that the word loses part of its concrete meaning in these constructions. Take for example the word *pied* 'foot'; used in isolation, it designates a well-defined part of the human body, very special in form; grouped with the name of an object, in expressions such as *le pied d'une table*,

---

[14] It is interesting that Meillet speaks of *je laisse venir* being two rather than three distinct words, as if the subject pronoun *je* has been so completely grammaticalized as to escape even his notice. The statement is unchanged in the 1921 reprinting. One wonders as well whether there actually exists solid evidence of *laisser* having its 'full grammatical value' in this construction in earlier times, or whether Meillet is assuming this based on the overall historical plot of grammaticalization as he has been outlining it.

d'une chaise, d'une lampe 'the foot of a table, chair, lamp', or *le pied d'une montagne* 'the foot of a mountain', the word loses its concrete value entirely, and only an abstract element of it remains: part of an object which supports and is in contact with a load-bearing surface. As Wundt has amply shown, we must not speak of metaphor in cases of this sort, as we unfortunately continue to do; the term is inappropriate.[15] We are actually dealing with another word; and, in Russian for example, in this case the word used is not *noga* 'foot', but the derivative *nožka* to designate the 'foot' of a piece of furniture. Inversely, the group of words often has a more precise, more concrete meaning than the joining of the component words would lead us to expect. When we speak of a *pied de lampe*, we no longer hardly think of a foot, in the abstract sense just defined, or of a lamp, but of an object of a particular nature which bears this name; we can on reflection represent to ourselves the two elements of the group, we have perhaps a vague feeling of them; but, on the whole, *pied de lampe* is the equivalent of a word, one designating one particular object. The grouping can be such that one of the words receives no actual grammatical characteristic: if in Ottoman Turkish, we want to talk about a garden of the Pasha's which is not familiar to the interlocutors, we say *Paşa'nın bahçesi* 'the Pasha's garden', with the sign *ın* of the genitive; if we are in a locality where the 'Pasha's garden' is known to all, the word *Paşa* will not take an ending, and we have, in a group bearing a single inflection, *Paşa bahçesi*; here there are almost no longer two distinct words, but a set locution. In the languages of the Far East, such as Chinese or Vietnamese, which have no affixes and where therefore nouns cannot be formed by derivation, it is by grouping together two words, each of which loses its proper signification, that we obtain nouns for persons or things; take for example in Vietnamese *phép* 'authorization' and *toán* 'to count'; we have a word *phép toán* meaning 'calculation, arithmetic'; with *bắn* 'shoot', we have *phép bắn* 'a shot', etc.; likewise *thầy* 'teacher' forms the nouns for the liberal professions; if *phép thuoc* is 'medicine', *thầy thuoc* is the 'doctor', etc. In sum, the habitual grouping deprives the words of both their expressive force and the expressive force of their union, and even their proper concrete value.

The words thus grouped by meaning are most of the time [391] juxtaposed to one another. From then on they behave in pronunciation approximately like one long word. We know that the way in which words are joined in the fluent pronunciation of sentences does not correspond to the word breaks as they appear in the ordinary writing of the modern languages. The convention has been established that every separable element having a role of its own in

---

[15] See for example Wundt (1900: 526).

the sentence is isolated in writing from every other element; this clear and convenient practice is founded uniquely on the role which the words play in the sentence and on the way in which they behave in it, and takes no account of pronunciation. For example the French definite article, which could not in any case be used on its own and which is always part of a group of nouns, is written separately because it can be separated from the noun which it determines, and we can say: *les enfants* 'the children', *les petits enfants* 'the little children', *les pauvres petits enfants* 'the poor little children', etc. From the point of view of pronunciation, *les enfants, les petits, les pauvres* each form a single word in these groupings. The definition of the *phonetic word* does not correspond to that of the *syntactic word*. The word group tends to constitute more or less a single phonetic word.

Now, numerous observations have shown that the same elements are pronounced shorter in proportion as the word they are part of is longer: in French the *â* of *pâté* is much shorter than the one in *pâte* 'dough', and the *â* of *pâtissier* 'pastry chef' and especially of *pâtisserie* 'pastry' is shorter than that of *pâté*.[16] The shortening has serious consequences: the vowel quality is often altered; a shortened vowel tends to close or, if it is already closed, can drop out completely. The accessory words grouped with others tend on this account to shorten and to change pronunciation. Moreover, both because of the shortening, and because, being accessory, they are pronounced without effort and heard without special attention, they are neglected, stripped of intensity, they are no longer more than half articulated. The history of languages shows that, as a result, accessory words have aberrant phonetic treatments. Against the principle of the constancy of phonetic laws there have often been invoked the special treatments which accessory words present. The argument obviously does not hold up; accessory words are found in particular conditions which determine particular pronunciations: their constituent elements, being shortened and weakly articulated, are exposed [392] to weakening or disappearance in cases where the elements of a principal word remain intact or undergo quite different modifications. In the past the rule of the constancy of phonetic laws was challenged based on the fact that English *th* remained voiceless at the start of almost all the words of the language, but became voiced in the article *the*; we now know that the initial voiceless consonants of accessory words are subject to voicing through a sort of weakening specific to these words; besides English, the phenomenon is seen for example in Irish, Scandinavian and Armenian; and it is not restricted to the Indo-European languages; it has been found in Samoa for example.

---

[16] See for example Grégoire (1899).

The phonetic alterations undergone by accessory words are often very profound. If we did not have the form of Gothic *himma daga* 'this day, today', we might struggle to believe an earlier *hiu tagu* 'this day' became Old High German *hiutu* (Modern German *heute* 'today'), and that *hiu dagu* 'this day' became Old Saxon *hiudu* 'today'; the doubts which could remain are relieved by the parallel passage of *hiu jâru* 'this year' to *hiuru* (Modern German *heuer*) or by that of *hînaht* 'tonight' to *hînet* in Middle High German, to *heint* 'today' in Modern Bavarian. The stress falls on the first syllable of the compound, on the demonstrative which contains the essential idea, namely the indication that it is about what is closest; the rest of the word has been reduced to almost nothing and has become unrecognizable.—The accessory words have come no longer to resemble the principal words even where, originally, they were identical. Thus in an ancient Greek dialect, Boeotian, words in long -*a*- have a genitive plural in -*âôn*, without contraction; but the corresponding article contracts -*âôn* to -*ôn*, and we have for example *tôn drakhmâôn*: in place of one single inflection, we have two distinct inflections, one for principal words, the other for the article.

The weakening of the meaning and the weakening of the form of accessory words go hand in glove; when both of them are fairly advanced, the accessory word can end up being nothing more than an element deprived of any proper meaning, joined to a principal word in order to mark its grammatical role. The change from a word into a grammatical element is accomplished.

[393]

***

The constitution of grammatical forms by progressive degradation of formerly autonomous words is rendered possible by the processes which we have just summarily described, and which consist, we have seen, in a weakening of pronunciation, of the concrete signification of the words and of the expressive value of the words and word groups. But what provokes it is the need to speak with force, the desire to be expressive. The history of negation furnishes an illustration of this principle.

Negation is expressed in common Indo-European by a little accessory word *ne* which subsists clearly in Sanskrit *na*, Slavic and Lithuanian *ne*, and Gothic *ni*, for example. But this very brief little word, which tended to be unaccentuated and which in Lithuanian and in Russian came to be closely grouped with the principal word it bears upon, rapidly became very unexpressive. Where it was necessary to insist on the negation,—and speakers almost always feel the need to insist, because most of the time we speak in order to act upon others in some manner, and we do what it takes in order to touch them, speakers were led to reinforce the negation *ne* with some other word.[17] This is what happened in Latin for example; just as German, in order to say *no*, came to say *nein* 'not one', Old Latin said *noenum* 'not one', instead of *ne*. Being an accessory word, *noenum* underwent a particular treatment and ended up as *nôn*. But thenceforth 'not one' was no longer found in *nôn*, and Latin *nôn* is not sensibly more expressive than Sanskrit *na*, Slavic *ne* or Gothic *ni*. French was led to reinforce the negation *ne*, which issued from *nôn* by a particular treatment of the accessory word, by means of little words such as *pas* 'step', *point* 'point', *mie* 'crumb'. We know how *pas* lost all of its proper meaning in sentences where it was an accessory of negation—a meaning perfectly preserved in the isolated word *pas* 'step'—, how *pas* on its own became a negative word, serving to express negation, and how as a result French *pas* is in its turn no longer expressive and calls forth a new reinforcement through accessory words; we are led to say *pas du tout* 'not at all', *absolument pas* 'absolutely not', or to have recourse to completely new phrases, such as the current slang expression: *tu parles s'il est venu!* 'my foot he came!'[18] a strongly expressive way of saying: 'he did not come'. [394]—The history of the German negation *nicht*, which etymologically signifies 'not a thing', is parallel to that of the Latin and French negation.—Languages thus follow a sort of spiral development: they add accessory words to obtain an intense expression; these words weaken, degrade and drop to the level of simple grammatical tools; new words or different words are added for purposes of expression; the weakening begins again, and so on without end.[19]

The grammatical categories which are subject to being expressed by means of words which have become grammatical elements are, as a consequence of what has just been said, those which have a certain expressive character; that at least is what takes place in languages which have grammatical forms characterized by affixes welded to words. Languages like Chinese and even more Vietnamese, which have no affixation, are led to express more categories by accessory words which are often called empty words.[20] But, in the

---

[17] The view that 'most of the time we speak in order to act upon others' seems uncontroversial today, but is innovative for the linguistics of the time. Classically, philosophers and practitioners of grammar and poetics characterized the essential purpose of language in terms of speakers representing the world in their minds, and of expressing their representations; rhetoric was the study of 'acting upon others' by using language to persuade them. Even William Dwight Whitney (1827–1894), who introduced many aspects of modernism into linguistics and whom Saussure wrote that he 'revered', identified 'the impulse to communicate as the governing principle of speech-development' (1875: 294), where communication involves others but does not equate with 'acting upon' them.

[18] The French expression literally means 'You're talking if he came'.

[19] As discussed by McElvenny (2020: 203–204), the 'spiral development' recapitulates an image used by Gabelentz (2016 [1891]: 269).

[20] Traditional Chinese grammar recognized an opposition between 虚字 *xūzì* 'empty' characters or words and 實字 *shízì* 'full' characters or words. The former term refers to particles and other morphemes with purely grammatical meaning, while the latter term refers to content words.

THE EVOLUTION OF GRAMMATICAL FORMS   133

Indo-European languages, categories such as the present and aorist of verbs, which simply express facts, are not likely to be characterized by the progressive welding of accessory words. Or if accessory words intervene, it is only secondarily, and after the weakening process is complete, as we shall see. It is different with categories which have a more intense signification and which as a result call for a clear and strongly characterized expression. The history of the perfect and the future are instructive in this regard.

By the perfect is meant a category with a very strong meaning, which indicates the action in so far as it is achieved, the result attained by the action, and not the action itself in its development and its duration or the act pure and simple. A meaning of this sort was expressed in Indo-European by a very particular type, with endings and root vowels specific to it, which in addition presented in many cases a reduplication of an initial part of the root, hence in Greek *leloipa* 'I left', etc.[21] This formation, very exceptional and hence very expressive, was not maintained over the course of the historic development of the Indo-European languages, in part because the meaning was weakened and degraded all the way to that of the [395] present, as in Latin *memini* 'I remember' or Gothic *man* 'I think', or to that of the preterite, as in Latin *cecimi* 'I sang' or Gothic *haihald* 'I held'; and in part because the type's structure was too specifically Indo-European to survive the ancient period of Indo-European: the general changes which were produced in the system did not permit the continuation of the conditions of formation which the Indo-European perfect required.[22]

But the form, in disappearing, left a gap. For the need was felt to mark clearly the achieved action, the result of which was envisaged. This was done most often by the grouping of a nominal form attached to an accessory verb.[23] And the reason is easy to see: the action achieved is already no longer a process, but a thing; hence it is properly expressed by a noun rather than a verb, since what the verb properly expresses is a process. This tendency is particularly manifested in the passive, and that is why the compound forms which serve to express the perfect first appear most often in passive form: Latin has *dictus est* 'it was said', starting from a period prior to the historic period (the process is moreover common not only to Latin and Osco-Umbrian, but also to Celtic,

---

[21] The present tense form is *leipō* 'I leave'.
[22] The second half of this sentence is a vacuous rhetorical flourish which amounts to saying that things happened as they did because conditions were such that they happened as they did.
[23] The nominal (noun) form referred to is the perfect (or past) participle. Although grammars list the participle as a form of the verb, it is inflected in the way that nouns and adjectives are.

which attests to the relatively great antiquity of the innovation).[24] And only much later, in the period in which the Romance languages were constituted, did an active type, of completely different structure, appear: *habeo dictum* 'I have said'. When this type was constituted, it had a great expressive force: I possess something which is said. This very striking process is found also in Germanic, after the most ancient period of the language (there is no trace of it in the Gothic of the fourth century after Christ), no doubt through an imitation of a Latin way of speaking which seemed striking and convenient; from this imitation of a way of grouping words, we cannot conclude that Germanic borrowed a grammatical form from Latin: grammatical forms properly so called scarcely seem to be borrowed; and, at the moment when the imitation could have taken place, the type *habeo dictum* still no doubt counted as two words felt as clearly distinct: it was not yet a grammatical form, but a grouping of words. With time, the type *j'ai dit* 'I have said' was unified and, early on, in French, it is purely and simply a way [396] of expressing the accomplished action, where the value of *ai* 'have' or of *dit* 'said' is no longer recognized; but then the group too ceases to be expressive; it loses its value as a perfect and becomes a simple preterite; and, since it then is in competition with the simple preterite, *je dis* 'I said', which is much less clear, with a more complicated and partly special formation, inflected moreover in a peculiar way (*nous dîmes* 'we said', *vous dites* 'you said', *ils dirent* 'they said'), it is sometimes ambiguous (*je dis* 'I say/said', *il dit* 'he says/said', *vous dites* 'you say/said' serve both as the present and the preterite), the simple preterite tended to disappear: it has today entirely vanished from use in Paris and in the whole region where French is spoken in the Parisian manner, which is to say in a radius of two to three hundred kilometres around Paris.[25] The progressive weakening of the value of the type *j'ai dit* has ended in making it into a simple preterite, with no remnant of its value as a perfect. The cycle has now run its course, and, to give itself a perfect, French will have to have recourse to some new phrase, the birth of which we cannot foresee.

Phenomena analogous to those observed in the history of Latin and the Romance languages, and notably in French, have occurred in many other languages, independently. For example, the Indo-European perfect had almost

---

[24] *Dictus est* is literally 'said it-is'; its perfectivity lies with the participle *dictus*. In Latin, the present passive 'it is said' is *dicitur*.

[25] The simple preterite remained in use—indeed still remains—in certain contexts, notably the recounting of historical events, in the speech of a highly educated elite, which Meillet is not the only linguist to treat as non-existent because it is reckoned as artificial, not natural.

entirely disappeared from use in Persian in the time of Darius; it was suppleted by a nominal form of the passive type, with a very clear passive value; to indicate what is accomplished, one said *ima tya manâ krtam* 'here is what has been done by me', with *krtam* here meaning 'done'. But there still survives in Old Persian simple preterites to express the act, and *akumâ* signifies 'we did', where it is about expressing the fact pure and simple. Later, the simple preterite was eliminated; there remained only the ancient compound form; but it took on an active character, and in Persian *kard* signifies 'he did'; *man* in *man kardam* has taken the value of a subject case; *kardam* 'I did' was inflected, which produced the impression of a single form in which the old participle was no longer recognized in any way; for the meaning, *kardam* is a simple preterite and no longer has the signification of the perfect, any more than does Modern French *j'ai fait*.

In a totally different form, the Slavic languages offer an exactly parallel development. At an ancient date, we find in them a simple preterite such as *budixŭ* 'I awoke' and a [397] compound perfect: *budilŭ jesmĭ* 'I have awakened' (with perfect value), literally 'I am the awakener'. The perfect value already no longer appears except in weakened form at the time of the most ancient texts, and, in the modern Slavic languages a type such as *voz-budil* in Russian, or *wz-budzilem* in Polish is a simple type with pure and simple preterite value. In many of the principal Slavic languages, notably in Russian and in Polish, there is no longer even any preterite other than the ancient compound perfect; the simple preterite has long since ceased to be used.

The evolution is thus the same in many languages, it would not be difficult to add other examples to those we have just passed in review. The perfect tends to be expressed by compound forms, of nominal character; as soon as they have entered into current usage, these forms tend to lose their perfect value; they degrade to the level of simple preterites; at the same time they lose their nominal character and appear as verbal forms. Then, being in general more regular than the ancient forms of the simple preterite, they tend to replace them.

The future or the durative present would give rise to remarks of the same order as those which have just been presented regarding the perfect.

Even in languages which have complicated conjugation, there can be no expression of future actions by particular grammatical forms. Such is the case with the Semitic languages and with many of the ancient Indo-European languages, for example. Early Germanic had no future, and still today we can hardly say that German has a future. To indicate an action to come, recourse is often had to forms which indicate an intention to do something; the grammatical form which had this meaning in the common Indo-European from which all the Indo-European languages have descended was the subjunctive mood; and so we find that, in Latin for example, forms such as *erit* 'he/she/it will be' or *dicet* 'he/she/it will say', which, through their origin, are subjunctives, have taken the value of the future and no longer even have any other value in Latin in historical times; comparative grammar alone alerts us that Latin *erit* and *dicet* were, in prehistoric times, subjunctives. In a more recent period of the development of certain Indo-European languages, the verb *vouloir* 'want' became an auxiliary for expressing the future; [398] in the mouths of many French people, *je veux faire* 'I want to do' already forms a group with a meaning weakened enough to be the equivalent of a sort of future. In English *I will make*, the development is still further advanced. In the southern Slavic languages and in Modern Greek, the future is expressed by means of a verb signifying 'want', but so degraded in form and meaning that only the linguist can now recognize it. In Modern Greek for example *thelô ina* 'I want to', reduced to *thelô na*, *thena* and simply *tha*, no longer offers any clue to the verb signifying 'want'. Elsewhere words signifying 'must' can be used, as in English, *I shall make* or in Modern Western Armenian *bidi anem* 'I shall do', literally, 'there is necessity that I do'; and then the accessory word can be reduced and become unrecognizable; instead of *bidi*, we find simply *di* in a number of Armenian dialects. It is by this means that the Romance languages obtained a future when the old Latin future became too weak, too inexpressive: *facere habeo*, which is the original of (*je*) *ferai* 'I shall do', signifies 'I have to do', in other words 'I must do'. The infinitive fused with the verb signifying 'to have'; *avoir* 'to have' took an inflection of its own, different from that of the isolated verb; when saying *je finirai* 'I shall finish', a French speaker does not think of *finir* 'finish' and of *ai* 'I have'; in saying *nous finirons* 'we shall finish', the speaker does not think of *finir* and of *ons*, and there could be no question of analysing *j'aimerai* 'I shall love' or *je viendrai* 'I shall come'. Consequently, these forms lost all expressive value. Since we are most often tempted to speak of the future with some particular expression, of desire, expectation or necessity, French came to refashion new futures for itself which still have a force of expression: a near future: *je vais faire* 'I'm going to do', where *je vais* 'I'm going' is already no longer anything but an auxiliary, and where the meaning of *aller* 'to go' is no longer perceptible; *je veux faire* 'I want to do', where the meaning of *vouloir* is still quite perceptible; *je dois faire* 'I must go', where *je dois* is hardly more than an auxiliary, but where the meaning of necessity is clear; *j'ai à faire* 'I have to do', etc. The future is not a necessary form; but in the languages where it exists, it is constantly remade.

Where there is a conjugation which expresses time, an explicit form is needed for expressing an action which is presently happening. But if one wants to insist on the duration of the action, complex expressions are often used which then go on to furnish simple forms. [399] English *I am making* is a current example of this fact. In all the present-day dialects of Armenian, the *present* is expressed by forms which no longer have any particular expressive value, but which were compound forms expressing duration. The type *sirum em* of most Russian Armenian dialects signified 'he is to love', and the type *g sirem* of most Turkish Armenian dialects is the result of the alteration of a complex form: *kay ew sirê* 'he stands and he loves', where *kay ew* has been reduced to *ku* and *ku* to *kə*; the pronunciation *g* of the old *k* is a particularity of the Armenian dialect of this region. The expression *kay ew sirê* expressed very strongly the duration of the action; the modern form *g sire* means no more than 'he loves' and is not sensibly less a single form in speakers' intuition.

Examples of this sort could be multiplied: the need for expression always causes groups to be created which, through usage, lose their expressive value and then serve as grammatical forms, devoid of force.

This shows how illegitimate it is to speak of *synthetic* and *analytic* languages. It is not in order to analyse that compound forms are used; it is for purposes of expression; and it is not in order to synthesize that we have unified forms: the unified forms result from a bringing together which in fact takes place between words grouped in a habitual way. When wishing to express oneself with force, one gives each notion a separate expression; one does not say *je ferai* 'I shall do', but *j'ai la volonté de faire* 'I have the will to do' or *il faut que je fasse* 'it is necessary that I do' or *je suis sur le point de faire* 'I am on the brink of doing'; this is not a matter of logic, but of a feeling to be rendered and of an action to be exerted on an interlocutor. And if *je veux faire* 'I want to do', *je dois faire* 'I must do', *je vais faire* 'I am going to do' no longer clearly express will, necessity, proximity, it is because, from the fact of their ordinary grouping, the words *veux* 'want', *dois* 'must', *vais* 'go' have lost their proper meaning, their expressive value, and have become simple auxiliaries while waiting to become one with the following infinitive. The Roman who said *facere habeo* 'I have to do' was doing no analysis, any more than the Frenchman who says *je ferai* 'I shall do' is doing a synthesis. Analysis and synthesis are logical terms which are entirely misleading about the real processes. The 'synthesis' is a necessary and natural consequence of the use which is made of groups of words.

[400] Words are moreover not alone in being subject to becoming grammatical elements; the way of grouping words can become a process of grammatical expression. In Latin, where the grammatical role of each noun is indicated by the noun's form, there is no necessary word order: for 'Peter hit Paul' one can say: *Petrus Paulum caedit*, or *Paulum Petrus caedit*, or *caedit Petrus Paulum*, or *caedit Paulum Petrus*, etc. The order is not indifferent; it serves to indicate certain nuances: depending on whether *Petrus* or *Paulum* is put first, attention is drawn onto one or the other word; but the order in no way indicates the words' grammatical roles. In French or English, on the contrary, it is the respective place of the words which indicates their role, and in exchanging the place of *Peter* and *Paul* in *Peter hits Paul*, the grammatical role of the two names would also be changed. Here, a word order which has for some reason become habitual has acquired the character of a 'morpheme', the mark of a grammatical category.[26] The expressive value of the word order which is seen in Latin has been replaced by a grammatical value. The phenomenon is of the same order as the 'grammaticalization' of this or that word; instead of it being a word used in a group with others which take on the character of a 'morpheme' through the effect of habit, it is a way of grouping words. Here again, there is a genuine creation of new grammatical tools, and not a transformation. The whole effect that French and English draw from word order to mark the relations of parts of the sentence with one another is a creation of these languages: neither Latin nor ancient Germanic offered anything comparable.

Paris, Collège de France.
A. Meillet

---

[26] The term 'morpheme' originated (as Russian морфема) in work of the 1880s by Jan Baudouin de Courtenay (1845–1929) (see Mugdan 1986). Meillet keeps it in quotation marks because it would not have been familiar to the broad audience aimed at, though perhaps also because he is significantly extending its use by applying it to word order.

6
Roman Jakobson, language unions, and structuralism in Russia

Encounter or misunderstanding?

Patrick Sériot

6.1 Introduction

It is now currently acknowledged that structuralism was not born in Paris or in New York in the years after World War II,[1] but that it has an older, more complex, more varied, more contradictory, and more puzzling history. It is also a received opinion that Roman Jakobson (1896–1982) was an early promoter, if not the founding father of structuralism. He is often presented in the western world as an American scholar. Yet, Jakobson was born in Moscow in 1896. His attachment to Russian culture remained important to him, to the point of having this simple epitaph in Russian written on his tombstone at Harvard: 'Roman Jakobson, russkij filolog' (a 'Russian philologist').

Not all of Jakobson's works in Russian or Czech have been translated into English, although almost all of them are now available, with the recently published Volume IX of his *Selected Writings* (Jakobson 2013–2014). There is nonetheless a whole area of his activity during his Czechoslovakian period (1920–39) that remains poorly known. It is precisely this untranslated area that will be discussed here, because it sheds new light on the tumultuous and tortuous history of the emergence of structuralism in Russian intellectual culture, which in the 'West' is known almost only for its literature and political ideology. *Rossica non leguntur*:[2] it is a great misfortune that the Russian language is so little known in the 'West'. The history of linguistics, most often

---

[1] It is, however, the main argument of Dosse's (1991) book, in which structuralism is essentially summed up in the Parisian quartet Foucault / Lacan / Lévi-Strauss / Barthes.

[2] 'What is (written) in Russian is not read'. The origin of this expression is 'Graeca sunt, non leguntur', common in the Middle Ages about monks who quoted Greek without understanding it or refused to read it. It was taken up in Russia in the nineteenth century, to lament the fact that works written in Russian were not read and known in the 'West'.

assimilated to that of Western linguistics, loses the possibility of seeing itself in the mirror of its other self: the linguistics of Eastern Europe. Translating Russian linguistics, philosophy of language, and semiotics should help to correct this distorted view.

Roman Jakobson's 1931 text which is presented in this volume, *K kharakteristike evraziiskogo iazykogo soiuza* (*The Eurasian language union*), has not yet been translated into English. Along with several of Jakobson's articles dealing with the same issues in the same period, it has remained almost unnoticed. It is my view that this text helps to answer a paradoxical question: was Jakobson, this supposed founding father of structuralism, a structuralist in the 1930s? In other words, what is the relationship between unions of language and structuralism? What is at stake here is the notion of *affinity*.

Linguistics and philosophy of language were the object of a passionate discussion in Russia more than in other countries at the beginning of the twentieth century: should *similarities between languages* be explained by contact in time (genealogical filiation from a common ancestor) or without contact (typology)? Jakobson added a third possibility, which is not a variant of the second: *teleology*. This, which he thought was specific to 'Russian science',[3] was to serve as the basis for his geopolitical vision of the Soviet territory, for his 'orthogenetic' biological model of the evolution of languages, and for one of his most original theses: the transformation of the rhetorical couple metaphor/metonymy into a fundamental principle of language, well before he published his 1941 book on aphasia. Two main themes will be discussed here: Russia and the natural sciences.

I will attempt to explain the kind of criteria and principles underlying Jakobson's argument by exploring its intellectual sources in a world where modernity blends intimately with a resolutely anti-modern universe: German *Naturphilosophie* of the early nineteenth century and the holism of the early twentieth century. Or: is claiming the existence of a breakthrough enough to achieve it? This investigation allows us to question the specificities of the reflection on language in 'Russian thought': is it 'radically different' from its Western counterpart, or is it only a local variant?[4] Was there a specific

---

[3] In 1929 Jakobson wrote an article 'Über die heutigen Voraussetzungen der russischen Slavistik' [On the contemporary prerequisites of Russian Slavic studies], which was not included in the *Selected Writings* in his lifetime, where he presents 'Russian science' as a unique epistemological domain and Russia as a structural whole: 'the conception of Russia as a structural whole'; 'Russian theoretical thought has always been characterized by certain specific trends'; 'One could characterize the Russian environment as hostile to positivism'. This highly controversial text has recently been published in his *Selected Writings* as Jakobson (2013–2014 [1929]).

[4] On a more specific study of this question, see Sériot (2007).

intellectual climate in the 1920s–30s in Russian culture, both in the Soviet Union and in some émigré circles?

6.2 Language unions

At the turn of the 1920s and 1930s, Jakobson, a Russian émigré who lived in Czechoslovakia, had in mind, in the midst of the economic crisis, a project which occupied him intensively for about three years: to prove, using phonology, the ontological existence of Eurasia, in other words the Soviet Union as a total, organic, natural territorial unit. What is at stake is the theory of 'language phonological unions', a special aspect of the notion developed in 1923 by Nikolay Trubetzkoy (1890–1938) of 'language union' (*iazykovoj soiuz, Sprachbund*),[5] a little-known episode in the history of phonology. This paper aims to present some of the paradoxical aspects of the epistemological, philosophical, and ideological foundations of Jakobson's conception of the Eurasian phonological language union, based on the discourse on language and sign in Russian culture.

The thesis put forward here in this introductory essay is threefold:

— Jakobson's theory of phonological unions of languages is very different from other works of areal linguistics of that period, despite appearances;
— it is not structuralist;
— it can be understood and only finds its coherence on the basis of the Russian émigrés' Eurasianist theory, thus revealing, in this particular case, an inextricable link between science and ideology.

Let us briefly recall that 'Eurasianism' is an ideological and political movement that issued from Russian emigration in the inter-war years. It was founded in Sofia in 1921 by a small group of four Russian intellectual émigrés: the linguist Nikolay Trubetzkoy, the geographer Pyotr Savitsky (1895–1968), the art critic Pyotr Suvchinsky (1892–1985), and the theologian Georgy Florovsky (1893–1979). The fundamental idea of this movement was that the Russian Empire, which had become the Soviet Union, corresponded to a *natural totality*, which was neither Europe nor Asia, but a separate continent, a 'world apart', and that this very continent, this closed unity, was characterized by a certain number of elements which united it and radically differentiated

---

[5] See Trubetzkoy's (1923) 'The Tower of Babel and the confusion of tongues', English trans. in Trubetzkoy (1991: 147–160).

it from other territorial units (mainly from Europe). It was an accumulation of ethnic, economic, anthropological, human, geographical, cultural, linguistic, etc. features (on Eurasianism, see Böss 1961; Laruelle 2008; Sériot 2014; Goldsmith and Laks 2019).

The part of the Western intellectual world which stems from the tradition of the Enlightenment is accustomed to explaining the evolution of phenomena by the criterion of causation: in other words, what comes next is the consequence of what went before. In Russia, however, language change has often been thought of in terms of 'development tendencies' (Trubetzkoy) or 'goal orientation' (Jakobson). Yet, there is more: if, for Antoine Meillet (1866–1936), an analogy of forms between unrelated languages is not a serious scientific object of inquiry (Meillet 1931), for Trubetzkoy and Jakobson on the contrary, taking for granted that no resemblance can be due to chance, it was evidence of *affinity*, that is to say, a *tendency to attraction*.

This difference in approach to both comparative diachrony of languages and their geographical distribution has resulted in a rich tradition of linguistic typology in Russia, for example Viktor Khrakovsky's (b. 1932) school in Leningrad. But what is less well known is the intellectual origin of the idea that *any similarity of form is necessarily significant*.

This origin is twofold. On the one side it comes from German *Naturphilosophie* of the Romantic era, which blurred the border between the natural sciences and the sciences of culture (or of 'mind': *Naturwissenschaften/Geisteswissenschaften*). The Russian variant in the twentieth century links languages to a particular 'landscape' (or *Landschaft*), refusing any randomness in their distribution. A second source is an amazing collusion between the Cratylism of the rejection of arbitrariness and a virulent anti-Darwinism which issued in Russia from an orthogenetic biology called 'nomogenesis', or development based on *laws*.

These two intellectual streams, united by the rejection of chance and the passionate pursuit of 'unitotality' (*vseedinstvo*) of the objects of research and of a synthesis of knowledge, are the key to explaining the peculiarities of the philosophy of language in Russia that hinder the understanding of some particularly ambiguous texts by Jakobson or Trubetzkoy, rather different from those most widely read and commented on in the 'West'.

6.3 The Eurasian phonological language union

Jakobson discussed Eurasia as a phonological union in the following works, for a total of about one hundred pages (most of them were written around 1931):

- 'Remarques sur l'évolution phonologique du russe comparée à celle des autres langues slaves', *Travaux du Cercle linguistique de Prague* II (*TCLP-II*) (1929);
- *K kharakteristike evraziiskogo jazykovogo sojuza* (1931a) [Literally: For a characterization of the Eurasian language union];
- 'Über die phonologischen Sprachbünde',[6] *TCLP-IV* (1971 [1931]a);
- 'Principes de phonologie historique', *TCLP-IV* (1971 [1931]b);
- 'Les unions phonologiques de langues', *Le Monde Slave, 1* (1931b);
- 'O fonologicheskikh iazykovykh soiuzakh', in *Evraziia v svete iazykoznaniia*, Prague (1931c) [On phonological unions of languages];

eventually, a later text:

- 'Sur la théorie des affinités phonologiques entre les langues', *Actes du 4e Congrès international de linguistes* (Copenhagen 1936) (published in 1938; Jakobson 1971 [1938]).

At the end of his life, Jakobson came back to his ideas on the 'space factor' in his *Dialogues with Krystyna Pomorska* (Jakobson and Pomorska 1980).

The fundamental work is a fifty-nine-page booklet: *K kharakteristike...*, published in Russian in 1931 by the Editions eurasiennes in Paris. To bring to light or prove the existence of the 'Eurasian language union', Jakobson selected three fundamental features: correlation of softness,[7] polytony,[8] and territorial continuity.[9] Once he had differentiated languages with phonological softness from languages without it, Jakobson delimited more or less concentric geographical *zones*:

---

[6] In his articles in German, Jakobson used the term *Sprachbund*, coined by Trubetzkoy at the 1928 Congress in The Hague, and not *Sprachenbund*: it does not consist in languages that belong as such to associations, but rather in parts of languages defined by distinctive phonological features, parts that can be detached from the whole and so become integrated into a new group made up of other parts of other languages.

[7] Consonant softness should not be mistaken for palatalization. The result of the palatalization of [t] is [č] (a *change* in point of articulation towards the front palate), whereas the consonant softness is a raising of the tongue on the *same* point of articulation. The hard/soft opposition is *not relevant* in English: the [t] of *total* and the [t'] of *tin* are in complementary distribution; they are contextual variants of the same phoneme /t/, one before a front vowel, where the tongue is raised (the 'soft' variant) and one before a back vowel, where the tongue is not raised (the 'hard' variant). In Russian, however, these same two [t]s can be found before any vowel, front or back; their opposition is thus phonologically *relevant*: the different phonemes /t/ ('hard') and /t'/ ('soft') are correlated; for example, /tok/ ('current') ~ /t'ok/ ('it flowed'). The hard/soft correlation can also be found in word-terminal position: /dal/ ('he gave') ~ /dal'/ ('long distance'). Interestingly, in his text Jakobson at times speaks of *palatalization* for softness and of *palatality* for palatalization.

[8] Polytony is a difference in tone pitch with phonological value, opposing two otherwise identical vowels. Swedish, Serbo-Croatian, Ancient Greek, and Chinese are examples of polytonic languages.

[9] This is why Jakobson rejected the Irish exception: Irish Gaelic is characterized by the hard/soft correlation *and* absence of polytony, but the break in territorial continuity invalidates any Irish claim to being part of the phonological union of Eurasian languages. In his review of Jakobson's *K kharakteristike...*, Meillet (1931) cited the Irish phenomenon as a strong counter argument.

1) All languages characterized by phonological hard/soft correlation. For Jakobson, this covered all languages spoken in Eurasia except those of the Soviet Far East (*Dal'nii Vostok*)[10] and included 'overflows' westward (Polish, Latvian, Lithuanian) and eastward (Japanese).
2) Polytonic languages. Here Jakobson's border comprises the entire Baltic region, including several Scandinavian languages. On the other side—and here Jakobson declared the relation *symmetrical*—are the polytonic languages of southeast Asia.
3) A strip (or zone) entirely surrounding this area and defined exclusively in negative terms: languages that are *neither* polytonic *nor* characterized by a hard/soft correlation, e.g. French or English.
4) An even more peripheral band characterized by polytony, among other features; this covers the central African zone, where Bantu languages are spoken.

This set of 'features' is supposed to bring to light the essence or singular specificity of Eurasian languages.

6.4 Breaking up language families

After this brief presentation, we can begin to study the epistemological foundations of the notion of language union. It is necessary to ask why it was so important for Jakobson to have an overall view of phonological relations among the world's languages and to discover natural ties in the spatial relations of *contact* (or even absence of contact) between phonological systems. We will have to examine how components defined as intrasystemic (i.e. Jakobson's relevant features) can be considered operative *outside* and *across* system boundaries.

Jakobson's main argument is that there are phonological features—that is, intrasystemic ones—that exceed system boundaries. Those phonological features 'spread like an oil stain' (Jakobson 1971 [1938]: 236), a simile that Jakobson used regularly in his writings on this topic. The primary feature of interest to him in this connection is the hard/soft correlation of consonants, which, he explains, *overflows the boundaries* of Eurasia (it can be found, for

---

[10] It is difficult to draw the exact border of Palaeo-Siberian languages like Chukchi or Yukaghir. But this was not Jakobson's main point. Like most Eurasianists, all his attention was focused on the overall view of the whole and the border between Europe and Eurasia.

example, in eastern Estonian dialects)[11] or else *constitutes* itself *that border* (e.g. the one separating Romanian proper from its eastern dialects, namely Moldavian):

> The study of the geographical distribution of phonological facts shows that several of these facts usually go beyond the limits of one language and tend to unite several contiguous languages, independently of their genetic relationships or the absence of these relationships.
>
> (Jakobson 1971 [1938]: 244)

6.5 A geometric vision of geography

In direct contrast to Serge Karcevsky (1884–1955), who based much of his reasoning on the concept of asymmetry, Jakobson and Trubetzkoy were fascinated by *symmetry*. For them an object existed if—or because— it has a symmetrical structure. But while for Trubetzkoy this symmetry was abstract (for example, as he saw it, the vowel systems of all languages were symmetrical),[12] for Jakobson symmetry was located in *space*, on a real territory. Jakobson's symmetrical layout is marked by his *centre/periphery* opposition, which brings to light the 'centrality' of Eurasian languages and the 'peripheral nature' of western European ones, defined exclusively by negative features. While Jakobson's reasoning looks very much like it belongs to linguistic *geography*, it was actually based on a *geometric* view of space.

In the dialectology of Jules Gilliéron (1854–1926) or the Italian neo-linguists, the centre/periphery opposition occupies a prominent place. But for them, the term *centre* is used for any region in which linguistic innovation occurs. Since linguistic changes have no reason to all occur in the same place, there is no region that is central with regard to all its linguistic features. The notions of 'centre' and 'periphery', which never refer to more than one feature, must therefore be considered as relative (on this point, cf. Ivić 1970 [1963]: 95). This is not the case in Jakobson's linguistic geography, in which this opposition is absolute: there are languages that are *in themselves* central or peripheral. In 1938, he comes back to this key idea:

---

[11] For Jakobson, Estonian and the Baltic languages (Latvian and Lithuanian) do not belong to Eurasia.
[12] See Trubetzkoy (1985: 117); French translation: Trubetzkoy (2006: 150).

A language can at the same time belong to different phonological affinities which do not overlap, just as a local dialect can have particularities linking it to various dialects. While the kernel[13] of the above-mentioned association[14] contains only monotonic languages (without polytony), its two peripheries: the eastern one (Japanese, the Dungan dialect of Chinese) and the western one (Lithuanian and Latvian dialects; Estonian) belong to two large associations of polytonic languages (i.e., languages capable of distinguishing the meanings of words by means of two opposing intonations).

(Jakobson, 1971 [1938]: 243)

Or, in 1931:

Polytony, in any of its forms, is absolutely foreign to Eurasian languages. Eurasia is thus symmetrically bordered by unions of polytonic languages: in the north-west by the Baltic union, in the south-east by the Pacific union. This is another example of the symmetrical structure of the eastern and western ends of the continent, to which Savitzky has drawn attention ...

(Jakobson 1931a: 16–17)

But Jakobson's geometric symmetry is puzzling, because he does not take isometry into account: the Baltic union covers a much smaller area than the Pacific union; at most, there is an approximate homomorphy. Moreover, Jakobson has nothing to say about what can be considered the crucial component in thinking on symmetry, that is, where the *axis* is situated, or even if there is one. It seems that Jakobson's geometric representation of space in the 1920s–30s can be traced back to the German geographer Carl Ritter (1779–1859) and from there to Pythagoras' and Plato's metaphysics of world harmony and order (see Plato's *Timaeus*). Attempting to use symmetry as a principle for ontologically proving the profound, intrinsic reality of discovered objects amounts to knowing *how to make sense* of geometric relations, to *attribute meaning* to what is hidden.

In fact, Jakobson's main argument is that the spatial distribution of phonological features is not random, but *corresponds* to other, non-linguistic phenomena (on the theory of correspondences, see Sériot 1993: 100):

We have pointed out that the association of softening languages is combined with an association of polytonic languages in the West as well as in the East.

---

[13] Jakobson uses the word kernel (in French *noyau*) here in the sense of a geometric centre.
[14] It is the union of Eurasian languages. In French Jakobson uses the term *association de langues* to translate *iazykovoi soiuz*.

> It is unlikely that this symmetry of the two borders of the same association is due to mere chance.
>
> (Jakobson 1971 [1938]: 246)

Jakobson does not formulate any hypothesis. If the facts precede the enquiry, if they are waiting to be discovered, his method of investigation is thus a pedagogy of the eye, supposed to make us *see* this dazzling *fact*, that there are naturally central objects and others naturally peripheral, and that moreover this relation of centre and periphery is symmetrical. There is even a space beyond the periphery: this kind of non-being of the languages which know neither hard/soft correlation nor polytony, a strictly negative definition of what most languages of Europe are.

6.6 The same and the other

More than 2000 years of philosophy lie behind the question of whether two things are similar or different. Jakobson's thinking on this subject does not offer any philosophical revelations, but it has the advantage of being explicitly confined to linguistics, although this does not exclude the problem of resemblance by ways of common properties or common origin from the broader debate on innate and acquired features.

What is an affinity between languages? 'Affinity' is a key term, whose deep ambivalence necessarily draws our attention. Originally, this term belongs to biology. It designates the ability of copulation between different species to lead to fertilization and viable hybrids. One thus speaks of sexual or physiological affinities. The question here is which latent metaphorical system Jakobson used when *constructing* his 'phonological affinities', all the while claiming to have *discovered* them, to have defined a resolutely new object of study, to have brought about what, following Gaston Bachelard, would be called an epistemological break (see Bachelard 2002).

It is against the background of questions of hybridization and language purity that Jakobson's use of the term 'affinity' in the 1920s and 1930s acquires meaning, and it does so by contrast. Jakobson established an explicit opposition between affinity (in Russian *srodstvo*) and kinship (*rodstvo*). For him, affinities are resemblances that in no way depend on genetic kinship but do not pertain to typology either. They are not inherited but acquired through spatial contact, convergence, parallel development, and/or harmonious spatial distribution.

In a 1958 article entitled 'Typological studies', Jakobson made an even sharper distinction between affinity and typology. He classified similarities between languages into three types, defined by object of study, method, and whether or not these involved time–space coordinates (1958 [1971]: 524); see Figure 6.1.

method	object	factor
genetic	kinship	time
typological	isomorphism	(neither time nor space)
areal	affinities	space

Figure 6.1 Classification of similarities between languages, according to Jakobson (1958 [1971]: 524)

An affinity is therefore not a state, as in typology, it is something that occurs, a dynamic process.

6.7 Preformationism

For Jakobson, dynamic development was based on a principle of *preformation*: languages converge not by adaptation but through the development or use of rudiments *already present* in them. Just as in Trubetzkoy's thinking, languages follow a particular 'evolutionary logic', so in Jakobson's theory they only come together because of a propensity to do so: 'Languages only accept foreign structural components when those components correspond to their own developmental tendencies' (Jakobson 1971 [1938]: 241).

This idea of preformation had been developed by Trubetzkoy in relation to what he called the wholeness of Eurasia:

> Eurasia represents an integral whole, both geographically and anthropologically. The presence within it of geographically and economically diverse features, such as forests, steppes, and mountains, and of natural geographical connections between them makes it possible to view Eurasia as a region that is self-sufficient economically. By its very nature, Eurasia is historically destined to comprise a single state unity.
> (Trubetzkoy 1925: 6; English trans. in Trubetzkoy 1991: 165)

The notion of preformation, which is sometimes considered the equivalent of *predestination* in philosophy of history, is clearly biological, that is, *naturalist*.

It is enlightening to contrast that notion with the one developed by a contemporary of Jakobson's, Joseph Vendryès (1875–1960). Vendryès' term was *predisposition*, although by this he meant not a 'tendency' to unite or resemble each other, but practical similarity of the sort that facilitated 'combinations' or hybridization:

> The basis of pidgin English is Chinese—a grammar-poor language. Strictly speaking, [pidgin English] is Chinese that uses English words. Using English vocabulary, which lends itself remarkably well to the purpose, sentences are built whose word order perfectly reproduces Chinese word order. This gives rise to an odd combination that proves the aforementioned *affinity* between the two idioms. In this case there is indeed a particular language at the basis of the mix, but the very nature of that language—the fact that it is virtually devoid of grammar—particularly *disposed* it to the role that fell to it.
> (Vendryès 1979 [1921]: 323; my italics, PS)

Not enough attention has been paid to the fact that the notion of affinities as an innate disposition to match up (a biochemical metaphor) was the dividing line between Jakobson and the vast majority of linguists studying language contact in his time. In Jakobson's thinking (in contrast to Sanfeld's or Pisani's) there was no room for the notion of 'substrate', and there was no notion of 'articulatory base' (in contrast to van Ginneken's thought). Meanwhile, the notion of space, which had been used unsystematically by Hugo Schuchardt (1842–1927) and Jan Baudouin de Courtenay (1845–1929; see the notion of 'border bilingualism'), was geometric in Jakobson's thinking: a Platonic and Pythagorian notion of *order and harmony*. We begin to get a glimpse of the gulf that lies between Jakobson and Meillet,[15] despite the former's repeated, superficial curtseys to the latter. For Meillet, change was caused both 'socially' and internally, and only occurred within language families. Jakobson's idea of change was one of teleological development in which unrelated languages converged by means of affinities.

The notion of affinities was pulled back and forth in conceptual history between resemblance and attraction. The originality of Jakobson's position, founded on his interest in anti-Darwinian orthogenetic biology, was to maintain that resemblance was *explained* by attraction.

---

[15] Meillet's review of Jakobson's work on the Eurasian language union (Meillet 1931) is a model of intellectual misunderstanding.

6.8 On the sources of typology: *similarity without a common ancestor*

In the 1930s, Jakobson had an explicit target: 'naturalism' in linguistics. What does that mean?

> The doctrine of Schleicher, the great naturalist in the field of linguistics, has been undermined for a long time, but one can still find many traces of it. ... Is it necessary today to remember that language belongs to the social sciences, not to natural history? Is it not an obvious truism?
> (Jakobson 1971 [1938]: 234)

Jakobson's target is 'orthodox evolutionism':

> There is a tendency to explain the grammatical and phonetic similarities of two languages by their descent from a common ancestor-language, and to consider only the similarities which may be explained in such a way that it remains without any doubt the most stable element of this doctrine.
> (Jakobson 1971 [1938]: 234)

> The similarity of structure is independent of the genetic relationship of the languages in question and can connect either the languages of the same origin or of different ancestry.
> (Jakobson 1971 [1938]: 236)

Now, we can pose the problem in the following terms: What is the value, or the explanatory power of the resemblance of form? Does it rely on *chance*, on *cause*, on a *hidden plan*? Or: Why are similar things similar? A way of tackling this puzzling question is a close reading of the way so-called 'bourgeois science' was presented in the Soviet Union in the 1920 and 1930s. Was it, strictly speaking, idealistic or materialistic?

A first step on the way to solving the problem in our linguistic field is the important paper which Ernst Cassirer (1874–1945) wrote in New York a few days before he died (Cassirer 1945). He drew attention to the striking similarity between the French naturalist Georges Cuvier (1769–1832) and Jakobson and Trubetzkoy's structuralism. His argument relies on the common epistemological attitude they shared: the 'law of correlation of the parts in a whole'. For them, what is true for the organs in their relation to the organism they belong to is also true for the phonemes inside the phonemic system of a given language. Willingly or not, Cassirer had the intuition that Jakobson and

Trubetzkoy's implicit mode of reasoning was the very naturalistic model they explicitly refused.

We shall now go a little bit further. The great German writer Johann Wolfgang von Goethe (1749–1832) is known abroad mainly for his literary works. Nonetheless, he saw himself essentially as a scientist-naturalist. His anti-Newtonian *Farbenlehre* (*Colour theory*) was for him more important than his *Die Leiden des jungen Werthers* (*The Sorrows of Young Werther*). Goethe was a promoter of *idealistic morphology*, the main theses of which can be summarized as follows:

— two forms may be similar without any contact either in space or in time;
— no similarity in form can be due to mere *chance*.

The consequence of those two principles is that there exists a *hidden plan* to be discovered and exposed. I will now try to show how this idealistic morphology is a useful clue towards figuring out some features of Jakobson's work that distinguish it sharply from 'classical' structuralism.

6.9 The theory of types

How can we explain and justify the similarity of objects which look like one another? There are three main possibilities:

1) a common ancestor;
2) teleological convergence;
3) harmony and transcendence.

Jakobson and Trubetzkoy chose the last two possibilities and rejected the first. Their reason for doing so is that similarity with a mechanical cause does exist but is *meaningless*. By contrast, similarity of pure form, without any *contact* whether in time or space, means that there is some plan, some design, a hidden teleology which governs those correspondences of form. Here we are confronted with an important and irreconcilable opposition between a positivist attitude, which considers that a similarity without contact is not interesting in the least, and an idealist morphology, which strives to unmask the hidden reason of similarity.

The first approach, for instance, will not be interested in the phenomena of doppelgangers, those people who look like each other, without having a common origin. Their resemblance is due to pure chance, and therefore does not have any bearing on the only issue which has a value: reconstructing the common origin. Meillet is a concrete example of this epistemological attitude:

> The classification according to the general traits of structure was found to be devoid of any practical or scientific utility; it is just an amusement, of which no linguist could ever take advantage.
> (Meillet 1921: 76–77).

On the opposite side, Soviet biologist Aleksandr Ljubischev (1890–1972), who during his whole life professed a very explicit Platonism without ever getting into political trouble, constantly maintained the opinion that no similarity of form can be due to chance: if frost patterns on a frozen windowpane look like tree leaves, if the shape of a seashell resembles that of a galaxy, all those phenomena can be summed up by a common rationale: *Eto ne sluchajno!* ('It is not by chance!').[16]

In the 1920s, Jakobson was deeply interested in a non-Darwinian biology which was becoming increasingly popular in the Soviet Union: the nomogenesis of Lev Berg (1876–1950). Nomegenesis is a theory which claims that evolution is governed, determined, and regulated by *laws* (in Greek *nomos* = law); it is a variant of *orthogenesis*, a general view of biological evolution which rejects any randomness. In a letter to Viktor Shklovsky dated 26 February 1929, Jakobson wrote: 'I read Berg's book on nomogenesis with passionate interest' (letter published in Toman 1994: 61). In later years, he recommended this work to Noam Chomsky several times (Toman 1994: 23).

In *Nomogenez*, published in 1922, Berg explicitly rejected Darwinian theory. Drawing support from Owen's theories, he emphasized the notion of *convergence*, that is, the independent acquisition of similar characteristics by unrelated organisms (Berg 1922: 105). But whereas Owen was trying to understand homologies, Berg overturned the value scale. The focus of his research was *analogies*, and he sought to show that, in diametric opposition to Darwinian theory, evolution did not proceed by divergence from a common ancestor but rather by the convergence of unrelated organisms living in the same environmental conditions.

Another source for Jakobson's ideas in the inter-war period is the theory of types of Nikolay Danilevsky (1822–1885). Danilevsky was an extreme nationalist and anti-Western thinker, both a historian and a biologist. He is known in Russian intellectual historiography for his book against Darwin (1885)

---

[16] Some of Ljubischev's works were reprinted under Yuri Lotman's supervision in the Tartu semiotic journal *Trudy po znakovym sistemam* (now *Sign Systems Studies*) in 1977.

and his book against Europe (1869). Both are extremely aggressive. Jakobson ranked Danilevsky among the 'wonderful fruits' of Russian philosophy due to his anti-positivism (Jakobson 2013–2014 [1929]: 218). Danilevsky proposed a theory of *closed types*. In this domain, he followed very closely Cuvier, who maintained that the living world was divided into four *types* (*embranchements*), totally different from one another and impenetrable to one another. This theory of closed types was important for Jakobson and Trubetzkoy, who used it in their work on linguistics to prove that the Russian (or 'Eurasian') culture was totally alien to the 'European' one. Thus, for Trubetzkoy there is a clear opposition between the continuous and the discontinuous in languages. For instance, he claims that Russian and Mordvinian, which are totally unrelated genetically, present a phonemic *continuity* (they belong to the *same type*), whereas Russian and Czech, linked by an obvious kinship, display a discontinuity (they are members of two *different* phonemic types).

Goethe, the main representative of idealistic morphology, thought that all plants go back by 'metamorphosis' to an ideal, primordial proto-plant (*Urpflanze*), which is not a common ancestor, but an ideal prototype. Trubetzkoy and Jakobson share Goethe's concept of archetype, but they add to it the very different principle of closed type, borrowed from Cuvier.

6.10 The enigma of similarities

In our quest for the little-known sources of Jakobson's way of thinking, another unexpected candidate appears: Paracelsus (1493–1541). In the Renaissance, a common cure for headaches was to eat walnuts. What is the *link* between the two, walnuts and headaches? It is the *similarity* between the form of a walnut and the form of the human brain. If one thinks that no similarity of form is due to chance, then it is normal that there is something superior which links walnuts and the brain. This kind of medicine—known as *sympathetic medicine*—makes sense (and has its delusional efficacy) if one accepts the premise that form *is* a content. My point is that Jakobson took this question of similarity of form very seriously. Let us take his definition of poetry: 'The poetic function projects the principle of equivalence from the axes of selection to the axes of combination' (Jakobson 1960: 358).

In this very famous but very intriguing formula, Jakobson highlights the important role he assigns to similarities and contiguities in verbal art. A clue to how to understand this enigmatic formula is given surreptitiously by Jakobson in a paper from 1956 where he writes:

> The principles underlying magic rites have been resolved by Frazer into two types: charms based on the law of similarity and those founded on association by contiguity. ... This bipartition is indeed illuminating.
>
> (Jakobson 1971b [1956]: 258)

What Jakobson found in the work of the British anthropologist James Frazer (1854–1941) is the principle of *sympathetic magic* in 'primitive' cultures, divided into magic by contact and magic by resemblance. Here is the passage from Frazer's *The Golden Bough* which is decisive for our discussion:

> If we analyse the principles of thought on which magic is based, they will probably be found to resolve themselves into two: first, that like produces like, or that an effect resembles its cause; and, second, that things which have once been in contact with each other continue to act on each other at a distance after the physical contact has been severed. The former principle may be called the Law of Similarity, the latter the Law of Contact or Contagion. From the first of these principles, namely the Law of Similarity, the magician infers that he can produce any effect he desires merely by imitating it: from the second he infers that whatever he does to a material object will affect equally the person with whom the object was once in contact, whether it formed part of his body or not. Charms based on the Law of Similarity may be called Homoeopathic or Imitative Magic. Charms based on the Law of Contact or Contagion may be called Contagious Magic.
>
> (Frazer 1911 [1890]: 52)

Little by little we begin to piece together the parts of the puzzle:

similarity → metaphor (syntagmatic axis)
contiguity → metonymy (paradigmatic axis)

A next step in this reconstitution of the origins of Jakobson's ideas in the inter-war period is most likely the *Naturphilosophie* of the first half of the nineteenth century. The notion of *function* was soon to emerge. It was on this basis that the British anatomist Richard Owen (1804–1892) developed the opposition between *homology* and *analogy* that from then on dominated comparative anatomy, especially after it was redefined in the theory of evolution. In 1843 Owen systematized the opposition in *Naturphilosophie* between *affinity* and *analogy*, except that the word *affinity* was replaced by *homology*. Organs or body parts that had the same *function* in different animals regardless of their origin (e.g. wings in birds and wings in insects) were *analogous* while organs of the same origin in different animals and regardless of form or function were *homologous* (e.g. birds' wings and whales' pectoral fins).

I wish to draw attention to the striking parallelism of argumentation in Jakobson and Richard Owen: the opposition between homology and analogy in the philosophy of nature in the middle of the nineteenth century is used by Jakobson to support the idea of difference between language families and language unions. In this regard, Jakobson's 1931 *K kharakteristike...* is of fundamental significance. Jakobson's main idea is that language unions are more important, or more real, than language families as a way of explaining the existence of Eurasia. In that respect, Jakobson goes further than Trubetzkoy. Thus, despite the obvious genetic link between Russian and Czech, those two languages belong to two completely different cultural worlds, and this difference is based on the fact that Czech does not have the hard/soft phonological correlation, whereas all the languages of Eurasia possess it. It is also a way of contrasting Romanian and Moldavian.

This opposition is reinforced by a fascination for symmetry. Here, as in Platonism, geometry is a means of interpreting geography. Jakobson's comment about the symmetrical position of the Baltic and south-east polytonic unions on both sides of Eurasia is the same as in Ljubischev's *Eto ne sluchajno!* ('It is not by chance!'). Another example of this overwhelming role of geometry and symmetry is Jakobson's interpretation of the place of the articles in Western European languages, shown in Figure 6.2.

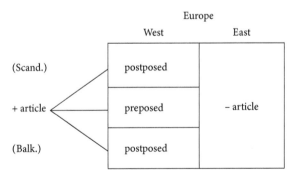

Figure 6.2 The position of articles in Western European languages according to Jakobson

In order to link Jakobson's interest for symmetry and similarity, we have to turn now to Greek philosophy, more exactly to Empedocles' formula: τὸ ὅμοιον τοῦ ὁμοίου ἐφίεσθαι. This formula is traditionally translated differently in each language. In English it is usually rendered: like is only known by like/like produces like. But in French it is: seul le semblable attire le semblable. The Russian version is also different: podobnoe stremitsja k podobnomu ['Like aims at/aspires to like']. I think a more or less adequate translation of ἐφίεσθαι would be 'refers to'.

This philosophical principle led to a dispute in physics in the seventeenth and eighteenth centuries about 'action at a distance'. According to the concept of action at a distance, bodies act on each other without any material mediator, through the void, and at any distance. An example of a force considered as an example of such action is Newton's force of universal gravitation. In short-range interactions, by contrast, forces can be transmitted only through specific material intermediaries. The subject of the dispute is contactless action. Jakobson transposes the dispute from physics to linguistics: action without a contact in space becomes for him similarity without a contact in time.

It is now possible to understand that Jakobson strove to build a synthesis, or an ambiguous mix between:

a) the Romantic values of *Naturphilosophie* and
b) the principles of anti-positivistic and anti-Darwinian natural sciences.

His emphasis on *function* masks a fascination with the necessary relation *form/content,* which was the 'mainstream' of Russian intellectual thought in the years 1920 to 1930 from Aleksandr Potebnja (1835–1891) and Aleksei Losev (1893–1988) to Joseph Stalin through Nikolay Marr (1864–1934).[17] If *a form without content is not a form*, one understands the impossibility of the arbitrariness of the sign for Jakobson. In addition to quoting Joseph de Maistre (1753–1821)—'Let us therefore never speak of chance and arbitrary signs' (Maistre 1980 [1821]: 103)[18]—Jakobson relies heavily on the neo-Platonic principle of the *link*, which he calls *metod uvjazki* ('the method of linkage'). We can thus reconstruct Jakobson's axiological scale of values, shown in Figure 6.3.

---

[17] Aleksandr Potebnja, a Ukrainian linguist and philosopher of language, was the main figure to introduce Wilhelm von Humboldt's thought in Russia; Aleksei Losev was a religious philosopher, a fierce critic of structuralism (see Losev 2003); Nikolay Marr was the famous Soviet linguist whose 'New theory' in total opposition to the Neogrammarians was abruptly overthrown by Joseph Stalin in 1950 (see Samuelian 1981; Thomas 1957).

[18] Jakobson frequently cited this line from *Les Soirées de Saint-Petersbourg* in his writings in the 1930s, and he came back to it in the *Dialogues* at the end of his life (Jakobson and Krystyna 1983: 88). De Maistre was one of the main anti-revolutionary thinkers in France, much like Edmund Burke in Britain.

– *Metonymy*	+ *Metaphor*
Horizontal axis	Vertical axis
Syntagmatic axis	Paradigmatic axis
Combination	Selection
Contiguity	Similarity
Prose	Poetry
Pasternak	Maiakovsky
Realism	Romanticism
Language family (*Sprachfamilie*)	Language union (*Sprachbund*)
Magic by contact	Magic by similarity
Divergence from a common ancestor	Convergence from a difference
Mechanics	Function
Causality	Goal, Purpose
(Phylogenesis)	Nomogenesis
Randomness / Chance	'Conformity to an inner law' (*Zakonomerost', Gesetzmäßigkeit*)
Chaos	Order

Figure 6.3 Jakobson's axiological scale of values

We can now conclude this long story. The basis of Jakobson's unity of thought in the 1920s and 1930s is the idea of likeness without contact:

— cause is replaced by purpose
— *therefore*, language unions are more real than language families
— magic by similarity underlies the metaphor
— *therefore*, links without contact are more important than 'mechanical' links.

The general premise is that any form of similarity is significant.

The texts by Jakobson in the inter-war period are at the crossroads: they are both echoes of an anti-Darwinian biology and an attempt at synthetizing the idealistic morphology of German romanticism with Neo-Platonism.

The thesis that I wanted to put forward here is that the emergence of European structuralism between the two World Wars is similar to a painful birth. One can distinguish different lineages, different lines of force. It is regrettable that most textbooks on the history of linguistics present Jakobson and Trubetzkoy as the spiritual sons of Saussurean thought.[19] In fact, the notion of *totality* (*celostnost'*, German *Ganzheit*), which Jakobson and Trubetzkoy constantly employed—that is, a totality of facts that need to be extracted from reality, and which then pile up on top of each other to constitute a whole whose ontological reality is supposed to be obvious—seems to me to be fundamentally different from the notion of system in Saussure, who, by contrast, meticulously constructs his object of inquiry from a certain *point of view*. It is in this way that for him neither a phoneme nor the syntax of a language is indebted to questions of ontology, because they are *constructed models*. The point of view is what makes it possible to select from the continuum of reality a certain number of discrete features that are relevant to the objective pursued by the theory. By contrast, in the empiricism of the Prague Circle linguists, at least in Jakobson and Trubetzkoy's work, the facts are already present in the real. The difference between the facts that are waiting to be extracted from the real and the point of view that we have on them is never theorized in Jakobson and Trubetzkoy.

It is thus this empiricist attitude (which does not preclude the extreme sophistication of the methods used to bring the objects to light) which makes it possible for the émigré Russian proponents of the *Sprachbund* theory to think that systemic elements can 'spread', like an 'oil stain', beyond the limits of the systems. As a union of languages is not itself a system, in the 1930s the distinctive features in Jakobson are still—in the texts that deal with the spatial distribution of 'structural features'—elements of *substance* and not of strict *relation*. They belong to a holistic vision of accumulation and globality, and not to a systemic vision of structure, where any local change modifies the whole. For Jakobson and Trubetzkoy, a union of languages is *not a structure, but a totality*.

The problem of affinities greatly exceeds the transfer of terms from one discipline to another. In fact, the issue is as much how a research object is defined, what its boundaries are, as it is the extremely ancient philosophical problem of sameness and difference. The most surprising result is that Jakobson's solution was perfectly in line with nineteenth-century naturalism, despite his denials and claims to the contrary.

---

[19] Non-affiliation is suggested, however, by Tullio de Mauro (1972 [1967]) in his 'Notes', published as an appendix to Saussure's *Cours de linguistique générale*, as well as by Françoise Gadet (1995).

The Eurasian language union

Roman Jakobson (1931)
Translated by Patrick Flack

1. Language union

In the current hierarchy of values, the question *where to?* is rated more highly than the question *where from?* The hallmark of national identity is now self-determination rather than genetic indicators; the idea of caste has been replaced by that of class; in public life, as in scientific discourse, sharing common functions or a unity of purpose has overshadowed the importance of a common origin. The *purpose*,[1] that ugly duckling of the ideology of the recent past, is being gradually and universally rehabilitated.

Until recently, the comparative method was used in the science of language almost exclusively to elucidate the common historical legacy of related languages. But when we resort to the comparative method nowadays, we are interested as much in the independent existence and characteristic evolutionary trends of the branches of a language as in its primitive, common stem. Both the comparison of divergences in the life of related language branches and the study of similar forms of evolution—so-called *convergences*—can equally shed light on the purposefulness of linguistic transformations. That said, the convergent evolution of related languages constitutes only a special case. The similarities between features that evolved independently in neighbouring languages of different origins is yet another question that has entered the field of current linguistic problems. It is becoming increasingly clear that common paths of development can be found even in languages that start from completely different points: dissimilar materials can give rise, through different means, to structures of the same type. Next to the traditional notion of languages of *common origin*, the notion of languages *oriented towards a common purpose* is thus emerging.

---

[1] [Translator's note:] We translate *cel'* (goal, objective) by 'purpose', to highlight the coherence with *celestremitel'nost'* (purposefulness) used in this and the next paragraph.

The International Congress of Linguists in The Hague (De Boer et al. 1928) approved the following proposal by Nikolay Trubetzkoy:

> We call 'language group' any set of languages that are connected by a significant number of systematic correspondences. We have to distinguish two types of language groups—language unions on the one hand, language families on the other. It is very important to differentiate these two concepts. (see *Actes*) [4][2]

These notions were first delimited by Trubetzkoy in his article 'The Tower of Babel and the Confusion of Languages' (Trubetzkoy 1923). He takes Bulgarian as an illustration: it belongs both to the family of Slavic languages (along with Serbo-Croatian, Russian, Polish and others) and to the union of Balkan languages (together with Modern Greek, Albanian and Romanian). Language families, on the one hand, are characterized by a common heritage of lexical and grammatical features, and by phonic concordances that point to a common source and allow the reconstruction of common proto-forms. Language unions, on the other hand, are characterized by similarities in the structure of two or more neighbouring languages and by parallel changes in independent language systems.

Unions of states are distinguished according to their nature and size. For example, there are political, economic and military unions. Military unions are in turn distinguished by the character and scope of their tasks (offensive or defensive alliances, alliances against a single or against any 'peace-breaker'). A given state can be simultaneously linked with different partners from alliances of various types and sizes. In a given language, several systems are correlated: its sound shape, its inventory of verbal forms (morphology) or of forms of word-groups (syntax), its vocabulary, its phraseology. These are closed systems that constitute the different *planes* of a single language; language is a system of systems. As in the case of state unions, some language unions have a single plane, others have several. Within a single language plane, structural similarities of varying degrees are possible. A single language can thus belong to different language unions (which can be concentric or simply intersecting), depending on its different planes and features. While morphological similarities, i.e. verbal forms,[3] are typical of the above-mentioned union of Balkan languages, syntactic similarities characterize the languages of the Romano-Germanic Western world. The German linguist Walter Porzig even

---

[2] [TN:] Our translation is based on the original Russian version, published in 1931 (Jakobson 1931a), not the modified version published in the *Selected Writings* (Jakobson 1971a: 144–201). The numbers in square brackets indicate the pagination of the original version.

[3] Besides morphological similarities, there are also similarities between the languages of the Balkan Union in terms of syntax, lexical meaning, and sound shape (cf. Selishchev 1925a).

suggests interpreting these languages syntactically as separate dialects of a single language—the *language of the West* [*Sprache des Abendlandes*]. According to him, one of the most pressing and rewarding goals of Indo-European linguistics is thus to write the syntax of this 'language of the West' (Porzig 1924: 150). [5]

2. The Eurasian language union in contemporary science

Eurasia is an aggregate of specific features—soil, vegetation, climate—, a typical 'multi-featured' region, a particular, singular and integrally whole geographical world. These are the conclusions of the Russian geographical science of the last decades, such as they are synthetically summarized in the works of Pyotr N. Savitzky.

With every passing year, we are discovering with increasing clarity (as this is the direction that the most advanced scientific research is taking) that correlations or strictly lawful relations[4] exist between phenomena that belong to different spheres. Of course, these relations are not to be understood in terms of a perfect coincidence of the boundaries of these phenomena. Instead, the lines that demarcate associated phenomena are bundled into clusters. Phenomena can be related either chronologically or geographically. In either case, the fact that several domains are correlated does not constrain the internal laws of each of them. On the contrary, it is impossible to discover a correlation without a prior immanent study of each of these domains. This is a necessary precondition. Each domain must be studied according to the structural diversity of its own concrete manifestations—its historical diversity in the light of the lawfulness of its evolution, its territorial diversity in the light of its zonal lawfulness. The diversity of one area cannot be deduced mechanically from the diversity of another, there is no one-to-one correlation between superstructure and base. The aim of science is to grasp the interlinking of phenomena from different planes and to discover the lawful framework that underpins these multi-plane interconnections. Let us call this method of research the *method of linkage*, thereby raising this little word [*uvjazka*] from the standard Russian vocabulary to a scientific level. One of the manifestations of this method is the notion of a *place of development* ([*mestorazvitie*] the term and concept stem from Savitzky 1927: ch. IV), which binds a socio-historical context and its territory in a single totality.

Does the shared living place of the Eurasian geographical world differ from similar living places and, above of all, from those of the neighbouring

---

[4] [TN:] 'lawful' is a translation of the Russian *zakonomernyj*: it is for example commonly used to translate the equivalent German term in Kant (*gesetzmässig*).

European and Asian worlds? If so, in what aspects does it differ? Economic geography, in accordance with the results of physical geography, has established the integrally whole character of the Eurasian world. The historical destiny of Eurasia confirms its indissoluble unity. Studies of racial coefficients in blood samples have revealed the existence of an essential anthropological difference between the peoples of Eurasia and Europeans or Asians. Finally, having overcome its long and dangerous dependency [6] on the genealogical tree of languages, ethnology is now establishing the distinctive hallmarks of the Eurasian cultural sphere (see Trubetzkoy 1927 and Zelenin 1929).

In his article 'On the Turanian Element in Russian Culture', Trubetzkoy convincingly demonstrated that there is a close relationship between the structures of the Turanian and Russian spiritual worlds on the one hand, and a close relationship between the Turanian spiritual world and Turanian languages on the other (Trubetzkoy 1927: 34–53).[5] A new scientific problem, which Antoine Meillet (1928) clearly formulated in his approving review of Trubetzkoy's article, results logically from these two rapprochements: the internal relation between the structure of Russian and of Turanian languages must be brought to light. In other words, the question of the structural community of Eurasian languages arises.

Savitzky (1929) was the first to compare the dialectal division of the Russian linguistic world with data from physical geography. His study highlights an extraordinary parallelism between the most important climatic isolines of Cisuralia and the most important Russian isoglosses (i.e. the boundaries of the dialectal phenomena that serve, because of their particularly useful attributes, as the basis for the classification of Russian dialects).[6] The unexpected fact that the Russian dialectological map reproduces the characteristic features of the zonal composition of the Eurasian geographical world is an incentive to broaden our research framework and to compare, in addition to the Russian linguistic block, the whole linguistic diversity of Eurasia with the data of general geography. Here again, our initial question arises: is there any unity in this multilingualism (so confusing to Europeans)? What is that unity? A haphazard, chaotic jumble, or a lawful construction, a harmonious union?

If this question has arisen so late in science, the fault lies with the fact that the predominance of genetic interests over functional problems has riveted

---

[5] The Turanian or Ural-Altaic languages include the Uralic (Finno-Ugric and Samoyed branches) and the Altaic (Turkic-Chuvash, Mongolian and Manchu-Tungus branches) language families. Scientists have not yet definitively elucidated what links the Uralic and Altaic languages: a family relationship or a union?

[6] [TN:] Jakobson uses indifferently the Russian terms *dialekt*, *narečie* and *govor*, all of which we translate by 'dialect'.

the attention of the majority of linguists onto separate families of languages (we leave aside more general philosophical considerations). Specialists of Russia have studied Russian only in the context of Slavic languages, and not in the context of the languages of Russia. The problems of the convergent evolution and diverse interactions of the languages of Russia, [7] i.e. precisely the set of questions that would have brought linguistics into the disciplinary field of synthetic studies of Russia, has remained in the shadows.

In spite of the centuries-old bonds between East Slavic and Finno-Ugric languages forged by their close cohabitation, Alexander Pogodin (1929) notes that, until recently, 'Russian science has not understood sufficiently the importance of Finno-Ugric linguistics'. Pogodin contrasts the great successes of the present period with the episodic, unsystematic research on Finno-Ugric languages before the revolution: 'there is something very positive in the uninterrupted and undeniable development in Soviet Russia that has incorporated a multitude of new materials and new questions and has welcomed into its ranks new scholarly forces that previously remained outside scientific communication'. The situation was and is more or less similar in the case of the other non-Russian languages of Russia.

It is particularly characteristic of contemporary Russian linguistics to compare Russian with geographically contiguous languages that have a different origin. If such comparisons were previously almost exclusively reduced to the problem of lexical borrowing, now the circle of problems is widening. The changes undergone by Russian when it is adopted by non-native speakers are now being studied, as witnessed by the publications of Afanasy Selishchev on Russian among national minorities in the Volga regions (Selishchev 1925b, 1927), by the materials collected by Alexander Georgyevsky on 'The Miscegenation of Languages in the Soviet Far East', by the remarks of Evgeny Polivanov on the adaptation of Russian to the linguistic habits of minorities, etc. Reciprocal influences between neighbouring languages are now also being studied, not only in the field of lexicography, but also in phonetics and grammar. Let us mention, for example, Konstantin Baushev's (1929) work on the influence of Russian on the literary syntax of Votjak or Selishchev's reflections on the impact of indigenous languages on the phonetics of Siberian Russian dialects. The question of the influence of Finnish on the phonetic composition of northern Great Russian had already been raised in the past, but only now, with Trubetzkoy's work on the disintegration of the general unity of Russian (where he analyses the phenomenon of 'tsokanie'),[7] has this influence been precisely brought to light (Trubetzkoy 1924b: 293). Influence

---

[7] [TN:] Dialectal pronunciation in certain parts of Russia (north and Siberia) that replaces [tch] with [ts] (neutralization of the tch/ts opposition).

is only one aspect of the problem, it is only the most straightforward result of linguistic cohabitation. There are cases where it is difficult to decide what we are facing: a borrowing or the result of convergent evolution. Borrowing and convergence, as I have already written, are not mutually exclusive and cannot be categorically opposed. What is important is not a borrowing itself, but its function from the point of view of the borrowing linguistic system; it is important that there is a demand [8] for the novelty in question, and that it is accepted by the borrowing system, in accordance with the possibilities and needs of its evolution (Trubetzkoy 1927: 96–98). Borrowing is, for the most part, only a special case of convergence. The essential problem, when it comes to the comparison of neighbouring languages, is thus that of convergence. As far as the languages of Eurasia are concerned, a new step in this direction has been taken by Dmitry Bubrikh (1929). This scholar, who is both a Slavist and a Finnologist, has highlighted the proximity of the phonological systems of Great Russian and Mordvinian[8] and has shown that this rapprochement cannot be reduced to a unilateral action. Such partial comparisons anticipate the answer to the question of the common features of all the languages of Eurasia.

In his very comprehensive work concerning the connection between beliefs and taboo words among Eurasian peoples, Dmitry Zelenin (1929) has discovered 'a comparative uniformity of verbal taboos among Eurasian peoples of different origins. ... Concerning taboos, they have more words in common than different ones'. The functional peculiarities of taboos in the languages of Eurasian peoples are so original that scientific models built on the study of taboo words outside Eurasia are not applicable to Eurasian material. 'In our explanation of the psychology and genetics of taboo words, we have been able to adhere only partially to J. Frazer's theory, and more often than not we have been obliged to depart from it. We are inclined to explain this phenomenon by the difference between the Eurasian cultural cycle and the culture of the other countries on the basis of which Frazer developed his theory' (Zelenin 1929: 4). Zelenin describes the role of forbidden words in the mythology of Eurasian peoples, the representations of the relationship between a name and its bearer, the function of substitute words and secret languages, the relationship between verbal prohibitions and word production. In other words, his work highlights the common Eurasian characteristics of a speaker's attitude towards words. Where there is a common appreciation of the word, a unity of linguistic culture, it is natural to assume direct correspondences in linguistic structure.

[8] A phonological system is the inventory of sound differences by which a difference in meaning can be realized in a given language.

3. The alphabet of phonology and the problem of phonological geography

Given that the sound shape[9] of language is the linguistic aspect that is most studied at present, [9] it is in this area that the study of similarities between neighbouring languages can prove particularly fruitful. Of course, great methodological caution is necessary.

Not all similarities are equivalent, there are several types. Two languages can use similar phonic material, but the role of that material in both languages may differ. In a given language, the difference between two sounds can be used to distinguish the meaning of words; this is called a *phonological* difference. In this case, linguists speak of two *phonemes.*[10] In another given language, these two sounds may be present, but they cannot be found in the same position and the choice of the one over the other is conditioned by the phonetic environment. In this case, they are considered as two combinatorial variants of the same phoneme. Examples: in Russian *i* and *u* are two different phonemes (cf. *Igor'* [Igor]—*ugor'* [eel]), while in Kabardic they are two combinatorial variants of the same phoneme, which is realized as *i* after some consonants, as *u* after others. In Russian, the phoneme *e* is realized as a closed *é* before soft consonants, i.e. it is pronounced with more tongue lift (*éti-* [these]), but before a hard consonant, it is realized as an open *è*, i.e. it is pronounced with less tongue lift (*ètot-* [this]).[11] In this case, the closed *e* and the open *e* are two combinatorial variants of a single phoneme, whereas in French or Italian, for example, these two sounds can appear in the same place, they can distinguish two words by their meaning and constitute thus two different phonemes. Compare the French words *dé* (dice), *lé* (cloth) with a closed *e* and *dais* (canopy), *lait* (milk) with an open *e*. When comparing the phonetic structure of two languages, it is important to make sure that sounds that are similar in appearance are also similar in function.

That said, such an analysis is not yet sufficient, as it would not be very fruitful to make a comparison only between the scattered phonemes of two languages. The phonological inventory of a language should not be represented as a mechanical sum of phonemes. Phonemes are always found in certain relationships, they constitute a system. It often happens that a given phoneme of a language is, in of itself, identical to that of another language,

---

[9] [TN:] We use the term 'sound shape' to translate *zvukovoj stroj*, as this is the translation used by Jakobson himself, for example in *The Sound Shape of Language* (Jakobson and Waugh 1979).

[10] We call phonemes the members of a phonological opposition that are indivisible into other smaller oppositions. A very simplified definition of a phoneme could be: a sound capable of distinguishing the meaning of words in a given language.

[11] The concepts of *softness* and *hardness of consonants* are explained in section 5.

but what differs is the place taken by each of these phonemes [10] in the corresponding phonological system. Let us compare, as an example, the vowel systems of three different languages:

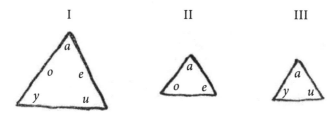

The first and second systems have the phonemes *o* and *e*, but their position is different. In language II, they form the base of the triangle: *o* is the lowest vowel in the system from an acoustic point of view, *e* is the highest; in language I, *o* and *e* are 'mid rank' phonemes, while *u* plays the role of the lowest phoneme, and *i* that of the highest. By virtue of their function in the system, the vowels *u* and *i* of language I are closer to the vowels *o* and *e* of language II than the apparently identical phonemes *o* and *e*. System III offers a closer parallel to system II. These two systems of three phonemes are phonologically identical; however, in system II the low phoneme is realized as *o*, in system III as *u* and, furthermore, the highest phoneme is realized in one case as *e*, in the other as *i*. When comparing the phonological structure of two languages, one must take into account not only the relation of the sounds to the phonological system, i.e. the system of significant sound differences, but also the relations of the phonemes within this system. First of all, it is essential to highlight a characteristic variety of inter-phoneme relationships, their so-called *correlation*. Two correlated phonemes have common acoustic properties and one differential property: one of two phonemes is endowed with a certain acoustic feature, the other, on the contrary, is deprived of it; the same property can distinguish several pairs of phonemes in the same system. By virtue of the repetitive nature of this relationship, the differentiating property is, as it were, bracketed and abstracted from specific phoneme pairs by linguistic thought. As such, it can be conceived of independently of any given phoneme. Similarly, the common features of each pair of phonemes can be abstracted as well: this substrate, in turn, constitutes a real unity in the phonological system. Here are some examples of phonological correlations:

> *Quantitative correlation of vowels.* [11] In several languages, e.g. Czech, Hungarian, Latin, Serbian, Ancient Greek, there is a reciprocal opposition between vowel length and its absence, i.e. brevity. For example, in

Serbian, *ā* (long *a*) and *ă*, *ō* and *ŏ*, *ē* and *ĕ*, *ū* and *ŭ*, *ī* and *ĭ* are opposed. The quantitative distinction of vowels in these languages allows us to differentiate words by their meaning. Compare, for example, the Czech words: *mili* [they were washing]/*milí* [charming]/*míli* [mile (Acc.)]/*mílí* [mile (Instr.)]. The differentiation of vowels according to their length and brevity exists in linguistic thought independently of the concrete vowel pairs that realize the quantitative correlation. This fact is illustrated by quantitative or metrical versification, which is based on the alternation of length and brevity. Finally, in the phonological systems of these languages, one finds the idea of vowels as such, independently of their quantitative differences. For example, the idea of *a* exists apart from any connection with length and brevity. A valuable clue in this regard is that one can rhyme identical long and short vowels in these languages.

Dynamic correlation (of intensity): strong accentuation/absence of accentuation. Example: Russian pairs: *á/a* (unaccentuated), *ú/u*, *í/i*. Differentiation of word meanings: *rúki* [hands (Noun. pl.)]/*rukí* [hand (Gen. sing.)], *múka* [torment]/*muká* [flour]; *zámki* [castles]/*zamkí* [locks], *pláču* [I cry]/*plačú* [I pay]; *pálite* [you shoot]/*palíte* [shoot!]/*poletí* [fly!] (this last example gives, in consistent phonological spelling: /pàl'it'i /—/pal'ít'i/'/pal'it'í/).

Every language contains a small set of correlations, which determine its phonological composition to a significant degree. The Russian phonological system includes: firstly, a dynamic correlation that is incompatible with the quantitative correlation of vowels; secondly, two consonantal correlations, of timbre (consonant softness/hardness)—which will be discussed in more detail in section 5—and of sonority. The differential feature of the last correlation is the presence or absence of voice during the pronunciation of consonants (voiced–voiceless). The correlation of consonants by sonority is a means to distinguish words: *da* [and]/*ta* [that one], *žar* [heat]/*shar* [ball], *b'ju* [I hit]/ *p'ju* [I drink].

Polish has the same two consonantal correlations as Russian, but no vowel correlations. Czech has a correlation of consonants by sonority and a quantitative vowel correlation. In Czech, the accent falls on the first syllable, in Polish on the penultimate. Thus, in these two languages, unlike in Russian, the place of the accent is externally conditioned and cannot be used to differentiate the meaning of words. Consequently there is no dynamic phonological correlation at the level of the word [12] (cf. Jakobson 1923: 26 ff, Baudouin de Courtenay 1922: § 27). The phonological system of the Štokavian dialect of

Serbo-Croatian includes, besides the consonantal sonority correlation, two vowel correlations: melodic and quantitative. The melodic correlation has the particularity of differentiating the direction of vocal pitch: two types of melodies are opposed. In Štokavian, vowels with a rising intonation are opposed to those with a flat intonation. The clearest realization of this contrast is the opposition between a rising and a falling intonation of vowels. In a melodically correlated language, two words can be pronounced identically and be distinguished only by the melody of the vowels.[12] Here are some examples from Vuk Karadžić's dictionary:

Ascending accent in the 1st syllable	Descending accent in the 1st syllable
sela = Gen. sing. village	*sela* = Noun. pl. villages
basma = embossed cloth	*basma* = incantation
sjenica = tit	*sjenica* = gazebo
bacati = throw	*bacati* = stab (prick)
luka = grassland	*Luka* = Luke

In the phonology of the Štokavian word, the 'accentuated–unaccentuated' correlation does not exist. The place of the accent is determined externally, as in Czech and Polish. The accent in Štokavian falls on the syllable with a rising intonation, but if this is absent in the word, it falls on the first syllable.

The presence of a melodic correlation (*polytony*) or its absence (*monotony*) implies a series of particularities in the phonological structure of a given language. For example, a polytonic language necessarily has a quantitative correlation of vowels, whereas in a monotonic language this correlation is incompatible with the 'accentuated–unaccentuated' correlation. In short, polytony (and consequently monotony) clearly determines the character of a phonological system. [13]

While the general principles for describing phonological systems are now well established, we still lack accurate descriptions of the phonological systems of many specific languages. The traditional descriptions of the phonetic makeup of different languages are mostly not very useful for phonological interpretation. In each case, the linguistic material needs to be reconsidered

---

[12] The Serb linguist Radovan Košutić (1919) points out that in Russian there are two different syllabic intonations that correspond orally to Serbian: in Russian open syllables (ending in a vowel), the accent is usually ascending: *idú*, while in closed syllables (ending in a consonant) the accent is descending *idút* (Ch. 2). Thus, in Russian, a vowel with an ascending accent and the same vowel with a descending accent are combinatorial variants of a single phoneme, whereas in Serbian they are two correlated phonemes.

from another point of view. And until this indispensable descriptive work is done, the most urgent linguistic task of the present day, namely the mapping of phonological phenomena and the classification of the world into phonological zones, cannot be carried out. The development of *phonological geography*, a new scientific discipline with a great future, is thereby greatly hindered.

That being said, the fragmentary material that is available to comparative phonology does already provide a basis to affirm that the isolated existence of a language or a family of languages within its own boundaries does not fully account for the basic principles of its phonological structure and, in particular, of its various correlations. Phonological language unions or isophones (the boundaries between phonological phenomena) of large dimension are more typical than phonological islands. Mapping specific correlations geographically promises to produce a picture in which large areas that extend beyond the boundaries of individual languages predominate over a fragmented 'mosaic' constellation, over fragmented correlations. I have tried to divide the contemporary Slavic linguistic world into zones based on phonological correlations, while noting that languages of different origins may belong to the same zones (Jakobson 1929: 79, 109). A typical example of this is the phonological proximity of Modern Greek and Bulgarian (intensity correlation, etc.) as well as the phonological proximity of Hungarian and Czechoslovakian (quantitative correlation, accentuation at the beginning of the word, similarities in the inventory of consonantal phonemes, etc.). Work on the delineation of correlation areas promises to be particularly fruitful.[13] [14]

Linguistics must take into account the spatial distribution of phonological unions. It is far too easy otherwise, when studying neighbouring languages whose history is not well known, to mistakenly interpret the marks of a

---

[13] Rudiments of phonological geography can be found in Father W. Schmidt's (1926) captivating book *Language Families and Language Groups of the World*. Phonological criteria play only a secondary role for the author in his classification of the globe into linguistic zones, they are ancillary to grammatical (morphological and syntactic) criteria. But in studying the geographical distribution of sound phenomena, Schmidt does try to separate phonological from non-phonological facts, i.e. phonemes from combinatorial variants (cf. his remarks on pp. 274, 282). Without doubt, this is to his credit. Schmidt not only records different types of linguistic structures and their distribution, he also compares linguistic areas to cultural areas. Even as a resolute opponent of evolutionism, the author could not however resist the original sin of evolutionism: European egocentrism remains the essential pivot of his work. He sets up a scale of ethnological cultural circles: *Urkulturen, fortgeschrittene Kulturen, weiter fortgeschrittene Kulturen, Hochkulturen*. Linguistic phenomena, especially phonological phenomena, are evaluated on this scale. The fact that the absence of certain phonological differences, of certain groups of phonemes, is compensated for by the presence of other phonological differences, by other ways of grouping phonemes is not taken into account. Instead of linking the absence of certain correlations of a linguistic system with the positive structural features of that system, Schmidt explains it by the poverty of its culture (e.g., p. 530). In contrast, he considers the presence of certain phonolog-

phonological union as genetic symptoms and to assume the existence of a language family instead of a language union. This has happened to many attempts to systematize various exotic languages: when an exotic phonological feature that was unusual from the point of view of European linguistics was detected in a set of neighbouring languages, it was taken as the mark of a common origin.

4. The monotonic character of Eurasian languages and the neighbouring unions of polytonic languages

A telling example of the zonal nature of phonological correlations is the geographical distribution of polytony.[14] The largest [15] language union by polytony is a group of languages of diverse origins in the Pacific Ocean. These include the Sino-Tibetan language group (Chinese, Tibetan, Burmese, Thai, etc.), the Vietnamese and Malay groups, as well as Japanese and Ainu. One also finds large language unions characterized by polytony in Central Africa and America.

Finally, the languages of the Baltic coast also constitute a union of polytonic languages. This union is smaller in size than the polytonic unions mentioned above, with a much lower degree of polytonic use. However, it is remarkable that a whole group of Baltic languages of different origins are characterized by the use of polytony. These include Swedish, Norwegian, most Danish and some Baltic German dialects, northern Kashubian, Lithuanian and Latvian,[15] Livonian and Estonian (cf. Jakobson 1929: 60). Some examples of the

---

ical facts, especially facts specific to European languages, as the mark of a high level of culture. While establishing an inventory of vowels in Indo-European languages, the author writes: 'There is something particularly refined and profound in the fact that within this linguistic group it is the vowels, those lightest and most fluid elements of the language, the most suitable for expressing formal relations, that can be called upon to the highest degree to play this role' (pp. 540, 533, 537). If we see things this way, the diversity of directions of linguistic evolution is replaced by a difference in the degree of evolution. The notion of 'language group' is, at first sight, similar to the notion of 'language union', but since neither divergence nor convergence are sufficiently taken into account in the evolution of languages, the 'group' becomes, next to the 'family', a genetic notion. This notion proves to be applicable only to the languages of the most primitive cultures (p. 521), and the specific features of the group are interpreted as a kind of palaeontological indicators. Consequently, the author, studying the geographical distribution of these specific features, does not hesitate to mix different temporal planes, and to assimilate, for example, the phonological peculiarities of Ancient Greek, Gothic, Old Slavic and those of present-day languages: Baltic, Caucasian, African (pp. 291 ff).

[14] If the movements of the voice vary and take different directions and the opposition of these directions distinguishes the meaning of words, then, according to Durnovo, we call this language polytonic. Also included in the category of polytonic languages are those whose phonologically distinct melodies are limited to the syllable (musical syllabic stress) and those in which the melodies of whole words are opposed, without a precise syllable location (musical word stress). In these languages, the phonological syllabic accent is a special case, it can only appear in monosyllabic words (cf. Polivanov 1928: §33).

[15] The third branch of the same family, Prussian, which disappeared in the eighteenth century, was also polytonic (see Fortunatov 1895).

distinctive roles of melodic correlation in the languages of the Baltic area are:[16]

		Ascending accent on the 1st syllable	Descending accent on the 1st syllable
Swedish	giftet	poison	marriage
	regel	rule	lock
Norwegian	kokken	cook	stove
Danish	trykker	press	printer
North German	brüt	it cooks	fiancée
Northern Kachubian	čöüka	I crawl	crawling
Lithuanian	suditi	judge	salt
	dviém	by two (Instr.)	with two (Dat.)
Latvian	seju	I was sowing	I attached
Estonian	kaevu	in the well (Acc.)	of the well (Gen.)

[16] In all the Baltic languages except the Latvian-Lithuanian family, melodic correlation is a recent evolution. Thus, there is no polytony outside the states surrounding the Baltic: it is absent from Germanic languages, or indeed from the closest relatives of Norwegian, namely Icelandic and the Faroese dialect; moreover, it tends to disappear in north-western Norwegian dialects. Neither the southern Kashubian dialect, nor Kashubian's closest relative, Polish, nor Estonian's cousins, the other Finnish languages, know it.

It should be pointed out that we include here in the category of polytonic languages not only languages that have a proper melodic correlation, but also those with a correlation between 'vowels interrupted in the middle or at the end by a glottal stop/vowels without glottal stop'. This 'discontinuity' correlation can be considered as a variant of the melodic correlation. The discontinuity correlation, which is also present in some of the languages of the Pacific polytonic union, is widespread

---

[16] Sources of the examples: for Swedish and Norwegian: Kock (1901: 7, 23), for Danish: Ekblom (17), for North German: Leskien and Brugman (1882: 11), for North Kashubian: Lorentz (1908: 147; cf. Lorentz 1903:, 90), for Lithuanian: Kurschat (1876: 60), for Latvian: Endzelīns (1922: 57), and for Estonian: Polivanov (1928: 202). [TN: The source 'Ekblom' is missing from Jakobson's bibliography and it is impossible to determine what text he was referring to. The incomplete references have been retained in this translation.]

on the south-west and south-east coast of the Baltic Sea. The Danish languages of West Schleswig and its neighbouring islands have a melodic correlation, the other Danish dialects, with a few exceptions, have a discontinuity correlation (cf. Kock 1901: 28 ff.). Some of them apparently have both melodic and discontinuity correlations (see Ekblom, pp. 16-17, 20-21). The discontinuity correlation is also found in north-western Lithuanian dialects (see Gerullis 1930: XLVI ff.) and in Latvian; in some languages it coexists with the melodic correlation, whereas in others the latter is absent (see Endzelīns 1922). Finally, Livonian, which is part of the Finnish family but is embedded in the Latvian context, has a discontinuity, but no melodic correlation (see Kettunen 1926: §§6-8).[17]

Polytony, in any of its forms, [17] is absolutely foreign to Eurasian languages. Eurasia is thus symmetrically bordered by unions of polytonic languages: in the north-west by the Baltic union, in the south-east by the Pacific union. This is another example of the symmetrical structure of the eastern and western ends of the continent, to which Savitzky has drawn attention (Savitzky 1927: 47).

Serbo-Croatian—with the exception of its south-eastern periphery (see Broch 1903: 48) and of the neighbouring Slovenian dialects of the Krajina (see Tesnière 1929: 90 ff.)—forms a polytonic isolate, a rare phenomenon in the universe of languages. It must be considered that Serbo-Croatian phonology is a typical archaism, as it has preserved a Proto-Slavic framework. It is what remains of a once immense mass of Indo-European polytonic languages. The history of the loss of polytony by these languages, coupled with the history of their migration, constitutes one of the most interesting problems of historical phonology.

At present, neither Europe, with the exception of the union of Baltic languages and the Yugoslav linguistic isolate, nor Asia, with the exception of the Pacific union, have polytonism. But do the languages of Eurasia also differ from the *monotonic* languages of Europe and Asia in their phonological correlations?

---

[17] The Baltic polytonic union is bounded in the south and north by languages with a particular correlation that use different methods of syllabic division to differentiate the meaning of words. In his article on phonological systems (published in the fourth volume of the *Travaux du Cercle Linguistique de Prague*), Trubetzkoy mentions this correlation in Standard German, in a part of German dialects and in Dutch. For a description of a similar correlation in Lappish, see Lagercrantz (1923, 1926, 1928). The complexity of Lappish phonology consists in the fact that in some dialects the mentioned correlation is combined with a quantitative correlation of vowels. In addition, in some others, it is combined with a quantitative correlation of consonants.

5. Consonantal opposition of timbre in the languages of Eurasia and neighbouring regions

The feature that distinguishes the languages of Eurasia from the monotonic languages of its neighbouring places of development is the phonological use of differences in consonantal timbre. In Great Russian, for example, twelve consonantal phonemes are phonologically opposed to the same number of corresponding phonemes, which differ only by their timbre. These are the so-called hard consonants: *r, l, n, m, d, t, z, s, b, p, f* and their correlative so-called soft consonants: *r', l', n', m', d', t', z', s', b', p', f'*.[18]

In Great Russian, the difference between hard and soft consonants is one of the main ways to differentiate the meaning of words. To give a few examples: *byt* [daily life]/*byt'* [to be]/*bit* [beat]/*bit'* [to beat], *mat* [obscene language] / *m'at* [crumpled]/*mat'* [mother] / *m'at'* [crumple], [18] *myl* [(he) soaped] / *myl'* [soap!]/*mil* [nice]/*mil'* [mile' (Gen. Pl.)], *rov* [ditch]/*r'ov* [roar], *ves* [weight] / *ves'* [all], *pilu* [saw (Acc. Sg.)]/*pil'u* [(I) saw], *volna* [wave] / *vol'na* [free (fem.)], *gorka* [slide]/*gor'ko* [bitter], *stenka* [wall] / *Sten'ka* [diminutive of *Stepan*: 'Stephen']. One also finds verses that rely on the opposition of hard and soft consonants:

Ja videl	I have seen
Vydel	The transformation
Vësen	of springs
V osen'	In autumn
	Xlebnikov (Khlebnikov),

The opposition of hard and soft consonants plays a very important role in other Russian languages. Belarusian has the same pairs as Great Russian, except that the place of the pairs *t–t', d–d'* is occupied by *c–c', dz–dz'*, and that Belarusian dialects of the south-west do not know the opposition *r–r'*. The Ukrainian inventory of hard and soft consonantal pairs differs from Great Russian through the absence of the soft phonemes *b', p', v', f'*;[19] the soft phoneme *r'* is also absent in some dialects.

For Russian speakers, consonantal softness is a common, self-evident linguistic category and, especially if they are not an expert in linguistics, it is

---

[18] Only the sibilants *c* and *j* are not in an oppositional pair. The difference between *g* and *g', k* and *k', x* and *x'* does exist in Russian, but it has no phonological role, it does not serve to differentiate the meaning of words.

[19] Examples: *robit* [work (Gen. Pl.)] / *robit'* [do!], *nis* [nose] / *n'is* [he wore] ('indicates only the softness of the consonant) *tik* [the current] / *t'ik* [it flowed], *sinu* [son'! (vocative)] / *sin'u* [blue (Acc. Sg.)], *lisa* [fox] / *lis'a* [cow with a spot on its forehead], *rad* [happy] / *r'ad* [series]. The softness correlation in literary Ukrainian is described in detail by Synyavsky.

difficult for them to imagine either that the majority of foreign languages do not use this means to distinguish words, or that in many languages soft consonants, if they exist, are only a combinatorial variant that is not distinguished in linguistic thought. Even Russians who are initiated in linguistics are often surprised by the fact that Europeans do not hear the difference between soft and hard consonants. I have experienced this several times with Czechs and Germans: when I pronounced 'žar'–žar, Rus'–rus, krov' krov' and so on, my interlocutors stated that I had uttered the same word twice. Vasily Tredyakovsky wrote in 1752 already that, no matter how much one explains to Europeans the essence of consonantal softness in Russian, 'one can never change their pronunciation, so that they are not able to assimilate it, unless by blessed chance' (Tredyakovsky 1849: 30).

Literary Polish and southern Polish dialects use the entire phonological inventory of the softness correlation pairs that are present in south-western Belorussian with, in addition, [19] the pairs k/k' and g/g'. Northern Polish dialects are characterized by the absence of the phonemes p', b', f', v', m' (see Nitsch 1915: 270 ff.); most of these dialects do not have the phonemes k', g' (1915: 276 ff.).

Polish and East Slavic languages provide material to analyse several typical varieties of the softness correlation. Let us compare four vowels with the same aperture: *u, y, ü, i* (*ü* is a sound conveyed in German spelling by *ü*: *dünn, früh*, in French by *u*: *tu*). Each vowel has its own tone. The pitch of this tone is determined by the size and shape of the resonator (the channel that goes from the glottis to the lips). These vowels differ, from an objective acoustic point of view, by the pitch of their individual tone. From *u* to *i*, the pitch of each vowel's tone rises gradually. If a phonological system has only three vowels of the same aperture: 1. *u*, 2. *y* or *ü*, 3. *i*, then the two oppositions (1.–2. and 2.–3.) are on the same plane and the only differential property is the pitch. If, instead, all four series are present, then two planes of opposition are distinguished: the vowels *ü* and *i* are opposed to the vowels *u* and *y* as hard to soft, the vowels *u, ü* are correlated to the vowels *y* and *i* as dark to light. These are two distinct and independent differences in timbre: one is the *hard/soft* opposition, the other the *light/dark* opposition. Neither of these differences can be reduced to the other. There is no doubt that there is a difference in principle between these two differential properties from the point of view of subjective acoustics. Characterizing these properties in terms of objective acoustics is a more complex problem, but for the moment, this is irrelevant to us.

What has been said in relation to vowels is also applicable in broad terms to the timbre differences of consonants, i.e. to differences in the acoustic pitch of consonants. In the opposition between hard and soft consonants, hard consonants are considered as having normal timbre, while soft consonants constitute a category with an additional feature. In the opposition of dark and light consonants, light consonants are considered normal, whereas darkness is deemed to be an additional feature. If there is a threefold opposition of consonants (dark-hard–light-hard–light-soft), this opposition is considered as a gradation on the same plane: normal consonants are opposed to high-pitched (soft) consonants on the one hand, to low-pitched (dark) consonants on the other hand. Oppositions of consonants by timbre on two planes, i.e. involving four types of consonants, are very rare. Polivanov mentions [20] four phonological varieties of *k* and *g* in some Japanese dialects: dark-hard, light-hard, dark-soft and light-soft (Polivanov 1928: 103). High pitch consonants are produced by reducing the resonant cavity space. The main way to reduce resonance is by elevating the tongue towards the hard palate (*palatum*). Conversely, to lower the timbre, the resonance space must be increased, which is achieved by rounding and advancing the lips (*labialization*).[20]

The consonantal phonemes of literary Russian are divided into five groups according to their point of articulation, i.e. according to the active organ that is most involved in the articulatory work to produce the consonant:

1. *Postlingual consonants*, which are articulated with the back of the tongue. Occlusives: *k, g*; fricatives: *x* (occlusive consonants are produced by closing the organs of speech and preventing air from escaping; to articulate fricatives, a narrow slit is left for the air to escape).
2. *Mediolingual consonants*, which are articulated with the middle part of the back of the tongue. They are called palatal, in reference to the organ that is passively involved (hard palate). If the middle part of the tongue rises towards the posterior part of the hard palate, the consonants are called postpalatal, if it rises towards the anterior part, they are called prepalatal. In literary Russian there are no postpalatal consonants (*k', g', x'* are not independent phonemes). The prepalatals are: j and i (in the Muscovite pronunciation), the phoneme that corresponds to the letter щ (e.g. *šči, obščij*), as well as its corresponding voiced phoneme (e.g. *doždik, drožži*).

---

[20] Consonant labialization has been well described by Yakovlev (1923: 49 ff).

3. *Prelingual consonants*, which are articulated with the front part of the tongue (the blade according to English phonetic terminology). Occlusives: *c, č*, fricatives: *s, z, š, ž.*
4. *Apical consonants*, which are articulated with the tip of the tongue. Occlusives: *t, d*; fricatives: *n, l, r.* Prelinguals and apicals have the particularity of bringing the active organ closer to the dental area in the upper part of the oral cavity. This includes the upper incisors, the gum and the adjacent part of the hard palate. For this reason, prelinguals and apicals [21] are often grouped into the common category of dentals (cf. Broch 1910: §15).[21]
5. *Labial consonants*, which are articulated through the movement of the lips. Occlusives: *p, b*; fricatives: *v, f, m.*

If the articulation of a prelingual, apical or labial consonant is accompanied by a raising of the middle part of the tongue towards the hard palate, which produces an acoustic impression of softness, that complementary articulatory work is called *palatalization*. Palatalized consonants differ from similar non-palatalized consonants only through this additional articulatory work (and correspondingly, at the acoustic level, only through their higher timbre). Naturally, if a language has a series of 'palatalized/non-palatalized' consonantal oppositions, the differential property, i.e. the presence or absence of complementary articulatory work (and acoustically, the difference in timbre) is abstracted from the consonant pairs themselves, and, in turn, the common substratum of a pair is abstracted from the differential property (e.g., *s* is abstracted from its hard and soft variants). In other words, a consonantal softness correlation is given. This correlation is distinguishable if the opposition of timbre involves consonants of several articulatory series. Thus, in Great Russian we have prelingual, apical and labial palatalized consonants, while in the majority of Ukrainian dialects there are palatalized consonants of the first two series.

In the production of prelingual or palatal consonants, by contrast, the elevation of the middle part of the tongue towards the hard palate is not complementary but essential articulatory work. It is true that this articulatory work also causes an acoustic impression of high timbre. But mediolingual and hard consonants, which are identical in their mode of articulation despite belonging to different series, are not only mutually opposed by timbre, but also by their characteristic noise (and therefore, from an articulatory point

---

[21] It was Nikolay Trubetzkoy who drew my attention to the importance of differentiating between prelingual and apical consonants in order to analyse the consonantal softness correlation.

of view, by the place of the main articulatory work). Which of these two motor-acoustical differences, timbre or characteristic noise, constitutes then the differential phonological property of the opposition?

If a given language has an opposition between palatalized consonants and non-palatalized consonants of the same series and, in addition, an opposition between mediolingual [22] and non-palatalized consonants of a related series, these oppositions are considered to be related by timbre and are part of the softness correlation. Examples: 1) Polish dialects, where palatalized labials are opposed to hard labials, but where mediolinguals are opposed to hard postlinguals, prelinguals and the apical *n*; 2) Ukrainian dialects, where palatalized prelinguals correspond to hard prelinguals, but where other prelinguals correspond to apicals. The Hutsulian dialects of Bucovina and Bessarabia belong to this type. The great mass of Ukrainian dialects, by contrast, corresponds to the Great Russian type: all soft consonants, which are phonologically opposed to the corresponding hard consonants, are realized as *palatalized* sounds, not palatal ones.

If a language has no palatalized consonants but does have mediolingual consonants that are opposed to hard consonants of *different* series, then it is, of course, the difference in timbre and not the difference in characteristic noise (or points of articulation) that is highlighted. For example: 1) some Polish dialects that are deprived of the phonological softness of labials oppose the postpalatal variety of mediolinguals to postlingual hard consonants, while the prepalatal variety of mediolinguals is opposed to prelingual hard consonants and the apical *n*.[22] 2) In some Western Ukrainian dialects (e.g., Lemko, Galician intelligentsia), the soft equivalents of prelingual and apical consonants are realized as mediolingual consonants.[23] Let us consider a language with the following structure: the mediolingual *t* is in the same relation to the apical *t* as the mediolingual *s* (susurrant *s*) to the prelingual *s*. In all these 'relationships',

---

[22] Polish dialects without the phonological pairs *k* / *k'*, *g* / *g'*,—which occupy the whole Polish territory north of the following line: Lower Wieprz–Vistula–Grójec–Sochaczew–Vistula–southern frontier of the Krajna (Nitsch 1915: 276 ff.)—, must be considered as an intermediate type between languages with or without softness correlation. If only the pair *n* / *n'* were missing, there would be no 'double-ranked' hard consonants, corresponding to the mediolingual consonants, and these languages would have to be classified into the same type of languages without the softness correlation as, for example, Czech. The association between voiced consonants (*r, l, n, m*) and noisy consonants is too weak for the apical *n* to be clearly opposed to prelingual noisy consonants on its own. This is why we are inclined to treat northern Polish dialects as lacking the softness correlation. Similarly, the Slovakian Spiš dialects belong to this phonological type, which have mediolingual consonants that correspond to the hard *l, n* and prelinguals (cf. Stieber 1929: 111 ff, 122 ff).

[23] It is to Vasil Simovich, an excellent connoisseur of Ukrainian dialectology, that I owe this information on the expansion of palatal and palatalized consonants in Ukrainian dialects. This information substantially corrects the demonstrations of Zilinsky (1913: 350), which have been repeated without verification by several linguists.

similar timbres are opposed, while the characteristic noise (conforming to the points of articulation) of the hard *s* and *t* differ. In this case, we are again in the presence of a softness correlation.

If, in a given language, the mediolingual consonants correspond to hard consonants, all belonging to a *single* series, then there are no conditions that allow the highlighting of timbre, i.e. to attribute the differential property of the oppositions specifically to a difference in timbre. Under these conditions, mediolingual consonants are considered simply as one articulatory series, and the consonants of the mediolingual series constitute—in relation to the consonants of the other series, as well as all the other consonants of different series—, *disjunct* or non correlated phonemes. The Slovak inventory of mediolinguals, for example, is reduced to the phonemes *t', d', ň, l'*; Czech has the same series of phonemes except *l'*. The relationship of Czech *t'* to *t, k,* or *c* is the same as the relationship between *s* and *x*, etc. All these phonemes are disjunct. As a result, there is no softness correlation of consonants in either Czech or Slovak (see footnote 41).

From the point of view of their phonological relationship, there are transitional spaces between authentically Slovak and purely Ukrainian dialects: these are the eastern Slovak dialects, which have lost the quantitative correlation that is also foreign to Ukrainian, and the peripheral Subcarpathian Ukrainian dialects (Rusyn), which have lost the correlation of intensity, which is foreign to Slovak. Some Rusyn dialects that are closer to Slovakian phonology have reduced the use of the softness correlation: soft endings have become hard (Durnovo et al. 1915: 70). Nevertheless, it is the presence or absence of phonological consonantal softness that clearly separates Slovak and Ukrainian. It is precisely this phenomenon, remarks Olaf Broch, 'that defines the typical contrasts in the phonological structure of the various Slavic languages; a typical case of this contrast can be found at the frontier of the Ugro-Russian and eastern Slovak languages, which, it should be remembered, is not an ethnographic boundary' (Broch 1910: §178; see also Broch 1897).

The softness correlation has disappeared in Kashubian (see Lorentz 1925: 72–85) as well as in High and Low Sorbian (Shcherba 1915: 183). In the eastern Sorbian dialect, the former category of hard/soft pairs, according to Shcherba's observations, is disappearing. Only voiced dentals have a soft equivalent, but [24] these 'are on their last leg' (Shcherba 1915: 30). Shcherba has noted some characteristic signs of the fading of the softness correlation: young people tend to replace the soft *l'* with a European neutral *l* (Shcherba 1915: 29); *n* is easily substituted to *n'*, and 'analysing this combination puts natives in an awkward situation' (Shcherba 1915: 22); *n'* 'is not perceived as soft, so if this softness is not realized in the transition to the following vowel, i.e., in the absence of a subsequent vowel, then it is the previous transient high sound, perceived as *j*, that acquires greater importance'. It is indeed the difference in vowels, to which consonantal timbre oppositions are transposed, that acquires importance (Shcherba 1915: 184).

In the South Slavic region, only the eastern Bulgarian dialect has a phonological opposition of soft and hard consonants. But even there, its use is very limited and much narrower than in any Russian dialect. Only in some eastern Bulgarian dialects do we find pairs of soft consonants at the end of words. In the other dialects, the softness correlation is found in front of hard vowel phonemes—in most eastern Bulgarian dialects, only in front of *a*.[24] In these languages the softness opposition is at the threshold of phonemicization. A characteristic indication of this fact is a widespread tendency to replace the phonological opposition of consonants with a phonological differentiation of subsequent vowels: in eastern Bulgarian, *a* after a soft consonant tends to turn into a diphthong (the monosyllabic combination of two vowels): *ea*.

Broch points out that 'in Serbo-Croatian there is no alternation of hard and soft consonants, as there is in Russian' (Broch 1910: 68). The same can be said of eastern Bulgarian on the one hand, Slovenian on the other. Thus, *the consonant softness correlation encompasses the entire East Slavic linguistic universe, as well as the eastern areas of the West and South Slavic domain. But it is alien to the western periphery of the Slavic world.*

The language of *Russian Gypsies* is very close to Russian phonology. While the language of Ukrainian Gypsies reproduces the phonological structure of Ukrainian (Barannikov 1928: 59), the language of Great Russian Gypsies [25] is reminiscent of Great Russian in some of its phonological features.[25] The most characteristic similarities are the presence of a softness correlation, the inventory of consonants that realizes that correlation, and its relationship with the vowel system. This system consists, as in Russian, of the phonemes *i, u, e, o, a*. As in Russian, the phoneme *i* is realized with *i* after soft consonants, *y* after hard ones. In Russian, only hard consonants without soft correlates combine with the phoneme *e*, which in this case is realized as a sound with a posterior articulation (*užé, cep*). In Gypsy, the phoneme *e*

---

[24] The degree of softness in eastern Bulgarian varies between 'semi-palatalization' and the level of Great Russian. The inventory of correlated consonants is broad: there is the entire Great Russian inventory, but also *c—c'*. On the comparison of eastern Bulgarian consonantal softness and the facts of western Bulgarian, see Miletić (1903: 39-40); Mladenov (1915); Broch (1910: 72 ff, 152); Jakobson (1929: 55 ff, 76 ff).

[25] I have used mainly the description of the phonological characteristic of the language of the Great Russian Gypsies provided by Maxim Sergyevsky (1929a)—from which all examples are taken.

also occurs after hard consonants with a soft correlate but is realized as an anterior sound after soft consonants, as a medial-anterior sound after hard dentals (except for *l*), and as a medial sound after other hard consonants. The difference between postlingual and corresponding soft consonants is externally conditioned: *ž, š, c* and *dz* are always hard, *č* and *dž* always soft. The remaining dentals and labials are divided into two phonological variants: soft and hard. The opposition 'softness–hardness' is present before the phonemes *i, e, a, o*, but even within these limits, the conditions under which this opposition is realized are particular to each consonant category. Examples: *ferlóti/týkno; cyt'én'te / léste; rat'á/uštá; tat'óla / tató; tykn'ín'ko / paný; romn'én/javné; čen'á / čináva; čur'í/ryč; sas'á; pas'ováva/sóno; kiriv'í / lavýna; bel'v'él'/veš; grub'ováva / bibo*. Gypsy words mostly end with a vowel, or else with a liquid or nasal consonant (Sergyevsky 1929a: 98); of all the soft consonants, only *l'* and *n'* are used at the end of the word: *bel'v'él'/balvál; č'ergén'/romnén*. What is characteristic here is that *the consonantal softness correlation exists in the dialects of the Gypsies that live among the eastern Slavs and Poles* (see Kopernicki 1925: III ff.), *but is absent in other Gypsy dialects (Danubian and others), as well as in other languages of the Indian branch.*

The opposition of soft and hard consonants is profoundly alien to all western Romance languages, without exception. It suffices here to recall how difficult it is for a French or Italian learner of Russian to pronounce soft consonants. Jan Baudouin de Courtenay (1908: 584) reports an eloquent example: a French woman who came to Russia was aware of the difference [26] between soft and hard consonants in Russian but could not grasp what exactly this difference consisted in. When pronouncing Russian words, she replaced the soft consonants with hard consonants (e.g., *bel* instead of *p'el, de* instead of *t'e, rugi* instead of *ruk'i*): she replaced the characteristic feature of a consonantal correlation, softness, with another one, specific to French: sonority.

Only the Romanian group, a linguistic island at the easternmost periphery of the Romance world, knows a consonant softness correlation. The eastern part of this 'island' is occupied by Moldavian. The Carpathians form the western border of Moldavian, the Soviet Republic of Moldava its eastern periphery (see Weigand 1909: 10 and map no. 65). Maxim Sergyevsky (1929b) has devoted a substantial study to the languages of the Republic of Moldova. Moldavian is characterized by a combination of the following features: 1. soft *s', z'* in various positions and 2. mediolingual occluders that originate from the asyllabic *p, b + i* groups (Weigand 1909: 12). In some of the languages described by Sergyevsky (Rybnitsa district and others), these occlusives apparently correspond to softened *t*, *d*. The author states that they 'almost coincide acoustically' and 'in some individual pronunciations can truly coincide' (Sergyevsky 1929b: 87). Characteristically, peasants do not distinguish these consonants in writing despite the adopted standard spelling, and thus write, for example, май дини ар арди... [*maj dini ar ardi*] when etymologically it should be written май дине ар арде... [*maj dine ar arde*]— Sergyevsky transcribes *g'in'i ar ard'i...* (1929b: 96). In the same dialects *s'*, *z'* are realized as palatalized anterolinguals. In Sergyevsky's examples, we find *s'*, *t'*, *n'*, *r'* (*ais'* = Romanian *aici*, *z'ern'* = Romanian *viermi*, *or'* = Romanian *ori*) at the end of the word; both these consonants, along with *z'*, *d'*, *l'*, can be combined with the phonemes *a*, *o*, *e*, *i*, whereas soft labials are combined only with *e*, *i*.[26] [27]

Another type of Moldavian dialect studied by Sergyevsky (e.g., Ananiv district) differs from the first one in that the combinatorial reflexes '*p*, *b*, + asyllabic *l*' are 'a bit further away from *t'*, and *d'* from an articulatory and acoustic point of view, i.e. they are apparently opposed to postlinguals, as soft consonants are opposed to hard ones (e.g. окь [*ok*], кептин [*k'eptin*]). Another peculiarity is that the phonemes *s'*, *z'* are realized as mediolingual fricatives (Sergyevsky 1929b: 96).

The softness correlation, which is present in Moldavian and literary Moldavian, is foreign to literary Romanian. The question as to where the boundary of the softness correlation is located exactly in the Romanian group must be answered by the specialists of Romanian who are able to identify, in the diversity of dialectal phenomena, the systematic phonological set of Romanian languages. However, we can already say that, as far as the softness correlation is concerned, the Romanian group forms a parallel with the Bulgarian dialectal group: *from east to west, the softness correlation fades, then finally disappears completely.*

The Finno-Ugric group is also divided into two types: eastern, where phonological consonant softness is present, and western, where it is absent.

---

[26] The Moldavian vowel system is very similar to that of literary Russian. Moldavian has 5 accented and 3 unaccented phonemes. The light vowels are soft (and, therefore, characterized by anterior articulation) after the soft consonants (*i, e, ja*) and hard (characterized by more posterior articulation) after the hard ones (*y, è, a*) (cf. Sergievskij 1929b; Kurylo 1929: 218). The difference consists in the fact that in Russian only uncorrelated hard consonants combine with *e*, while in Moldavian correlated hard consonants also combine with *e*; another difference is that in Russian the basic variants of the phonemes are *i, e*, while in Moldavian they are *y, è*. For example, in Russian the word can only start with *i* and not with a *y*, while in Moldavian it is the opposite: *yntreg, jin, jibovnik*. Thus, in Russian one can find only *i* after *k*, while in our Moldavian dialect one also finds *y*: *kynina*. One more difference: the unaccented phoneme *a* in Russian corresponds to Moldavian *e* (posterior e).

From this point of view, the languages of the Finnish branch[27] are particularly significant. Permian languages, i.e., 1. *Votjak*, or Udmurt (see Emelyanov 1927), 2. Komi (*Zirian* and *Permyak* variants), have an autonomous consonantal softness correlation. The hard *t, d, n, l* are opposed by corresponding soft mediolingual consonants, but hard *s, z*, in some languages are opposed by mediolingual consonants, while in others they are opposed by palatalized anterolingual consonants. Thus, the inventory of correlated consonants of the Permian languages coincides entirely with two western varieties of Ukrainian 'hard *r*' dialects, one where soft *s* and *z* are realized as mediolinguals (see p. 23), and one where soft sibilants are not palatal, but palatalized (see p. 22). To illustrate the differentiating role of the softness correlation in Permian languages, I provide here some examples from the book of Georgy Lytkin (1889), in Russian characters: пас [*pas*]: [sign],/пась [*pas*]: [fur coat]; сам [*sam*]: [profit]/сям [*s'am*] : [custom]; сысь [*sys*]—: [rot] / сись [*s'is*]: [wax]; сой [*soj*]/[arm], сёй [*s'oj*] / [clay]; роз [*roz*] / [ear] / розь [*roz*] : [orifice]; ут [*ut*] : [roll], уть [*ut*] : [sight]; код [*kod*]: [drunk] / кодь [*kod*]: [similar]; нэм [*nem*]: [century], нем [*n'em*]: [nothing]; нур [*nur*]: [snack]/нюр [*n'ur*] [28]: [swamp]; лань [*lan*]: [silence], лян [*l'an*]: [enclosed]; ул [*ul*]: [branch]/уль [*ul*]: [wet]; пел [*p'el*]: [thumb] / пель [*p'el*]: [ear].

Softness correlation plays an even more important role in the phonological system of the two variants of *Mordvin*: Erzya and Moksha (cf. Bubrikh 1929; Evsevev 1928; Shakhmatov 1910). The following consonantal phonemes have corresponding soft phonemes: *t, d, n, l, r, s, z, c, dz*. Bubrikh's examples are: *is't'a, v'ed'ams, pan'an, mol'an, vad'r'a, s'ado, z'aro, c'ora*. All soft Mordvin consonants, as in Great Russian, are palatalized.

The same correlation exists in some of the dialects of the *Cheremis* (Mari) grasslands, e.g. Malmyž and Permian (Wichmann 1923; Beke 1911: 104 ff.). In these Cheremis dialects, where the independent consonantal softness correlation is absent, there is a syllabic softness correlation that is typical of Eurasian Turkic languages. We will examine these dialects later, in connection with the differences in timbre of Turkic languages (pp. 33–34).

Karelian dialects are characterized by a rich phonological gradation. In the Karelian dialects of Tver, there is a phonological softness correlation not only for anterolingual, apical and labial consonants, but also for postlingual ones. It thus surpasses, from a numerical point of view, the inventory of phonemes of Great Russian. In southern Karelian languages, the anterolingual (*s, z*) and

---

[27] Where the source of the phonological data is not indicated, it is due to Dimitry V. Bubrikh (1929).

apical (*t, d, n, l, r*) consonants enter into the softness correlation. The Olonets languages, along with eastern Ludes languages that are in close contact with them, form an intermediate type between the presence and total absence of a softness correlation. Their inventory of pairs is: *t/t', d/d', n / n', l/l', r / r'*. If these soft consonants were realized as mediolinguals, soft and hard would be considered as two different articulation points (mediolingual and apical), and, as in Czech, there would be no correlation of timbre. But in the languages in question, soft consonants are not palatal, they are palatalized. They are not distinguished from hard consonants by their point of articulation and, it seems, differences in timbre are thus felt as such. It is characteristic that new borrowed words from Great Russian retain *s', z'* and soft labials in these languages. A language without softness correlation (e.g., Czech) cannot reproduce the independent softness of a foreign language. It is easier to increase the inventory of correlated phonemes than to assimilate new disjunct phonemes.

In the far north of the Karelian Republic, in the Ukhto-Karelian dialect, there is no consonantal softness correlation. Neither Lappish nor the main body [29] of Finnish (the language of the Finns in Finland) knows it. Soft consonantal phonemes have recently appeared *in the eastern regions of Finnish*— partly within Finland itself (near Saimaa), but mainly outside of it (around Leningrad)—following the loss of the final *i*: the palatalized *t', d', n', l', r'* and, in some dialects, also *s', k'*, etc. See below for a parallel dialectal innovation in Estonian. Apart from this innovation, Estonian has no phonological consonantal softness. Livonian, which occupies northern Courland, also lacks it (Kettunen 1926).

The softness correlation is also foreign to Hungarian, i.e. the western representative of the Ugrian branch of the Finno-Ugric family. Like Czech, Hungarian has the disjunct mediolingual phonemes *t', d', ň*; formerly, it also knew the mediolingual *l'*, but as in the case of Czech, it has lost it. According to Castrén's (1849) indications, one of the eastern offshoots of the Ugrian branch (in the Ob' region), Ostiak, has 8 correlated consonant pairs: *t–t', d–d', n–n', l–l', č–č', dž–dž', k–k', g–g'*. Examples: *tul*: [stupid], *t'ul*: [button]; *tada*: [empty], *t'ad'a*: [father]. No sufficiently reliable data are available to verify whether the endangered Vogul, another member of the Obugrian group, knows phonological consonantal softness.

The *Samoyed* languages, which are close relatives of the Finno-Ugric family, also have a consonantal softness correlation. According to Castrén, the Yuraks, the most numerous ethnic group of the Samoyeds, who migrate between Arkhangelsk and the mouth of the Yenisei, possess the following pairs of consonants by softness and hardness: *t, d, n, l, r, s, z, c* (Castrén 1854: §§ 20, 23, 29, 31, 33, 35, 37, 39; cf. also Lehtisalo 1927: 28 ff). The realization of the soft phonemes, as we can see, corresponds to that of literary Ukrainian (anterolinguals are palatalized, and mediolinguals correspond to apicals).

Having examined, firstly, three branches of the Indo-European language family, Slavic, Indian and Romance as well as, secondly, the Uralic language family (Finno-Ugric and Samoyed), we come to the conclusion that there are two phonological types, each of which is very clearly related to its geography. Languages and dialects that have consonantal softness correlation form a compact territorial group. Given that this group is made up of representatives of different branches, we are entitled to speak of a language union, which we call the Eurasian language union. This union is opposed by another type: languages and dialects that do not have a phonological [30] opposition of consonants by softness and hardness. These languages belong to the same families, or even branches of families, as the languages of the first type, but they are geographically situated outside the territory of the Eurasian language union. Depending on their spatial location, they are either European (the majority of Romance languages, the south-western periphery of the Slavic world, the north-western periphery of Finnish languages, Hungarian and Danubian Gypsy languages), or Asian languages (the majority of Indian languages).

Turkic languages are characterized by what is called *vowel harmony*. Vowels form a series of pairs, where each paired vowel is then distinguished by its timbre. Thus, two categories of vowels are in mutual opposition: 'hard' vowels of low timbre; and the corresponding 'soft' vowels of high timbre. Example: the Kazakh-Kyrgyz vowel system:

Hard vowels	Soft vowels
a	e
o	ö
y	i
u	ü[28]

In these languages, all the vowels of a word belong to the same category as its first vowel. If the first syllable contains a soft vowel, all other vowels

---

[28] When pronouncing *ö*, the position of the tongue is the same as when pronouncing *e*, and the position of the lips is the same as for *o*. When pronouncing *ü*, the tongue position is the same as when pronouncing *i*, and the lip position is the same as for *u*.

are soft; if it is hard, then all the following ones are hard. Along with other contemporary Russian linguists, Galimdjan Sharaf (1927) has highlighted in his interesting work 'Palatograms of Tatar Sounds Compared to Russian' an important phenomenon in the phonological structure of a whole set of Turkic languages. In these languages, there are consonant pairs next to vowel pairs, all of which are opposed by hardness and softness. Moreover, vowel harmony is indissolubly connected with consonant harmony: some words are formed of soft consonants and soft vowels, the others of hard consonants and hard vowels. This is called syllabic *synharmony*. Sharaf (1927: 98–99), Yakovlev (1930: 61) and others have shown further that it is inaccurate to examine pairs of opposing Turkic vowels as an autonomous phonological category [31] and consonant pairs only as a complementary variation.[29]

Next to vowel softness correlation, consonantal softness correlation constitutes an integral part of a *softness correlation of syllables*. In languages of this type, although the consonantal softness correlation is not independent but is rather part of a larger set of correlations, it is nevertheless a phonological fact, an element of the phonological system. To take some examples from Kazakh-Kyrgyz: *al* [take]/*el'* [wrist]; *ak* [white] / *ek'* [sit (imperative)]. Softness in languages with vowel harmony is used to differentiate whole words and not phonemes. This is why in some Turkic writing systems 'a common soft sign is used for all the sounds of a word, as if it were enclosed in parentheses' (Sharaf 1927). In the Latin script built on this principle (the Kazakh alphabet of Tyuryakulov), words have the following appearance: *al/'al*; *aq / 'aq*. In the Russian spelling, the traditional soft sign can of course be used as a prefix: ал/ьал; ак/ьак. Other examples of this spelling are Tatar words: ана [mother]/ьана [here we are], etc.

The syllable-softness correlation has been found in the following Turkic languages: *Tatar, Nogai, Kazakh, Kyrgyz, Bashkir, Turkmen* (Sharaf 1927: 97; Yakovlev 1928: 60 ff.), the language of the *Bessarabian Gagauz* (Moshkov 1904: XXVII), *Azerbaijani* (according to the Azerbaijani grammar of Polivanov and Gasanov) and in the majority of *Uzbek* dialects.[30] On the other

---

[29] In his detailed description of the phonological character of the differences between Tatar consonants according to softness and hardness, Sharaf refers, among other things, to the ability of both hard and soft consonants to play the role of interjections (*r!, š'!, m'!, s'!*) and to onomatopoeia that are made up of only hard consonants or only soft consonants (*klt / k'l't', mrt, t'r ',* etc.).

[30] Syllabic harmony is characteristic of all Uzbek languages that are not Iranianized (Polivanov 1929: 517; 536). Polivanov includes in this category: 1. the Uzbek group itself, to which the majority of the peasant dialects of Uzbekistan belong, including those of the semi-nomadic Uzbeks; 2. the non-Turkmenized northern Uzbek languages (in the Turkestan and Tchimkent districts, with the exception of the Ikan and Kara-Bulak dialects); and 3. Turkmenized Uzbek dialects (Ikan, Kara-Bulak and some others).

hand, it should be mentioned that there is no softness correlation either in Ottoman Turkish, which belongs to the same south-western group of the Turkic family as the languages of the Turkmen and Gagauz of Bessarabia (Samoylovich 1922: 5–6), nor [32] in the Ottomanized language of the Dobrudja Gagauz. This was pointed out to me by authoritative Turkologists: Jan Rypka, a professor at Charles University in Prague, and Tadeusz Kowalski, a professor at the Jagiellonian University in Krakow who pays great attention to the problem of consonantal softness, as demonstrated by his research on Karaim. Thus, *in the Turkic group, we find a close parallelism with the division of the Indo-European and Finno-Ugric linguistic worlds into two types: the Eurasian type, that has a correlation of consonantal softness, and the non-Eurasian type, which lacks it.*[31]

The phonological structure of the language of the north-western Karaites, who live in the districts of Ponevej, Trok and Vilna, is very instructive in this regard. This Turkic language, which is very well described in Kowalski's book, has undergone a very curious evolution—from a syllabic softness correlation to an independent consonantal softness correlation. Example: kunlardan [of servants]/k'un'l'ard'an' [of days] (Kowalski 1929: XXX). In this language, practically all consonants with a labial, apical, anterolingual or postlingual articulation point are in a softness correlation. The emergence of the softness correlation in Karaim closely parallels the Russian-Polish phonological evolution. I will not dwell in detail on the characteristic features of the Russian-Polish transformation of Proto-Slavic phonology,[32] but I would like to mention one thing: the Proto-Slavic phonological system had the same syllabic softness correlation as Turkic languages with syllabic harmony (with the difference that, in Proto-Slavic, this correlation did not serve to distinguish a word, i.e. it did not have a syntactic function—a function which it does have in languages with vowel harmony—, but this is not of interest to us at the moment). The Russian-Polish type of modification of the Proto-Slavic phonological system consists in the fact that the consonantal softness opposition acquired an autonomous role. Therefore, the vowel softness opposition lost its importance, and a clear tendency to unify vowel phoneme pairs differentiated by timbre became visible in both Russian and Polish. [33] In an opposite type of modification of Proto-Slavic phonology, which we observe

---

[31] Unfortunately, there is no data on a whole set of Turkic languages present in Eurasia. Do the consonants of these languages differ according to softness (e.g., in Iakut, Altaic-Tatar, etc.)? In all these languages, vowel harmony is rigorously observed and the parallel discovery of consonant harmony is theoretically very likely. It could be that vowel harmony is a particular manifestation of syllabic harmony.

[32] I have tried to elucidate this question in Jakobson (1929: ch. VII) and elsewhere.

in the West and South Slavic languages (especially in Czech, Serbo-Croatian and Slovenian), consonantal softness correlation is lost, a fact which conditions the persistence of a vowel softness correlation. Among Turkic languages, it is Turkic-Ottoman that has undergone the latter type of evolution, whereas there is a complete analogy with the eastern variant of Slavic evolution in the language of the north-western Karaites. In this language, vowels that follow soft consonants coincide with the corresponding vowels of the hard syllable.[33] We can compare, for example, the Russian change from *e* to *o* before hard consonants (*s'óla, id'óm*) with the same phenomenon in Polish before hard labials.

Chuvash, a close relative of Turkic languages, occupies an intermediate place between languages that have syllabic softness correlation (Tatar type) and languages that have independent consonantal softness correlation (Russian type). As in the Russian type, the Chuvash *s–s'* opposition is independent of the following vowels, so that the soft *s'* variant often combines with hard vowels, and the hard *s* combines in turn with soft vowels (Egorov 1930: 51). The other consonants follow the Tatar type; i.e. as far as softness and hardness are concerned, they form an indissoluble whole with their adjacent vowels. But what is characteristic here is that Tatar palatalized consonants 'have a harsher acoustic effect than the corresponding sounds of Chuvash, which in this respect are close to the Russian consonants and, apart from some nuances, coincide with them' (Egorov 1930: 54). This, it seems, is to be related to the above-mentioned tendency of Chuvash to develop an independent consonantal softness correlation.

Of all the eastern Finnish languages, *Cheremis* (Marian) respects vowel harmony the most consistently. Cheremis dialects that do not have an autonomous consonantal softness correlation (see above) are visibly closer to the Tatar phonological type: consonantal timbre forms a coherent whole with the timbre of the vowel phoneme of the same syllable. The presence of syllabic harmony in Cheremis [34] has often been mentioned by researchers (see, e.g., Lewy 1922: 36–37). Ramstedt, describing the High Cheremis dialects, explains that in a heated discussion neutral vowels are dropped, consonants become syllable heads and differences in the timbre of these consonants are

---

[33] To be more precise: after soft consonants, soft vowels were replaced by the corresponding variant of the vowel phonemes of the hard syllable, which was located at the absolute beginning of the word and was felt in linguistic thought as the basic variant of the corresponding phoneme. Only at the absolute word beginning was the vowel softness correlation retained, because in this position the phonological difference could not be transferred to the consonants.

used as an independent way of differentiating words. Examples: *tr* (with syllabic *r*: dropped hard neutral vowel) [peace]/*tr'* (with syllabic *r'*: soft dropped neutral vowel) [border]; *š* (syllabic hard consonant: dropped initial hard neutral vowel) [reason], *š'* (syllabic soft consonant: dropped initial soft neutral vowel) [no] (Ramstedt 1902: IX, X). If we take into consideration that, in this language, the opposition in timbre of the pairs of consonants *t, n, l* occurs independently of their vowel environment, we will notice a transition from a syllabic softness correlation to an independent consonantal softness correlation—which can be compared to a similar phenomenon in Chuvash phonology. According to Paasonen, who studied the Cheremis dialect of the Bir district of the Ufa governorate, the objective degree of consonantal softness in a soft syllable coincides with the degree of palatalization in Volga Tatar and is lower than in Chuvash, which in turn is lower than the softness of Mordvin consonants (Paasonen 1901: IV–V). Characteristically, when Cheremis speak Russian 1. the softness of Russian consonants weakens, 2. they have a tendency to unify syllables by tone, e.g., *l'es', n'et'* (Selishchev 1927: 67).

In *Mongolian* dialects, consonants before *i* are palatalized. Three phonological changes caused this extra-phonological fact to become an independent softness of consonants: 1. Final *i* were dropped, while the softness of the preceding consonants was retained. 2. First syllable *i* were assimilated to the vowels of the following syllables (the so-called 'break'). The phoneme *i* was replaced by *a, e, o,* etc. The trace of this *i* is the softness of the preceding consonant. 3. Consonants were dropped between *i* and its following vowel. The result was the 'contraction' of both vowels into a single long vowel: *i + a*, which contracted into *e*, etc. The preceding consonant remained soft.[34] [35]

Some Mongolian dialects consistently preserve consonantal softness in all these categories of cases, while in other dialects the scope of independent softness is restricted. As far as the available materials allow us to judge, consonantal softness correlation is widespread in the Mongolian linguistic world. A typical example of a Mongolian dialect that consistently preserves consonantal softness before a vowel that is replaced or dropped without replacement

---

[34] Vladimirtzov compares the completion of the formation of long vowels from vowel combinations with a simultaneous process of transition undergone by Mongolian tribes 'from a hunter-gatherer's life to nomadic life, which caused great changes in their life in general. Various tribes at various times adapted in different ways to the conditions of their new nomadic life on the steppe, a life which in the end most Mongolian tribes adopted. Under these conditions, the process of phonetic evolution must have been faster, and new words, as well as old ones, took on new forms as they were adapted to the requirements of the new life taken on by words in relation to nomadic everyday life and the nomadic conditions on the steppe' (Vladimirtzov 1929: 241).

are either the *Ordos* (Mostert) or the *Dagu* dialect, which occupies a large part of northern Manchuria and is beautifully described in Nicholas Poppe's monograph. All three of the above-mentioned factors cause consonantal softness in the Dagur dialect (Poppe 1930: 119ff., 142). Conversely, the *Khalkha* dialect, surveyed in the major work of Boris Vladimirtzov (1929), does not have soft consonants at the end of words, but does have them before *i* that has changed into another vowel (fracture, constriction). In this dialect, there is an oscillation: in some cases, consonants are soft, in others, under unspecified conditions, they are hard.

The Dagur and Khalkha dialects belong to the eastern Mongolian branch. The representative of the western branch, the *Kalmyk* dialect, is also characterized by soft consonants (before a dropped *i*). Vladislav Kotvich notes the presence of the soft consonants *n, l, r, v, k* (Kotvich 1929: 51).

In the case of Mongolian dialects, Poppe speaks of a palatalization of consonants (Poppe 1930: 120, 142), while Vladimirtzov talks of the combination of a consonant with a very short and weak transitional soft sound, which he denotes by a superscript small *i* (Vladimirtzov 1929: 56, 176, 200). This disagreement can be overcome if one highlights that, in Mongolian dialects, the main articulatory work ceases before the additional one, i.e. between the palatalized consonant and the broad vowel (*a, e,* etc.). Mongolian dialects have developed a distinct transitional vowel element, close to the non-syllabic *i*—a phenomenon that commonly accompanies strong palatalizations (cf. Broch 1910: §185). That phonological softness is indeed realized here by a strong palatalization is demonstrated by Poppe: because the softness is independent, the degree of palatalization is much higher than in the position before *i*, where softness is externally conditioned. That said, Dagur combinations with *i* remain close to Russian: for example, in the word *biteg* (letter) *b'* is pronounced almost as in *bit'* (to hit) and is very far from *b* in German *bitte* (Poppe 1930: 142). [36]

Let us take stock of our geographical overview of monotonic languages that also possess a phonological consonantal softness. These languages are spread over three plains: the White Sea-Caucasian plain, the East Siberian plain and the Turkestan plain, which correspond to the core area where the geographical features of the Eurasian world are also present (cf. Savitzky 1927: 8ss, 1921: 131). The south-western periphery of this phonological union is occupied by the *western confines of the Eurasian steppes*, which extend along the shores of the Black Sea from Odessa to the Balkans. Finally, it seems that, in the east, monotonic languages with a softness correlation cover 'the Mongolian core of the continent', which, given a series of other features, also belongs to Eurasia (Savitzky 1927: 50).

The mountainous region bordering the White Sea-Caucasian plain from the south-east is mostly occupied by the languages of the High, or North, Caucasian group.[35] The phonological peculiarities of the languages of Eurasia are here present: differences of consonantal timbre play a significant role in these languages. But—this is a typical peripheral phenomenon!—these differences are partly modified, partly exacerbated.

The same type of softness correlation as in Russian, Mordvin, etc., is found in *Abkhaz* and in the *Eastern Kiech* dialects. There is a corresponding correlation in *Lak* and *Chechen* too, the only difference being that the category of consonants with a high timbre is formed here, from the sound-production point of view, in a different way. These are the so-called 'emphatically soft' consonants.

Another kind of deviation from the canonical timbre correlation of languages of the Eurasian plains is a 'darker' correlation of consonants in North Caucasian languages. In terms of objective acoustics, we can state here that the opposing consonants are not those of high and normal timbre, but rather those of normal and lower timbre. This correlation holds in all western Caucasian languages and in many Dagestan languages. In some languages, like Kabardian, it serves as the only timbre correlation, in others it coexists with a softness correlation of one type or the other; example: Abkhazian.[36] [37]

Transcaucasian languages, such as Armenian and the Kartvelian (Georgian) group, are devoid of timbre differences in their consonants. The transitional nature of this area, geographically and ethnographically, between Eurasia and its neighbouring places of development, has already been repeatedly pointed out (Savitzky 1928: 90; Svyatopolk-Mirsky 1929; Zelenin 1929: § 87). There are no further timbral differences in the Iranian languages of the Caucasus (Ossetian, Tat) or in the Iranianized Uzbek dialects.[37]

Far Eastern Palaeo-Asian languages confirm Savitzky's thesis that the Far East is situated outside the Eurasian world (Savitsky 1927: 51). These languages are divided into two phonological types. Chukchi (Bogoraz 1899) and

---

[35] I derive information on timbre differences in these languages from oral communications with N. S. Trubetzkoy and from the works of Yakovlev (1923, 1928, 1930). Trubetzkoy (1924a) provides a classification study of these languages.

[36] In Kabardian, there are eight pairs of opposing dark-light consonants: for example *beg'* = infantile illness, *beg* = spider (I indicate the labialization of consonants through a hard sign). In the Abkhazian phonological system, there are dark and soft correlates for five light-hard consonantal phonemes, only soft correlates for six, and a dark correlate for only one such consonant.

[37] This includes a number of urban Uzbek accents (Tashkent, Dzhizak, Samarkand, Katta-Kurgan, Ura-Tube, Parsha, Bukhara) and a group of transitional Fergana accents (Polivanov 1929).

Yukaghir (Yokhelson 1898) do not distinguish consonants by timbre. Even the Russian Far-Eastern dialects that have been subjected to Yukaghir influence (Bogoraz 1901) tend to noticeably reduce the use of softness correlations. In this respect, the easternmost point of the Russian linguistic world is similar to its westernmost point, i.e. the region of the Rusyn dialects. Glyak, which covers the northern part of Sakhalin and the lower Amur has a soft consonant correlation as well as polytony, according to anecdotal evidence provided by Lev Sternberg (1900).[38] It thus belongs to the Pacific polytonic union and is especially close to Japanese in the composition of its correlations: Japanese accents, except in the north-east, are characterized by polytony and by a softness-hardness difference of consonants (Polivanov 1928: 169ff).

A similar phenomenon occurs on the north-western frontier of Eurasia: here, too, an isoline of soft consonants is embedded in a polytonic language union. The distinction of consonants by softness and hardness is characteristic of Lithuanian, where it seems to be a component (result) of a softness correlation of syllables (cf., e.g., Kurschat 1876: 14, 24 et passim). According to Larin, in the Lithuanian accents that neighbour Slavic ones, palatalization 'is more distinguishable and universal than in other Lithuanian accents, because of Polish and Russian influence' (Larin 1926: 115). An independent softness of consonants exists in Latvian as a dialectal phenomenon. It is especially widespread in [38] eastern Latvian accents,—Endzelins presumes a Russian influence (Endzelins 1923: 90). This phenomenon, which appeared as a result of the loss and elimination of *i*, demonstrates, along with an analogous eastern Finnish phenomenon, that the development of the isoline of softness correlation is still progressing, or at least, was progressing until recently.

6. A consolidated phonological characterization of the Eurasian Language Union

The prevalence of syllabic synharmonism in the eastern fringes of the Turanian linguistic world[39] (in particular, in the languages of the Manchu-Tungus branch) still needs to be investigated, but we can already legitimately speak of a Eurasian language union, without prejudging the degree of closeness of its isophones with other Eurasian isolines in some segments.

---

[38] The following Gilyak consonants are paired by softness and hardness: *ts, ch, s, z, b, n, l, v*.
[39] Alkor (1930) remarks that 'almost all the specifically Tungus consonants can be palatalized or not', but it is unclear whether this concerns phonological softness. The descriptions of Tungus languages by Russian scholars have unfortunately not been published yet.

The composition of phonological correlations in the Eurasian Union languages is characterized by a combination of two features: 1. monotony, and 2. timbral oppositions of consonants, which manifest themselves, with the exception of the Caucasian periphery of Eurasia, in the form of a softness correlation. Outside of the territorially continuous group of languages that we have called the Eurasian language union, no language possessing this combination of phonological features exists at present on the mainland of the Old World, i.e. on the continent that makes up Eurasia. Only among the languages of some islands neighbouring this continent in the far west of the European world is there *one* language that has the said features, namely *Irish*, which has both monotony and a phonological opposition of soft and hard consonants (see, e.g., Sommerfelt 1922, 1924–1927).[40] [39]

In the far north-west and, correspondingly, in the far north-east, the Eurasian language union is neighboured by groups of monotonic languages without timbre differences in their consonants: on the one hand, Loparian, the Ukhto-Karelian dialect, Finnish (except for its eastern margin), and the Finnish-Swedish dialect; on the other hand, the Chukchi-Yukagir type of Palaeo-Asian languages.[41] In the north-west and throughout the east, the Eurasian union is bordered by polytonic unions, the Baltic and the Pacific unions. Finally, to the south-west and south, the neighbours of the Eurasian union are again monotonic languages that do not distinguish consonants by timbre: the main body of languages of Europe, Ottoman Turkish, the Kartvelian group and the Indo-European languages of the Middle East (Armenian and the Indo-Iranian group).

So far, we could establish only one noticeable divergence between the phonological boundary and the foreign isolines that define the contours of Eurasia: at its Polish confines, Eurasian isophones turned out to be more aggressive than both physical or geographical features and historical boundaries. But, firstly, a comparison of Polish accents presents the vivid picture of a weakening softness correlation, i.e. it reveals the transitive, local character of Polish phonology (cf. above), and secondly, we can find another curious indication, again linguistic, of a Polish bias towards the east. The specific tendencies of a given linguistic whole often find themselves condensed in literary language. The Russian orientation of the phonological evolution of

---

[40] The phonological composition of Eurasia is defined by a *positive* feature (the presence of timbre correlations). This is all the more significant since that it has to this day not been possible to find a single positive phonological feature common to all European or all Asian languages.

[41] The same type seems to be joined by those eastern Japanese accents in which there is neither polytony, nor quantitative correlation of vowels, nor softness correlation of consonants (see Polivanov 1924).

Polish literary language is clearly and convincingly demonstrated by Lehr-Spławiński (see, e.g., 1929: 192ff.). Literary Polish has eliminated a number of phonological distinctions that were alien to the East Slavic system, all the while preserving some phonological differences that have a correspondence in the Russian language world, despite the fact that these differences were eliminated in the surrounding Polish dialects that pressured the literary language.

The local, transitional nature of Romanian and Bulgarian phonology is even more visible. These are dialectal groups with very unevenly distributed consonantal timbre differences: in some dialects these differences are used quite thoroughly, in others there is a sharp tendency to reduce the use of softness [40] correlations, by limiting to a minimum either the number of consonants that are opposed by softness and hardness, or the inventory of phonetic combinations in which an opposition is realized. The difference between soft consonants and corresponding hard ones is partly eliminated, and the difference in timbre is partly replaced by some other differential sign. Finally, the zone where softness correlation is reduced neighbours the regions of dialects where this correlation does not exist at all.

At the junction of the Eurasian Union with polytonic unions, polytonic languages that have a phonological softness of consonants play the role of a connecting node to the Eurasian world. Such languages are Lithuanian, Latvian—with its dialectal softness—, and to a lesser extent Estonian—with its Revalian 'semi-softness'—on the eastern edge of the Baltic Union; most Japanese dialects and Hilä on the northern edge of the Pacific Union.

Curiously enough, the combination of consonantal softness correlation with polytony is relatively alien to Slavic languages, and in those cases where such a combination did occur every effort was made to eliminate it (see Jakobson 1929: 51, 59). Thus, for Slavic languages, the preservation of a softness correlation is tantamount to the adoption of the Eurasian complex of phonological features.

The phonological features of languages that neighbour the Eurasian world deserve special attention. It is not infrequent, in the areas neighbouring the geographical boundary of the consonantal softness correlation, to find mediolingual voiced consonants that are homogeneous in their mode of production with consonants of related series. The area of this phenomenon in southeast Europe is considerable: Czech, Slovak and Hungarian (mediolingual consonants t, b, which correspond to the anterolinguals t, e), Serbo-Croatian (mediolingual consonants, which correspond to the anterolinguals *ch*, *g*), Albanian with its dialectally distinct mediolingual consonants (see Weigand

1913: 10), some west Bulgarian and Romanian accents that lack softness correlation.

7. History of the Eurasian Language Union

We have characterized the phonological features that unite the languages of Eurasia in a static perspective, but our problem is not thereby completely solved. The Eurasian language union possesses its own history and, in particular, its own historical phonology. The boundaries and, indeed, [41] the very features of a language union change like the boundaries and features of a single language. We have information about the history of Slavic, Romance, Finno-Ugric, Turkic and Mongolian languages. The specific question is how, when, and in what connection did those of these languages that are related to the Eurasian area assimilate, develop or retain the softness-hardness consonantal opposition? In my paper 'Remarks on the Phonological Evolution of Russian in Comparison with the Other Slavic Languages', I tried to identify the basic types of evolution of Slavic language and the tendencies that underly each of these types (Jakobson 1929). Now, the Eurasian type of evolution of Slavic language should be compared with the evolution of the non-Slavic languages of Eurasia (not only the result, but precisely the course of their evolution itself!). And finally, as we have noted above, the results of comparative-historical phonology are to be compared to the history of language migrations. Without becoming acquainted with the *formation* of a language union, one cannot really grasp its essence, or grasp the relationship of a linguistic environment to its territory. We have considered a series of homogeneous phenomena; the Eurasian branches of several language families attached to Eurasia are endowed with softness and hardness consonant pairs, whereas the non-Eurasian branches of the same families are not. Hence, there must be a transformation process of a language into a Eurasian one, a Eurasian course of linguistic evolution. And if this process exists, then we must provide a synthetic characterization of it.

The fate of the non-Eurasian members of Eurasian language families shows us how languages are introduced to places of development that neighbour Eurasia. A process of Europeanization is very visible here. The history of the western outposts of the Slavic linguistic world is instructive in this regard. The age of disintegration of Proto-Slavic (tenth to eleventh century) radically transformed the phonological composition of all Slavic dialects. The common Slavic syllabic softness correlation was displaced. The eastern path of the evolution of Slavic languages—the development of an independent softness correlation of consonants—was opposed in the West by a tendency to abolish the timbre differences of consonants. At a phonological crossroads, Czech chose a path which found a parallel in German (see Jakobson 1929: 55). The history of the phonological evolution of Czech, from the age of the disintegration of Proto-Slavic to the end of the Czech Middle Ages (at the beginning of the fifteenth century), is essentially the history of a thorough eradication of consonantal differences of softness and hardness. Jan Hus witnessed the dying of the last vestiges of this distinction. He himself defended the language's original archaism, pathetically [42] declaring that 'those Prague citizens and other Czechs deserve to be scourged who speak half-Czech and half-German' by eliminating the distinction between *li–ly*, by using a neutral, *European*, *l* instead of a hard *l*, and *i* instead of *y*.[42] The indignation of Hus was in vain, as those Czechs who spoke *more Teutonicorum* gained the upper hand.[43] After the collapse of Proto-Slavic, Lusatian and Kashubian tried to assert a consonantal softness correlation.[44] But in the further course of the evolution of these languages, the softness correlation was dropped. Polabian, by contrast, a language embedded in the Germanic context, consistently enforced a consonant timbre distinction, giving it an important grammatical role. By the beginning of the eighteenth century, it had fourteen pairs of consonantal phonemes contrasted by softness and hardness (see Trubetzkoy 1923: 131, 161). It was not the softness correlation, but its bearer, Polabian itself, that was abolished. A language doomed to disappear often allows itself risky phonological experiments which are inaccessible to a language that is destined for wide expansion.

If we go beyond the limits of a single language or language family in interpreting the history of the phonological opposition between soft and hard consonants, we find that a language union is no less fluid in outline and internal structure than a state, for instance.

The alphabet of the earliest Turkic monuments, the Orkhon inscriptions carved on stones in the seventh and eighth centuries, was used by the Turks as early as the sixth century. This alphabet clearly displays pairs of soft and hard consonants: *g, k, d, t, s, p, l, n, b* are written using a series of letters for

---

[42] Soft *l* was replaced in Czech even earlier by the European *l*.
[43] The distinction of consonants by softness and hardness is so foreign to Czech linguistic thought that the founder of Czech historical grammar, Jan Gebauer, did not notice the influence of this difference on one of the fundamental phonetic changes of Archaic Czech, the so-called 'mutation'. A linguist with Russian linguistic experience, Alexey Shakhmatov (1898) was required to correct this lacuna.
[44] They also partially unified pairs of vowels with different timbre.

soft syllables, another series for hard syllables.[45] [43] Further, there is reason to suppose that Proto-Turkic or Proto-Altaic, itself the ancestor of a linguistic family conventionally called Altaic (cf. note 2), was characterized by syllabic synharmony.

Comparing indications from the historical phonology of languages that border the Altaic linguistic world, we find that, at different times, these languages passed through a stage of phonological attraction to the Altaic linguistic core. That is the case of the dialects of the Finno-Ugric branch, which adopted synharmonism, to a higher or lesser degree (Szinnyei 1922: 41–44). Proto-Slavic, having already separated itself from other members of the Indo-European family but not yet having been subjected to dialectal division (see Trubetzkoy 1922: 218 ff.), unified its syllables consistently. Step by step, the harmony of phonemes within a syllable was established: the language contrasted two standard types of syllables, soft and hard (Jakobson 1929: 20 et passim). The southern neighbours of the Altaic languages developed an independent consonantal softness correlation directly. The thorough pairing of soft and hard consonants in seventh century Chinese is attested (Karlgren 1915: ch. 2). This correlation temporarily penetrated into the Indo-Iranian group as well. Trubetzkoy demonstrates the presence of the soft and hard consonant pairs t and e, t and e aspirated, n and s at least in Old Indian.

Nowadays the zone of monotony is wider than the zone of phonological softness of consonants, and it is softness that is the most typical component of the Eurasian combination of phonological features. Initially, by contrast, the zone of softness correlation was wider, and the zone of monotony was narrower—and at that time monotony was the main component of Eurasian phonology. Later the zone of softness of consonants narrows, and the features and limits of the modern Eurasian language union gradually emerge. Middle Indian no longer has softness correlation; Chinese lost it at the turn of the past millennium; at the same time the timbre distinctions of consonants on the south-west margin [44] of the Slavic world disappear: first in Serbo-Croatian and Slovenian, then in west Bulgarian, Czech and Slovak (Jakobson 1929: 36–37, 51–57). We do not have data that would allow us to date the

---

[45] It is curious that western scholars consider exclusively in this pairing of consonantal letters the denotation of the timbre of adjacent vowels. The Danish linguist Vilhelm Thomsen thus writes that 'the specific sound of the consonant was in most cases absolutely the same' (Thomsen 1894: 17). Dark-soft and dark-hard vowels were denoted in the alphabet of the Orkhon inscriptions by several different letters. Only light-soft and light-hard vowels are denoted by single letters. Only two further letters are thus necessary to convey this difference in writing. It is thus impossible to assume that, instead of this simple device, a frightful number of complementary consonantal letters were introduced only to denote just two soft vowels. Russian linguists correctly inferred that the alphabet of the Orkhon inscriptions reflects in fact a syllabic synharmonism.

standardization of a unified neutral timbre of consonants in the western languages of the Finno-Ugric and Ottoman Turkic families. The narrowing of the zone of phonological consonantal softness is accompanied by another phenomenon, a sort of reaction against the former: both the western and the eastern outposts of the Eurasian linguistic world strengthened the role of the opposition of consonants by softness and hardness. In the course of the first centuries of the present millennium, they introduced an independent consonantal softness correlation instead of a syllabic softness correlation. The new boundaries of the phonological union were thereby reinforced.

Let us mention a few dates: in Mongolian dialects, the phonological events that spawned an independent timbral opposition of consonants date approximately to the thirteenth and fourteenth century (Vladimirtzov 1929: 184, 241; Poppe 1930: 109). The western sector of this phonological 'marker' of Eurasia was formed somewhat earlier. In Polish (Rozwadowski 1915: 340–341) and in eastern Bulgarian (see, e.g., Shchepkin 1906: 86 et passim), the independent softness correlation of consonants originated during the eleventh century. With regard to Russian, the epoch of great upheavals and reforms that ended with the establishment of a new correlation throughout the entire language corresponds to the twelfth to thirteenth century (Trubetzkoy 1924b: 294 et passim). According to Bubrikh's hypothesis, Mordvin had independent consonantal softness already in the eleventh century, and Karelian acquired and developed this correlation during the first half of the current millennium.

The Turkic dialects of western Eurasia, namely parts of the Kipchak-Polovtsian dialectal group, also underwent a similar phenomenon. In Radlov's (1887) opinion, Polovtsians continued to live in Crimea for a long time, and the Karaites, who emigrated from Crimea to the north-west, brought with them the Polovtsian dialect that they have preserved to this day. Through extensive comparisons, Kowalski has proven the thesis of a close kinship between Western Karaim and ancient Polovtsian (Kowalski 1929: L). Western Karaim is the only living branch of the Kipchak-Polovtsian group of Turkic languages. Kowalski dates the emigration of the Karaites from the northern coast of the Black Sea to the fourteenth century (Kowalski 1929: XVII). The resettlement in Poland of Armenians who spoke a Kipchak dialect that is very close to Karaim, in his opinion, dates to the same time. Monuments of this now extinct dialect, which were written in the sixteenth or seventeenth centuries using the Armenian [45] alphabet, have been preserved. Kowalski found striking similarities between Armenian-Kipchak and Karaim, indicating the genetic proximity of both dialects. By comparing the two dialects, he discovered an important fact: Armenian-Kipchak transformed its syllabic softness correlation using the same methods as the north-western Karaim dialect. Kowalski does not exclude the possibility that in the dialect of the north-western Karaites this transformation is due to Belarusian influence (Kowalski 1929: XLVII). Under this assumption, we would have to attribute the Armenian-Kipchak transformation of total syllabic harmony into a harmony of consonants to Slavic influence. That would mean that the two dialects would have experienced independently but contemporaneously a similar and complex process that has no parallel in any other Turkic dialect, even though many Turkic dialects were also exposed to Russian influence. The striking similarity of their inherited phonological inventory would correspond to a surprising similarity in their acquired inventory. Would it therefore not be simpler to attribute the consonantal softness correlation that characterizes both dialects also to their inherited inventory? True, the monument of the Polovtsian dialect of thirteenth and fourteenth centuries, the Codex Cumanicus, does not seem to contain indications of this phenomenon. But, for all their closeness, there are dialectal differences between Armenian-Kipchak and north-west Karaim, on the one hand, and the language of the Codex on the other hand. In any case, the question of the territorial identity of the Kipchak-Polovtsian dialects as they are reflected in the Codex remains open to this day (cf. Bang 1911). In the context of the phonological evolution that Slavic and Finnish languages of western Eurasia were going through in the beginning of this millennium, it is very probable that the dialects of the Kipchak-Polovtsian group had a tendency to transform syllabic synharmonism into a harmony of consonants.

Within the Slavic territory, the transformation of the softness correlation of syllables into a corresponding correlation of consonants spread from the south-west in the direction of the north-east. The dialects from which modern Great Russian is derived acquired the new correlation several decades later than the dialects that gave rise to Ukrainian. Southern dialects solved their cardinal phonological problems independently, through trial and error, without a ready-made model. Hence the struggle of contradictory phonological tendencies, hence the inevitable oscillations and complications. These internal phonological conflicts could not fail to leave an imprint on the sound system of Ukrainian. In the northern zone of the Russian linguistic world, by contrast, possible conflicts were pre-empted. Dialects of this zone assimilated [46] southern solutions to phonological problems even before their appearance. This ensured a seamless reconstruction of their phonology (Jakobson 1929: 63–67. 79).

In sum, the Great Russian softness correlation is a standard type. It is systematically used in the interest of the differentiation of word meanings, both lexically and grammatically. It is realized very broadly, before almost all vowels and at the end of the word. Labial consonants are included in this correlation, along with dentals. The Great Russian phonological softness of consonants achieves an exclusively complementary function. As a consequence, mediolingual consonants do not play the role of phonological softness here. In general, the oppositions of consonants by softness and hardness are clearly distinguished from differences by point of articulation. In addition, differences in the timbre of consonants are sharply separated from the timbre differences of vowels: phonologically, consonants are opposed by softness and hardness, vowels by lightness and darkness. The tendencies that characterize the Eurasian language union achieve their most mature form in the phonological shape of Great Russian. As such, it is no coincidence that the phonology of Great Russian forms the basis of literary Russian, i.e. the language with the most general Eurasian cultural mission.

8. Consonantal softness in European science and letters

Western grammars of Russian have always stumbled over the difficulty of conveying to Europeans the profoundly strange (to them) phonological opposition of hard and soft consonants. European phoneticians, and *in their footsteps*, Russian phoneticians have often confused different concepts: softness with platalization, palatalization with palatality (cf. above), phonetic and phonological softness. In essence, consonantal softness was first defined scientifically at the beginning of the present century in the works of the Russian linguist Alexander Tomson (1927). But even in 1927, this scholar remarks that there is still an insufficient understanding of the question in the European specialized literature (for example in the new edition of the first volume of the Comparative Slavic Grammar by Vondrák 1924). This led Tomson (1927) to provide a German summary of his conclusions on this set of problems.

When the speakers of languages that do not possess a phonological softness of consonants try to describe languages that possess that category, [47] they very often deform the material, introducing alien linguistic experiences into it. Thus the German Caucasianist Adolf Dirr (1928) does not notice the soft consonants in Abkhazian, and only Russian researchers (Marr 1926; Yakovlev

1928) avoid this omission. Russian and native researchers (see Bubrikh 1927) have uncovered and corrected significant phonological shortcomings in the interpretation of the eastern Finnish languages by Finnish scholars. Characteristically, in many cases Russian linguistic literature initially adopted and repeated the kind of mistakes made by Western scholars. Thus, for example, the traditional doctrine of European Turkology about 'vowel harmony' was adopted in Russian scholarship, despite the fact that, as we saw, it is inapplicable to a number of Turkic languages in Eurasia: in these languages, vowel harmony is only a component of a more complex phonological phenomenon, namely syllabic vowel harmony. In this case, it is mainly the work of indigenous Turkic scholars that has led to radical revisions of the foundations of Turkic phonology. The Tatar linguist Sharaf, who in the above-mentioned study analyses Tatar consonantal pairings by softness and hardness extensively, refers to the observations of Akhmerov, Alparov and Validov on Tatar and to the works of the prominent Kazakh writer and linguist Akhmed Baytursunov on Kazhak-Kirgiz. Polivanov's excursus in 'On the Designation of Japanese Palatalized Consonants in Russian Practical Transcription' is also very interesting in this regard (1928: 169ff.). The pairing of consonants by softness and hardness in Japanese is very similar to the corresponding Russian correlations. But Edwards (1903) has overlooked the presence of this correlation in Japanese and treats the Japanese soft consonant as a combination of the consonants *s* and *j*. The European transcription of Japanese words is also designed according to this false interpretation. Curiously enough, Russian practical transcriptions used to be a blind imitation of European transcriptions: *pya* [*rua*] was transcribed by Russians as *pua* or *pia* [*ria*],—while the simplest and most accurate way to reproduce that Japanese syllable would be the Russian *ря* [*rja*].[46] Polivanov's transcription, which is nowadays accepted by Russian Japanologists, is based precisely on this last principle. The circular route to Japanese through Europe was thus replaced by a more direct route from Russia. We see a similar process in relation to the languages of national minorities in Eurasia.

Polivanov's transcription of Japanese speech is instructive from another point of view. It once again illustrates the high [48] suitability of the Russian Cyrillic alphabet, as compared to the Latin alphabet, for the transcription of a language that possesses an independent opposition of consonants by softness and hardness. It is not without reason that, next to many Russian tribes, this alphabet was adopted by eastern Finnish tribes, Moldavians and Russian

---

[46] Following the European transcription, we continue to write *Kioto* instead of *Kjoto*, etc.

Gypsies.[47] The efforts by Nikolay Yakovlev to deduce a formula for constructing the most economical alphabet in number of letters is very interesting in this regard (Yakovlev 1928). The author establishes that, with regard to the transmission of the difference of consonants by softness and hardness, the Russian alphabet perfectly matches the formula, i.e. it achieves maximum economy by denoting soft consonants by adding letters for the subsequent vowel phonemes (*я, ё, ю, и* [*ja, ë, ju, i*]) and by using the additional symbol'. Yakovlev goes on to demonstrate that this system of writing is the most convenient and advantageous also when applied to the similar phonology of the eastern Finnish languages. He suggests that the principles of this writing also be used for the languages of the High Caucasus that have one or two consonantal timbre correlations

An analysis of the attempts to Latinize the Belarusian script can serve here as a clear illustration of the uneconomical nature of the Latin alphabet for a language with an independent soft consonant. For example, if we rewrite in Cyrillic the first pages of a Belarusian book printed in the Latin alphabet—*Włast, Karotkaja istoryja Biełarusi* (Vilnius 1910)—and compare both versions, it appears that just the loss of the Russian system of 'additional' vowels increased the Latinized text, compared to *Cyrillic*, by about 7.5%. In other words, for every hundred pages of text, those Belarusians who took fancy to the Latin alphabet added seven and a half pages of wasted paper, typesetting and printing ink—a useless waste to please Westerners. No matter how one transcribes the spelling, there is still a surplus expense inherent in the transition from Russian or, for example, East Finnish languages to the Latin alphabet. Not only that, but the Latin transmission of softness of consonants is defective because of a lack of unity of principle that has a particularly harmful effect on the teaching of grammar. In Russian script, the phonological softness of consonants is symbolized by the letters *зь, зя, зё, зю, зи* [*z', zja, zë, zju, zi*], whereas in the Latinized Belorussian text four completely different devices are used [49] to denote softness: 1. Soft and hard *l* are rendered by two different letters: 1 = soft *l*, *ł* = hard *l*. 2. The softness of other consonants that are in a position not before a vowel are denoted by a special superscript sign, e.g. *kniaz', Rus', dzien'*. 3. The difference of all consonants, except *l*, by hardness and softness before the phoneme *i* is conveyed by two different letters for the phoneme *i*: *y* after hard consonants, *i* after soft ones (this corresponds to the Russian denotation). Examples: *kniazi, dni*. 4. The softness of these same

---

[47] The verse anthology of the Karaite poet O. A. Kobeckogo 'Irlar' (Kiev 1904), the only secular book in western Karaim, is printed in the Russian alphabet.

consonants in front of all other vowels is represented through the insertion of the letter *i* between the consonant and the vowel: *kniazia, kniaziu, kniaziom*. Such diversity is quite irrational and can be eliminated to a greater or lesser extent if one generalizes the transcription of consonant softness by means of superscript signs, but in this case one would need many typographic combinations of consonantal letters with superscript signs, and lines would literally crawl with awkward prefixes that are moreover hard to write. Attempts to adjust the Latin alphabet to the phonology of the Eurasian languages have either repeated the history of Trishka's caftan[48] or must alter that alphabet so radically that it is left only with bits and pieces, emptying the slogan of Latinization of its meaning.

9. The Tasks Facing Eurasian Linguistics

All these considerations constitute only an *outline*, a preliminary work plan. The next tasks are now to investigate in detail and then to map the phonological use of consonantal timbre distinctions in the languages of Eurasia and neighbouring areas. The following issues need to be considered:

1. In a given language, does timbre correlation appear as an opposition between consonants with reduced (dark) or normal (light) noise, or as an opposition between normal consonants (hard) and consonants with increased natural noise (soft or 'emphatically soft'), or, finally, does the language combine both correlations and contrasts dark-hard with light-hard and light-soft? [50]
2. Are the consonants of a same timbre opposed to a consonant of another timbre independently or in combination with an opposition of two categories of adjacent vowels, so that the carriers of the correlation are not actually distinct phonemes, but rather syllables?
3. In a given language, how many consonantal phonemes are mutually opposed to each other by timbre, i.e. are paired consonantal phonemes, and how many are single consonant phonemes, i.e. are not involved in timbral correlations.
4. How significant is the articulatory and thus acoustic difference between consonants of a given timbre and correlative consonants of another

---

[48] Referencing the long usage of the Latin alphabet for certain languages of this kind does not prove anything: are there no bad historical examples that should not be repeated? The possibility of using the one or other alphabet for a given language must be analysed from the point of view of its internal expediency.

timbre in a given language?[49] If consonants in a given language are paired by softness and hardness, which consonants are the soft correlates of the anterolingual and apical consonants—the mediolingual or the palatalized anterolingual and palatalized apical?

5. How large is the inventory of timbre correlation in a given language, i.e. in how many and in what categories of phoneme combinations can consonants be contrasted by timbre? Thus, for example, in Great Russian the timbre of consonants is externally conditioned (i.e. the softness correlation is not realized) before the following phonemes of the same word: before *e*, before an unstressed *a* if it does not belong to the ending, and in most combinations with consonants.

6. How often does each of the phonemes correlated by timbre actually appear in speech, and how significant is the functional burden of timbre correlation in a given language, i.e. to what extent is timbre correlation used to distinguish: 1. lexical meanings (example: *byt–bit*) and 2. grammatical meanings (example: *bit–to beat*)?

7. To what extent a given language uses the contrasting of consonant timbre for grammatical declensions (alternations): Examples: *nes-u, nes'-ot, nes'om, nes-om.*

The answers to these questions will allow us to determine the extent to which we are able to apply the one or the other correlation of timbre in different languages and dialects to explain the main feature or features of that correlation in Eurasian languages. We are convinced that mapping these data will again reveal the symmetry [51] of the zonal principle of the distribution of phonological properties. Further it will be necessary to proceed, in the comparative study of the Eurasian languages, from an accounting of correlations to other problems of phonological structure, such as the determination of the comparative prevalence of different types of systems of vowels both within and beyond Eurasia. It is very likely that a comparison of the Eurasian and neighbouring geographical worlds in light of these problems, and then of morphological and syntactic problems, will enrich with new features and clarify the concept of the Eurasian language union.[50] All this, [52]

---

[49] From this perspective, the comparison of the palatograms of Tatar and Russian soft and hard consonants realized by Sharaf (1927) is very interesting. We find further useful palatograms for comparison in the works of Bogoroditzkij (Great Russian; 1909), Sinyavsky (Ukrainian; 1929), Benni (Polish; 1917) and Mladenov (Bulgarian; 1915).

[50] Already at the time this article was being printed, we became aware of the important conclusions arrived at by Nikolay S. Trubetzkoy in the study of the geographical distribution of declension. 'In general, declension is a relatively rare phenomenon, and unknown to most languages on the globe. The geographic area of declension is fairly limited. It covers all of Eurasia, and extends somewhat beyond

of course, will require the close cooperation of specialists in various disciplines (Slavic studies, Turkology, Finno-Ugric linguistics, Caucasian studies, etc.). This work can only be accomplished satisfyingly through a knowledge of the huge mass of materials on Eurasian languages that has been collected in recent years but of which, unfortunately, only a relatively small proportion has been made public so far.[51]

its limits. In the east, it includes the language of the Eskimo and apparently some North Canadian Indian languages, in the west it includes almost all Slavic (except Bulgarian), Baltic, Finnish, Lappish and Hungarian languages; further, in a very weakened form, declension is present in German and Dutch, but further, in Romance languages as well as in English and Danish it is already absent. In Africa and Asia, there is no declension. The boundary is between Ottoman and Arabic, Armenian and Kurdish, Azeri and Persian, Karakirghiz (and also Uzbek) and Iranian, and further between Mongolian and Tibeto-Chinese. Declensions are most strongly developed in the Ugro-Finnic languages (e.g., Hungarian has 21 cases) and in the eastern Caucasian languages (up to 30 or more cases). In second place come Samoyedic and Altaic languages (Turkish, Mongolian, and Tungus-Manchurian), and in third place are Slavic languages together with Lithuanian and Latvian. Of the Slavic languages, the most strongly developed declension is Great Russian (cf. such case differences as *stakan čaju–vkus čaja, govorju o lese–živu v les*u), which thus reaches the level of the Turkic languages in this respect; in Bulgarian, declension of nouns has disappeared altogether, in pronouns it is preserved to a small extent (as is the case in other languages of the Balkan union); in Serbian declension is corrupted (in the singular, the difference between dative and prepositional is abolished, in the plural between dative and instrumental); in the other Slavic languages (Polish, Czech, Slovak, Lusatian, Slovak, Ukrainian, and Belarussian), declension is more developed than in Serbian, but less than in Russian". The comparison of the phonological phenomena considered above with the morphological observations of N. S. Trubetzkoy allows us to formulate the following statements: 1) there are, on the main continent of the Old World, specifically central and specifically peripheral phenomena; 2) all Eurasian languages are characterized by central phenomena (consonantal timbre differences, monotony, declension); 3) central phenomena are unknown to all non-Eurasian languages, except for intermediate languages directly neighbouring Eurasia; 4) peripheral phenomena characterize particularly the Romano-German zone of Europe and the whole south and south-east of Asia.

[51] The diverse materials collected recently on the Finnish, Turkic, Mongolian, and Caucasian languages of Eurasia are still waiting to be published. But from that which has been published, much is absent from European libraries. Even this fragmentary study could not have been written had it not been for the rich collection of Russian books and journals available in the Slavonic Library of the Foreign Ministry of the Czechoslovakian Republic and for the amicable collaboration of its director, Vladimir Tukalevsky. I wish thereby to express my profound gratitude to him and to all those who helped me through their advice, remarks, and bibliographical corrections.

7
Louis Hjelmslev on the correlational structure of language
The place within the system

Lorenzo Cigana

7.1 Introduction

It is safe to say that *General structure of linguistic correlations* is a cornerstone of the linguistic and epistemological thinking of Louis Hjelmslev (1899–1965) and is among the most important contributions to markedness theory of the 1930s. Despite having been conceived before glossematics—the general theory of language elaborated in 1935 by Hjelmslev, together with Hans Jørgen Uldall (1907–57)—the text was subjected to continuous retouchings: a life-long process testifies to Hjelmslev's striving for a definitive formulation of the principles laid out in the text, as well as to their importance for glossematics itself. Hjelmslev's paper is a clear example of both the formalist stance of glossematics and the combinatorial approach that came to define structuralism as such.

In what follows, we first address, in section 7.2, the issue of the uneven philological status of this text, a result of its tortuous editorial history. Our account of this background is of more than mere anecdotal interest, since it allows us to frame Hjelmslev's paper within the broader historical context of its conception. In section 7.3, we discuss the theoretical tenets of the paper. Seven basic tenets are identified that need to be kept in mind in order to fully appreciate the reach of Hjelmslev's proposal: going beyond a mere description of markedness phenomena, his goal was to identify the laws that govern the structure of any linguistic system, leveraging their logical form in order to establish a procedure for the immanent analysis of such systems. In section 7.4, we outline the main points of Hjelmslev's argument. Conclusions are drawn in section 7.5.

7.2 A troubled history

The paper presented here is not Hjelmslev's original contribution of 1933 but a cumulative result of many additions and reformulations carried out on a core text, 'Bidrag til læren om grammatiske systemers almindelige bygning', a lecture on the structure of grammatical systems given at the Copenhagen Linguistic Circle on 27 April 1933 (cf. Gregersen 1991, I: 220ff; Gregersen 1991, II: 86ff; Cigana 2018).

The central aim of the lecture was to identify the laws by which a linguistic system constitutes itself as such. This is a topic that Hjelmslev had already adumbrated in his first work, *Principes de grammaire générale*. In this book, he formulated a set of basic assumptions, which together formed a working hypothesis on the nature of linguistic systems. At base was the distinction between 'semantemes' (essentially: roots) and (inflectional) morphemes (1), which were both 'grammatemes' to be described synchronically and panchronically in terms of functions (2), as they group into categories (3), which are always provided with meaning (4) and governed by a form of rationality ('prelogic') that does not coincide with classical normative logic (5). Many of these assumptions were further elaborated in other lectures on related topics given in the same period: the structure of grammar and the relationship between grammar and logic on 24 June 1933; the relevance of linguistics for the theory of thought, discussed at the *Selskab for Filosofi og Psykologi* on 16 February 1933 (cf. Gregersen 1991, I: 220); the internal structure of the category of case on 18 May 1933 ('Foreløbige Undersøgelser vedrørende kasus (i tilslutning til meddelelsen på sidste møde)');[1] and, finally, the morphological theory of Sergei Karcevsky (1884–1955) on 26 May 1933.

The stance adopted in the *Bidrag* continued a line of research begun in 1928, as stated by the author himself in the 'Note to the reader': while the *Principes de grammaire générale* closes by stating the need for further criteria for distinguishing between categories of semantemes and categories of morphemes, the 1933 lecture focuses on the latter and their internal structure, trying to establish the laws governing the 'possible number and mutual relationships of morphemes within one and the same paradigm' (cf. § 1).

Hjelmslev prepared a manuscript out of the *Bidrag* lecture, which was intended to be published in the very first issue of the *Bulletins du Cercle Linguistique de Copenhagen*, a publication modelled on the proceedings of the

---

[1] Most likely a discussion on the state of art of his research on case, published later under the title *La catégorie des cas* (1935–1937).

Société de linguistique de Paris. Hjelmslev's goal was clearly, on the one hand, to turn his lecture into a manifesto for the newly born Copenhagen Linguistic Circle (established in 1931) and, on the other, to distinguish the Copenhagen Circle's position in structural grammar both from that of the Prague Circle and that of Viggo Brøndal (1887-1942), cofounder of the Copenhagen Circle and the most Praguian-oriented among his members (cf. Basbøll forthcoming: 7-8, § 16.2.3; cf. Gregersen and Jensen forthcoming, § 5.2).

Moreover, two important dates were approaching as Hjelmslev prepared the manuscript: the Third International Congress of Linguists (Rome, 19-26 September 1933), and the Second Conference of Phonetics (London, 22-26 July 1935). Both were perfect events at which to present Hjelmslev's programme, and he did indeed intend to showcase his theory in Rome;[2] hence, arguably, the sense of urgency—and of incompleteness—which permeates the contribution.

All his efforts came to nothing, however, as the submission was rejected by the editorial board:

> An enriched manuscript of such communication, in French, was submitted to the Bulletins, yet it was rejected by a majority decision of the editorial board during the meeting of June 24, 1933, without further circulation of the manuscript and at the proposal of only one member, who was absent at the plenary meeting of April 27.
> ('Introduction', photocopy deposited in the archives of the Linguistic Circle, cf. Gregersen 1991, II: 89)

The scarcely veiled reference is to Viggo Brøndal, whose decision was, however, supported by two further members of the Copenhagen Linguistic Circle: Louis Leonor Hammerich (1892-1975) and Kaj Barr (1896-1970). While Brøndal's rejection was, so to speak, categorical, Barr and Hammerich explained their decisions, declaring Hjelmslev's proposal too hurried.[3] Hjelmslev took Brøndal's rejection as an attempt to hamper both his theory and position within the Circle:

> This much has been clear to me since 1931 and I originally established the Linguistic Circle in the hope that we could be a collective with a grammatical

---

[2] Letter to Karcevsky of 19 November 1931, cf. Gregersen and Jensen (forthcoming: § 5.2.).
[3] In their eyes, the contribution was 'a dazzling improvisation. It works like a shock, and that is why it is dangerous. One may hope that it will be very significantly modified, mostly for Hjelmslev's own sake. A piece of technical excellence and clarity, it is knowledgeable and learned. Yet also resentful and fierce, daring, earth-shaking, not enough thought-through, unfinished, inconclusive' (Linguistic Circle's archive, LK adm 18:1, cf. Gregersen 1991, II: 90).

theory, a hope which was laid waste by Brøndal. I now have new hope for phonematics.

(Hjelmslev's archive, folder 31, cf. Gregersen and Jensen 2022)

Hjelmslev bowed out of attending the Third International Congress of Linguists in Rome, leaving Brøndal free rein. Through this dispute, a lasting feud was born,[4] which remained unresolved until Brøndal's death in 1942 and which made any collaborative projects in the domain of general grammar impossible. The story of the feud with Brøndal has been told many times (Zilberberg 1985; Rasmussen 1987; Larsen 1988; Gregersen 1991, II: 86 ff.; Gregersen and Jensen 2022Larsen and Nault 1993; Fischer-Jørgensen 1997: 33 ff.; Ablali 2017: 72 ff.; Gregersen and Jensen 2022): we discuss it here only insofar as it represents the basis of the unfortunate editorial history of Hjelmslev's paper. The main reason behind the feud was most likely competition between Hjelmslev and Brøndal, both academic and conceptual.

Despite Brøndal's rejection, Hjelmslev carried on working on his hypothesis, sustained by a new member of the Circle who, on many levels, made all the difference: Hans Jørgen Uldall (1907–57). Shortly after their first meeting, the two linguists began elaborating Hjelmslev's model into a general description of languages based on purely distributional criteria and according to the principle of linguistic isomorphism. While Uldall focused more on expression, Hjelmslev, who was trained as a field phonetician and anthropologist, worked mostly on grammar and cross-linguistic comparison, trying to spread his ideas on linguistic correlations further in other venues, such as (1) the cycle of twelve lectures given at the University of Aarhus (Hjelmslev 1972 [1934]), in which such issues are dealt with in great detail; (2) his book on case (Hjelmslev 1935–1937); (3) the paper 'La structure des oppositions dans la langue', presented in 1937 at the Eleventh International Congress of Psychology (Paris, 25–31 July 1937) and published in the *Proceedings* (Hjelmslev 1937); (4) 'Note sur les oppositions supprimables', a contribution in homage to Trubetzkoy, in which Hjelmslev tries—not without difficulty—to bridge the gap between his own views on markedness and those of the Prague Circle; (5) the lecture to the Copenhagen Linguistic Circle of 17 April 1941 on the internal structure of the

---

[4] Earlier divergences have been highlighted by Rasmussen (1987), concerning the evaluation of Otto Jespersen's stance, the controversial interpretation of the runic inscription 'mauna' on a comb found in Setre (Norway), dated to the seventh century AD, and the edition of *Acta Linguistica. Revue internationale de linguistique structurale*, founded through the joint efforts of Hjelmslev and Brøndal in 1939, at a time when their clash had already been consolidated. Other instances of confrontation could also be mentioned. Although hardly more than anecdotal in themselves, these divergences serve to show how the relationship between the two linguists was never uncomplicated.

category of comparison (cf. Hjelmslev 1946), which would also be included in the reworked version of the 1933 paper (cf. here § 4). Last but not least, (6) a lecture given at the Circle on 2 June 1949, with the very same title as the paper itself, *Structure générale des corrélations linguistiques*[5]—another clear sign of Hjelmslev's commitment to have his own research shared and acknowledged. However, despite these coordinated efforts, the cornerstone of his approach remained buried in Hjelmslev's drawer.

In 1942, on Brøndal's death, Hjelmslev suddenly had free rein in many departments (not least in the editorial board of *Acta*, cf. Rasmussen 1987: 46 ff.) and planned to pick up the text again:

> On November 12, 1942, at the decision of the extraordinary general assembly, a change took place in the composition of the Bureau and the Bureau immediately agreed for the publication of the manuscript in the actual *Mélanges*, along with the additions deemed necessary by its author.
> ('Introduction', photocopy deposited in the archives of the Linguistic Circle, cf. Gregersen 1991b: 89)

Hjelmslev reworked many points of his original manuscript, revamping it in light of theoretical advances made in the 1940s, notably the notions of 'commutation' and 'connotation' (see below, § 85; cf. Cigana 2023) and a neater formal classification of morphological categories (*Mot et morpheme*, unpublished), and adding updated cross-references. However, he never got as far as publication in 1942, nor, indeed, later on. Reasons for this include (1) non-content related factors, such as those apologetically referenced by Hjelmslev in a letter to Uldall of 1949;[6] (2) lack of time, since, from the 1940s onwards, Hjelmslev was occupied with securing the epistemological foundations of his new theory, glossematics, by returning to and updating another idea— that of 'participation' (cf. Cigana 2014, 2022a)—which was included in the latest version of the glossematics, the *Résumé of a Theory of Language*

---

[5] Cf. *Bulletins du Cercle Linguistique de Copenhague* 1941–1964 (8–31): 257 (B49).
[6] On 1 August 1949, Uldall wrote to Hjelmslev from Tucuman: 'What has happened about your afhandling about the participative system? If it hasn't been printed yet, couldn't you send me a carbon copy? I need it badly' (Hjelmslev's archive, folder 34: 34_Uldall_440). To which Hjelmslev replied: 'My "thesis on the participative system" is nearly identical to the one titled "Structure générale des corrélations linguistiques". The manuscript has been lost, along with many others, presumably at the publishers—for which reason we currently have a sad case pending; I think that it will lead to our leaving Munksgaard. Unfortunately, I do not own a carbon copy, only an incomplete draft, almost inaccessible to others. This whole story of the lost manuscript has got on my nerves; it is for the same reason that the *Bulletin* has not come out yet. Otherwise, there is nothing particularly new: everything remains essentially unchanged' (Letter dated 15 August 1934, in Hjelmslev's archive, folder 34: 34_Uldall_450; translation is ours).

(cf. Fischer-Jørgensen in Uldall 1967 [1957]: xxi, n. 3); (3) a shift of focus, as the original emphasis on general grammar moved progressively into the background, making space for the elaboration of a broader, fully-fledged semiotic model. Different steps may be identified within this process, from the emphasis on grammar, to the study of expression (phonematics/cenematics with Uldall), to a combined model—a first glossematic linguistic theory, to a more complete and general semiotic version. Accordingly, the original partial model of grammatical correlations had to be revised, its reach and role within the picture reframed with every step. Finally, (4) perfectionism, which is possibly the main reason in Hjelmslev's case. In fact, he kept reworking his ideas (and his terminology, cf. Basbøll forthcoming: § 16.1.2) throughout: hence his reluctance to publish a definitive version of his theory on linguistic correlations and hence the pervasive presence of this topic in his writings. The result is that the paper, which could have discussed an up-to-date version of this part of the theory, appeared only posthumously, portraying the theory as it was back in 1935, while the most advanced version was incorporated in the *Résumé of a Theory of Language* (1975)—an unfortunate outcome reverberates in the theory's later reception. Algirdas J. Greimas (1917–1992), one of the most important French semioticians and disseminator of Hjelmslev's thought in France, refers to Brøndal on a topic—the so-called 'square of oppositions'[7]—he would have possibly credited to Hjelmslev if he had only known about Hjelmslev's contribution. It is surely not by chance that the same contribution went largely unquoted in many attempts to address the origins of the theory of markedness (Battistella 1996; Greenberg 2005 [1966]), having been re-evaluated only in relatively recent times (Zilberberg 1985; Andersen 1989, 2001; Vykypěl 2006; Skafte Jensen 2012).

There might, however, be another important reason for this: Hjelmslev's contribution is not a theory of markedness, or, at least, it is not limited to this. Its domain is significantly wider.

7.3 Tenets of a theory on the formation of linguistics systems

Hjelmslev's (1973 [1933]) paper has usually been considered within the history of markedness theory (see references quoted in the previous section). Quite rightly so, as the paper indeed discusses a way to describe markedness-phenomena such as syncretism and neutralizations found in particular languages (A) on the basis of a general principle (A'). His principle, maintained in partial reaction to Ferdinand de Saussure's (1857–1913) assertion of the purely

---

[7] Cf. Greimas (1976: 21) and Svend E. Larsen (1986: 63). It is worth mentioning that Greimas also quotes Robert Blanché's logical hexagon as a complementary source (ibid.).

negative structure of language based on oppositions,[8] was initially drawn from Lucien Levy-Bruhl's (1857–1939) insight on 'prelogical mentality' (cf. Lévy-Bruhl 1910, 1922, 1927) encompassing any human symbolic institution, such as rites, totemic beliefs, language, etc. Later on, the principle was termed the 'law of participation' (Hjelmslev 1935: 102) and formalized on a purely linguistic basis, freeing it from its socio-cognitive constraints and ideological biases (civilized vs. primitive). But since (A') is only attainable on a theoretical level, this issue is actually approached from a slightly different point of view, concerning how general grammatical categories constitute themselves within the structure of language (B).

It would be tempting to explain the shift from (A) to (A') and (B) in terms of a generalization: language-specific markedness phenomena (A) are described through a common principle (A') which, in turn, is said to hold true for language in general (B). However, once we have reached the core of Hjelmslev's argumentation (§ 46 ff.), we realize that what is put forward here is not just a theory of markedness,[9] nor a theory of the functioning of language, whose oppositional mechanism is indeed held to apply at all levels (morphosyntax, semantics, phonology),[10] rather it is (C) a metatheoretical framework for the identification of the overarching principle of analysis for structural linguistics. This principle is found in the so-called 'analysis by dimensions' (§ 48, later called 'free articulation', cf. Hjelmslev 1975; Cigana 2022: 262 ff.; Vykypěl 2006).

Issue (A) is then approached through (C), which is the reason why Hjelmslev can claim that 'our work has no forerunners' (§ 14) and why the different theories on linguistic oppositions developed from 1930 onwards can hardly be brought into alignment.[11] This difficulty arises not because of the phenomenon itself, however 'Protean' (cf. Greenberg 2005 [1966]: 11) it may be, but because of the quite different epistemological presuppositions those models build upon, *constituting* the corresponding phenomenon in quite different ways.

In Hjelmslev's view, at least seven interdependent assumptions can be identified:

---

[8] Cf. Karcevsky (2000 [1927]: 21): 'It has become a commonplace to affirm that linguistic values only exist by virtue of their opposition to each other. In this form, such an idea leads to an absurdity: a tree would be a tree only because it is neither house, nor horse, nor river. ... Pure and simple opposition necessarily leads to chaos and cannot serve as a basis for a *system* ...' (translation ours).
[9] This under the proviso that the label 'markedness' only gained currency later on. When Hjelmslev speaks of the 'mark', it is to object to both the term and the model behind it. The result is a theory of markedness without the mark.
[10] A claim foreshadowed by the changing of the title, from general structure of grammatical systems to general structure of linguistic correlations.
[11] The constellation of models changes according to the point of view. When it comes to markedness (1), the competing theories include at least Jakobson and Trubetzkoy's vs. Hjelmslev's vs. Greenberg's models (cf. Sørensen 1949; Andersen 1989). When it comes to the combinatory possibilities for linguistic systems (2), the theories to be contrasted are mostly Hjelmslev's and Brøndal's (Greimas').

1. Hierarchy: the analysis is conceived as a progressive division aiming to establish closed inventories of minimal elements. On the plane of content, grammatemes are divided into semantemes (roughly: stems) and morphemes, which can be expressed by so-called 'formants' (cf. § 58). In turn, morphemes belonging to different categories are treated as semi-minimal units ('taxemes') and further reduced to glossemes, the formal equivalent of distinctive features (cf. 4). This procedure relies on the idea that open, productive sets can be described in terms of combinations of closed classes of virtual elements. This insight was further expanded in accordance with the hypothesis of isomorphism, developed in 1934, according to which the content-side (signified) and the expression-side (signifier) of a language constitute two parallel hierarchies to be analysed through the same method, albeit yielding different results. The strong deductive stance entailed by this conception was first adopted in 1937 (cf. Fischer-Jørgensen in Uldall 1967 [1957]: v); the far-reaching consequences of its adoption have been insightfully examined by Andersen (1989: 28 f., 43, 2001: 22 f.).
2. Form: elements are established through positional criteria, that is, in terms of functions and can be manifested by a wider range of different realizations in the actual usages (contextual variants). In the case of Hjelmslev, the Saussure-inspired notion of the 'place within the system' is taken up quite literally: each unit is distributed in a corresponding category in relation to its likelihood of occurring in a given position within the chain, and further identified by the oppositions (correlations) it enters into with all other units of the same category.[12]
3. Immanence: substance is only taken into account as an epiphenomenon, in as much as it is said to 'manifest' the form. A model that does not share an immanent stance is less likely to draw a clear line between the formal elements and their manifestations, often endorsing a statistical treatment of units (thus an inductive stance) or pushing the reduction out of the formal domain; for instance, analysing phonemes into phonetically distinctive features. Conversely, it may be claimed that Hjelmslev's principle of analysis into correlative classes was developed in order to maintain the description on a formal (ideal), purely qualitative level.[13]

---

[12] This represents a major difference from other approaches. Jakobson's criticism of Hjelmslev's treatment of *Wortgefüge* (cf. Jakobson 1936: 27–29), for instance, reflects such difference.

[13] The issue concerning the structuralist attitude towards statistics has yet to be properly addressed. A generic assessment such as the one by Haspelmath (in Greenberg 2005 [1966]: ix) is unsatisfactory,

4. Reduction: the method of plotting units within dimensions was formulated here from a theoretical point of view and applied in Hjelmslev (1935–1937). This method, however, is neither purely taxonomic nor merely synthetic: its function is to provide the means to reduce the system of semi-minimal elements (taxemes) in terms of possible combinations of minimal elements (or 'glossemes': α, A, β, B, γ, Γ and later Γ$_2$). These are said to be 'parts of dimensions' functioning like the formal counterparts of the distinctive features.[14] While originally entailing both formal and substantial considerations (cf. 1935, where the method relies on the so-called 'semantic zone' for the mapping of grammatical correlations), it was revamped on a purely formal basis later on (cf. Hjelmslev 1970 [1957]: 106–107).

5. Uniformity: the reduction to glossemes serves as the basis for uniform cross-linguistic comparison (cf. Cigana and Polis forthcoming). The same inflectional category of fundamental morphemes may be manifested in different ways across languages (e.g. case in Polish and Hungarian) and even within one and the same language (e.g. English case in nouns vs. pronouns); moreover, a single case may cover quite different functions across languages, or not occur at all (e.g. ablative in Latin and Finnish vs. Polish). Concrete instantiations cannot be taken as a solid ground for comparison, nor can semantic patterns or phonetic features.[15] On the contrary, formal configuration is claimed to provide a viable basis for comparison, as form is general: categories and elements realized in different languages can be compared via their articulation, i.e. the parameters needed to describe them (descriptive universals): internal organization, position or 'value' covered by the given member within the category. As further explained in Hjelmslev (1935), the same category may instantiate different inventories of elements (cases), but those inventories always lead back to a uniform framework, entailing the same dimensions (1, 2, or 3) and different combinations of the same values (α, A, β, B, γ, Γ, cf. Hjelmslev 1935, and Γ$_2$ later on, cf. Hjelmslev 1975), which reflect markedness-patterns. Individual cases may then be compared on the basis of their combinatory value.

since it leaves unexplained interesting cases in which a bridge between the structural and the statistical views was indeed attempted (Spang-Hanssen 1959).

[14] 'These end-points we call *glossemes*, and if we assume that one taxeme of expression is usually manifested by one phoneme, then a glosseme of expression will usually be manifested by a part of a phoneme' (Hjelmslev 1961: 100).

[15] This insight seems to foreshadow a criticism of the semantic maps method (see Cigana and Polis forthcoming).

6. Organicity: a strong emphasis is put on the need for accounting for the internal cohesion of the system. In Hjelmslev's eyes, this is achievable through describing each element simultaneously in terms of all relevant parameters (dimensions).
7. Graduality: an innovation which Haspelmath mistakenly attributes to Greenberg;[16] in Hjelmslev's model, binarism is rejected in both its qualitative ('only two features') and quantitative version (also called dualism: 'only two members for each opposition') as an unacceptable a priori restriction, while actually being just one among multiple possibilities. In this respect, Hjelmslev's model resembles Brøndal's more than Jakobson and Trubetzkoy's theory, as it puts forward up to six (or seven) possible mark-values for any given dimension, ranging from a maximally marked or, in Hjelmslev's terminology, *intensive* (α) term, through moderately marked/unmarked values (β/B, γ/Γ) to a maximally unmarked, 'vague' or *extensive* term (A)[17] (see the translation, 3. §§ 14-43).

The product of this framework, the theory of linguistic correlations discussed as early as 1933, was taken up in greater detail in 1934 (cf. Hjelmslev 1972 [1934]), implemented in the domain of grammatical case in 1935-1937, reframed in an early formulation of glossematics dated 1936 (called 'cenematics', cf. 'Synopsis of an Outline'), concisely presented in 1937 at the *Onzième Congrès International de Psychologie* (Paris, 25-31 July 1937, cf. Hjelmslev 1937) and compared with the Prague model in a tribute to Nikolai Trubetzkoy (cf. Hjelmslev 1970 [1939a]). It was only briefly mentioned in Hjelmslev's *Omkring Sprogteoriens Grundlæggelse* (1943), yet meaningfully presented as a universal procedure also applying to expression, as he himself endeavoured to prove in a number of complementary works on the phonemic pattern of Danish (Hjelmslev 1973 [1951]) and of French (Hjelmslev 1970 [1948]). Finally, it appeared posthumously in 1973, although not in a definitive form, as can be seen from the many calls for more material to be added and the abundance of warnings about the provisional nature of the research.

---

[16] 'Another important innovation of Greenberg's is the scalar conception of markedness. This means that markedness it not just a binary opposition 'unmarked vs. marked', but that we rather have a scale from maximally unmarked through moderately marked to maximally marked, and when comparing two categories, we can (or rather, have to) say that one is less marked and the other is more marked' (Haspelmath in Greenberg 2005 [1966]: xv).

[17] These stances need to be accounted for simultaneously in order to avoid rushed comparisons, both interdisciplinary and cross-disciplinary. For instance, Brøndal's and Hjelmslev's models cannot be compared by the sole fact that each includes six elements, since the definition of such elements is quite different. The same holds true in the comparison between such models and Blanché's oppositional geometry or the prototype-theory.

In what follows, we will address the main aspects of Hjelmslev's theory by reconstructing his argumentation.

7.4 The structure of the paper

The paper is organized into three main sections, the formulation of the problem (A), the method of investigation (B), and the application (C). The first section, the densest and longest, is further divided into three subsections, concerning the general formulation (A1, § 6 ff.), its relevance for actual linguistics (A2, § 13 ff.), and the examination of three concurrent models (A3, § 14 ff.): those of Peshkovsky (3a), Karcevsky (3b), and Jakobson (3c). The structure of the first section is mirrored by that of the second, further articulated in the domain of investigation (B1, § 56 ff.), questions to ask (B2, § 70 ff.), and procedure (B3, §§ 80–86). Finally, the section concerning the 'facts', not by coincidence the shortest, seems more like an appendix: the numbering of paragraphs is here substituted by a heading which reads 'system of two terms', clearly presupposing that others were meant to be introduced, mirroring the structure of *La catégorie des cas* (1935–1937) and the rich material discussed in *Sprogsystem og sprogforandring* (1972 [1934]).

This is how the paper was structured in its author's mind; but readers may find it preferable to approach it following a different division:

1. (§§ 1–5) Hjelmslev clarifies the philological status of his contribution. This part was probably added around 1944 or later, as the communication of 1941 is mentioned, along with further sections II and III, used to discuss empirical data (cf. § 5, n. 2), which were referred to as 'dated back to 1943'.

2. (§§ 6–13) The general framework of the paper is sketched out. The goal is set of describing the internal organization of morphological systems, where 'morphology' is intended to denote the inflectional mechanism as opposed to the derivational. As in 1933, a criterion for such distinction is foreshadowed in that inflection is said to be both associative and syntagmatic, whereas derivation is purely associative (cf. § 57). However, the distinction clearly requires something further: if 'associative' and 'syntagmatic' were defined in purely functional terms, they would be indistinguishable, as both inflection and derivation deal with associative sets of elements which may occur in a given position within a chain. Instead, the two concepts are interpreted pragmatically, as it were, in connection to the speaker: a paradigm counterintuitively represents something that depends on the speaker's intentions (free choice), whereas a syntagma represents a fixed pattern (bound choice).

A second distinction is taken up between semanteme (themes and roots as combined elements) and morpheme (combining elements), in accordance with early positions in his *Principes de grammaire générale* (Hjelmslev 1928). The mutual relationships (correlations) between morphemes belonging to one and the same category are then said to be the object of the paper, under the proviso that a category—much like language in general—may form different systems (properly 'configurations', see §§ 70–79 below): gender may be realized as a two-member system (as is the case in most Romance languages), a three-member system (as in German), or a four-member system (as in Danish, once abstraction is made between the particular systems of nouns and pronouns). An exhaustive comparison, however, cannot be a matter of purely quantitative consideration, as systems consisting of the same number of elements may distribute these quite differently (that is, elements may have different 'values'). Hence the need for both a quantitative and a qualitative approach, only achievable by assuming the existence of a law which governs the mutual relationship between the terms of a given system (cf. § 11). What were later to become known as the 'laws of solidarity' (cf. Hjelmslev 1935: 125), stating the proportion between the number of elements and their relations—and thus the possible systems[18]—are foreshadowed here in opposition to Hjelmslev's early position as expressed in a letter to Brøndal dated 4 December 1931 (cf. Gregersen 1991, I: 222). Finally, the difference between *état abstrait* (abstract state, or language in general) and *état concret* (concrete state, or a given historical language), which served as the basis for Hjelmslev's theory of general grammar (cf. Hjelmslev 1928), is here combined with the Saussurean tripartition between synchrony, diachrony, and panchrony, resulting in a quadripartition in which pansynchrony and pandiachrony (i.e. the general theory of system and of change, called respectively 'panchrony' and 'metachrony', from 1934) are opposed to 'idiosynchrony' and 'idiodiachrony' (systems and changes within particular languages). The solution to the problem of the mutual relationships (correlations) is said to explain how particular languages (that is, given systems of categories) are organized and change over time, only if formulated on a general level (cf. § 12).

3. (§§ 14–43) The core of Hjelmslev's argumentation is a long critique of the three models proposed by Peshkovsky, Karcevsky (2000 [1927]), and

---

[18] Technically, the possible combinations of glossemes on each dimension: for instance, the occurrence of a combination of marked (α), unmarked (A) and relatively marked (β or B) is said to be impossible. These must not be understood as a priori restrictions, but as logical conditions for description, accounting for *possible* occurrences and syncretisms (and not only for actually occurring phenomena; cf. Hjelmslev §§ 13, 44, 45).

Jakobson (1932). The somewhat far-fetched dialectical fashion followed by the exposition is instrumental in bringing forth contrastively the respective tenets: accounting for the logical basis of three-member systems, Karcevsky's model compensates for the faults of Peshkovsky's, which correctly identifies the intrinsic feature of linguistic oppositions—vagueness—but fails to extend it beyond two-term systems. In turn, Jakobson succeeds in further qualifying this vagueness, yet ends up in an inconsistent network of binary divisions as he tries to reduce this vagueness to contradictory features (Andersen 1989: 24). The central idea of this section is, however, the diagram introduced by Hjelmslev (Figure 7.1) in order to chart Karcevsky's mapping, which would become the signature of Hjelmslev's abstract approach, deemed to be full of 'useless subtleties' by Trubetzkoy.[19]

Figure 7.1 Hjelmslev's sublogical diagram

A category is seen as a box or frame, divided into logical fields according to standard logical oppositions, contradiction (producing a two-field box) and contrariety (producing a three-field box)—the only option which can be generalized. The box and its fields account for the unity of the fundamental meaning associated with any grammatical category and its logical nuances (see Figure 7.2). The way members are arranged in opposition to each other within a category, however, is said to depend on the intrinsic[20] functioning of language, which defies logical oppositions (cf. especially § 22, 23, 27). This arrangement is only transposed[21] upon the diagram, which serves as a register of sorts in order to map the overlapping quality which defines linguistic correlations. The result is a set of six (later seven) possible correlates, from the maximally marked or intensive (α), which is said to concentrate their possible usages (variants) on one field of the diagram only, to maximally unmarked (A), in which the entirety of the diagram is filled (cf. § 32), enabling the unmarked

---

[19] 'Niktemnye subtil'nosti' (Trubetzkoy 1975: 439), cited in Rasmussen (1987: 51).
[20] Called 'prelogic' in 1935. In the actual version of the 1933 paper, there are only mentions of the 'alogical' or 'illogical' structure of language (see also Hjelmslev 1972 [1934]), maintained following on from positions expressed in 1928.
[21] Such transposition depends on the so-called 'sublogic', further discussed in 1935 (cf. Cigana 2018, 2022a). Interestingly enough, Benveniste (1949) also relies on it in his description of Latin prepositions.

term to 'stand for' the marked one by sharing its features (the field they have in common; see for instance Figure 7.3).

In addressing Hjelmslev's version of markedness, Andersen (1989) rightly points out the importance of this diagram, representing the 'reference potential' of a term (Andersen 1989: 24, 31, 2001: 44–45, 47–48): in a couple like *man: woman*, a rather standard example of markedness patterns, the marked term has a precise (concentrated, intensive) meaning, insofar as it can stand for only a specific class of referents, while the unmarked correspondent stands for a wider range of referents, including the categorical meaning (man as human being). While substantially correct, this reading is somewhat limiting: 'reference potential' is only applicable to content-descriptions and easily paves the way for referential interpretation, which is quite remote from Hjelmslev's framework. The diagram originally represents the category itself, while the boxes allow for the registering of the range of realizations (variants) in which each term may be manifested—in other words, its possible distribution. What Jakobson conceived in terms of possession vs. non-possession of a feature (mark) is here reinterpreted on a purely distributional basis, as a correlation (participation) between a vague or *extensive* term, which allows for a broader registration of variants, and a precise or *intensive* term, which tends to concentrate its variants on a part of the diagram:

> For a more detailed description of the system of oppositions, cf. La Catégorie des Cas [1935–1937] p. 98 ff. Any opposition is by principle considered as a participation. Letters α β and γ denote the intensive members, while A B and Γ the extensive members, whose variation range is broader.
>
> (Hjelmslev 1970 [1948]: 219).

4. (§§ 44–55) Hjelmslev concretely formulates his own proposal. Substitution (rectified to 'commutation' in 1942) decides which element belongs to a given category, and, this being the only criterion, all elements are equal in that respect, hence the need to distinguish them qualitatively. Their different ways of positioning within the category provides the solution; yet, since systems may exist which include more than three elements, the requirement is formulated for a description that combines these two conditions. A dichotomic analysis (*à la* Jakobson) produces a simple model, in which all elements can be classified, albeit in respect to different features (represented by the nodes of a hierarchy). The alternative is an analysis by *dimensions*, in which the elements are arranged within a system of up to three (or more, after 1942) 'sides' of the category itself. The advantage is that all elements can be described in

terms of their position in all parameters simultaneously, respecting the functional facts such as possible syncretisms and neutralizations which are said to occur between extensive (unmarked) and intensive (marked) terms. An important result of this stance is that markedness becomes a built-in feature of Hjelmslev's analysis. Systems consisting of more than one dimension are not included in the paper but discussed in *La catégorie des cas* (1935–1937), to which Hjelmslev refers (cf. § 81, n. 70).

The reader is also given a clearer view of the functional phenomena, by distinguishing an ideal level from its manifestation: commutation and syncretism are said to be flip sides of a single phenomenon, the mutual correlations existing between the elements of a category, while Jakobson's *Vertauschung* (*i.e.* the *actual* replacement of the marked term by the unmarked correspondent in a given context) is said to manifest such features.[22]

5. (§§ 56–69) This section marks a different step in the paper's flow: Hjelmslev here seems to slow down the pace, cautiously limiting the reach of his previous insights to categories of inflectional morphemes, while insisting repeatedly on the provisional nature of his research (which nevertheless would be expanded afterwards). He addresses both terminological and theoretical issues (grammateme/semanteme/morpheme vs. formants; inflection vs. derivation; associative vs. syntagmatic relations, cf. §§ 6–13). Such definitions allow for the reframing of certain phenomena such as suppletion, which is ruled out as a case of synonymy in which one and the same semanteme is expressed by different theme-formants (§ 60), while transfers (§ 62, later called 'conversions') are taken into account. Transfers would play an increasingly important role as a necessary presupposition for the study of both morphological content and structural semantics: see, for instance, the transfer of case into prepositions for which Wüllner and Bernhardi were acknowledged (cf. Hjelmslev 1935: 107).[23]

6. (§§ 70–79) The procedure for charting the functional pattern of a given system ('configuration', *C*) is explained as it presupposes three coordinated steps:

---

[22] This distinction coincides with the one Coseriu insightfully draws between 'neutralization' and 'neutralizability' (cf. Coseriu (1992 [1988]: 220–221). Although revamped in 1943, with the introduction of a panoply of terms such as 'latence', 'implication', 'overlapping', 'fusion', Jakobson's terminology kept on changing.
[23] This allows for an appreciation of the close similarity of Hjelmslev's (1935–1937) theory of case and Brøndal's (1940) theory of prepositions, cf. n. 5 of this introductory essay.

1) The extensional (*Ext*), in which elements are studied according to their role of extensive/intensive as well as in relation to their realized variants (*V*, cf. § 73), as replacements occur by overlapping of contextual variants (a given element *A* can replace another *B* by sharing the same contextual variant *a*, being susceptible to occurring within the same context).
2) The step in which 'syncretisms' (*S*) are studied, which are stipulated to occur exclusively between an intensive and an extensive element, thus depending 'on the structural relationships between the terms' (§ 73).
3) Such intracategorial factors are compensated for by the investigation of the paradigmatic intercategorial context, insofar as 'dominances' (*D*) are considered. The term 'dominance' is intended to imply a pressure exerted by an element belonging to a category A upon elements belonging to a concurrent category B resulting in the establishment of a syncretism: for instance, in German and Latin, the neuter gender is said to dominate the syncretism between the nominative and accusative cases (cf. § 75). Unfortunately, dominances are not discussed in more detail in the paper—they receive a proper discussion in 1934, where an intensive dominant is said to entail a simplification (reduction by syncretism or by defectivation) in the dominated category, whereas an extensive dominant is said to engender a complexification (or 'specification', cf. Hjelmslev 1972 [1934]: 113 f.).

Ext, *S*, and *D* in turn presuppose the setting up of the 'inventory' (*Inv*, cf. § 78) of elements for each category, by running the commutation test, which possibly leads to the distinction between a normal system and particular systems (cf. §§ 6–13).

Finally, in conformity with his stance on the general issue of form vs. substance, Hjelmslev resolutely denies the possibility that the *intensional* step (*Int*), that is, that concerning the substance of the content of the elements, should be prioritized over the extensional step (§ 79), while conceding the convenience of keeping the two orders together for practical investigation:

> from a theoretical point of view, it is the question *Int*. that presupposes the question *Ext*. and not vice versa. From a practical point of view, however, we believe that it is useful to take into account both of the questions simultaneously: the investigation requires to a certain extent that we consider them together.
>
> (§ 79, cf. also § 84)

The same consideration will return in 1957, as the purely formal nature of the method is laid out (cf. Hjelmslev 1970 [1957]: 106–107).

7. (§§ 80–end) The scheme of the procedure is set down, anticipating the applicative moment of section C ('Facts'). This section is possibly the patchiest and most disorienting one, because of the repeated claims about the provisional state of the art as well as the unfulfilled promise of many more applications to come. In fact, only one relatively simplistic case (French comparison, cf. also 1934) is actually discussed, and, even then, in a rather dismissive way. The scheme is pursued in other complementary works on the topic, such as Hjelmslev (1972 [1934], 1935–1937, and 1975). In the present paper, notable remarks concern (1) the necessity of identifying each category within its respective systemic context (nominal classes or verbal classes) and through a purely functional—that is, morphosyntactic—criterion, as further elaborated in 1936 (cf. Hjelmslev 1970 [1938]); and (2) a section foreshadowing the notion of connotation, probably dated 1942 (§ 85, cf. Cigana 2023) and circumscribing the description to a specific state of a language, identified 'dia-systematically' (i.e. in terms of geographical, historical, and stylistic coordinates).

Finally, in the sample case—the system of French comparison—the tools discussed so far are implemented. The category is said to be logically articulable to three degrees of 'intensity'[24] (Figure 7.2) and to be set up as a two-term system, since, for French, Hjelmslev does not acknowledge, beside the positive, the separate existence of both comparative and superlative, but only of a single complex content-element labelled 'comparative-superlative'.[25]

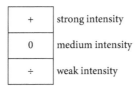

Figure 7.2 The sublogic diagram of comparison

---

[24] Which, according to Hjelmslev, is the fundamental meaning (*Grundbedeutung*) of comparison.
[25] His reasons for this are unclear, but relate to the fact that in French the difference between comparative and superlative 'is often, but not necessarily, expressed by a difference of articles (definite article in opposition to zero-article), but never as a difference inherent to the category of comparison' (cf. § 86, C, Inv.).

In 1934, this feature serves as the basis for contrasting the French category of comparison with other systems (German, Danish; cf. Hjelmslev 1972 [1934]) and is resolved by admitting that each system can be differently *oriented*.[26]

The conclusion is put forward that, in French, the comparative-superlative plays the role of the intensive term (α), while the positive is extensive, or unmarked (A), being able to replace the former in some contexts, such as periphrastic usages.

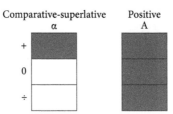

Figure 7.3 Participative correlation between French morphemes

An investigation of syncretisms (S) and dominances (D) is not undertaken, as these are said to be non-occurring.

7.5 Concluding remarks

Overall, Hjelmslev's paper, while offering a thorough discussion of the underpinnings of the models considered, does not offer a complete overview of his model: many important notions, constituting indispensable tools of his theory—such as 'tension', 'optimum', 'insistence', and even 'orientation' (cf. Cigana 2022a: 158 ff.)—are missing, despite having been developed in the same period. A complete presentation is thus deferred to other occasions, mostly between 1935 and 1937.[27]

It is not by chance, then, that, in *Omkring Sprogteoriens Grundlæggelse* (1943), when referring to the method discussed here, Hjelmslev explains:

> the science of categories, however, presupposes such a comprehensive and such a closely coherent apparatus of terms and definitions that its details cannot be described without its being presented completely; it cannot therefore, any more than the science of units which determines it, be treated in the prolegomena of the theory.
>
> (Hjelmslev 1961, § 20: 101)

---

[26] Which could reflect, inter alia, the not particularly surprising phenomenon of inversion of markedness-values within the same category in different languages, called 'conditional' (Greenberg 2005 [1966]: 24) or 'reverse markedness' (cf. Haspelmath in Greenberg 2005 [1966]: xv).

[27] The other important publications having coincidentally also appeared posthumously (cf. Hjelmslev 1972 [1934]; 1975).

We touch here on a limit of structural thinking: a qualitative science of linguistic categories as envisaged by Louis Hjelmslev remains beyond the scope of contemporary linguistics, as the reconstruction of the general paradigmatic structure of language is hardly among its desiderata. Moreover, the gap that separates the whole theory discussed here from concurrent models, be they contemporaneous or successive, concerned with general morphology (both dependency and constituent-oriented) or just with contemporary markedness-oriented descriptions is considerable. As we have seen, the paper discusses a single topic—the hypothesis regarding the laws which govern the constitution of a grammatical category—on three different levels (A–A', B, C, see above), approaching markedness phenomena insofar as they reveal the very principle of such laws. It is safe to say that it does so in a very elaborate way, if not in a fashion that seems quite remote from linguistics or concrete data. However, even in its sketchy style and with a high level of abstraction and density, *General structure of linguistic correlations* is a prime example of the stance Hjelmslev adopted as early as 1928, approximating Saussure's realization of the need to tell linguists what they are doing when describing languages.

Here we touch upon a second important point of structuralist thinking, typical of Hjelmslev's own approach. According to such a stance, facts in themselves are said to be blind: they need to be placed within a systematic context in order to become meaningful and within a theoretical framework to acquire an explanation. Hence, the particular attention given in the paper to the logical nature of the operations carried out by linguists: correlations—much like form in general—are conceived both as a feature of language to be accounted for and as a result of the linguist's metalinguistic activity, tasked with distinguishing and comparing linguistic elements. In so doing, a linguist is often led implicitly or explicitly to ground his own operations according to a more or less classical logical framework (see, for instance, Cantineau 1955). While drawing attention to this aspect, Hjelmslev shows the inadequacy of a classical framework, deemed too normative and narrow for the real needs of linguistics. Binarism, for instance, looks simpler and more intuitive, and thus might easily be considered correct by both the speaker's and the linguist's feeling; yet it offers a solution that is too simple, since it leaves out some oppositional possibilities which could explain markedness-related phenomena.

Overall, this paper provides a vivid portrait of the structuralist mindset, allowing, at the same time, for a reframing of many common interpretations: the comprehensively formalistic approach, in particular, so appreciable in the text, is not adopted for its own sake but linked to a strong epistemological stance that acknowledges the necessarily constructive nature of any linguistic description. Such epistemological awareness is what makes structuralist thinking so relevant and current for the contemporary humanities.

General structure of linguistic correlations

Louis Hjelmslev (1933)
Translated by Lorenzo Cigana

Note to the Reader

§ 1. After the publication of my work, *Principes de grammaire générale*, in 1928, my research was focused on the domain of general grammar, with special attention paid to the issue of the general structure of morphematic categories: possible number and mutual relationships of morphemes within one and the same paradigm.[1] During the Second International Congress of Linguists, held in Geneva in 1931, I found great support and inspiration in some rather detailed conversations with Serge Karcevsky and some other members of the Prague Linguistic Circle. On 27 April 1931 I presented a first result of my research to the Linguistic Circle of Copenhagen in a communication entitled *Structure générale des systèmes grammaticaux*.[2]

§ 2. An enlarged manuscript of that presentation, in French, was then offered to the *Bulletin* of the Linguistic Circle of Copenhagen, but in June 1933 it was rejected by decision of the editorial board. In 1942 the *Board of the Circle* decided to publish it immediately.

§ 3. The significant delay in the publication of this little paper of mine is thus due to circumstances beyond my control. In this situation I thought it useful to reproduce the text as it was written in 1933; the first part of this work (I) reproduces the text in its entirety, with the addition of some footnotes indicating their later inclusion.

§ 4. The first part includes (as in the manuscript of 1933) some paragraphs on the category of comparison which were only briefly included in my original oral presentation in 1933. Along with some added remarks that are not found

---

[1] [Translator's note:] The following typographical conventions are used in footnotes: footnotes with no brackets were in the original manuscript, square brackets mark footnotes added later by Hjelmslev, and curly braces mark notes added by 1973 editors. I thank Una Canger for the invaluable help in revising the translation.

[2] {'*Structure générale des corrélations linguistiques*'. Paper published for the first time in *Essais linguistiques* II (1973), on the basis of a manuscript found in Louis Hjelmslev's archives. In what follows, without further mention, notes in brackets have been added to the first draft by Louis Hjelmslev himself}.

here, they were presented as a special communication (*Notes sur les degrés de comparison*) announced at the Circle's Board in 1935 and presented in a plenary session on 17 April 1941.

§ 5. The second and the third parts of the paper (II–III) date back to 1943 and serve to clarify my present position concerning the problem.[3]

Morphematic correlations

(June 1933)

A. Problem

1. Formulation of the problem

§ 6. In what follows the aim is to discuss the general problem of the *structure of grammatical systems*.

§ 7. We here take the term *grammatical system* in the limited sense developed by the linguistic tradition. The grammatical systems that we are concerned with are: the system of case, that of number, that of gender, of degrees of comparison, of articles,[4] of persons, of voices, tenses and aspects, of modes. The systems enumerated are all *morpheme categories* of the *inflectional type*.[5] Within our framework, the term *inflection* is opposed not to *agglutination, isolation* and *polysynthecism*, but to *derivation*. We thus use of the term *inflection* in a rather broad sense: without taking into account the typological differences between languages, we consider any morpheme that does not display features of a *derivational* element as inflectional.

This delimitation of our field of investigation is still rough and provisional,[6] yet it will suffice for the time being.

§ 8. Each of the aforementioned categories, wherever it occurs, consists of two or more members that, by the very fact of belonging to the same category, contract a reciprocal relationship called *correlation*. There will thus be a correlation between nominative, accusative, genitive and dative, which are all members of the category of case. Likewise, there will be a correlation between

---

[3] {Among Louis Hjelmslev's papers there is no manuscript that contains the clarifications mentioned. He probably never wrote sections II and III.}

[4] Only where the morphematic nature of the category of articles is unquestionable. Cf. further herein.

[5] Cf. L. Hjelmslev, *Principes de grammaire générale* (Det kgl. danske Videnskabernes Selskab, Hist.-fil. Meddelelser XVI, 1928).

[6] The final precisions are provided in chapter B1.

singular and plural, both members of the category of number; or between masculine, feminine and neuter, all members of the category of gender, and so forth. By the very fact of contracting a correlation, the members of a category *form a system* and can be qualified as *terms* of a system. It is important to make clear from the very beginning that *one and the same category can form different systems* in those languages in which it is realized.[7] While the category of case is found invariably in Sanskrit, Latin and German, the *system* of cases is different in each of those languages, since the number of cases varies and the correlations contracted by them are specific to each language, to the extent that no case can receive the same, identical definition in all languages. The terms used to indicate grammatical cases—such as 'genitive', 'dative' and so forth—possess a precise value only within a single, well-defined language: these values depend on the correlations, and these in turn depend (largely, if not exclusively) on the number of terms included in each system.

What holds true for the category of case is also valid for any other grammatical category. The *system* is thus the specific form in which a *category* is realized; such a form is defined by the number of terms and by the correlations they mutually contract. The problem of the structure of grammatical systems can thus be traced back to the more specific problem of the *correlations* or *mutual relationships contracted by members that belong to one and the same system*.

§ 9. Since grammatical systems vary across languages, a comparative procedure will turn out to be the only means to uncover the general principle governing the different realizations, whenever possible. Moreover, it is not just a matter of comparing systems that differ only quantitatively (i.e. systems that entail numerically different inventories of terms like the system of cases in Sanskrit, Latin and German); it is first and foremost a matter of investigating systems that realize different categories but include the same number of terms, in order to check whether terms belonging to such systems behave functionally in the same way.

§ 10. Let us begin with the simplest imaginable possibility: a system consisting of only *two terms*. A case system may include two cases, for instance the nominative and the genitive of ordinary substantives in English and in Scandinavian. A system of comparison may include two degrees (like in French). A system may have two numbers like the singular and the plural; two genders, like masculine and feminine in nouns and adjectives of French or like animate and inanimate in some languages, including a certain hypothesized state of

---

[7] Or rather: in each linguistic state in which the category is realized.

Indo-European. Although quite rare, a system of two persons is also possible. This system can be found in an archaic state of Danish where the distinction is drawn between two personal forms of the verb, namely a second person form (*est*, 'you are', *fikst* 'you had', etc.) and an undifferentiated form serving simultaneously as first and third person (*er* 'I am, he is', *fik* 'I had, he had'). We can have a system consisting of only two voices, like the active and the passive, or a system of two tenses, present and preterite, which are the only two non-periphrastic forms in English, German and Scandinavian languages; or a system consisting of only two modes, like the system in English that on a purely formal level includes only an indicative (*is, has*) and a non-indicative, which serves simultaneously as subjunctive, imperative and infinitive (*be, have*).

§ 11. In comparing these systems, the question arises whether what they share is merely the *quantitative* fact of including two terms, or whether there also is a *qualitative* fact at play: is there some law that governs the mutual relationship between the two terms, valid for all systems consisting of only two terms? Is the relationship between two terms always the same in passing from one system to the next? Or does each system present a different set of conditions that require different laws?

§ 12. The same problem arises also for more comprehensive systems: systems with three terms [three cases, as in the personal pronouns of French, English and Scandinavian languages; three numbers, as in Ancient Greek; three genders, like masculine, feminine and neuter; three degrees of comparison, as in Latin, Greek and English; three persons, as in Latin, Greek and German; three voices, as in Ancient Greek; three tenses, as in literary Hungarian which includes (besides the present tense that also indicates future), two non-periphrastic forms of the preterite, namely an imperfect and a 'perfect'; three modes, as in Modern Danish which distinguishes an indicative, for instance *er* or *har*, an imperative, for instance *vær, hav*, and a subjunctive-infinitive, for instance *være, have*] or with four terms (suffice it to recall, for instance, the four cases acknowledged in many languages by traditional grammar: nominative, accusative, genitive and dative). Systems that are *more complex*, like the case systems of Latin, Sanskrit and, even more so, the case systems of Finnish, Hungarian and of some Caucasian languages, or the system of grammatical gender or 'nominal classes' of Bantu; the tense and aspect systems of Ancient Greek, Latin and French can also be cited. Examples can be multiplied. For each one of these types of systems we would wish to know whether or not identity of number is accompanied by an identical or analogous configuration of the terms, in fact universal or limited by conditions depending on a general principle.

2. The significance of the problem

§ 13. It should be obvious that the solution to this problem constitutes one of the most natural and urgent tasks for a scientific grammar. The general problem that we have just formulated is a *pansynchronic* problem coming from general grammar, whose goal it is to identify the laws governing the morphological structure of human language and to provide the possible and the necessary conditions required by this structure.[8] Within this science we shall hardly find a more central problem than the one here presented. In fact, inflection (in our sense of the word[9]) has always been at the core of grammatical research;[10] general grammar is thus faced with the obligation to account for the laws that govern the structure of inflection. Yet, in pursuing its own goals, general grammar also aims at more far-reaching goals: results achieved by general grammar will have decisive repercussions in other branches of linguistic studies. Once the general laws that govern the structure of inflection have been identified, the knowledge of these laws will allow us to present for the first time the *pandiachronic* problem of possible changes and of necessary changes, to explain observed changes and to predict those that are likely to occur under given circumstances. Moreover, such pandiachronic research will lay the foundations for the scientific grammar of each language, meant to effectively replace the vague groping of traditional grammar. Every grammar of the state of a given language, every idiosynchrony the description of which is not limited to a sterile enumeration of the forms, but which aims at explaining observed facts,[11] will find its foundations in the general theory: the concrete system of the given language is explained in light of general principles of the abstract system of language. Finally, the idiodiachrony, or the description of changes undergone by a given language, will find in the pandiachronic theory the means of explanation: the change in a concrete system is explained by the general laws that handle the changes. We thus believe that any grammar, be it 'descriptive' or 'historical', theoretical or practical, will benefit from knowledge based on the contribution provided by the general grammar, and that the investigation of a general problem like the one that interests us here is of great importance for linguistics.

---

[8] Cf. *Principes de grammaire générale*, pp. 101–107.
[9] In the sense we use that term, cf. above, § 7.
[10] We know that the general problem of inflection is also behind that of 'parts of speech'. In this respect, cf. *Principes de grammaire générale*, pp. 198–204, 296 ff.
[11] Cf. *Principes de grammaire générale*, pp. 55–57.

The problem is thus compelling and demands an urgent, albeit temporary, solution.

3. Previous hypotheses

§ 14. Our work has no forerunners. Not only has no solution been found for our problem until now, it has not even been addressed. We know of no research, be it comparative or general, that was carried out in this order of ideas. At most, we hope to glean what we can, here and there from single language grammars, from suggestive remarks presenting some principles of a general scope. And yet, apart from some recent works to which we shall return shortly, we have not been able to pick out in the entire grammatical literature from ancient times to modernity, any contribution of this kind that deserves serious attention. It is possible of course that we have missed some passages—even more so since the analytic history of the grammatical science has yet to be written. Lacking such guidance, one can easily get lost in the far too boring maze of tradition. If some attempts have been made in this direction, they have almost certainly fallen into oblivion: they have simply not found any resonance within the trends that direct the evolution of our science. It would not be sufficient to say that the problem at stake has been poorly investigated: it has not even been addressed by classical linguistics. Such is the paradox of grammar: a science that can boast of a two-thousand-year-old tradition has not addressed even the most important, the most urgent problems—not even problems whose solution might have provided the most decisive consequences, also for diachronic studies, have been approached. It has long been maintained that the grammatical system of a language is nothing but the fortuitous outcome of blind evolution. We have forgotten to ask ourselves how to explain the indisputable fact that a language, while being subject to constant alterations, always retains the ability of forming systems. The discussion concerning the general laws that lay at the root of language's organizing power has been disregarded as futile; the very existence of such laws was often denied—and most of the time implicitly. This prejudice has severely hampered any empirical approach.

§ 15. The only works that contribute a solution to our problem are some idiosynchronic sketches of quite preliminary character that are quite recent. There are in all three, and they all stem from authors of Russian origin, and they all deal with modern Russian. It seems that studies of fundamental problems of synchronic grammar have early on occupied researchers specifically in Russia.[12]

---

[12] Jakobson traces the modern attempts that we are talking about back to a tradition inaugurated by Aleksandr C. Vostokov (1831), a tradition that had in Filipp F. Fortunatov one of his most important supporters (*Charisteria Guilelmo Mathesio quinquagenario*, Prague 1932, p. 75).

In discussing these contributions, we must keep in mind that their aim is not the general theory. The two—to which we shall first turn—do not even aim at studying the structure of correlations the way they can be observed in the Russian language; they just touch upon the problem, and it occurs only marginally in their presentations.

3a. Peshkovsky's hypothesis

§ 16. In his Russian syntax—a work which in many respects is one of the most advanced among current scientific grammars[13]—*Aleksandr Matveevic Peshkovsky* briefly expounds his theory concerning the problem we are dealing with here.[14] It seems that this doctrine closely continues the essential points that in this respect are at the bottom of Russian grammatical tradition.

Peshkovsky begins with the category of comparison which, according to him, in Russian includes three morphological 'categories':[15] the positive, the comparative and the superlative. Peshkovsky observes that only the comparative and the superlative indicate a comparison or rather a 'degree' of comparison, whereas this idea is absent in the positive. M. Peshkovsky interprets this fact by saying that in relation to the comparative and the superlative the positive has a 'zero meaning', and it constitutes a 'zero category':[16] it is the very absence of signification that constitutes the true signification (better 'value') of the positive. Peshkovsky compares this zero in the signified with the same 'zero-ending' that was also observed by Ferdinand de Saussure in the plane of the signifier.[17] From this fact Peshkovsky concludes that 'zero-categories' (i.e. the terms of a category) contract a constant mutual relationship and that they thereby are constantly susceptible of being mutually compared in our consciousness. He observes that such 'zero-categories' proliferate in the Russian language: thus, the indicative represents the zero-mood, the imperfective aspect represents the zero-aspect, the neuter is the zero-gender, and so forth.

---

[13] Cf. our *Principes de grammaire générale*, p. 111.

[14] A. M. Peshkovsky, Русский синтаксис в научном освещении, 3rd ed., Moscow-Leningrad 1928, p. 30 ff. Peshkovsky exhibits a somewhat excessive use of the term 'category'. He thus calls 'categories' what we would call 'morphemes', i.e., the members of a category. Such use is justified only insofar as morphemes are conceived as classes that include different variants, like Peshkovsky does. (It seems that Peshkovsky thinks above all about variants in the plane of the signifier: from that point of view, the Russian comparative admits the variants -ee (учтивее), -e (лéгче), -ше (стáрше), and so forth*, just like Latin comparative admits different variants such as *iust-ior, min-or*, and so forth. It would be justified to think also of those variants that can be observed in the plane of the signified, i.e., the particular variants that can be assigned to the comparative in the same way.

*{Russian examples are given sometimes in Cyrillic, sometimes in the Latin alphabet. To avoid issues of transliteration we have generalized the use of Cyrillic; *Essais linguistiques* II, p. 64, N.o.E.}.

Concerning the meaning of our term 'morpheme', cf. below.

[15] Нулевое значение. In Saussurean terminology one would say 'value' rather than 'meaning'.

[16] Нулевое категория.

[17] *Cours de linguistique générale*, 2nd edition, p. 123 ff.

§ 17. It is clear that Peshkovsky's observation is just a first approximation, and that it requires more precise details based on a thorough examination. The results of our research will show that the definition of 'zero' cannot be maintained and must be replaced by another. Nonetheless Peshkovsky's observation contains a certain truth, overlooked until now by the majority of grammarians, and it is not specific for Russian: Once given the necessary clarification, his observation can undoubtedly be generalized. In fact, it seems that within a morphological system there is often at least one term susceptible to a precise semantic definition, and at least one or several terms (the ones called 'zero' by Peshkovsky) that, in comparison with the precise ones, allow for a relatively vague, blurred or confused definition: there are *precise terms*, and there are *vague terms*. Moreover—and this is even more important—it seems that *a system is often organized on the opposition between the precise terms on the one hand and on the vague terms on the other*. This is the *first hypothesis* inferred from Peshkovsky's observation.

§ 18. Peshkovsky's brief remarks are not sufficient for a definition of the opposition between two precise terms, nor of the opposition between two vague ones; however, they prove to be useful for an understanding of all the cases where a vague term is opposed to a precise one. That is to say that Peshkovsky's doctrine proves to be particularly fruitful for the description of *systems with two terms*. Although still quite sketchy, his observation seems to be largely realizable in a system of two aspects like the Russian one:[18] the imperfective is the vague term opposed to the perfective, which is the precise one. A quick glance at the provisional examples mentioned above (§ 10) will suffice to show to what extent this idea is valid:

	precise term	vague term
Case: English, Scandinavian (substantive)	genitive	nominative
Comparison: French	comparative	positive
Number:	plural	singular
Gender: French (substantive, adjective)	feminine	masculine
Person: Danish (verb)	2nd person	1st-3rd person
Voice:	passive	active
Tense: English, German, Scandinavian	preterite	present
Mode: English	imperative-subjunctive	indicative

---

[18] We temporarily ignore the problem of deciding whether the system of Russian aspect really consists of only two terms.

These examples are quoted with utmost caution. The examination to which they shall later be submitted will allow us to specify the different cases that are observed. For the time being they suffice to show that the observation made by M. Peshkovsky concerning systems with two terms has every chance of being generally usable. In fact, they allow us to formulate a *second hypothesis* according to which *every two-term system is based on the opposition between a precise term and a vague one*. It can hardly be questioned that there is a certain truth in this hypothesis.

§ 19. The situation is more complicated when it comes to systems consisting of more than two terms. But here again it is clear that the opposition between precise and vague terms is repeated for a vast majority of cases. Even in the more complicated case-systems, the nominative most often maintains the role as an undecided case or a 'zero' case; the same role is maintained by the singular in a system that includes a dual number besides the plural; likewise for the positive in a system that includes a superlative along with the comparative; the same role is often assigned to the third person in a system comprising three grammatical persons; this is also the case for the present tense in a system comprising three tenses and so forth. There may be cases in which two terms out of three are 'vague'. Now, if Peshkovsky is right in assigning the vague role to the neuter form of Russian gender, and if it seems reasonable to do so also to the neuter form of systems similar in German and Latin, it must also be stressed that in languages such as French the masculine is also vague. It seems that in such systems there is only one precise term: that is the feminine.

We find this quite important. The consequences to be drawn from these hypotheses is that linguistic correlations are often vague and imprecise oppositions, and as a consequence *it would be a mistake to want to reduce them to a rigorous principle of the logico-mathematical type*. It is not the first time that we observe that language does not obey formal logic. Yet, Peshkovsky's observation allows us to note this in a more precise and more concrete way. It shows that in standard morphematic correlations it is not a matter of a logical opposition between *a* and *non-a*, but most often of a more confused opposition between a precise term and a vague one.

3b. Karcevsky's hypothesis

§ 20. The ideas put forward by Serge Karcevsky are rather different. Compared to Peshkovsky's theory, they have the advantage of giving a rather accurate account of systems that are more complex. Their main drawback, however, is that they reduce linguistic facts to a quasi-mathematical scheme that agrees poorly with the empirical observations made by Peshkovsky. Karcevsky says:[19]

> [I]n grammar, subdivisions always come in twos or threes; each subordinating class includes only two or three subordinated classes. Thus, the specification of the idea of 'resultativity' only requires two aspects: the positive (the perfective) and the negative (the imperfective); the verb is either modal or non-modal (*verbum infinitum*); the modal verb includes three modes; the indicative includes three tenses; the present-future form includes three persons and each person two numbers. Two correlative values contract a contrary opposition; but when they come in threes, the third term is neuter and as such is opposed to the other two.

§ 21. It is clear that Karcevsky denies the existence of systems that are the result of a single subdivision and include more than three terms. An examination of the facts will show whether this hypothesis holds or not. Setting aside this question for the time being, we notice that Karcevsky only recognizes two possible types of systems:

(1) + − a type of system that includes a positive and a negative term, opposed as contraries
(2) + − 0 a type of system that includes the same terms, with the addition of a neutral term, opposed to the two contrary ones

§ 22. The tool which Karcevsky here provides us with in order to register two-term systems and three-term systems does not account for the linguistic opposition between precise and vague terms. It makes it necessary to transform this opposition to a logical opposition between contrary terms and between contrary terms and neutral ones. This feature lessens the usefulness of the tool itself: in all the cases where the hypotheses established above (§§ 17–19) can be verified, Karcevsky's schema accounts only indirectly for linguistic facts by transformation. The disadvantage resulting from this is above all that the choice of establishing which term is the positive and which the negative will be arbitrary: since the opposition that defines them is a contrary opposition, it follows logically that they are absolutely equal, and that they operate on the same level.

---

[19] Cf. *Système du verbe russe*, Prague 1927, p. 22 ff.

§ 23. Despite this disadvantage, we do not consider Karcevsky's attempt as futile. On the contrary, it is informative in showing what happens—and what must necessarily happen—when a linguistic opposition is transformed into a logical opposition: for a two-term system that satisfies our second hypothesis (§ 18), the transformation can only be carried out by converting an opposition between a precise term and a vague one to an opposition between contrary or contradictory terms. As far as three-term systems satisfying our first hypothesis (§ 17) are concerned, the transformation will necessarily require that, two of three terms are defined as contraries: since the existence of a neutral term comes in between these two, they can no longer be interpreted as contradictory. Now, since the interpretation according to contrariety is still possible also for two-term systems, this interpretation can be generalized—which is exactly what Karcevsky does by claiming that 'two correlative values are in opposition as contraries'.

In order to carry out the logical transformation suggested by Karcevsky we have to set up the semantic or conceptual zone of the given category and divide it in the only logical way: into two contrary fields and an intermediate one, as follows:

Here the fields, + and − contract a contrary opposition; the field 0, whose semantic content has to be defined as 'neither + nor −', is opposed to both + and − taken together, constituting a contradictory opposition. Likewise, + and 0 taken together constitute a contradictory opposition in relation to −. The same holds true for − and 0 taken together, which constitute a contradictory opposition in relation to +. This is nothing but elementary logic, and yet it is useful to insist on it in order to show what is in fact behind Karcevsky's reasoning.

§ 24. We now only have to place the systems of two and three terms that are concretely observed in languages on this diagram, and we shall obtain the following graphic representation, which perfectly realizes Karcevsky's reasoning:

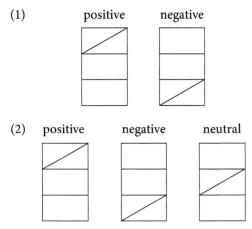

The positive and the negative terms each occupy one of the two contrary fields of the semantic zone assigned to the category, whereas the neutral term occupies the intermediate field.

§ 25. In order to provide some examples, it is sufficient to transpose the previously discussed systems in the light of Peshkovsky's ideas on to the logical system grafted on the above established schema. We do not know if Karcevsky would subscribe to all these applications; however, the principle still holds. We thus have the schemes (1) and (2) on p. 237 (cf. § 18).[20,21,22]

§ 26. It should be obvious that such a logical scheme will account only poorly for the real facts. Yet it provides something that was missing in Peshkovsky's model: the logical criterion behind systems consisting of three terms.

§ 27. Peshkovsky's and Karcevsky's theories have both proven to be useful: in fact, they complement each other. Peshkovsky's doctrine accounts at least approximately for the specific character of linguistic oppositions; however, since no logical basis is provided, it fails to describe systems consisting of more than two terms. Karcevsky, on the other hand, provides the logical basis, allowing us to explain three-term systems. However, since it fails to investigate how such systems are realized in language, his theory requires the real

---

[20] It should be remembered that the choice between the positive and the negative is arbitrary.

[21] Karcevskij defines the Russian nominative as "zero case" (op. cit., p. 18) and the Russian indicative as "zero mode" (p. 136). On the other hand, it is true that Karcevskij sometimes oscillates between the two definitions of "zero" and of "negative" (cf. for instance op. cit., p. 18 note, and p. 141, where the indicative is defined as "negative mode or zero mode"). This reveals the problems that arise when it is a question of moving the vague terms into a logical schema, a difficulty that increases when it comes to systems consisting of two or more vague terms. We do not know if it was such occasional oscillations on the part of Karcevskij that induced Jakobson to believe that he considered all oppositions to be binary (Charisteria Mathesio, p. 76)—an interpretation which is not compatible with Karcevskij's own description. There is, on the contrary, a profound and interesting difference between Peškovskij's and Karcevskij's view concealed in Jakobson's theory.

[22] The 3rd person is indeed defined by Karcevskij as "neither the one nor the other" (p. 132).

systems to be transformed into logical ones, underlying as it were, but also further removed from linguistic facts.

(1)

	positive	negative
case	genitive	nominative
comparison	comparative	positive
number	plural	singular
gender	feminine	masculine
person	2nd person	1st-3rd person
voice	passive	active
tense	preterite	present
mode	imperative-subjunctive	indicative

(2)

	positive	negative	neutral
number	plural	dual	singular
comparison	superlative	comparative	positive
person	1st	2nd	3rd
tense	perfect	imperfect	present
gender	feminine	masculine	neuter

§ 28. Neither of the two authors, however, has managed to motivate systems consisting of more than three terms: Peshkovsky does not discuss them; Karcevsky explicitly denies their existence. We shall examine this possibility in due course. Our investigation will show the necessity of acknowledging the existence of more complex systems that derive from a single subdivision—systems that can only be motivated by applying simultaneously both tools provided by Peshkovsky and Karcevsky. In order to give a true explanation of the linguistic facts we have to account for their specific nature without losing sight of a single moment of their possible illogical or alogical character; on the other hand, we should not leave it at that: we also have to find a logical landmark that will allow our thinking to register the facts. In our opinion, each of the two aforementioned theories thus contains its own relative grain of truth.

3c. Jakobson's hypothesis

§ 29. In his recent work on the structure of the Russian verb, Roman Jakobson[23] pursues the tradition represented by Peshkovsky, while (tacitly) opposing

---

[23] 'Zur Struktur des russischen Verbums', in *Charisteria Guilelmo Mathesio oblata*, Prague, 1932, pp. 74–84.

Karcevsky's doctrine.[24] Jakobson links Russian grammatical tradition to that part of the doctrine of the Prague Linguistic Circle which defines 'phonological' correlations by the opposition between a *marked* correlative series and an *unmarked* one.[25] There can be no doubt, on the other hand, that on this point the phonological theory of the Prague Linguistic Circle has the same origin as Peshkovsky's grammatical theory. In so far as these different hypotheses can be verified, one and the same principle will appear to govern both the phonematic and the morphological structure. It is a generalization and unification that constitutes the goal of Jakobson's important efforts inaugurated in this first 'tentative and innovative' outline of a structural grammar.[26]

§ 30. Jakobson deals exclusively with two-term systems, claiming that no more complex systems can result from a simple subdivision. Thus, if a category includes three terms, it must be explained as resulting from a double subdivision. Provided that this hypothesis cannot be verified without exceptions (which is almost certain in the first place), the tool provided by Jakobson will only be usable for two-term systems. Such a restriction resembles the one imposed by Peshkovsky, and indeed the two theories coincide on this point: Jakobson's model merely adds some clarification, which nevertheless will prove to be useful.

§ 31. The main clarification consists in the definition of 'unmarked', given by Jakobson, which reformulates Peshkovsky's 'zero' category (called 'vague term' in our provisional terminology). As noted above, it is not a matter of the logical opposition between *a* and *non-a*. According to Jakobson, the marked (precise) term signals the presence of a meaning *a*, whereas the unmarked (zero, vague) term *does not* indicate the presence of this meaning *a*: this term refrains from signalling whether *a* is present or not. To that Jakobson adds—and this seems to us very important—that this general definition of the unmarked term implies two more specific possibilities: 1) under certain circumstances, the unmarked term can be used to signal the *absence* of *a*;[27] 2) under different circumstances, it can be used to signal the *presence* of *a*, thanks to a rule of *replacement* (*Vertauschung*) according to which an unmarked term

---

[24] Cf. above, § 25, note 21.
[25] For these definitions, cf. Nikolay S. Trubetzkoy in *Travaux du Cercle linguistique de Prague* 4 (1931a), pp. 97 ff. and the *Project de terminologie phonologique standardisée* prepared by the Prague Linguistic Circle, ibid., pp. 313–314 [Prague Linguistic Circle 1931].
[26] Cf. op. cit., p. 74 note.
[27] Cf. op cit., p. 74.

can serve as a substitute for the marked term.[28] Thus, Russian feminine is marked, whereas the masculine is unmarked; Russian тёлка is feminine and means 'female calf', whereas телёнок is masculine and simply means 'calf'. Now, when телёнок is used, it may refer, according to circumstances, to a male calf (the meaning of *non-a*) or to a female calf (the meaning of *a*, admitted by the rule of substitution). It goes without saying that Jakobson's remark applies not just to Russian. The same holds true, for instance, for Latin *equos* and *equa*. It is indeed a general principle.

§ 32. This clarification allows us to go beyond the notion of 'zero' used by Peshkovsky. Let us try, on the basis of Jakobson's indications, and by employing Karcevsky's ideas to the extent possible, to move further forward and to be even more precise. According to Peshkovsky, the value of a 'zero-term' will be the very 'absence of meaning'. We were immediately able to realize that this is not exact, and that it is the absence of *precise* meaning that one has to say. Jakobson's remarks allow us to understand the nature of this lack of precision: it is a sort of whimsical hesitation between different meanings enclosed within the semantic zone assigned to the category in question. Let us take up our diagrammatical representation, and we shall have a closer look at what Jakobson is telling us: one term can be qualified as 'marked'; it occupies one field of the zone—let us say the field *a* in order to avoid the arbitrary choice between positive and negative imposed by Karcevsky's doctrine; there is another term, called 'unmarked', which, depending on the circumstances, can occupy any field of this zone: either the field *a*, by substitution (which will establish an occasional synonymy with the 'marked' term), or the contrary field *b*, by contrast, or even the field *c*, which comes in between the other two as the 'neutral' one of the zone. It should be obvious that more possibilities should be added: either *a* and *b* simultaneously, or *a* and *c*, or *b* and *c*, or *a* and *b* and *c*—the extreme case in which the whole zone is filled in an absolutely indecisive way, without any possible degree of precision. From a certain point of view this last possibility is the main one, because it encompasses all the others, and because that is the one that occurs in isolation, out of context (which of course does not mean that it cannot occur in particular contexts). It represents, so to speak, the 'lexical' value of the term.[29] So we have:

[28] Cf. op cit., p. 83.
[29] Cf. Jakobson, op. cit., p. 83.

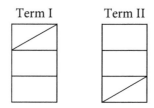

Theoretical variants of the term II

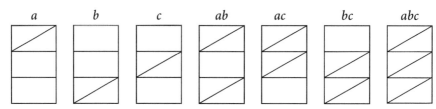

Term I (the 'precise', 'marked' term) will be called more exactly the *intensive* term (symbol: >), whereas term II (the 'zero', 'vague' or 'unmarked' term) will be called the *extensive* term (symbol: <). The extensive term has the capacity of extending its meaning on the whole zone; the intensive term, on the other hand, entrenches itself in a single field without crossing the boundaries.

§ 33. All this is still pure theory. It is the logical consequence to be drawn from Jakobson's suppositions. Yet it is highly probable that, *insofar as our second hypothesis (§ 18) turns out to be verifiable*, the facts will fit these diagrammatical configurations. Let us return to our provisional examples of two-term systems (§ 18) and let us at first note the inaccuracy of Peshkovsky's formulation according to which the idea of comparison or of degree would be missing in the positive, characterized by the absence of meaning. Definitely not. The positive has its own meaning, which is the general meaning of any degree of comparison. In order to be more precise, we should be able to specify the nature of the very notion of 'comparison', i.e. to define its semantic zone as a whole. But even without this precision it seems absurd to consider the positive as being outside of the category of comparison and devoid of content, stripped of signification. If Peshkovsky were to be taken literally, any two-term system would include a term without a proper meaning: the nominative, the singular, the masculine and so forth would all be devoid of content. However, what distinguishes all those forms from each other, what ensures the identity of each one of them and prevents us from confusing them, is the fact that they belong to a given category. The positive can be defined as a degree of comparison by the very fact of contracting a correlation with the comparative, it is likewise by correlation with the genitive, the plural, the feminine respectively that the nominative is defined as a case, the singular as a number, the masculine as a gender.[30] Thus, every one of these extensive terms possesses the particularity of carrying the meaning of the whole zone in a rather indecisive or 'vague' way, as we have just said, and as a consequence of admitting the meaning of any field of that zone, according to circumstances. Thus, to mention only some clear yet still provisional examples, the singular may indicate the idea contrary to that of the plural (field *b*), or it can indicate the same idea that is otherwise assigned to the plural (field *a*), or the intermediary field (field *c*) or any other combination of the fields. Likewise, the masculine is opposed to the feminine, or it can replace it, or even indicate the whole gender in a more or less vague way. The present tense, in its turn, may oppose the preterite, replace it, or it can more or less suspend the very indication of tense. All this does not prevent the singular from being a number (in the grammatical sense), the masculine from being a gender and the present from being a tense: rather, they are respectively a number, a gender, a tense *without specification*.

Such perspective seems to be more realistic and more practicable than Jakobson's: instead of marking them as marked and unmarked, one should say, 'intensive' and 'extensive'. The extensive term is not characterized by the absence of something, but rather by the capacity of occupying any part of the zone. This is what results directly from observation. Jakobson's 'mark' is merely an artifice introduced by the theoretician in order to explain something that can ultimately be described in a better or simpler way without it. The 'mark' is a superfluous invention and a useless complication. It suffices to transfer the facts on the register of the zone and to observe what happens.

§ 34. In order to outline how these systems behave according to Jakobson's theory, it is useful to summarize in a concise schema the full system established by Jakobson in order to explain the Russian verb. In our schema, which of course should not exempt the reader from referring to Jakobson's original contribution, the symbol ∶ (our sign for correlation) is interposed between the two terms of a correlative couple; the symbol ∷ means 'is subdivided into';

---

[30] {The manuscript reads 'plural as a number, feminine as a gender'.}

between the two terms of a correlative couple, the one that Jakobson qualifies as 'marked' is written in *italics* (and will everywhere assume the first place in the couple), and the one he considers the 'unmarked' term is in roman type. So we have:

I Aspect ('verbal classes'):
perfective : imperfective
imperfective :: *iterative* : non-iterative (only in the preterite)

II Voice ('genus'):
intransitive : active (in the broad sense)
intransitive :: *passive* : reflexive (only in the participle)

III 'Conjugation system'
syntagmatic forms : infinitive
syntagmatic forms :: *participle* : finite verb[31]
participle :: *predicative* : attributive[32]
      attributive :: case-correlates
participle[33] :: *neuter* : non-neuter
      non-neuter :: *feminine* : masculine
participle[31] :: *plural* : singular
finite verb :: *'mode of arbitrary action'*[34] : indicative
    indicative :: *preterite* : present
- *preterite* :: *neuter* : non-neuter (only in the singular)
- non-neuter :: *feminine* : masculine
- *preterite* :: *plural* : singular
- present :: *personal* : impersonal (= third person)
- *personal* :: *first person* : second person
- present :: *plural* : singular

§ 35. In this schema, we have left out some correlations that receive a special place in Jakobson's system, and which also from the start seem partly

---

[31] It is important to note that, according to Jakobson, the existence of a correlation *participle* : adjective should also be taken into account.

[32] This correlation only occurs in the passive participle. In the active participle, Jakobson identifies a different correlation: *gerundive* : attributive.

[33] Only attributive participle and passive predicative participle.

[34] *Modus der willkürlichen (willkürhaften) Handlung.*

contestable: they are some sub-correlations that occur within the *'mode of arbitrary action'*. In order to discuss them properly, we have to go into some detail with both Jakobson's presentation and Russian grammar. But these details will serve to throw light on certain principles.

[§ 36.] Jakobson calls *'mode of arbitrary action'*[35] that which is usually called *imperative*. Jakobson avoids using the traditional notion of *imperative*: he clearly does this in order to account for the multiple usages of the Russian imperative, in which the hortative value traditionally assigned to this mode is absent.[36] The Russian imperative can in fact be used in cases where other modern European languages require the indicative; in particular circumstances it may even replace the Russian indicative; it evidently encroaches on its domain.[37] These substitutions thus lead us to define the Russian imperative as the extensive term in opposition to the indicative. In fact, this is the option we would choose, not just for Russian but for all other languages whose modal category is structured in a similar way. To us it seems obvious that an imperative which counts among its usages the meanings of a hortative and of a descriptive imperative[38] must be defined as a form that occupies the opposite fields of the zone assigned to the category of mode, thus contracting a relation of participation with the indicative. We shall return to this. Jakobson does not follow this route; he defines the 'mode of arbitrary action' as the marked term of the modal correlation.[39] A reason for this may be that he, on the one hand follows Peshkovsky's tradition in which the indicative is the 'zero mode'; and on the other hand, Jakobson follows Bühler in basically distinguishing the representational language (*darstellende Sprache*) from its triggering function (*Auslösungsfunktion*). Such a distinction, however, pertains to *speech* and has no importance for the description of the linguistic

---

[35] In Karcevsky's formulation, who actually follows the traditional terminology by calling 'imperative' the form at issue (op. cit. p. 137–141, cf. mostly p. 139: 'From the particular feature of the relationships between the speaker and the interlocutor, to which the imperative form corresponds, a new value is formed: that of an act imposed on the interlocutor, thus more or less arbitrary from the point of view of the interlocutor').

[36] Incidentally, Karcevsky's formulation (cf. note 35) is not restricted to anything specific: it applies to the imperative of any language. This means that Jakobson's terminology seems to fit poorly with his own intentions.

[37] For examples, cf. Karcevsky, op. cit., p. 140; Jakobson, op. cit., p. 78; Holger Pedersen, *Russisk grammatik* (Copenhagen 1916, p. 161). Pedersen's examples are particularly instructive.

[38] Cf. Latin *ubi data occasiont, rape clepe tene* (Plaute, *Pseud*. 138); *cetera rape trahe fuge late* (plaute, Trin. 291). There is no difference of principle between these usages and those of Russian imperative.

[39] On p. 81, however, Peshkovsky speaks of an unmarked imperative. We have to admit we did not understand this point, which blatantly contradicts the rest of the essay.

system.[40] It will not conceal the fact that the Russian language possesses only one *form* for the hortative and for the descriptive imperative—a form that thus displays two variants. These variants may, if required, be distinguished in compliance with the functions identified by Bühler. Jakobson is, however, of the opinion that the hortative variant (for which he reserves the name 'true imperative' or simply 'imperative') is the only one that admits sub-correlations. If we are not mistaken, the renowned Russian linguist confuses on this point *language* and *speech*. The network of correlations that constitutes the grammatical system (in this case, the 'conjugation system', as Jakobson calls it) does not depend on stylistic variants: this would be a *contradictio in adiecto*. Only the form admits sub-correlations, even if these may be used only under specific stylistic conditions.

§ 37. According to Jakobson, the imperative admits only three sub-correlations:

1) the correlation between Russian forms of the type двинем 'let us move', пойдём 'let us go' (traditionally: first person plural of the imperative) (marked form) and those of the type двинъ 'move (you)', пойди 'go (you)' (traditionally: second person singular of the imperative). Nor does Jakobson acknowledge a difference of person or of number: he defines this correlation with the special term of *Mitbeteiligungskorrelation*. However, a clarification should be made. Jakobson observes correctly that the marked form always coincides with the first person plural of the indicative (двинем 'we move', пойдём 'we go'). He explains this by saying that the first person plural of the indicative replaces the corresponding marked form. Here it is not a matter of substitution, but of something else: a syncretism between indicative and imperative in the first person plural. The form in question does not replace anything since there is nothing to replace. It is here a matter of two variants of one and the same form: an imperative variant of the first person plural. Let us observe *en passant* that the existence of such a form, straddling the indicative and the imperative (hortative), discredits from a grammatical perspective the usefulness of Bühler's stylistic distinctions. Moreover, thanks to the correlations of person and number contracted by forms like двинем, пойдём, etc., Jakobson's so-called *Mitbeteiligungskorrelation* can be reduced to a complex correlation between the second person singular of the imperative, on one hand, and the first person plural of the indicative-imperative (syncretized), on the other.

---

[40] In fact, this distinction is reduced to what Karcevsky correctly remarks: 'The imperative, being the expression of actively volitional act of the speaker, belongs to affective language', 'the indicative is an objective and intellectual mode' (op. cit., p. 137, 141).

§ 38. 2) The correlation of number: plural (marked) ∶ singular (unmarked). In this case, the example двинъте 'move (you-plur.)' ∶ двинъ 'move (you-sing.)' can be accepted without any problem. However, one may wonder why Jakobson here classifies the opposition двинемте 'let us (you and me) move' ∶ двинем 'let us (me and him or me and you) move': in our opinion, this is not a difference of number but a difference between the inclusive and the exclusive person, a difference known in many languages in the first person plural; it is thus a difference of person and not of number.[41]

§ 39. 3) The correlation of 'intimacy': двинъ-ка (familiar form) ∶ двинъ.[42]

§ 40. Let us now return to the system set up by Jakobson. This system is only composed of correlative couples, or two-term correlations, whose structure is invariantly the same: each couple includes a marked term and an unmarked one. The relationship that gathers the correlations is no less simple: every correlation takes its fixed place in the system as superior and/or inferior in relation to other correlations. The system is thus conceived as a *hierarchy* in which each correlation and each correlative couple represents a specific level and in which each correlation (with the exception of the highest one) results from the subdivision of one of the two terms belonging to the correlation immediately above. It is a fact that the hierarchy has three entries, or rather three different hierarchies (the hierarchies of aspect, of voice—both including only two levels—and the broader hierarchy of 'the system of conjugation'). Every verbal form is thus defined by the place it occupies in these three hierarchies simultaneously. It is nonetheless true that this does not change the hierarchical principle behind the whole system (even if such a principle will have major consequences for the central part of the system, the 'conjugation system', where the hierarchy is the most complex).[43]

§ 41. Faced with such a hierarchical system, so simple and so uniform, one would first ask whether this system is not really subject to any other principle except for the two just mentioned: that of marked/unmarked and that of the upper and lower order. One would above all ask further whether there is not

---

[41] The fact, mentioned also by Jakobson, that the Russian desinence -те is not specific to imperative but that it can also be used in a relatively free way (cf. на́-те 'here (for you)', from the interjection на; по́лно-те 'enough', from по́лно, neuter predicative of по́лный 'full', and so forth) may lead one to question its inflectional nature. Another example of this free usage is provided by двинем-те, from двинем. In our opinion, however, Jakobson is right in considering this form inflectional: in nominal sentences, it belongs to the verb; in nominal sentences as well as in interjections, it is added to the predicate and can be considered as belonging to the zero-copula.

[42] The same considerations concerning -те also apply to -ка, cf. на́-ка, and so forth.

[43] No reasons are provided for the exclusion of aspect and voice from the system of conjugation. A reason might be that Jakobson conceives these forms as pertaining to derivation.

some rule that determines the relationship between these two principles. In fact, between the marked and the unmarked term, the one that lends itself to subdivision is sometimes the marked, sometimes the unmarked, sometimes both of them, and each one in its own way. It is hard to accept that the choice between the different possibilities would be completely random. Jakobson's theory has nothing to teach us concerning this question: on this point, it fails us. We are here facing a lacuna: we need a theory that is at the same time more solid and less mechanical. Moreover, it is impossible to think of a measure that enables us to fill this lacuna and to complete the theory. Ultimately one may wonder whether such a theory is sufficient to properly explain the facts.

§ 42. Another disadvantage of this model is that the same category occurs in different nodes of the schema. This jeopardizes the very idea of a hierarchy of correlations. Grammatical gender occurs both below the participle and the preterite; we also find it in the substantive. And wherever it occurs, the number of genders is three: this means that the double sub-correlation established by Jakobson (neuter : non-neuter and feminine : masculine) exhibits a specific solidarity between the two correlations it consists of. The grammatical number is located under the participle, the preterite and the present; this latter is found also in the substantive. It may be added that the correlation predicative : attributive, recognized in the participle in the 'conjugation system', is also found in the adjective, within inflection (provided that the distinction between conjugation and inflection is conceived the way Jakobson does). The same applies to the correlations of case, located under the attributive participle.

It thus seems inadequate to conceive of the grammatical system as a hierarchy where some correlations are subordinate to others. It is rather a question of a *network* of entangled correlations.

In order to grasp the extent of such entanglement, it seems appropriate to observe: that according to Jakobson, the correlation iterative : non-iterative occurs only in the preterite; that the correlation passive : reflexive is reserved for the participle; that it is only in the singular that the preterite (along with the predicative adjective) distinguishes gender. One might thus say that the preterite has the correlation iterative : non-iterative, and that the singular has the correlation of gender. But the idea of a hierarchy, of a stratification or of a one-way progression is untenable. The image of a network would agree better with the facts.

§ 43. A third disadvantage is that the system does not account for the reciprocal delimitation of categories: the system seems to form a single hierarchy of divisions and subdivisions. The category of person and that of gender thus include two layers that seem to be completely comparable to any other layer of the hierarchy: the 'personal' includes a sub-correlation first person ∶ second person, just as the present includes a sub-correlation personal ∶ impersonal, and as the indicative in its turn includes the sub-correlation preterite ∶ present. The non-neuter allows a sub-correlation feminine ∶ masculine, just like the participle and the preterite include a sub-correlation neuter ∶ non-neuter, and as the syntagmatic forms include the correlation participle ∶ finite verb. It seems to be a stratification that proceeds through uniform stages. This uniformity, however, seems to fit badly with the realities. Some of the forms considered belong to one and same paradigm, while others do not. The three grammatical persons thus constitute a separate category, since they belong to one and the same paradigm; the same is true for the preterite and the present, while there is an insuperable boundary between the category of person and that of tense. Likewise the three genders form a category which in its turn is clearly different from the category of tense. This is simply a pure truism, but it is a truism that seems to be undermined by Jakobson's theory. The various correlations established by Jakobson do not occur on the same level. There is an associative relation, and as a consequence a correlation, between the neuter and the feminine, between the neuter and the masculine, between the third person (the 'impersonal') and the first, between the third person and the second. These associative relations, these correlations are facts that must not be neglected by the theory. Jakobson's theory, dividing the categories according to the dichotomic principle, fails to give an adequate account of them: it blurs the boundaries that are clearly drawn in the object to be described.

§ 44. In our opinion, that which decides the number of members belonging to a category is the possible substitutions[44] of units occurring in a same place in the chain. Such a condition is satisfied by the three grammatical persons: the first person can replace the second, just as the second can replace the third in the same place of the given chain; this holds true for the masculine, which can replace the feminine, and the feminine, in turn, can replace the neuter.[45]

§ 45. This tight and specific relation which links together the terms of the same category as opposed to other categories, and which arranges them in a line where all the terms have, so to speak, the same rights. Such a relation

---

[44] [Nowadays we say *commutation(s)*.]
[45] Syncretisms and defective paradigms were on purpose provisionally left out of consideration.

is faithfully manifested by *syncretism*. Syncretism clearly constitutes a structural fact of the utmost importance. A structural theory which does not take syncretism into account would fit poorly with the realities that it set out to describe. It is not necessarily a matter of realized syncretism: syncretisms are undoubtedly only realized in well determined structural conditions that are still to be identified. It is rather a matter of *possible* syncretisms. We do not find that the Russian language, chosen by Jakobson as a sample to prove his theory, constitutes a suitable object for investigating syncretism. In order to identify laws of syncretism and to gather information that they may offer the theory, we either have to study a linguistic state in which syncretisms abound, or to adopt in the first place a comparative perspective, putting aside the idiosynchronic point of view where dangers are well-known and patent. It seems obvious that, as soon as syncretism is acknowledged as a fact, this will reveal the *equality of the terms* of a category. All else being equal, it seems that in a three-term system, in principle organized like one of three persons or of three genders in Russian, the possible syncretisms patently cross the demarcation line introduced by Jakobson's theory: in fact, in such a system syncretisms may occur *separately* between the third and the first person [cf. French (*il, je*) *parle*, as opposed to (*tu*) *parles*; German (*sie, wir*) *sprechen*, as opposed to (*ihr*) *sprecht*], and *separately* between neuter and masculine (cf. Latin *bonōrum* as opposed to *bonārum*; German *des* as opposed to *der*).[46]

These structural facts seem indisputably to demonstrate the *existence of categories consisting of three or more terms*.[47]

§ 46. What we have just said does not negate that a category with several terms under certain conditions can be analysed into smaller categories. This is quite probable for categories comprising a great number of terms. To see to what extent such an analysis is likely and even at times necessary it suffices to recall the case systems of Finnish, Hungarian and of many Caucasian languages, or the system of gender (nominal classes) of Bantu languages. There are even instances where such an analysis will clearly impose itself.

---

[46] Our argument would not be falsified even if the syncretism between the third and the second person and between the neuter and the feminine gender were non-existent. It is undeniable that the third person lends itself less readily to a syncretism with the second, and neuter less readily to a syncretism with feminine (cf. Latin *quae* as opposed to *quī*): this will be explained elsewhere. For the time being, suffice it to observe that such a syncretism may also occur, even if the conditions of their occurrence are specific and rare.

[47] More examples can be found in Jakobson's presentation: there is a triple correlation: adjective ⋮ participle ⋮ finite verb and another gerund ⋮ attributive participle ⋮ predicative participle (cf. above § 34).

§ 47. For such an analysis, two possibilities can be foreseen: an analysis by *dimensions* or an analysis by *subdivision*.

§ 48. The analysis by dimensions would consist in recognizing, within a given category, two or more sub-categories that intersect and inter-penetrate each other. The relationship between these categories would in principle be the same as the one that can be observed, for instance, between the cases and the numbers in Latin or in Russian:

	singular	plural
nominative		
accusative		
genitive		

Each sub-category would constitute a dimension of the upper category, and each member of the upper category would be decomposable into two entities, each one belonging to its respective dimension. For instance:

	c	d
a	1	3
b	2	4

where $1 = ac$; $2 = bc$; $3 = ad$; $4 = bd$.

§ 49. The analysis by *subdivision* consists in allocating the members of the upper category to two or more classes, of which at least one would include at least two members. For example:

	A	B
a	1	3
b	2	

where $1 = A^a$; $2 = A^b$; $3 = B$.

The operational difference between the two procedures consists in the fact that through the analysis *by dimensions*, two or more perfectly *coordinate* sub-categories are established *simultaneously*; whereas through the analysis *by subdivision*, two or more sub-categories are established *successively*, the second being *subordinated* to the first, the third to the second, and so forth (where applicable).

In a word: categories established through the analysis by dimensions form a *network*; categories established through the analysis by subdivision form a *hierarchy*.

§ 50. The reasons why a system of categories (and of sub-categories) has to be conceived as a *network* rather than as a *hierarchy* should be clear by now. Only the analysis by dimensions can account for the fact that members belonging to the same grammatical category are equals with respect to correlation, mutual substitution and syncretism, and that each member contracts the same independent and dependent relations as all the others. This is why, between these two possible kinds of analysis, our choice falls on the analysis by dimensions rather than on the analysis by subdivisions, which is chosen by Jakobson.

§ 51. As a final remark, let us explain a point of principle. The problem we are concerned with is not a *semantic* problem, but a *structural* one. This means that it cannot be settled by inductively ascending from single acts of *speech* to extract what they have in common. On the contrary, it is about describing the facts of *language*, by observing the *functions* directly. We now know which are the principal ones of these functions on one side, syncretism and substitution,[48] which are two complementary aspects of one phenomenon, that of correlation; on the other side, we have replacement, which reveals the membership of the terms of one category and which serves as a clue in establishing which term is intensive (marked) and which is extensive (unmarked). As long as the semantic facts are taken into account, they are considered as *values* and not as *meanings*. What we are aiming for is an *extensional* definition of each term, not an *intensional* one. It is the form, not the substance that counts.

§ 52. But one can suggest a different problem: one can aim at an intensional description of the meanings, attained by inductive observation of the speech acts. That is a perfectly legitimate problem. But it is a different problem.

These two questions lead to two different kinds of classification that do not necessarily coincide. They are complementary, and even if they are different, they do not contradict each other.

§ 53. This is how a logical classification of the Indo-European grammatical genders, based on intensional considerations can, in a natural and even necessary way, arrive at an analysis by subdivision where the inanimate gender is opposed to the animate gender, and where this last is subdivided into two subgenders: the feminine and the masculine. Such a classification of the genders may certainly be useful, yet it explicitly disregards the functional facts (syncretisms, substitution)—and this not by default, but by principle: it is based on different criteria and aims at different goals.[49]

---

[48] [Commutation.]

[49] Such a classification of genders has been common practice among Indo-Europeanists (A. Meillet, *Introduction à l'étude comparative des langues indoeuropéennes*, 5th edition, Paris 1922, pp. 156–157; *Linguistique historique et linguistique générale* I, Paris 1921, pp. 211–215). It is true that it is not based solely on facts of meaning, but also on facts belonging to the signifier: the inanimate gender differs from the animate gender by a difference in endings and in vocalism, and thus pertains to inflection, whereas the distinction between feminine and masculine pertains to the formation of themes. These arguments

§ 54. As for Jakobson, he is right to avoid referring to this particular theory, whose resemblance with his own system of Russian gender-forms is only superficial and external: in fact, they are worlds apart. Jakobson deals with the functional structure, not with the intensional analysis. Because we shall hardly be mistaken in assuming that the problem which the eminent Russian linguist poses himself is that of functional structure and by no means that of the intensional analysis. In our opinion it is even one of Jakobson's main merits to insist on the distinctly structural feature of substitution and to highlight the extensional connection between the terms of the paradigm.

§ 55. It is true, on the other hand, that throughout our argumentation we have been looking for a level of accuracy that has partially shifted the issue at stake and which in the end has led it to be formulated in a way that probably no longer corresponds completely to Jakobson's basic thoughts as they emerged from the study reviewed here. We are not absolutely certain that Jakobson will accept our conclusions. Is his point of view truly structural? Or are there behind some of his considerations, such as for example that of the imperative that was discussed above (§ 37), motives that stem rather from the problem of intension? Difficult to say. If we are right, Jakobson has committed himself in a truly commendable way to a new theoretical direction, but without drawing all the necessary conclusions from the chosen point of view. His theory seems to be inadequate and insufficient with regard to categories consisting of three or more terms. On the other hand, one should not forget that it is a first attempt down a road only just laid out.

B. Method of investigation

1. Domain of investigation

§ 56. We have provisionally limited our investigation to the domain of *inflectional morphemes*, by which we understand all morphemes without any feature typical of derivational elements.[50]

This delimitation of our object requires certain clarifications. The terms *morpheme* and *inflection* are at the current stage of research too poorly defined

---

seem to be too precarious: the signifier does not necessarily reflect the signified in an accurate way: the signified may change (both from the extensional and from the intensional point of view) without affecting the signifier, as the signifier may contain residues from a previous state of the signified. By relying on such arguments, the *synchronic* analysis of the primitive state of Indo-European may be jeopardized, since considerations concerning the hypothetical reconstruction of a previous state (pre-Indo-European) are introduced that are immaterial for the description of the mother-language conceived as a system of values.

[50] § 37.

to be adopted blankly as the basic notions in a solid theory. Before approaching this type of research, criteria should be provided that allow us to decide, in each particular case, whether a given element is a morpheme or not, and if so, whether its nature is inflectional or derivational. Since actual knowledge on this topic is insufficient, the research that we are about to undertake inevitably suffers from a deplorable uncertainty. The double issue of the nature of the morpheme and of inflection has not yet been settled; and the preparations for its solution are far from being accomplished.[51] Under these difficult circumstances, we are forced to take the following measures:

1. The field of investigation has to be reduced so that it only admits elements whose morphematic and inflectional nature seems a priori granted.
2. Before approaching the investigation we must look for approximative definitions in narrowing down the problem as much as possible, under the current conditions.
3. Even under this proviso, we must keep in mind and admit that our research is still *provisional*.

§ 57. Let us dwell on the second point. The operational provisional definitions that we wish to adopt are the following:[52]

Df 1* By grammateme we understand a minimal unit of the signified, with its own specific (explicit or implicit) expression in the signifier.

Df 2* By morpheme we understand a combining grammateme, and by semanteme a combined grammateme.

---

[51] For our part, we have submitted this problem to a careful investigation (cf. our remarks in *Principes de grammaire générale*, pp. 339–340), outlining a possible yet still provisional solution in a conference at the Copenhagen Society for Philology and History, on 9 April 1930. Our communication will be published elsewhere under the title *Mot et morpheme*. [Since 1930, we have reached results that to us seem more definitive and directly useful. However, it is impossible to approach this complex of problems in the present article. We hope to publish a completely revised version of that communication in a future volume of the *Travaux du Cercle linguistique de Copenhagen*.

Let us add that the implications to be drawn from these central issues about the structure of correlations allow for generalizations which have turned out to be by far less serious than we might have suspected back in 1931: in the following (?*) we shall see that our results concerning the structure of correlations allow for generalizations that by far exceed the domain of morphological inflection. This diminishes the importance of the observations to be given in § 57 ff. However, we have found it useful to retain this part of our previous work in order to justify our original choice of the field of investigation].

* {The references of this note and of the following one probably concern the sections II and III envisaged by the author.}

[52] [The numbering of the definitions given here and taken up later was added in 1943. The asterisk indicates the provisional nature of the definitions; this way we aim at avoiding a confusion with the definitions that we currently put forward as definitive (cf. further herein (?*); in the present paper there are not any definitive definitions replacing Df* 1–3).]

Df 3* We wish to define an inflectional category as a category whose nature is at the same time associative and syntagmatic, opposed for this very reason to the derivational categories and to the categories of semantemes, which only pertain to the associative order.

In the following, we will introduce some necessary and sufficient remarks to justify these definitions.

§ 58. *ad Df 1**: The grammatical analysis permits us to dissolve the spoken chain into minimal units, among which two species can be distinguished: the *semantemes* and the *morphemes*, according to the terminology adopted by Joseph Vendryès.[53]

Based on such an analysis we propose to make it clearer in two respects:

1. The term *grammateme*[54] is hereby introduced as a common denomination for both the semanteme and the morpheme.
2. We wish to reserve the terms *grammateme*,[55] *semanteme* and *morpheme* for units that belong to the signified. As for the units corresponding to the signifier, also called the *phonation* of grammatemes, the standard vocabulary already contains a sufficient number of unambiguous terms (*theme, root, stem; affix, formative* or *formant*,[56] further divided into *suffix, ending, prefix, infix*). The advantage of adjusting the terms suggested by Vendryès in this restricted and precise sense lies above all in that this terminology allows one to make a clear distinction between the signified and the signifier. For instance, the suggested terminology permits us to say that in English the formant (the ending) *-s* expresses alternatively three morphemes: the 'plural', the 'genitive' and the 'third person', and that the morpheme of 'plural' is expressed alternatively by different formants, such as *-s, -en,* etc This is how we would like to account

---

[53] Cf. *Le langage*, Paris 1921, p. 86.
[54] Since 1881, Jan A. Baudouin de Courtenay has introduced the term *morpheme* to designate any minimal unit provided with meaning (cf. *Versuch einer Theorie phonetischer Alternationen*, 1895, p. 6 ff, 10), by distinguishing between *semasiological morphemes* (namely what Vendryès calls *sémantèmes*) and *morphological morphemes* (or *wortbildende Morpheme*, called *morphèmes* by Vendryès). Cf. for instance Введение в языковедение, 4th ed., 1912, p. 12, and *Versuch*, p. 52). In this broader sense, the term *morpheme* has been used by many of his pupils (cf., for instance, Yevgeny D. Polivanov, who distinguishes between 'lexical or material morphemes' and 'formal morphemes' or 'formants', Введение в языковедение (Leningrad), 1928, pp. 6, 24). For our part, we do not follow this tradition. Vendryès' terminology has become international. [Cf. for instance Louis H. Gray's recent work, *Foundations of Language* (New York), 1939, pp. 150, 157. Leonard Bloomfield's terminology (*Language* (New York), 1933) is different: he distinguishes between *morphemes* or *lexical units* and *tagmemes* or *grammatical units* (what we call 'morphematic units' in our terminology); as can be seen the terms are, in this case, almost reversed.]
[55] Cf. our *Études baltiques*, Copenhagen, 1932, p. xj (statement by A. Sommerfelt).
[56] K. Brugmann, *Grundriss* II, 1, p. 8 ff. E. D. Polivanov, *loc. cit.*

for the facts observed by Otto Jespersen,[57] without resorting to his terminological distinction between *form* and *function*, which we find less clear and less useful.[58] The proposed terminology will likewise permit us, for instance, to distinctly identify three morphemes within the formant *-us* of the adjective in Latin constructions such as *bon-us dominus*, namely: 'masculine', 'nominative' and 'singular'. This is the only way to avoid overestimating the difference between the agglutinative type and the inflectional type (in the narrow sense), which is reduced to a difference in the signifier, and which bears no importance for the analysis of the signified. This way, we are able to work around a problem which has occurred ever so often in the domain of grammar: from the point of view of the analysis of the signified, the grammatical categories remain equally distinct in the inflectional type and in the agglutinative type; it is only from the point of view of the signifier that they can be confused.[59]

We are in great need of a terminology which will allow us to maintain these distinctions rigorously. *Our research is concerned with the signified, not the signifier.*

§ 59. Besides, there is hardly any need to insist on the necessity of taking into account the differences observed in the signifier in establishing the units of the signified. Without this precaution one will not take into consideration the differences between languages nor the proper linguistic facts.[60] In this respect, let us point out that without reducing the importance of this principle, the relations between signified and signifier can be of different kinds: a single unit of the signifier may correspond to a single unit of the signified (univocity); two or more units of the signifier can correspond to a single unit of the signified (synonymy); a single unit of the signifier can correspond to two or more units of the signified (homonymy); the expression of the signifier of a unit of the signified can be zero;[61] a unit of the signified can be expressed by the mere order of the units of the signifier.[62]

---

[57] *The Philosophy of Grammar*, p. 46.
[58] Cf. our *Principes de grammaire générale*, pp. 112 ff. [On the terminological issues here at stake, cf. *Acta Linguistica*, II, pp. 63 ff.].
[59] [This advantage of the analysis will stand out even more clearly if we consider that the commutation test is valid for both the content (signified) and the expression (signifier).]
[60] Cf. *Principes de grammaire générale*, p. 89. [Likewise, the differences observed in the signified must be taken into consideration in establishing the units of the signifier. In both cases, it is a matter of the commutation test carried out respectively on the content (signified) and on the expression (signifier). In 1931 we had not yet made this discovery, which is crucial for an understanding of the semiological mechanism of language.]
[61] Cf. F. de Saussure, *Cours*, 2nd ed., p. 123 ff., 163, 254 ff.
[62] Cf. *Principes de grammaire générale*, p. 125, references included.

§ 60. The discovery of the *grammateme*, which led to the abandonment of the *word* as basis of grammatical analysis, constitutes a decisive progress in modern grammar. This methodological change has created a number of advantages. Let us highlight just one that is of particular importance for our research: the phenomenon of suppletion (for instance: *je vais, j'irai, j'allais*) no longer poses a problem for grammatical analysis: it is obvious that it is a question of a peculiarity of the signifier which is of no importance for the analysis of the signified; all evidence points to it being one and same semanteme expressed by different themes (by different roots) depending on the circumstances; it is a simple case of synonymy, comparable to the synonymy existing between the different endings which express the 'plural' morpheme of English.

§ 61. *ad Df 2**. The second definition seems to be nothing but the logical consequence of the fact that the morphemes indicate the relations between semantemes.[63]

§ 62. However, this approximate definition does not allow for a decision to be reached in all the cases observed. Cases of transition are still numerous. In our opinion, the reason for this uncertainty is to be found in the fact that *what separates semantemes and morphemes is not a difference of meaning but a difference of function*. There are not only semantemes and morphemes, but there are also elements that can play the double role of semantemes and morphemes. There are in fact semantemes that correspond to the semantic zone assigned to each inflectional category, in the same language or another. The category of prepositions covers the same semantic zone as the category of case—which explains many genetic transfers between the two categories. It is this particular feature that makes the distinction between preposition and case-morpheme precarious in some circumstances (cf. for instance the French *de, à*; English *of*). Likewise, personal pronouns often seem to include semantemes that can be identified with elements that elsewhere play the role of morphemes of gender or of morphemes of person. Auxiliary verbs seem—by the semantemes that they include—to represent morphemes of mood, time, aspect and voice to the extent that *periphrases* can be confused with the inflectional category.

Such examples can easily be multiplied. Given that the actual state of our knowledge on this matter does not allow us to define the functional difference between semanteme and morpheme more precisely than we have done, if we assume our first principle (§ 56) the number of usable examples will shrink considerably. Despite this drawback, however, the stock of examples at our disposal is enough to allow for a provisional conclusion.

---

[63] Cf. Vendryès, loc. cit.

§ 63. *ad Df 3**. The difference between *inflection* and *derivation* is as evident as the one between semanteme and morpheme. And yet, at the actual stage of our knowledge, both are defined quite vaguely.

In our opinion, the difference between inflection and derivation should be looked for in the opposition between *syntagmatic relations* and *associative relations*.[64]

§ 64. Two kinds of syntagmatic relations can be distinguished: those that pertain to *speech* and those that pertain to *language*; the characteristic feature of the first kind, as opposed to that of the second, is freedom of combination.[65] In *language*, the syntagma represents a fixed unit, a part of which necessarily requires for the other. The most typical type of this kind is called *rection*.

§ 65. From the point of view of *language*, we deal with purely associative relations when it is a question of terms among which the speaker has free choice, and when the choice of a unit within a given chain is only conditioned by what the speaker wants to express. On the other hand, we are faced with a syntagmatic relation from *language* whenever the choice of term in a given chain is determined not by what one wants to say, but by mechanical facts of *rection*.

§ 66. On the basis of these definitions, it may be observed that a syntagmatic relation of *language* is quite rare; it occurs easily in combination with an associative relation, a choice that is at the same time free and limited to certain possibilities. Thus, it quite often happens that a preposition or a verb governs not just a single case, as in exclusion of all the others, but two or more cases, among which the speaker may choose freely according to what he wishes to say. Moreover, even if only one rection is required by the normative grammar, some violations of the law may occur; we are way too often prone to consider such irregularities as belonging to *speech*. That is too easy a solution. In order to avoid stating too lightly that it just is a matter of mere incidental improvisations, it is sufficient to note that what we call improvisations does have certain limitations: despite relative freedom, free choice is conditioned by rules. The norm always admits a relatively broad *latitude*: this is far from saying that the norm does not exist.[66]

§ 67. According to this principle, a sound method demands a prudent approach, that is: *to generalize the domain of associative relations as far as possible*.

---

[64] The distinction between *syntagmatic* and *associative* relations dates back to F. de Saussure: *Cours*, 2nd ed., pp. 170 ff. [For theoretical reasons, the term *associative* is here replaced with *paradigmatic*, cf. *Actes du IVe Congrès International de Linguistes*, p. 140, n. 3. No need to insist on the fact that our terminology, which we simply borrowed from Saussurean tradition, does not entail any psychologism.]

[65] Cf. F. de Saussure, *Cours*, 2nd ed., p. 172.

[66] [Cf. now *Cahiers Ferdinand de Saussure*, 2, 1942, pp. 42 ff.]

§ 68. Our third definition is based on such an idea. The choice of an inflectional morpheme is ordinarily conditioned by rection as well as by what the speaker intends to express. Wherever a category occurs that has an undeniable inflectional nature, there is rection[67] motivated by the semantic kinship between the governing term and the inflectional morpheme of the governed term; at the same time, the inflectional morpheme includes a meaning of its own, which is independent of the rection involved.

§ 69. Yet, our third definition is not less provisional than the second one. Here again, it seems that there is a semantic affinity, and even of a possible semantic identity between a derivational morpheme and an inflectional morpheme. What has been said about the difference between semanteme and morpheme applies also to the difference between inflection and derivation: *what separates them is not a difference of meaning, but of function.* There are elements that can play the double role of derivational morphemes and inflectional morphemes. In fact, for the semantic zone of every inflectional category one should in principle anticipate corresponding derivational morphemes, either in the same language or in another. Such a possible transition between the genitive and an adjective is possible and often observed, and also between certain cases and certain genders (mainly the neuter) on the one side and the adverb on the other. Here again, these difficulties demand a careful approach. As a consequence, our field of investigation has become even narrower, and our results even more provisional.

2. Questions to ask

§ 70. We have delimited our object. It emerges that in our material we have included only systems that unambiguously match our definitions. What remains is to clarify what questions we have asked of these materials in order to solve the general problem that occupies us. The previous discussion of our hypothesis has already shown to a certain extent what those questions are, and we just have to summarize them in a more systematic way.

§ 71. The main question, whose solution coincides with the result in each particular case, concerns the structure of a given system or the *configuration* contracted by the terms of that system. For each particular system considered, we will present the result of our research by the letter C (*configuration*).

---

[67] The role of rection has largely been overlooked by traditional grammar: rection is a decisive factor for all inflectional morphemes. Cf., in this regard, *Principes de grammaire générale*, pp. 153 ff.

§ 72. Such results can be attained by examining three orders of facts that represent just as many different questions whose solution is a necessary presupposition for our main question, namely:

§ 73. 1a. (*Ext*) the question of the *extensional* relationship contracted by the members of a system. The conclusions we have succeeded in drawing from our discussions about M. Peshkovsky's and Jakobson's hypotheses have already shown that replacements constitute a particularly valuable landmark in this respect: they are the facts that allow us to decide which terms are intensive (>) and which extensive (<). By presenting the results of our investigation we shall be able to recognize this basic feature and draw the ultimate consequences from it once more.

This very question can take on a quite different appearance if we—instead of insisting on the mutual relationship between the members—limit ourselves and study the possible variants of a given member (cf. above, § 32). Thus, we may also have:

1b. (*V*) that is the question of the realized *variants* of each term included in the system. This is a corollary of question *Ext*.

§ 74. 2. (*S*) The question of the *syncretisms* that are mutually contracted by the members of the system. It seems appropriate to postulate that a syncretism depends on the structural relationships between the terms.

§ 75. 3. (*D*) That is the question of the *dominance* exerted by certain members of the system determining syncretisms observed in other systems (for instance, in German and Latin the neuter gender dominates the syncretism nominative ~ accusative). It seems plausible a priori that dominance may also be functioning from the place occupied by the dominant term in the system.

§ 76. Besides these phenomena, we have also investigated that of *defectivation*: we assume that the relative place occupied by the different members within the system may determine, or concur in determining, the ways in which the reduction by defectivation of a given system may occur. It appears quickly, however, that the question is more complicated than one suspects a priori. That is why our results on this topic will not be included in the exposition of our investigations on this particular case. They will be found in a separate paragraph added at the end of our contribution.

§ 77. In fact, we believe that with the questions listed above we have exhausted the facts that may contribute to the solution of the general problem of the structure of morphematic systems. It would probably be appropriate to explicitly remark that we have not included the facts of *rection* in our investigation.

A first, quick glance has convinced us that, in regard to rection, no difference of principle separates the members of a system, and that the faculty of governing or being governed is not restricted to any particular place in the system as opposed to any other place.[68] It is true that this first impression is not necessarily correct; that is the question that is to be taken up again.

§ 78. It is thus primarily questions *Ext., S.* and *D.* that are presupposed by question *C.*

These questions presuppose, in turn, the question concerning the *inventory* of the morphemes that belong to a given category (here abbreviated *Inv.*). Experience shows that there may be difficulties in establishing exactly how many morphemes are included in a category. There are several reasons for this difficulty: the most evident one is the insufficiency of current grammar, which never conscientiously asks this question that is so vital for any research on the structure of systems. Furthermore, the solution to this problem depends on a clear distinction between morpheme and semanteme, as well as between inflection and derivation. Since we still lack the means to draw such distinctions in a proper way, the question concerning the *inventory* (or the *size*) of the system is always a delicate one, even more so as it is the most crucial one, representing the necessary starting point of any further research.

As a consequence, we have studied this question everywhere and with utmost care; we have tried to exhaust all the possibilities for each specific category and to include in it all the elements that appeared to belong to it. In addition, we have excluded from our investigation all cases that in this respect seem ambiguous. This feature contributes to narrowing down the domain of our investigation and to making our investigation rather tentative. On the other hand, we hope that the research that we have here undertaken and some other investigations that we anticipate, will serve to clear the way for a more definitive presentation concerning the methods to be employed in order to determine the inventory of a system. Time has not yet come for such a development. General grammar is a science still at its very beginning. We do believe, however, that we are carrying out a useful task in opening a trail in this unknown land.

§ 79. One may wonder whether the three aforementioned central questions also presuppose other questions, rather than the one concerning the inventory (or the size) of the system. In this connection, one should ask above all what is the position of the question concerning the *intensional definition*

---

[68] Let us note that rection is a fact more widespread than traditional grammar seems to show; cf. above, § 68, note 67.

of the semantic zone of each of the morphematic categories (we indicate this question with the abbreviation, *Int.*). Is this a question to be settled before one can approach the question *Ext.*? From a theoretical point of view, we do not hesitate to answer it negatively: extensional facts (such as the facts of substitution) can be investigated without first having touched upon the question of meaning. On the other hand, we do not think that the investigation of meaning can be carried out without previous knowledge of forms and functions. A meaning is always and necessarily a meaning of something, and the investigation of meanings presupposes the knowledge of the carrier of such meanings. Thus, from a theoretical point of view, it is the question *Int.* that presupposes the question *Ext.* and not vice versa. From a practical point of view, however, we believe that it is useful to take into account both of the questions simultaneously: the investigation requires to a certain extent that we consider them together, and the presentation of the results of the investigation will moreover win in clarity and insight, and it will be more accessible if the structural facts are projected on to a semantic matter. This way we do not seek to avoid the *Int.* question, even if it is decidedly peripheral; it will only be briefly touched upon, and the semantic interpretations given here will not be either discussed or further motivated. That is a task that will be taken up elsewhere.[69]

3. Procedure

§ 80. Our presentation reproduces the path of our investigation. This was naturally begun with a first survey of some specimens of systems, carefully chosen among those that to us seemed both the simplest and the clearest. This first survey has allowed us to draw certain hypothetical conclusions among which we have subsequently sought a generalization by attempting to verify them on more and more different flectional systems in different languages and suggesting—in reference to the basic problems that were mentioned above and which are still pending—the apparently indisputably identical nature as that of the systems that served as our starting point.

By presenting the results of this investigation, we thought it would be useful to avoid discussing in detail that which is not directly relevant for the principles of our investigation. What is important to establish at first is a survey in which one can easily orient oneself, a quick summary of the analysed material and the results which we have reached through this analysis. We thus leave

---

[69] [We have briefly and provisionally outlined these issues in a communication given at the Fourth International Congress of Linguists, cf. the *Actes*, pp. 140 ff., mostly pp. 148–149. Cf. remarks by Paul Diderichsen. We reserve the right to come back to these issues in a more detailed way in the near future.]

aside problems of details that have kept us busy during the investigation, and that should be treated in a less general treatise.

We have laid out our exposition as schematically as possible in order to meet such ends.

§ 81. For research as well as for the presentation of it, two procedures can be chosen: the classification principle can be chosen either for the *categories* (by investigating each inflectional category separately, for instance that of case, that of number, and so forth, across all languages under analysis, and by registering, for each one of them, all possible structures) or for the *size* (by investigating first those categories that consist of two members, subsequently those consisting of three members and so forth, taking samples of each size from all categories of all languages considered).[70] In our investigation, these two principles have served us alternately. For our presentation, we have chosen the last one, going from the simpler sizes to the more complex ones.[71] Several considerations have led us to this result. One of these considerations has been purely practical: we have undertaken a detailed investigation of the category of case, the results of which exceed the scope of the present work and which will be the object of a separate publication.[72]

That is also why no examples taken from the category of case will be found among the examples in this presentation.

§ 82. In agreement with what has been said above, for each size we will give, *at first*, the results from our *first* survey, in which it will be possible to grasp our principles and hypotheses along with some examples, and *secondly* a series of briefer *applications* which will serve as a basis for verification.

§ 83. It is obvious that for each example that we have examined, the object is always *the category studied in a given linguistic state*. In this respect, it is useful to give some clarifications about the delimitation of the *categories* and the *linguistic states*:

---

[70] To choose the principle of classification from within the *languages* (studying each single language separately) would be a less recommendable procedure when it is a question of establishing general facts on the basis of a comparative investigation. That would mean to separate facts that should be brought together.

[71] Besides, we consider it futile to include examples with more complex sizes, as they would require very detailed explanations which would in turn blur the results of our investigations. Cf. the following note.

[72] Our investigations on grammatical case have been presented as a special communication at the meeting of the Linguistic Circle of Copenhagen, on 18 May 1933, which followed the present communication. In fact, grammatical case represents the inflectional categories that offer a large number of examples of great complexity. Some of them were studied in detail in this special communication. [Cf. our work *La catégorie des cas*, 2 vol., in *Acta Jutlandica* VII, 1 (1935) and IX, 2 (1937).]

§ 84. 1. *Categories*. We have already pointed out[73] which kind of linguistic categories are relevant for our investigation. It seems clear that, in order to carry out this investigation in a proper scientific way, one should be able beforehand to define each of these categories in opposition to the others. Thus, one should be able to define the category of case, voice, person, gender, number, tense, mode, and others, such as the degrees of comparison, aspect and the article, to the degree that the general inflectional morpheme suggests that it be placed here.

From a practical point of view, it is simpler to deal with this question than the others mentioned above—whose solution is still pending. Faced with an element the inflectional character of which seems undisputed, one usually knows without any problem in which of the categories to place it.

However, definitions must be provided in order to prove that the chosen method is correct, and that the confidence with which we handle these questions does not merely stem from some habits inherited from an ill-founded tradition. Moreover, some borderline cases can be found that do not allow a univocal solution. We have not been able to completely avoid these borderline cases. Here again, we must limit ourselves to acknowledging the tentative character of our results.

Let us insist on the fact that, from our perspective, the question just mentioned is quite separate from the one concerning the *semantic* definition of linguistic categories (cf. *Int.*). The issue at stake here is not semantic but *functional*. Since experience shows that different functions may occupy the same semantic zone,[74] it follows that the functional (structural) definition of categories is in principle independent from their semantic content (value and meaning). On the other side it is true that this assessment only worsens our situation: while the semantic definition of at least some categories has been the object of scholarly discussions for centuries, the functional definition has hardly been considered in the classical theory. The problem that we have just pointed out has, as far as we know, been too poorly studied to allow even a conjectural and quite approximate solution.[75]

§ 85. 2. *The state of languages*: The states of languages are of different kinds (ancient and modern, common and regional, stylistically neutral or not, and so forth); all kinds of states are of equally relevant interest for our investigation. Let us make clear once and for all that, unless otherwise noted, the name

---

[73] Cf. above § 7.
[74] Cf. above § 62.
[75] [We have sketched a solution to this issue in *Actes du IVe Congrès International de Linguistes*, pp. 140–151] (*Essais linguistiques*, pp. 161–173).

of a language (such as 'French', 'German' and so forth) indicates the *common language* in its *modern state*. Generally speaking, *every one of our analyses is valid for the linguistic material described or included in the sources mentioned*; concerning the state of languages which are cited without an indication of sources our analysis is claimed to be valid for the material shown in current and commonly known treatises. These remarks are not just practical; they serve to express a principle: it is an overly widespread illusion that we can describe a language state in its entirety and in an absolute form; we describe only *what has been observed*, and shortcut generalizations—a clear inheritance from normative grammar—are not only dangerous, but clearly unjustifiable. Any statement concerning a 'language' or a 'linguistic state' only applies to the portion of a language and of a linguistic state that is included in the observer's perspective. A scholar is responsible for his deeds, and a sound method always requires an accurate circumscription of the object studied. This object is never a language in its totality.

§ 86. For every category studied in a given linguistic state, the aforementioned questions[76] will be discussed in the following order: *Int., Inv., Ext., S., D., C., V.*

It is for the sake of simplicity that the question *V.* is placed at the end as an explanatory support to the solution proposed to question *C*. The response to question *V* is already anticipated by the one given to question *Ext*.

The seven questions will not all be handled in all our examples. In order to avoid repetition, we shall explicitly discuss those questions that require an essential comment and the solution to which has not been implicitly given in the discussion of the other questions asked.

C. Facts

Systems with two terms
First survey
First series of observations
(1) Comparison in French

Int.—We suggest defining the semantic zone assigned to the category of comparison by the concept of *intensity*: the 'degrees of comparison' will be conceived as degrees of intensity. By relying on the conclusions we have drawn

---

[76] Cf. here 1.B2, § 70–79.

from Karcevsky's hypothesis (cf. § 23), the semantic zone can be represented as a unit consisting of three fields:

positive case (+):	strong intesity
negative case (−):	weak intensity
neutral case (0):	medium intensity, i.e. neither (clearly) strong nor (clearly) weak

We already know (cf. § 22) that qualifying the strong intensity as positive and the weak intensity as negative is a purely arbitrary choice: +, − and 0 are merely symbols that signal the relative logical position of a field; these symbols assert nothing absolute, and each one of them has no value if taken in isolation.

Inv.—In French the system of comparison comprises two terms: the *comparative-superlative* (*meilleur, pire, moindre; mieux, pis, moins, plus*) and the *positive* (*bon, mauvais, petit; bien, mal, peu, beaucoup*). The comparative-superlative is thus named because in languages that distinguish between comparative and superlative, it is given sometimes by the comparative and sometimes by the superlative; in French, the difference between these two possible degrees is often, but not necessarily, expressed by a difference of articles (defined article in opposition to zero-article), but never as a difference inherent to the category of comparison. We consider the form in *-issime* (cf. *rar-issime*) a derivate, not an inflectional element. We do not take periphrases such as *plus grand* into account since they are not inflectional. We can thus note that in French there is thus only a restricted number of themes that admit comparison: with regard to comparison, most adjectives are immovable (indeclinable).

Ext.—The comparative-superlative only indicates strong intensity (+). The positive indicates any degree of intensity (+, 0, −). Thus we have:

$$\begin{array}{ll} \text{comparative-superlative} & > \\ \text{positive} & < \end{array} \quad \text{(cf. § 73)}$$

Strong intensity, expressed by the comparative-superlative, can be absolute (*mes meilleurs souhaits*) or relative (cf. *ce livre est meilleur que l'autre; ce livre est le meilleur de tous*). On the other hand, it is characteristic of the French system that the comparative-superlative does not willingly lend itself to expressing the relative, strong intensity in cases where absolute intensity is not also conceived as strong. Of two things considered big—i.e. involving the quality of being little in a weak degree (tending to or reaching zero)—one can only with difficulty in using the French system indicate one as '*plus petite*' than the other: one must say '*moins grande*'. Through this feature, the French system is in clear opposition to the German system, cf. for instance: *Copenhague est moins grand que Paris—Kopenhagen ist kleiner als Paris*). Likewise, there can be cases in which German *schöner* is rendered in French with *moins laid*, and so forth. This principle, easily observed in the case of the comparative-superlative *plus* that belongs to the comparative periphrases, can be found (if necessary) in all the other comparative-superlative forms, so that in speaking of the moral qualities of two absolute rascals, nobody would ever say that one is *meilleur* than the other; the system invites one to say that one is *moins méchant, moins voleur* than the other. This is a very specific feature of the linguistic structure of French.

The intensity given by the positive may be of any kind since it may vary according to circumstances. This holds true for both the absolute and the relative intensity. By assigning a quality to an entity, nothing is implied about the intensity with which the entity possesses this quality. That is why the positive, unlike the comparative-superlative, allows any variation of degree: *très bon, peu bon, plus bon, moins bon* and so forth. According to circumstances, it may be a matter of strong, intermediate or weak intensity. The situation is different in the case of the comparative-superlative: the nuances of degree admitted by this form are all situated within the area of strong intensity: constructions like *beaucoup meilleur, (un) peu meilleur* only indicate different sections of the positive field, i.e. respectively the furthest and the closest to the neutral field; by definition, the comparative-superlative never crosses the limits of the field indicating strong intensity, and even (*un*) *peu meilleur* indicates a relative strong intensity.

S.—Syncretisms are non-existent.
D.—Dominances are non-existent.
C.—In going back to the scheme established above (§ 32) we see that the intensive term (here: the comparative-superlative) occupies only one field of the semantic zone, namely the field that by virtue of this very fact will be labelled as intensive and receive the denomination of *a*; conversely, the extensive term (here: the positive) has the capacity of occupying indifferently all three fields. The intensive term will be designated by α, while the extensive term by A; and since in the given example the intensive field coincides with the positive field, we can represent the system of French comparison with the following formula:

          + α comparative-superlative
          A positive

V.—The term A admits all the variants that are theoretically possible (§ 32). It would be pointless to give examples of this.

8
Émile Benveniste on the relation between linguistic and social structures
'Let us then consider that language interprets society'

Chloé Laplantine

8.1 Introduction

Émile Benveniste (1902–76) devoted most of his work to questions in Indo-European linguistics, and particularly to the study of Iranian languages. Among his contributions to this field are such books as *Origines de la formation des noms en indo-européen* (1935), *Noms d'agent et noms d'action en indo-européen* (1948), and *Le vocabulaire des institutions indo-européennes* (1969). Alongside this work—and inseparably from it—Benveniste reflected critically on general linguistics, on the notions and methods, the history and the future of the discipline and its relations to other disciplines.

Benveniste was a student of Antoine Meillet (1866–1936) and like Meillet his ideas about general linguistics were largely influenced by Ferdinand de Saussure (1857–1913). Benveniste is often considered a representative of European linguistic structuralism, but his theory of language can be seen as quite distinct from the considerations of other scholars identified with this intellectual trend. He developed a theory of *discourse* as an activity in which subjects constitute themselves in and through language (Benveniste 1966 [1958]: 259; English trans. 1971: 224) and, through their utterances, produce reality anew (Benveniste 1966 [1963]: 25; English trans. 1971: 22). Because Benveniste conceived of language as both a subjective invention of the individual speaker and a product of objective reality, he had an enduring interest in the diversity of experiences expressed in various languages as well as an interest in poetic language (see Laplantine 2011).

Chloé Laplantine, *Émile Benveniste on the relation between linguistic and social structures*. In: *The Limits of Structuralism*. Edited by James McElvenny, Oxford University Press. © Chloé Laplantine (2023).
DOI: 10.1093/oso/9780192849045.003.0008

In spite of these views which might appear to run counter to basic principles of structuralism, in particular to the objective and descriptive approach which often characterizes the works we label 'structuralist', Benveniste (1966 [1962]: 91–98, 1974 [1968a]: 11–28) saw his work as contributing to the structuralist intellectual movement. Nevertheless, here and there, explicitly or implicitly, Benveniste frequently puts forward views at variance with other formulations of structuralist doctrine. This is notably the case in his 'Structure de la langue et structure de la société' ('Structure of language and structure of society'), a paper he read at the conference 'Linguaggi nella società e nella tecnica' ('Languages in society and in technology') held in Milan, in 1968.[1] This paper, presented here, discusses whether and how 'structures' in such different domains may be compared and what relations may obtain between them.

8.2 Claude Lévi-Strauss: comparability of kinship systems and linguistic structures

In a letter which he sent to Roman Jakobson (1896–1982) in July 1948, Claude Lévi-Strauss (1908–2009) proposed a structuralist 'game':

> As a way of closing this letter which is already too long, I would like to propose a game: I will deduce, starting from the formal characteristics of kinship systems, the formal characteristics of linguistic structure, and I will say that:
>
> — the languages of South Asia have a simple structure from a logical point of view, but which brings into relation numerous elements whose position in the structure can be clearly determined;
>
> — the Indo-European languages have a simple structure from a logical point of view, but this structure is complicated by the fact that the multiple elements compete with each other to occupy the same position in the structure;
>
> — the American languages have a complicated structure calling on numerous elements, with several structural functions for the same element.
>
> I told this to Benveniste, who admitted that it was accurate, but thinks the parallelism is meaningless, because, he says, structuration only exists in language at the level of the differential elements and cannot be found at the level

---

[1] This conference was organized to celebrate the centenary of the birth of Camillo Olivetti. Roman Jakobson ('Language in relation to other communication systems'), Umberto Eco ('Codici e ideologie'), Ferruccio Rossi-Landi ('Problemi dell'alienazione linguistica'), and Lucien Goldmann ('Structuralisme génétique et analyse stylistique') also participated, among many others.

of grammar or vocabulary. Therefore he does not think that there are formal structures which are coextensive to the entire field of unconscious thought.
(Letter of 4 July 1948 in Jakobson and Lévi-Strauss 2018: 97)

Lévi-Strauss later presented this hypothesis to a broader audience in his article 'Language and the analysis of social laws', published in 1951 in *American Anthropologist*.[2] The article, which the author himself recognized as adventurous, gave rise to a controversy in the United States and France. There was an immediate reaction in *American Anthropologist* (Moore and Olmsted 1952); in France, the response came in such texts as André-Georges Haudricourt (1911–96) and Georges Granai's (1927–81) 'Linguistics and sociology' (1955), and Georges Gurvitch's (1894–1965) 'Le concept de structure sociale' (1955),[3] both of which appeared in the same issue of *Cahiers internationaux de sociologie*.

The hypothesis of a correspondence between kinship systems and linguistic structure finds its starting point in the idea that the social sciences, to be scientific, must borrow their methods from mathematics—Lévi-Strauss builds on Norbert Wiener's (1894–1964) *Cybernetics, or Control and Communication in the Animal and the Machine* (1948)—and further that language as a social phenomenon and as understood through the phoneme lends itself to such a scientific approach. Marriage regulations and kinship systems are, for Lévi-Strauss, susceptible of the same kind of analysis. The structures deduced by the linguist or the ethnologist are unconscious, and this is precisely what makes them ascertainable. They are also predictable and finite in number. Finally, the hypothesis of a correspondence between linguistic structures and kinship systems rests upon a theory of communication which assimilates the circulation of women and the circulation of words in society, seeing their common origin in the appearance of the symbolic function:

For words do not speak, while women do; as producers of signs, they can never be reduced to the status of symbols or tokens. But it is for this very reason that the position of women, as actually found in this system of

---

[2] The article (Levi-Strauss 1951) was subsequently published in French with the title 'Langage et société' in *Anthropologie structurale* (Lévi-Strauss 1974 [1958]).

[3] For example: 'His own theory of structures, which reduces them to models the ordering of which would call for the use of mathematics. Models borrowed from ethnology like those of kinship; from morphology; from phonology, erroneously identified with the whole of language; from political economy, in the form of Morgenstern-Neumann game models; from "relations of subordination", from political, religious, and mythological ideologies; all of these models are considered by Lévi-Strauss as "structures"; "communications", "exchanges", whether "transitive" or "cyclical" or both at once, are supposed to serve as the basis for "structures"' (Gurvitch 1955: 19). See also Lévi-Strauss (1974 [1956]: 379–400; English trans.: 1963: 324–345), which is a response to Gurvitch's text. For an analysis of the conflict between Lévi-Strauss and Gurvitch, see Jeanpierre (2004).

communication between men that is made up of marriage regulations and kinship nomenclature, may afford us a workable image of the type of relationships that could have existed at a very early period in the development of language, between human beings and their words. As in the case of women, the original impulse which compelled men to exchange words must be sought for in that split-representation which pertains to the symbolic function. For, since certain terms are simultaneously perceived as having a value both for the speaker and the listener, the only way to resolve this contradiction is in the exchange of complementary values, to which all social existence reduces itself.

(Lévi-Strauss 1951: 160)

In fact, Lévi-Strauss found himself in the middle of a passionate discussion about the notion of 'social structure', partly initiated by Alfred Radcliffe-Brown's (1881–1955) 'On Social Structure' (1940), which defines the concept in these terms: 'direct observation does reveal to us that these human beings are connected by a complex network of social relations. I use the term "social structure" to denote this network of actually existing relations' (Radcliffe-Brown 1940: 2). In the 1940s, Meyer Fortes (1906–1983) edited a festschrift entitled *Social Structure* (1949) in homage to Radcliffe-Brown, and George Murdock (1897–1985) published a work with the same title in that year (Murdock 1949).

Both Fortes and Murdock were interested in how social structure changes, in the invention of norms (Fortes) and regularity, and made liberal use of statistical methods in their studies. Murdock, who was interested in kinship systems from a comparative and statistical point of view, postulated, like Lévi-Strauss, a limited number of possible structures and aligned sociology with the natural sciences by hypothesizing laws: 'cultural forms in the field of social organization reveal a degree of regularity and of conformity to scientific law not significantly inferior to that found in the so-called natural sciences' (Murdock 1949: 249). The notion of 'social structure' is used by these authors alongside that of 'social organization', which can be found for example in the work of Franz Boas (1858–1942; e.g., Boas 1895) or Edward Sapir (1884–1939), where it determines an analysis in terms of 'patterning' and 'form'.

The study of social structure and linguistic structure in the work of Lévi-Strauss leads to the formulation of a totalizing model, an *order of orders*,[4]

---

[4] See Lévi-Strauss (1963 [1953]: 312 ff, 1974 [1956]: 390–391). Also: 'But when the anthropologist endeavours to create models, it is always with the underlying motive of discovering a *form that is common* to the diverse manifestations of social life' (Lévi-Strauss 1974 [1954]: 424; English trans.: 1963: 365).

which contains them and makes them comparable. Furthermore, each particular structure is a possible disposition within a totality which contains all possibilities and makes their occurrence predictable: Lévi-Strauss imagined a machine 'into which would be "fed" the equations regulating the types of structures with which phonemics usually deals, the repertory of sound which human speech organs can emit, and the minimal differential values, determined by psycho-physiological methods, which distinguish between the phonemes closest to one another'. This would make it possible to arrive at 'a sort of periodic table of linguistic structures': 'It would then remain for us only to check the place of known languages in this table, to identify the positions and the relationships of the languages whose first-hand study is still too imperfect to give us a proper theoretical knowledge of them, and to discover the place of languages that have disappeared or are unknown, yet to come, or simply possible' (Lévi-Strauss 1951: 157).

Benveniste's article 'Structure of language and structure of society' can be seen as a critique of structuralist conceptions and an attempt to go beyond them, possibly including a particular discussion of certain ideas proposed by Lévi-Strauss. The hypothesis of a structural analogy between language and society seems to be dismissed right from the beginning:

> Yet all of those who on many occasions, and even recently, have studied these relations are finally led to conclude that in reality no relation is to be found between language and society which would show an analogy in their respective structures. This is well known and immediately apparent. A quick look over the surface of the globe shows us languages with comparable structures serving societies which are very different from each other.
> (Benveniste 1974 [1970a]: 91–92).

Benveniste begins his article by posing a general problem: 'the relations between two vast entities, respectively language and society' (Benveniste 1974 [1970a]: 91)—and by reviewing the usual approaches to this problem so as to propose a way of going beyond them. This will consist in seeing language as the *interpreter* of society, an idea likewise formulated in the articles 'Sémiologie de la langue' ('Semiology of language';[5] Benveniste 1974 [1969]: 43–66; English trans. 1981: 5–23) and 'La forme et le sens dans le langage'

---

[5] 'The semiotic relationship between systems is expressed, then, as the relationship between *interpreting system* and *interpreted system*. It is this relationship that we shall propose on a grand scale between the signs of language and those of society. The signs of society can be interpreted integrally by those of language, but the reverse is not so. Language is therefore the interpreting system of society' (Benveniste 1981: 13, translation of 1974 [1969]: 54). Benveniste's term *interprétant* works, as in

('Form and meaning in language'; Benveniste 1974 [1967]: 215–238) dating from the same period. This development is announced in the opening lines of the article, where society is conceived as given along with language through the principle of intersubjectivity *I-you*, and language given along with society through communication:

> Language is, for a human being, a means, in fact the only means to reach another human being, to transmit a message to her or to him and to receive one in turn. Consequently, language poses and supposes the other. With language, society is immediately given. Society in turn only holds together by the common use of signs of communication. With society, language is immediately given.
>
> (Benveniste 1974 [1970a]: 91)

8.3 Antoine Meillet: 'changes in social structure give rise to changes in linguistic structure'

Benveniste refers rather indirectly to various recent attempts to compare language and society. For example, we can suppose that he is opposing the view of Antoine Meillet when he remarks, 'If one looks at historical evolution, one likewise finds language and society evolving separately' (Benveniste 1974 [1970a]: 92). Indeed, Meillet, in his inaugural lecture at the Collège de France in 1906, 'L'état actuel des études de linguistique générale' ('The current state of general linguistics'), spoke of language as a 'social fact' (Meillet 1921 [1906]: 16; see also Puech and Radzynski 1978), and posited that 'changes in social structure give rise to changes in linguistic structure' (Meillet 1921 [1906]: 18). For Benveniste, this position can be refuted. He gives as an example the social transformation occasioned by the Russian Revolution: 'Since 1917 the structure of Russian society has been profoundly modified, to say the least, but nothing comparable has occurred in the structure of the Russian language' (Benveniste 1974 [1970a]: 92). This example very likely echoes André Mazon's research into the influence of the Russian Revolution on the Russian language in *Lexique de la guerre et de la révolution en Russie* (*Lexicon of the War and the Revolution in Russia*) (Mazon 1920; see Jakobson et al. 2017), a work which had an important impact on linguists, as shown by a substantial review article by Jakobson (2017 [1921]: 113–172). For Mazon as for Meillet, the influence of social transformation on the language is to be observed primarily on the

---

'Structure de la langue, structure de la société', in relation to *interprété*, following, apparently, Saussure's distinction between *signifiant* and *signifié*; we have thus chosen to translate this pair of terms as 'interpreter' and 'interpreted', on the basis of 'signifier' and 'signified'.

level of the lexicon, and not on the deeper level of structure. Already in 1954 in 'Tendances récentes en linguistique générale' ('Recent tendencies in general linguistics'), Benveniste alluded to Meillet's hypothesis and the fact that it had not been followed up:

> Meillet wrote in 1906: 'It will be necessary to determine what social structure responds to and how, in a general way, changes in social structure are expressed in changes in linguistic structure'. In spite of certain endeavors (Sommerfelt), this program has not been completed, for just as soon as it was attempted to compare language and society systematically, disparities emerged. It appeared that the correspondence between them was constantly disturbed by the major fact of diffusion, in language as well as in social structure, so that societies of the same culture may have heterogenous languages, while languages very closely related may be used for the expression of entirely dissimilar cultures.
> (Benveniste 1971: 12–13; translation of Benveniste 1966 [1954]: 14–15)

Here, as in 'Structure of language and structure of society', we are led to think of Boas, and the notion of diffusion which introduces the dimension of historical change into anthropology, a dimension which allows him to demonstrate the erroneous character of racialist theories which attempt to establish correspondences between physical type, type of language, and type of culture. In his introduction to the *Handbook of American Indian Languages* (1911), Boas gave examples of multiple variables: 'Permanence of physical type: Changes in language and culture' (Boas 1911: 8); 'Permanence of language: Changes of physical type' (1911: 9); 'Changes to language and type' (1911: 10); 'Permanence of type and language: Change of culture' (1911: 10).[6] On the European side, the principle of the diffusion of languages is put forward by Saussure (1922 [1916]: 261–289) in the section of the *Course in General Linguistics* devoted to 'Geographical linguistics', and by Meillet (1928 [1918]) in 'Les langues de l'Europe moderne' ('The languages of modern Europe'). In both of these works we find the notion of 'extension of common languages' (Saussure 1922 [1916]: 280; Meillet 1928 [1918]: 103) mentioned by Benveniste:

> A quick look over the surface of the globe shows us languages with comparable structures serving societies which are very different from each other. This fact results from what is called the extension of common languages, occurring when a language is adopted by societies of different structures, structures which in principle are not destroyed or modified as

---

[6] Similarly, Benveniste gives the title 'Permanence of language, variation of society' to a part of his preparatory notes for the article 'Structure of language, structure of society'.

such. History also shows us, contrariwise, that languages distant in type from one another live and develop in societies which share the same social regime.

(Benveniste 1974 [1970a]: 91–92)

Benveniste again refers to Sapir in considering the independence of language and society, alluding to the famous formula 'When it comes to linguistic form, Plato walks with the Macedonian swineherd, Confucius with the head-hunting savage of Assam' (Sapir 1921: 234). which appears in the chapter 'Language, race, and culture' of *Language*, a chapter which must be understood in the context of Sapir's battle against racist ideologies, building on the positions staked out by Boas.

8.4 Language as a mirror

Finally, and this time in order to illustrate a conception of the correspondence between language and society, Benveniste brings up the image of language as a mirror of society:

> But other authors affirm, and it is no less obvious, that language is—as they put it—the mirror of society, that it reflects social structure in its particularities and its variations and that it is even most preeminently the index of changes which take place in society and in that privileged expression of society which is called culture.
>
> (Benveniste 1974 [1970a]: 92–93).

No precise reference is made here; perhaps Meillet is again being alluded to, or the Marxist conception of language which Voloshinov (2010 [1929]) attempted to develop in *Marxism and the Philosophy of Language*, to which the notions of 'reflection' and 'refraction' are central (see Sériot 2011: 83–96). In the manuscript notes for the article, the idea of language as mirror of society is associated with Karl Vossler (1872–1949), Walther von Wartburg (1888–1971), Father Wilhelm Schmidt (1868–1954), and Benjamin Lee Whorf (1897–1941):

> That will be the crux of my demonstration. Against the traditional conception which sees in language a witness [,] a 'mirror' of culture and society (Vossler

Frankreichs im Spiegel,[7] Wartburg[8]) and in another way Father Schmidt[9] who places in correlation the genitive and the structure

but I will also have to discuss Whorf...

I pose a homology between a fundamental property of language and an essential condition of culture: it is that of being meaningful by the same ~~instruments~~ elements of signification and the same mechanisms of signification.

Same elements of signification: the semantemes [units of 'semantics' in the sense in which I understand it].[10]

(Benveniste. Ms. PAP. OR. 46 [137]: 423 [84])[11]

Benveniste had already discussed Whorf in his manuscript notes concerning the proposition that time reference is absent from the Hopi language (see Laplantine 2020: 339–349). Whorf is here associated, but as a separate case, with the theory of language as mirror of society. For Whorf, language gives form to experience and allows the linguist to approach it, but is not exactly a mirror of it. Benveniste never completely refutes Whorf's positions but attempts to give them a more subtle formulation. For the question of Hopi time, he finds for example that, on the one hand, Whorf does not make a symmetrical analysis of European languages and Hopi, and, on the other, that he confuses the physics implicitly manifested by languages and the physics constructed by 'scientific' reflection. In manuscript notes for the article 'Structure of language and structure of society', Whorf appears as a step towards a theory of *interprétance* (Benveniste 1974 [1969]: 61 ff.; English trans. 1981: 17) that Benveniste is going to formulate:

> We must distinguish *society*, whose foundations and main characteristics are conscious because they are changed, they are destroyed or affirmed, they are promulgated!

---

[7] Vossler (1913). [ed. note]
[8] Wartburg (1922–1967). [ed. note]
[9] Schmidt (1926). [ed. note]
[10] 'C'est là que sera le nœud de ma démonstration. A l'encontre de la conception traditionnelle qui voit dans la langue un témoin, un "miroir" de la culture et de la société (Vossler Frankreichs im Spiegel, Wartburg) et d'une autre manière le P. Schmidt qui met en corrélat le génitif et la structure/ *mais il faudra aussi discuter Whorf...*/ je pose une homologie entre une propriété fondamentale de la langue et une condition essentielle de la culture: c'est d'être signifiante par les mêmes ~~instruments~~ éléments de signification et les mêmes mécanismes de signification. /Mêmes éléments de signification: les sémantèmes [unités de la "sémantique" au sens où je l'entends]'.
[11] All manuscript materials of Benveniste referred to in this chapter are held in the Archives of Émile Benveniste at the Bibliothèque nationale de France, Papiers d'orientalistes (PAP. OR).

and *language* whose structure and functioning are *unconscious*, since language is precisely what allows us to apprehend reality, to describe it, to understand it and to interpret it, and it is by means of language that we deal with society./

One must understand this: there is not on the one hand a <'pure'> experience and on the other a language into which we are free to transfer the experience, but the experience and the language are one, we can't make the experience without the language and the language models the experience. (Whorf goes too far in this direction but the principle is certain).[12]

(Benveniste. Ms. PAP. OR. 48 [160]: 382–383 [28–29])

8.5 Émile Benveniste: 'language is the interpreter of society'

It is interesting to note the way Benveniste's reflection proceeds in this note. The distinction between society as a set of conscious institutions and the unconscious functioning of language finds its source (perhaps not the only one) in Boas, who in the introduction to the *Handbook of American Indian Languages* distinguishes linguistic phenomena, which are unconscious, and ethnological phenomena, which give rise to 'secondary reasonings' (Boas 1911: 67), so that the study of language gives uncorrupted access to the history of the formation of ideas.[13] In France, it was Lévi-Strauss who relayed, diffused, and in a certain sense radicalized this distinction, in his search for the unconscious structures underlying phenomena, structures which could then be transposed to the interpretation of different orders of phenomena.[14] For Benveniste, it is the unconscious character of language and consequently its

---

[12] 'Il faut distinguer la *société*, dont les bases et les caractères principaux sont *conscients* puisqu'on les change, on les détruit ou on les affermit, ou les promulgue! / et la *langue* dont la structure et le fonctionnement sont *inconscients*, puisque la langue est précisément ce qui nous permet d'appréhender le monde, de le décrire, de le comprendre et de l'interpréter, et c'est au moyen de la langue que nous traitons de la société. // Il faut bien comprendre ceci: il n'y a pas d'une part une expérience <"pure"> et de l'autre une langue dans laquelle nous serions libres de transférer l'expérience, mais l'expérience et la langue ne font qu'un, nous ne pourrions faire l'expérience sans la langue et la langue modèle l'expérience. (Whorf va trop loin en ce sens mais le principe est certain)'.

[13] Boas (1911: 70–71) states: 'The great advantage that linguistics offer in this respect is the fact that, on the whole, the categories which are formed always remain unconscious, and that for this reason the processes which lead to their formation can be followed without the misleading and disturbing factors of secondary explanations, which are so common in ethnology, so much so that they generally obscure the real history of the development of ideas entirely'.

[14] 'If, as we believe to be the case, the unconscious activity of the mind consists in imposing forms upon content, and if these forms are fundamentally the same for all minds—ancient and modern, primitive and civilized (as the study of the symbolic function, expressed in language, so strikingly indicates)—it is necessary and sufficient to grasp the unconscious structure underlying each institution and each custom, in order to obtain a principle of interpretation valid for other institutions and other customs, provided of course that the analysis is carried far enough' (Lévi-Strauss 1974 [1949]: 33; English trans. 1963: 21).

permanence which allows it to apprehend the world.[15] Boas, seeing ethnological phenomena as obscured by secondary reasonings and reinterpretations, already had in view an activity of *interprétance*, but Benveniste makes of this activity a specific capacity of *discourse*: language is the interpreter of society, it gives form to experience, which does not exist otherwise. In this way Benveniste comes close to certain statements made by Whorf, who no doubt goes 'too far' in the sense that his conception of language leaves no room for discourse and subjectivation, and thus approaches a view of society as reflection of language (rather than of language as reflection of society).

Benveniste's critique of the conception of language as reflection of society is also developed in the article 'Deux modèles linguistiques de la cité', his contribution to a volume of *Mélanges* offered to Lévi-Strauss and published in 1970:

> In the incessant debate on the relations between language and society, the traditional view of language as 'mirror' of society is generally upheld. We cannot be too careful about using this kind of imagery. How could language 'reflect' society? These vast abstractions, and the falsely concrete relations into which they are placed can only give rise to illusions and confusions. In fact it is each time but a part of the language and a part of the society which is being compared in this way. With language, it is the vocabulary which plays the representative role, and it is on the basis of the vocabulary that one concludes—erroneously, for without any foregoing justification—about language as a whole. With society, it is the isolated atomic fact, the social datum, in so far as it is, precisely, object of denomination. We are sent back from one to the other indefinitely, the designating term and the designated fact only contributing, in this one-to-one pairing, to a kind of lexicological inventory of culture.
>
> (Benveniste 1974 [1970b]: 272)

8.6 Designation vs. signification

The discussion of the relations between language and society comes up in several of Benveniste's articles, and especially among the last ones he wrote. This theme, widely discussed by linguists and ethnologists in the twentieth century, and logically suited to a structuralist approach, allows Benveniste to interweave

---

[15] In his article, Benveniste (1974 [1970a]: 94) writes that '[l]anguage and society are, for human beings, unconscious realities': as principles, they cannot be changed. What human beings can change are, on the one hand, designations, and on the other, institutions.

several dimensions of his work, to develop the idea of language as interpreter, of discourse as intersubjective relation, and finally to insist on the signifying capacity of language. For Benveniste the representation of language as mirror of society depends on an atomistic conception of language and society, on a reduction of language to vocabulary and of linguistic activity to *denomination* or *designation* (language as nomenclature). Thus in 'Deux modèles linguistiques de la cité', Benveniste (1974 [1970b]: 272–280) shows by an analysis of linguistic forms in their relations, and notably by examining passages from ancient Greek and Latin authors, that Latin *civis, civitas* and Greek *polites, polis* do not refer to similar realities, but account for fundamental differences in the way the city as institution is conceived in the Greek and Latin worlds. It may appear surprising to find Benveniste criticizing the use of vocabulary as an approach to society: was he not the author of the two-volume *Vocabulaire des institutions indo-européennes* (1969), a work which would appear, precisely, to take vocabulary as evidence for the history of institutions?[16] But the project of the *Vocabulaire* as presented by Benveniste takes precisely the opposite view. In the introduction to this work he opposes an approach to language from the point of view of *designation* (which has recourse to a referent) and from the point of view of *signification*, an analysis where 'no extra-linguistic presuppositions come into play' (Benveniste 1969: 10), and which he practises both in the *Vocabulaire* and in articles like 'Deux modèles linguistiques de la cité'.

In the manuscript for the article 'Structure of language and structure of society', Benveniste refers to Meillet's (1905/6 text 'Comment les mots changent de sens';[17] 'How words change meaning'), noting however that though Meillet's view accounts for a necessary correlation between the transformation of the vocabulary and the society, it only deals with one aspect of language, and not the most fundamental one:

And so what do we observe?

Simply action *on the vocabulary*, which is obvious since it is the apparatus of designation which must adjust to changes in social reality and culture.

Meillet: How words change their meanings. That brings to light 1) diachronic condition 2) [restriction] to vocabulary 3) influence of the society on the lexicon./

---

[16] An English translation of this book was published in 2016 under the title *Dictionary of Indo-European Concepts and Society*. This title, unfortunately, misrepresents Benveniste's project.

[17] This article makes visible other strata of the discussion, referring for example to Arsène Darmesteter, Michel Bréal, Wilhelm Wundt, as well as to work on slang by Marcel Schwob and to Émile Durkheim's sociology.

But the core of language is its <formal> structure, the whole range of the distinctions it expresses and the connection between these distinctions. This structure changes little, and without direct relation to the changes of society.[18]
(Benveniste. Ms. PAP.OR. 48 [160]: 397[43]–398[44])

Benveniste thus declares invalid any attempt to compare the formal structure of language to the structure of society. The society changes, but this does not mean the linguistic structure will change: 'Since 1917 the structure of Russian society has been profoundly modified, to say the least, but nothing comparable has occurred in the structure of the Russian language' (Benveniste 1974 [1970a]: 92); 'Aside from violent changes, produced by war or conquest, the system of a language only changes very slowly, and under the pressure of internal necessities, in such a way that—and this is a condition which must be insisted on—in the conditions of ordinary life speakers are never conscious of linguistic change' (Benveniste 1974 [1970a]: 96).

8.7 Language as an activity

In another manuscript note, Benveniste again comments that the vocabulary is the most obvious index in language of the transformations of society, and the aspect of language most studied, but that it does not give access to the structure of language. To treat the relations between language and society, Benveniste proposes another approach to language, seeing it from the point of view of *communication*:

Conference in Milan
One must assign to language its true and only purpose, which is to serve the expression of messages, the only intersubjective tie.
Language is not a set of designations. At bottom language is not made to denote, but only to communicate. As for denoting one does one's best, and always in a manner which is incomplete, approximate, unstable.
Now it is in denoting that the relation with social structure is most clearly apparent, and not in the code according to which messages must be conceived

---

[18] 'Alors que constate-t-on ? /Seulement action *sur le vocabulaire*, ce qui est évident puisque c'est l'appareil de désignation qui doit s'ajuster aux changements de réalités sociales et de la culture. /Meillet: Comment les mots changent de sens. Cela met en lumière 1) condition diachronique 2) [restriction] au vocabulaire 3) influence de la société sur le lexique. // Mais le cœur de la langue est sa structure <formelle>, l'ensemble des distinctions qu'elle exprime et la liaison entre les distinctions. Cette structure change assez peu, et sans relation directe avec le changement de la société'.

nor in the structural base of the language (noun: verb distinction, existence of articles, gender and tense categories, clause structure, etc.)[19]

(Benveniste Ms. PAP.OR. 46 [137]: 377 [37])[20]

Though Benveniste wrote elsewhere that language is not an instrument of communication (see Benveniste 1966 [1958]: 258–259; English trans. 1971: 223–224), that 'long before being used for communicating, language is used for *living*',[21] if he prefers here to envisage language in terms of the intersubjective relation and the expression of a message rather than in terms of denomination, it is because he conceives language above all as an *activity*,[22] and seeks to propose another point of view on the relation between language and society, a point of view which he calls *semiologic* and which deals with the relation between sign systems.[23] This point of view allows him to envisage the impact of language on society, and, in his manuscript notes, to give his thinking a revolutionary turn:

Language is more and more at once the reality of language and the possibility of language. Because it becomes more and more language, it provides more and more elaborate forms which not only serve to interpret society but will contribute one day to transforming it.[24]

(Benveniste. Ms. PAP.OR. 46 [137]: 417 [78])

---

[19] 'Colloque de Milan /Il faut assigner à la langue sa véritable et unique fin, qui est de servir à exprimer des messages, le seul lien intersubjectif. /La langue n'est pas un ensemble de dénominations. Au fond la langue n'est pas faite pour dénommer, mais seulement pour communiquer. Pour la dénomination on s'arrange comme on peut, et toujours de manière incomplète, approximative, instable. /Or c'est dans la dénomination que le rapport avec la structure sociale se marque le plus clairement, et non dans le code selon lequel doivent être conçus les messages ni dans la base structurale de la langue (distinction nom: verbe, existence des articles, catégories du genre, du temps, structure des propositions, etc.)'.

[20] This manuscript note calls to mind the critique which Benveniste elaborates in his manuscripts on Baudelaire's language, where he opposes 'ordinary language' and 'poetic language'; 'ordinary language' (or 'signific language') has the sign for its unit and serves a referential function, while by means of 'poetic language' (or 'iconic language') the *poet* transmits a singular experience: 'Poetic language and more precisely poetics does not consist in saying but in *doing*. It aims at producing a certain effect, emotional and aesthetic' (Benveniste 2011: 400).

[21] 'bien avant de servir à communiquer, le langage sert à vivre' (Benveniste 1974 [1967]: 217).

[22] '*Vivre le langage* / Tout est là: dans le langage assumé et vécu comme expérience humaine, rien n'a plus le même sens que dans la langue prise comme système formel et décrite du dehors' (Benveniste. Ms. PAP. OR. 30, env. 2, f. 241): '*To live language* / All depends on that: in language assumed and lived as human experience, nothing has the same meaning as with language taken as a formal system and described from outside.'

[23] This problem is treated with the same conclusions, but from a different angle, that of the notion of sign (with the comparison between Peirce and Saussure) in 'Sémiologie de la langue' (Benveniste 1974 [1969]: 43–66; English trans. 1981: 5–23).

[24] 'La langue de plus en plus est à la fois la réalité de la langue et la possibilité de la langue. Parce qu'elle devient de plus en plus langue, elle fournit des formes de plus en plus élaborées qui non seulement servent à interpréter la société mais contribueront un jour à la transformer'.

8.8 Lévi-Strauss: circulation of words and women

Benveniste rules out any possibility of structural correlation between language and society, since their respective 'structures' are not isomorphic. Indeed, the basis of linguistic structure may be conceived as 'composed of distinctive units, and these units are defined by four traits: they are discrete, finite in number, combinable, and hierarchically ordered' (Benvensite 1974 [1970a]: 93). Nothing comparable is to be found in society, no unit comparable to that of language.[25] Benveniste defines the structure of society in terms of a double nature, composed of two systems of relations: the kinship system and the class system. This representation of the structure of society in two great relational systems may appear surprising; it would be interesting to determine where Benveniste gets this idea, which was perhaps in part inspired by the anthropology of Lévi-Strauss where kinship and language are conceived on the basis of a communicational model. It is the idea of 'relational system' which is interesting here. We may recall the words of Lévi-Strauss (1951) in the article 'Language and the analysis of social laws', mentioned in section 8.2:

> Now, these results have only been achieved by treating marriage regulations and kinship systems as a kind of language, a set of processes permitting the establishment, between individuals and groups, of a certain type of communication. That the mediating factor, in this case, should be the *women of the group*, who are *circulated* between clans, lineages, or families, in place of the *words of the group*, which are *circulated* between individuals, does not at all change the fact that the essential aspect of the phenomenon is identical in both cases.
>
> (Lévi-Strauss 1951: 159)

Further on, Lévi-Strauss sees women as *values*, in contrast to words which, reduced to their function as *signs*, have lost their original function as values (except in the case of poetic language). Finally, and before providing examples

---

[25] Benveniste does not mention the correlation which Lévi-Strauss would like to establish between Trubetzkoy's analysis of the phoneme and kinship systems: 'Like phonemes, kinship terms are elements of meaning; like phonemes, they acquire meaning only if they are integrated into systems. "Kinship systems," like "phonemic systems," are built by the mind on the level of unconscious thought. Finally, the recurrence of kinship patterns, marriage rules, similar prescribed attitudes between certain types of relatives, and so forth, in scattered regions of the globe and in fundamentally different societies, leads us to believe that, in the case of kinship as well as linguistics, the observable phenomena result from the action of laws which are general but implicit' (Lévi-Strauss 1974 [1945]: 47; English trans. 1963: 34).

illustrating the assimilation of linguistic structures and kinship systems, he proposes a primal scene for both language and kinship in the appearance of the 'symbolic function':

> As in the case of women, the original impulse which compelled men to exchange words must be sought for in that split-representation which pertains to the symbolic function.
>
> (Lévi-Strauss 1951: 160)

Seventeen years separate Lévi-Strauss's text from Benveniste's article, nevertheless the same notions are found in both: *communication, exchange*, and *value*. These are the three notions that Benveniste (1974 [1970a]: 101) indicates as 'essential' at the end of his article, notions which, as he notes, 'already extend our reflections beyond the traditional framework in which language and society are placed side by side'.

It is perhaps this dialogue with Lévi-Strauss that constitutes the main historiographic interest of Benveniste's article, which is not limited to its main thesis, 'language is the interpreter of society' (Benvensite 1974 [1970a]: 95), '[t]here is a metalanguage, but no metasociety' (1974 [1970a]: 97), a very important thesis which makes of language as discourse the interpreter of all the other systems, including itself, and a 'machine for producing meaning' (Benvensite 1974 [1970a]).

8.9 Language as production

The notion of 'production' must be underlined. We must keep in mind that Benveniste read his article before a congress entitled 'Linguaggi nella società e nella tecnica' ('Languages in society and in technology'), organized in honour of the centenary of the birth of Camillo Olivetti (1868–1943): this occasion for Benveniste's talk provides a social and economic angle to the question he deals with. The notion of 'production' recurs throughout the text, for example in a passage just preceding the one quoted: 'Language arises and develops in the human community, it is elaborated through the same process as society, in the endeavour to produce a means of subsistence, to transform nature and to multiply instruments' (Benveniste 1974 [1970a]: 95). But we can see that Benveniste transforms this notion, moving from the concrete production of goods to the immaterial production of language, which he develops as production of meaning, as 'enunciation' or utterance, the creation of linguistic forms and objects:

Language may be seen within society as a productive system: it produces meaning, thanks to its composition which is entirely designed for signification and thanks to the code which conditions its organization. It also produces enunciations indefinitely thanks to certain rules of formal transformation and expansion; it thus creates forms and patterns of formation; it creates linguistic objects which are introduced into the circuit of communication. 'Communication' should be understood according to the literal senses of things held in common and of circulatory movement.

(Benveniste 1974 [1970a]: 100–101)

The comparison between language and the economy is further supported by the image of 'circulatory movement' and of communication as 'common use'. Benveniste reminds us that the comparison had already been made by Saussure in relation with the notion of *value* (see Saussure 1922 [1916]: 115):

Already Saussure noted an analogy between certain notions belonging to economics and those which he founded, formulated, and organized for the first time in the process of linguistic communication. He pointed out that an economy like a language is a system of *values*.

(Benveniste 1974 [1970a]: 101)

Benveniste develops this analogy with economy by adding the notion of *exchange*, which he does not see, as we might rather have expected, in interhuman exchange (exchange of words, circulatory movement), but in the paradigmatic function of language: 'The paradigmatic axis of language is precisely characterized, with respect to the syntagmatic axis, by the possibility of replacing one term by another, one function by another, in so far, precisely, as it has a value by virtue of its syntagmatic use. And here we are very close to the characteristics of value in economics' (Benveniste 1974 [1970a]: 101). The manuscripts show that Benveniste was interested in the notions of *exchange value* and *use value* in Marx,[26] and that he was looking for analogies with the *sign* and the *word*:

---

[26] For example: '"La transformation des objets utiles en valeurs est un produit de la société, tout aussi bien que le langage" K. Marx (Extraits p. 270) / Il faut donc du temps pour que le producteur reconnaisse que les différentes productions ont dans l'échange, une *valeur*. Il faut aussi du temps pour que les différents énoncés ont un *sens*' (Benveniste. Ms. PAP. OR. 48 [160]: 50 [404]): '"The transformation of useful objects into values is a product of the society, just as language is" K. Marx (Extraits, p.270)/ It thus takes time for the producer to recognize that different productions have, through exchange, a *value*. It also takes time for different statements to take on *meaning*'.)

Do the Marxist concepts of exchange value and use value ('proper to the satisfaction of needs') correspond to the distinction between the *sign* as semiotic *value* and the word as a component of discourse?[27]

(Benveniste. Ms PAP. OR. 46[137]: 380[40])

This distinction between *sign* and *word* relates to the distinction made by Benveniste in 'La forme et le sens dans le langage' ('Form and meaning in language') (1974 [1967]) between two distinct domains of language, the *semiotic* (whose unit is the *sign*) and the *semantic* (whose unit is the *sentence*, which can be analysed into words). As we have seen, the sign is interchangeable within the paradigm, but a word in a sentence only has its own value, determined by the sentence.

In one of the preparatory notes for his article, Benveniste makes the notion of exchange a starting point for a reflection on the symmetry between linguistic communication and social communication, linking the reflection on value in Saussure, Lévi-Strauss, and Marx:

Notion of the exchange between speakers as 'interlocution'.
  Notion of the exchange between producers as 'interproduction'.
  It's the same conception of a relation between two subjects: relations of linguistic communication, symmetrical to the relation of economic communication.
  This is indeed the social-individual basis of Saussure's theory of the sign. We see for example in the theory of the exchange of women between two exogamous societies a symmetrical counterpart of the exchange of signs, of the circuit of communication.
  But whereas the exchange between speakers is mediated by the sign,
  the exchange between producers is mediated by the exchange value.[28]

(Benveniste. Ms. PAP. OR. 46[137]: 51[391])

We may find this manuscript note less than convincing; it should be considered an attempt rather than a fully worked-out thought, but it brings to light

---

[27] 'Les concepts marxistes de la *valeur d'échange* et de la *valeur d'usage* ("propre à satisfaire des besoins") correspondraient-t-ils à la distinction du *signe* en tant que *valeur* sémiotique et du mot en tant que composant du discours.'

[28] 'Notion de *l'échange entre locuteurs* comme "interlocution". / Notion de *l'échange entre producteurs* comme "interproduction". / C'est la même conception d'une relation entre deux sujets: relations de communication linguistique, symétrique de la relation de communication économique / C'est bien là le fondement individuel–social de la théorie du signe saussurien. On voit par exemple dans la théorie de l'échange des femmes entre deux sociétés exogamiques le symétrique de l'échange des signes, du circuit de la communication. / Mais, si l'échange entre locuteurs est médiatisé par le signe, / l'échange entre producteurs est médiatisée par la valeur–échange.'

the problems Benveniste was taking up, though they may appear somewhat remote fifty years later. Concerning the notion of 'production', we noted above that Benveniste speaks of language as a 'machine for producing meaning' (Benveniste 1974 [1970a]: 97). We should return to this image, derived, as we have noted, from economic discourse. Benveniste writes:

> If language is an instrument of communication or *the* instrument of communication, it is because it is endowed with semantic properties and because it functions like a machine for producing meaning, by virtue of its very structure. And here we are at the heart of the problem. Language makes possible the indefinite production of messages of an unlimited variety. This unique property depends on the structure of language which is composed of signs, of units of meaning, in great but always finite number, which enter into combinations governed by a code and permitting an incalculable number of enunciations—a number necessarily ever more incalculable, since the quantity of signs is always increasing and the possibilities of using and combining these signs increases in consequence.
> (Benveniste 1974 [1970a]: 97)

As we have seen, in speaking of the 'machine for producing meaning', Benveniste borrows from the economy the idea of a creative activity and applies it to language. Producing meaning is what discourse does by means of the interpretative capacity of language. Surprisingly, Benveniste justifies the idea of a production of meaning through the infinite combinatory possibilities of language. The representation of language as a combinatory system recalls Lévi-Strauss' vision of language, with the difference that in the latter's view the elements are necessarily finite in number. One might suppose that Benveniste is referring also and more directly to Noam Chomsky's (b. 1928) generative linguistics. Nevertheless, the representation of language as a combinatory system has little to do with the linguistics of enunciation developed by Benveniste, in which signs are not required to enter into different combinations to produce new meaning. When, in a 1968 interview entitled 'Structuralism and linguistics', Benveniste was asked by Pierre Daix to explain how Chomsky broke with structuralism,[29] he responded that '[Chomsky] considers language as production, which is completely different' (Benveniste 1974 [1968a]: 18). And further on, after pointing out that in the structuralist approach, 'one must start with data', he adds:

---

[29] Benveniste has just alluded to the extension of the structuralist approach to social phenomena, which, in his view, has weakened notions initially conceived for dealing with languages.

Whereas with Chomsky, it's exactly the contrary, he starts with speech as something produced. Now, how is language produced? Nothing is reproduced. There are a certain number of models, apparently. Now, each man invents his language and invents it all through life. And all men invent their own language on the instant and each in a distinctive way, and each time in a new way. To say good morning to someone every day of one's life is each time a reinvention. All the more so when we are dealing with sentences, it's no longer the constitutive elements which count, it's the complete organization of the whole, the original arrangement for which no model can have been given directly, so that it's the individual who fabricates it.

(Benveniste 1974 [1968a]: 18–19)

It is to be noted that Benveniste chooses a sentence-word, and what is more, a most ordinary and commonly repeated one, 'good morning', to illustrate the idea of linguistic invention. To say good morning every day of one's life is not to repeat the same 'good morning' for it is a new enunciation: 'nothing is reproduced'.[30] Language is no longer seen in terms of data but in terms of production (insofar as it is an invention). Although Benveniste does not speak here of 'combination', he does refer to organization and arrangement, notions which we also find in his research on poetic language (see Laplantine 2011: 217ff), along with others like 'assemblage' or 'junction', or even 'symphoria', 'symphronia', or 'sympatheme', terms he coins to describe an extended dimension of the 'syntagm' in the poem.[31] Benveniste thus pays particular attention to the 'syntagmatic' dimension of language, to its capacity for arranging elements in an original manner, which allows the subject to produce an enunciation which is each time new—or a poem. But when he speaks of sympatheme and rhyme, of new assemblages produced by the poet, or else of a suggestive language, it is the semantic dimension of language which he is bringing to light, the capacity of subjects to invent themselves by inventing their language. It is not words separated and ordered in an atomistic fashion that interest him, but the whole of discourse (the sentence) as produced by an enunciating subject, or

---

[30] It is interesting to note that the notion of production is used elsewhere by Benveniste, for example when he writes, 'language *re-produces* reality' (Benveniste 1971: 22; translation of 1966 [1963]: 25), adding, 'language is newly produced by means of language'. If it is a question of criticizing the representation of language as nomenclature, as an image of reality, the accent is placed on the activity of inventing reality effected by subjects through their discourse.

[31] 'En poésie le syntagme s'étend plus loin que ses dimensions <limites> grammaticales; il embrasse la comparaison, l'entourage très large, parfois la rime. On proposerait pour le renommer symphorie <sympathème ?> ou symphronie' (Benveniste 2011: 140): 'In poetry the syntagm extends further than its grammatical dimensions <limits>; it includes simile, the wider environment, sometimes the rhyme. To rename it, one might suggest symphoria <sympatheme?> or symphronia'.

by a co-enunciating subject (the listener or reader). The atomizing approach is exactly what he criticizes in a note entitled 'Differences of approach' concerning the method employed by Jakobson and Lévi-Strauss in their analysis of Baudelaire's poem 'Les Chats' (Jakobson and Lévi-Strauss 1962; see also Joseph, Laplantine, and Pinault 2020):

> One approach involves starting ~~from the poetic composi~~ <from the piece in> verse as a fact, describing it, taking it apart like an object. This is the analysis one finds ~~put into~~ applied to Les Chats in the fine article by Lévi-Strauss and Jakobson.[32]
>
> (Benveniste 2011: 186).

Here, as in the article 'Structure of language and structure of society' and other texts, Benveniste explicitly states a critique of structuralist method: the idea of an 'applied' analysis, which 'starts from facts', and which reduces language to an object which can be taken apart.[33] In Benveniste's view of poetic language, the poet produces a new semiology which the reader-listener must adjust to. The poem transforms the analyst (the subject) and the analysis (his discourse). Here we see that language is not only the interpreter of society, but above all of itself.

---

[32] 'Une approche consiste à partir de la composition poeti <de la pièce de> vers comme d'une donnée, de la décrire, de la démonter comme un objet. C'est l'analyse telle qu'on la trouve mise en <appliquée> aux Chats dans le bel article de Lévi-Strauss et Jakobson.'

[33] The questioning of the descriptive approach is also important. This is a major theme of his research on poetic language (see Laplantine 2011: 131 ff.). Description is not the only way language signifies, as Stéphane Mallarmé argues in *Crise de vers* when he opposes *décrire* (describe) and *dire* (say) (see Mallarmé 2003 [1897]: 259). In relation with what was said earlier about the reduction of language to the activity of naming, we might recall that Mallarmé also opposes *nommer* (to name) and *suggérer* (suggest) in a famous formulation: '*Nommer* un objet, c'est supprimer les trois quarts de la jouissance du poème qui est faite de deviner peu à peu: le *suggérer*, voilà le rêve' ('To name an object suppresses three-quarters of the pleasure we get from the poem, which comes from guessing little by little; to *suggest*, that is the dream'; Mallarmé 2003 [1891]: 405). In the interview 'Ce langage qui fait l'histoire' ('Language making history') which he gave in 1968, Benveniste refers to the literary experiments of the time: 'The whole signifying power of language is being put into question. What is at stake is knowing whether language is destined always to describe an identical world by identical means, simply varying the choice of epithets and verbs. Or whether other, non-descriptive means of expression may be envisaged, and whether another quality of signification would emerge from this break' (Benveniste 1974 [1968b]: 37).

Structure of language and structure of society

Émile Benveniste (1970)
Translated by Andrew Eastman

Ladies and gentlemen, I have here to deal with a subject which leads one at times to state the obvious, at others to pose a contradiction.[1] Indeed, I will be examining the relations between two vast entities, respectively language and society.

Language is, for a human being, a means, in fact the only means to reach another human being, to transmit a message to her or to him and to receive one in turn. Consequently, language poses and supposes the other. With language, society is immediately given. Society in turn only holds together by the common use of signs of communication. With society, language is immediately given. Thus each of these two entities, language and society, implies the other. It would seem that they can and even must be studied together, discovered together, because together they come into existence. It would also seem that from one to the other, from language to society, precise and constant correlations can and must be found, since one and the other arise from the same necessity.

Yet all of those who on many occasions, and even recently, have studied these relations are finally led to conclude that in reality no relation is to be found between language and society which would show an analogy in their respective structures. This is well known and immediately apparent. A quick look over the surface of the globe shows us [92] languages with comparable structures serving societies which are very different from each other. This fact results from what is called the extension of common languages, occurring when a language is adopted by societies of different structures, structures which in principle

---

[1] This is a new translation of Émile Benveniste's essay. Benveniste's text 'Structure de la langue et structure de la société' was published in the proceedings of the conference 'Linguaggi nella società e nella tecnica' (Milan, 14–17 October 1968) along with a translation into English entitled 'The structure of language and the structure of society' (Benveniste 1974 [1970a]). The translator's name is not indicated. We have consulted this translation in making our own.

are not destroyed or modified as such. History also shows us, contrariwise, that languages distant in type from one another live and develop in societies which share the same social regime. One need only look around today to see for example the situation of language and society in the eastern half of Europe, where we see Slavic, Finno-Ugric, Germanic, or Romance languages serving societies of essentially the same structure.

If one looks at historical evolution, one likewise finds language and society evolving separately. One and the same language remains stable through the most profound social upheavals. Since 1917 the structure of Russian society has been profoundly modified, to say the least, but nothing comparable has occurred in the structure of the Russian language.

From these oft-repeated observations arises the view so often expressed by linguists and anthropologists both, that society and the culture inherent to society are independent from language.

Sapir, a man who knew both aspects of these realities, affirmed that simple and complex types of languages of an infinite number of varieties can be observed at any level of culture, and that there is not, from this point of view, since they use the same language, any difference between Plato and a Macedonian swineherd. We are left to conclude that language and society are not isomorphic, that their structures do not coincide, that their variations are independent of each other, and to content ourselves with taking note of the discordance.

But other authors affirm, and it is no less obvious, that language is—as they put it—the mirror of society, that it reflects social structure in its particularities and its variations and that it is even most preeminently the index of changes which take place in society and in that privileged expression of society which is called [93] culture. It is hardly possible to reconcile these views. They show at any rate that the problem is far from simple and it is indeed the fundamental problem of the situation of language in society; they also show that the way this problem has been discussed up until now has not brought us any closer to a solution.

In reality these notions, language and society respectively, are immense and of a complexity which we have not finished exploring. The idea of seeking one-to-one correspondences between these two entities, according to which a certain social structure would correspond to a certain linguistic structure seems to reflect a very simplistic view of things. They are, naturally, non-isomorphic objects, as we can already see by the difference in their structural organization.

The basis of linguistic structure is composed of distinctive units, and these units are defined by four traits: they are discrete, finite in number, combinable, and hierarchically ordered.

The structure of society cannot be reduced to this schema; its nature is twofold. We find on the one hand a relational system, which is called the kinship system; and on the other another system of relation, of division, the system of social classes which is organized according to productive functions. Now, neither individuals nor the various groups of individuals can be transposed into units or groups of units comparable to those of language. The family is often spoken of as the cell of society. This is a metaphor which must not be allowed to mask the real situation. Society does not consist in an aggregate of such cells, an aggregate of families, and groups of families do not have the slightest analogy with the groupings of significant units in language.

We must then conclude that there is no correspondence either in nature or in structure between the constitutive elements of language and the constitutive elements of society. But in fact this is a rather summary point of view which we must go beyond. One must be aware of the implications involved in the notion of language and the notion of society when one sets out to compare them. And thus we must point out and correct a confusion made between two senses of the term language and of the term society respectively. [94]

On the one hand we have society as empirical, historical fact. We speak of Chinese society, French society, Assyrian society. On the other hand, there is society as human collectivity, ground and primary condition of human existence. In the same way, we have language as empirical, historical idiom, the Chinese language, the French language, the Assyrian language; and language as a system of significant forms, the primary condition of communication.

By making this first distinction, we separate two levels in each of the two entities, one historical, the other fundamental. We then recognize that the problem of the possible relations between language and society is posed at each of these two levels, and that two different solutions may thus be admitted. We have seen that, between a historical language and a historical society, no correlation of a necessary character can be posed; but at the fundamental level, homologies can immediately be perceived. Several characteristics are common to one and the other, to language and society—I repeat—at this level. Language and society are, for human beings, unconscious realities; both represent nature, so to speak, the natural milieu and the natural mode of expression, milieu and expression which cannot be conceived of as being other than they are and cannot be imagined as being absent. Both are always inherited, and in language use and in social practice at this fundamental level, it is difficult to imagine that either could ever have had a beginning. Neither can be changed at the discretion of human beings. What human beings see changing, what they can change, what they effectively do change in the course of history are the institutions, sometimes the entire form of a particular society, but not, not ever, the principle of society which is the ground and the condition of collective and individual life. In the same way, what changes in language, what human beings can change, are designations, which multiply, replace one another, and are always conscious, but never the fundamental system of the language. For if the constant, growing diversification of social activities, of needs, of notions requires ever new designations, a unifying force is necessary in turn to counterbalance it. Standing above classes, above [95] groups and particularized activities, a cohesive power holds sway which makes a community out of an aggregate of individuals and creates the very possibility of production and collective subsistence. This power is language and language alone. For this reason language represents a permanence at the heart of changing society, a durable phenomenon which binds ever-diversifying activities. It is an identity persisting through individual diversities. From this proceeds the deeply paradoxical double nature of language, which is at once immanent in the individual and transcendent to society. This duality is found in all the properties of language.

How then can we pose the relation between language and society so as to elucidate by the analysis of the one (language), the analysis of the other (society)? This relation will not be a structural correlation, since we have seen that the organization of human beings is not comparable to that of language. It will not be typological, for the language type, whether monosyllabic, polysyllabic, tonal or morphological, has absolutely no influence on the specific nature of society. Nor will it be historical or genetic, because we do not make the origin of the one depend on the origin of the other. Language arises and develops in the human community, it is elaborated through the same process as society, in the endeavour to produce means of subsistence, to transform nature and to multiply instruments.

It is in this collective work and through this collective work that language is differentiated and becomes more efficient, in the same way that society is differentiated in its material and intellectual activities. Here we envisage language simply as a means of analysing society. To this end we will pose them synchronically and in a semiological relation, the relation of interpreter to interpreted. And we will formulate these two closely interrelated propositions: first, language is the interpreter of society; second, language contains society.

The justification of the first proposition: language as interpreter of society, is given by the second: language contains society. This is verified in two ways: first, empirically, by the fact that language can be isolated, studied, and described for itself without referring to its use in society, nor to its relations with the social norms [96] and representations which make up culture. Whereas it is impossible to describe a society, or to describe a culture, apart from their linguistic expressions. In this sense language includes society, but is not included by it.

Secondly, and I will return to this point in a moment, language provides the constant and necessary basis for the differentiation between individual and society. I say language itself, always and necessarily.

Let us then consider that language interprets society. Society becomes meaningful in and through language, society is *par excellence* the interpreted of language.

In order for language to fulfil this role of interpreter which is first of all and from a quite literal point of view to bring the interpreted into existence and to transform it into an intelligible notion, language must fulfil two conditions with respect to society. Since society is human nature fixed in institutions and shaped by technology, by the conditions of production, society is apt to diversify or evolve constantly, at times slowly, at times very fast. But the interpreter must not change as such, while remaining capable of registering, designating, and even orienting changes which take place in the interpreted. This is a condition of general semiology. A semiological principle which I would like to pose is that two semiotic systems cannot coexist in a condition of homology, if they are of different natures; they cannot be mutual interpreters one of the other, nor convertible one into the other. That is indeed the situation of language with respect to society; language can receive and give a name to all the innovations that social existence and technological conditions produce, but none of these changes reacts directly on its own structure. Aside from violent changes, produced by war or conquest, the system of a language only changes very slowly, and under the pressure of internal necessities, in such a way that—and this is a condition which must be insisted on—in the conditions of ordinary life speakers are never conscious of linguistic change. Such change is only recognized retrospectively, after several generations, and consequently only in societies which preserve evidence of earlier linguistic states, societies possessed of writing.

[97] Now, what assigns to language this position as interpreter? It is that language is—as is well known—the instrument of communication which is and must be common to all the members of a society. If language is an instrument of communication or *the* instrument of communication, it is because it is endowed with semantic properties and because it functions like a machine

for producing meaning, by virtue of its very structure. And here we are at the heart of the problem. Language makes possible the indefinite production of messages of an unlimited variety. This unique property depends on the structure of language which is composed of signs, of units of meaning, in great but always finite number, which enter into combinations governed by a code and permitting an incalculable number of enunciations—a number necessarily ever more incalculable, since the quantity of signs is always increasing and the possibilities of using and combining these signs increases in consequence.

There are thus two properties inherent in language at its deepest level: the property of being formed of significant units, which constitutes its nature; and the property of being able to arrange these signs in a significant way, which determines its use. These two properties must be kept distinct; they require two different analyses and are organized in two particular structures. The link between these two properties is established by a third property. We have said that we have on the one hand significant units, secondly the capacity to arrange these signs in significant ways, and thirdly, we shall say, the *syntagmatic* property, which allows for combining them according to certain rules of consecution and only in this way. One must be fully persuaded that nothing can be understood which has not been reduced to language. It follows that language is necessarily the appropriate instrument for describing, conceptualizing, and interpreting both nature and experience, thus that compound of nature and experience which is called society. It is thanks to this power of transmuting experience into signs and reducing it to categories that language can take as its object any order of facts whatsoever and even its own nature. There is a metalanguage, but no metasociety.

Language surrounds society on all sides and contains it [98] within its conceptual apparatus, but at the same time, by virtue of a distinct capacity, it configures society by establishing what could be called the semantics of society. This is the part of a language which has most often been studied. It consists, indeed, above all but not exclusively, of designations, items of vocabulary. The vocabulary furnishes a very abundant material which has been liberally drawn on by historians of culture and society. The vocabulary preserves invaluable evidence of forms and phases of social organization, political regimes, modes of production which have been successively or simultaneously employed, etc. Since this is the aspect of the relation between language and society which has been most thoroughly explored, of language as set and system of designations, thus remaining constant at the same time as it is constantly renewed and enlarged, we will not dwell on it. We will limit ourselves to highlighting several features of this semantic capacity.

The facts which language provides from this point of view only take on their full value when they are brought into relation with each other and coordinated with their reference. A complex mechanism is involved, whose testimony must be interpreted with caution. The state of a society at a given period does not always appear reflected in the designations it makes use of, for these designations may often subsist while the referents, the designated realities have changed. This fact is frequently experienced and constantly verified, and the best examples of it are, precisely, the term 'language' and the term 'society' which I am now continually making use of. The diversity of references which can be accorded to each of these two terms is precisely what bears witness to and conditions the use which we are to make of these forms. What is called polysemy results from language's capacity to *subsume* under a constant term a great variety of types and consequently to allow for variation of reference within the stability of signification.

Thirdly, to move on to a somewhat different consideration, but which there are good grounds to insist on more particularly today, everyone speaks from himself. For each speaker, speech emanates from himself and returns to himself, each speaker determines himself as subject with regard to the other or others. However, and perhaps because of this, language which is thus [99] the irreducible emanation of the deepest self in each individual is at the same time a superindividual reality and coextensive with the whole collectivity. It is this coincidence between language as an objectifiable, supraindividual reality, and the individual production of speech which underlies the paradoxical situation of language with regard to society. Language, indeed, provides the speaker with the basic formal structure which makes possible the exercise of speech. It provides the linguistic instrument which ensures the double functioning, subjective and referential, of discourse; this is the indispensable distinction, always present in any language whatsoever, in whatever society or period, between I and not-I, operated by special indicators which are never absent from language and serve only this purpose, forms which in grammar are called pronouns, and which accomplish a double opposition, the opposition of 'I' to 'you' and the opposition of the 'I/you' system to 'he'.

The first, the 'I-you' opposition, is a structure of personal allocution which is exclusively interhuman. Only a special code, religious or poetic, authorizes the use of this opposition outside of the human milieu.

The second opposition, that of 'I-you'/'he', opposing person to non-person, accomplishes the operation of reference and founds the possibility of discourse about something, about the world, about what is not allocution. We have here the foundation on which the double relational system of language rests.

Here a new configuration of language appears, one which exists alongside the two others which I have summarily analysed; it is the speaker's inclusion in his or her own discourse, the pragmatic dimension which poses the person in society as a participant and unfolds a complex network of spatio-temporal relations which determine the modes of enunciation.

This time each human being positions and includes himself in relation to society and to nature and positions himself necessarily in a class, whether it be a governing class or a productive class. For indeed language is here considered as a human practice revealing the particular use which groups or classes of human beings make of language and the differentiations of the common language which result from it.

I could describe this phenomenon as an appropriation by certain groups or classes of the system of denotation [100] which is common to all. Each social class appropriates to itself terms which are in general use, and attributes specific references to them, thus adapting them to its own sphere of interest and often making them the basis for a new derivation. In turn these terms, charged with new values, enter the common language, bringing lexical differentiations into it. This process could be studied by looking at a certain number of specialized vocabularies which bear their reference within themselves, giving rise to a particular, relatively coordinated universe. This might be, for example—but I don't have time now to develop the example—the analysis of vocabularies specific to certain classes, like the vocabulary of the sacred in the language of the Roman pontifices. I have expressly chosen a language which is easy to analyse and has a fairly rich vocabulary, in which may be found both a large stock of specific terms and specific ways of combining them, a particular style, in sum all the characteristic traits of an appropriation of the common language effected by charging it with new notions, new values. This would be a way of verifying on a smaller scale the role of language within society insofar as this language becomes the expression of certain specialized professional groups, for whom their world is, preeminently, *the* world. By distinguishing, as we have tried to do, the different types of relations which bind language to society, relations allowing each to shed light on the other, we have had to do primarily with the mechanism which allows language to serve as the denominator, the interpreter of social functions and structures. But beyond this we get a glimpse of certain less obvious analogies between deep structures, between the very functioning of language and the fundamental principles of social activity. These are as yet only crude comparisons, vast homologies, the theory of which must be carried much further before they will bear fruit, but I think they are necessary and well-founded. I can only give a first approximation of them here by pointing out three essential notions.

Language may be seen within society as a productive system: it produces meaning, thanks to its composition which is entirely designed for signification and thanks to the code which conditions its organization. It also produces enunciations indefinitely thanks to certain [101] rules of formal transformation and expansion; it thus creates forms and patterns of formation; it creates linguistic objects which are introduced into the circuit of communication. 'Communication' should be understood according to the literal senses of things held in common and of circulatory movement.

Here we are in the sphere of the economy. Already Saussure noted an analogy between certain notions belonging to economics and those which he founded, formulated, and organized for the first time in the process of linguistic communication. He pointed out that an economy like a language is a system of *values*: this is another fundamental term. This analogy could give rise to long developments, but we can extend it to a third notion which is connected to that of value, the notion of *exchange*, which can be assimilated to paradigmatic exchange. The paradigmatic axis of language is precisely characterized, with respect to the syntagmatic axis, by the possibility of replacing one term by another, one function by another, in so far, precisely, as it has a value by virtue of its syntagmatic use. And here we are very close to the characteristics of value in economics. Saussure compared the salary-work relation to the signifier-signified relation, because on both sides a value is in play and because the two members of this binomial are of a wholly different nature and are brought together in an arbitrary relation. I am not absolutely certain that this is the best example one might find or that the relations between salary and price, salary and work are rigorously homologous with that between signifier and signified, but here it is not so much this particular example which is in question as the principle of comparison and what it shows us about how to apply certain criteria and certain notions common to language and to society.

It will thus suffice to put forward, with a view to future elaboration, these three basic notions, which already extend our reflections beyond the traditional framework in which language and society are placed side by side.

I have tried in a very cursory way to show that it is necessary and possible in the discussion of this vast subject to introduce essential distinctions and also to pose relations between language and society which are at once logical and functional: logical when we consider their significant faculties and relation; functional in that both language and society may be considered as productive systems each according to its nature. In this way underlying analogies may emerge from beneath surface discordances. It is in social practice and in the use of language, in the relation of interhuman communication that the common traits of their functioning are to be discovered, for the human being is, still and ever more, an object to be discovered, in the double nature which language founds and initiates within him.

References

Abel-Rémusat, Jean-Pierre (1822). *Élémens de la Grammaire chinoise, ou Principes généraux du Kou-wen ou style antique, et du Kouan-hou, c'est-à-dire, de la langue commune généralement usitée dans l'empire chinois*. Paris: Imprimerie Royale.

Ablali, Driss (2017). 'Louis Hjelmslev en toutes lettres: éléments de réponse au projet glossématique inachevé avec Uldall dans des lettres à Martinet, Jakobson, Benveniste et quelques autres', in Estanislao Sofia and Valentina Chepiga (eds), *La correspondance entre linguistes—une espace de travail*, 65-84. Louvain-la-Neuve: Academia/L'Harmattan.

Adelung, Johann Christoph, and Johann Severin Vater (1806-1819). *Mithridates oder allgemeine Sprachenkunde mit dem Vaterunser als Sprachprobe in beynahe fünfhundert Sprachen und Mundarten*, 4 (in 6) vols. Berlin: Voss.

Alkor, Jan (1930). *Proekt alfavita èvenkijskogo (tungunsskogo) jazyka*. Leningrad: Izdatel'stvo Akademii Nauk SSSR.

Alter, Stephen G. (2005). *William Dwight Whitney and the Science of Language*. Baltimore: Johns Hopkins University Press.

Amiot, Joseph-Marie (1776). 'Lettre sur les Caractères chinois', *Mémoires concernant l'Histoire, les Sciences, les Arts, les Mœurs, les Usages &c. des Chinois*, vol. I: 275-323. Paris: Nyon.

Andersen, Henning (1989). 'Markedness theory—the first 150 years', in Olga Miseska Tomić (ed.), *Markedness in Synchrony and Diachrony*, 11-46. New York: Mouton de Gruyter.

Andersen, Henning (2001). 'Markedness and the theory of linguistic change', in Henning Andersen (ed.), *Actualization*, 21-57. Amsterdam and Philadelphia: Benjamins.

Andresen, Julie Tetel (1990). *Linguistics in America 1769-1924. A Critical History*. London and New York: Routledge.

Andrews, H. A. (1943). 'Bibliography of Franz Boas', in *Franz Boas, 1858-1942. American Anthropologist (Memoirs)*, New Series No. 61) 45.3, Part 2: 67-109.

Angell, James Rowland (1907). 'The province of functional psychology', *The Psychological Review* 14.2: 61-91.

Arnauld, Antoine, and Claude Lancelot (1660). *Grammaire générale et raisonnée contenant les fondemens de l'art de parler, expliqués d'une manière claire et naturelle*. Paris: Pierre le Petit. (English trans.: *General and Rational Grammar: The Port-Royal Grammar*, Jacques Rieux & Bernard E. Rollin [trans.]. The Hague: Mouton, 1975.)

Ash, Mitchell G. (1995). *Gestalt Psychology in German Culture, 1890-1967*. Cambridge: Cambridge University Press.

Auroux, Sylvain (1973). *L'Encyclopédie: 'Grammaire' et 'Langue' au XVIIe siècle*. Tours: Mame.

Auroux, Sylvain, Anne Boes, and Charles Porset (1981). 'Court de Gébelin (1725-1784) et le comparatisme: deux textes inédits', *Histoire Épistémologie Langage* 3.2: 21-67.

Bachelard, Gaston (2002). *The Formation of the Scientific Mind: A Contribution to a Psychoanalysis of Objective Knowledge*. Manchester: Clinamen.

Balbi, Adriano (1826). *Introduction à l'Atlas ethnographique du Globe*. 1 + 1 vols. Paris: Rey.

Bally, Charles (1905). *Précis de stylistique*. Geneva: Eggimann.

Bally, Charles (1909). *Traité de stylistique française*. Heidelberg: C. Winter.

Bally, Charles (1913). *Le langage et la vie*. Geneva: Atar.

Bang, Willy (1911). 'Beiträge zur Kritik des Codex Cumanicus', *Bulletin de la classe des Lettres de l'Académie 2 de Belgique* 1: 13-40.

Barannikov, Alexey (1928). 'Pro dïalekt cigan Artemïvs'koï okrugi', *Naukovij zbírnik Leningradskogo tovaristva doslídnikív ukr. ist., pis'menstva ta Movi* 1: 53-61.

Barton, Benjamin Smith (1797). *New Views on the Origin of the Tribes and Nations of America.* Philadelphia: Barton.
Basbøll, Hans (2022). 'Developments in Northern and Western Europe: Glossematics and beyond', in B. Elan Dresher and Harry van der Hulst (eds), *The Oxford History of Phonology*. Oxford: Oxford University Press, 331–355.
Battistella, Edwin (1996). *The Logic of Markedness.* Oxford: Oxford University Press.
Bat-Zeev Shyldkrot, Hava (2008). 'Saussure, Meillet et le concept de grammaticalisation', in Michel Arrivé (ed.), *Du côté de chez Saussure.* Limoges: Lambert-Lucas, 39–50.
Baudouin de Courtenay, Jan (1895). *Versuch einer Theorie phonetischer Alternationen: Ein Capitel aus der Psychophonetik.* Strasburg: Trübner.
Baudouin de Courtenay, Jan (1908). 'Zur Frage über die "Weichheit" und "Härte" der Sprachlaute im allgemeinen und im slavischen Sprachgebiete insbesondere', in *Jagić-Festschrift: Zbornik u slavu Vatroslava Jagića*, 583–590. Weidmann: Berlin.
Baudouin de Courtenay, Jan (1912). *Vvedeniye v yazykovedeniye* [Introduction to linguistics]. Saint Petersburg.
Baudouin de Courtenay, Jan (1922). *Zarys historji języka polskiego.* Warszawa: Polska Składnica Pomocy Szkolnych.
Baushev, Konstantin (1929). *Sintaksičeskij stroj votskoj reči i genezis častic sojuznogo porjadka.* Moskva: Gosudarstvennoe izdatel'stvo.
Beke, Ödön (1911). *Cseremisz nyelvtan.* Budapest: Magyar Tudományos Akadémia.
Benni, Tytus (1917). *Metoda palatograficzna w zastosowaniu do spółgłosek polskich.* Warszawa: Towarzystwo Naukowe Warszawskie.
Benveniste, Émile (1935). *Origines de la formation des noms en indo-européen.* Paris: Adrien-Maisonneuve.
Benveniste, Émile (1948). *Noms d'agent et noms d'action en indo-européen.* Paris: Adrien-Maisonneuve.
Benveniste, Émile (1949). 'Le système sublogique des prépositions en latin', *Recherches structurales (Travaux du Cercle Linguistique de Copenhague* 5), 178–184. Copenhagen: Nordisk Sprog- og Kulturforlag.
Benveniste, Émile (1966). *Problèmes de linguistique générale.* Paris: Gallimard.
Benveniste, Émile (1966 [1954]). 'Tendances récentes en linguistique générale', in Benveniste (1966: 3–17). (Original in *Journal de psychologie normale et pathologique*, 51.1–2: 130–145.)
Benveniste, Émile (1966 [1958]). 'De la subjectivité dans la langage', in Benveniste (1966: 258–266). (Original in *Journal de psychologie normale et pathologique*, 55.3: 257–265.)
Benveniste, Émile (1966 [1962]). '"Structure" en linguistique', in Benveniste (1966: 91–98). (Original in Roger Bastide (ed.), *Sens et usages du terme 'structure' dans les sciences humaines et sociales*, 31–39. The Hague: Mouton.)
Benveniste, Émile (1966 [1963]). 'Coup d'œil sur le développement de la linguistique', in Benveniste (1966: 18–31). (Original in *Comptes rendus des séances de l'Académie des Inscriptions et Belles-Lettres, Année 1962*, 106–2: 369–380.)
Benveniste, Émile (1969). *Le vocabulaire des institutions indo-européennes*, 2 vols. Paris: Minuit.
Benveniste, Émile (1970). 'The structure of language and the structure of society', in *Linguaggi nella società e nella tecnica*, 459–469. Milan: Edizioni di Comunità.
Benveniste, Émile (1971). *Problems in General Linguistics*, Mary Elizabeth Meek (trans.). Coral Gables: University of Miami Press.
Benveniste, Émile (1974). *Problèmes de linguistique générale 2.* Paris: Gallimard.
Benveniste, Émile (1974 [1967]). 'La forme et le sens dans le langage', in Benveniste (1974: 215–238).
Benveniste, Émile (1974 [1968a]). 'Structuralisme et linguistique', in Benveniste (1974: 11–28). (Original: 'Un entretien de Pierre Daix avec Émile Benveniste. "Structuralisme et linguistique"', in *Les Lettres françaises* 1242: 10–13.)
Benveniste, Émile (1974 [1968b]). 'Ce langage qui fait l'histoire', in Benveniste (1974: 29–40). (Original in *Le Nouvel Observateur* 210 bis: 28–34.)
Benveniste, Émile (1974 [1969]). 'Sémiologie de la langue', in Benveniste (1974: 43–66). (Original in *Semiotica* 1 [1968]: 1–12, and 2 [1969]: 127–135.)

Benveniste, Émile (1974 [1970a]). 'Structure de la langue et structure de la société', in Benveniste (1974: 91–102). (Original in *Linguaggi nella società e nella tecnica*, 17–28. Milan: Edizioni di Comunità.)

Benveniste, Émile (1974 [1970b]). 'Deux modèles linguistiques de la cité', in Benveniste (1974: 272–280). (Original in *Échanges et communications. Mélanges offerts à Claude Lévi-Strauss à l'occasion de son 60e anniversaire*, Jean Pouillon and Pierre Maranda (eds.), 589–596. The Hague: Mouton.)

Benveniste, Émile (1981). 'The semiology of language', Genette Ashby and Adelaide Russo (trans.), *Semiotica* 37 supp.: 5–23.

Benveniste, Émile (2011). *Baudelaire*, présentation et transcription par Chloé Laplantine. Limoges: Lambert-Lucas.

Benveniste, Émile (2016). *Dictionary of Indo-European Concepts and Society*, Elizabeth Palmer (trans.). London: HAU Books.

Berg, Lev. (1922). *Nomogenez, ili èvoljucija na osnove zakonomernostej [Nomogenesis, or Evolution Based on Internal Laws]*. Petrograd: Gosudarstvennoe izdatel'stvo. (English trans.: *Nomogenesis, or Evolution Determined by Law*. Cambridge, MA: MIT Press, 1969 [1926].)

Bergounioux, Gabriel, and Charles de Lamberterie, avec la collaboration de Jack Feuillet, Anne-Marguerite Fryba-Reber, Daniel Petit, Georges-Jean Pinault, Pierre Swiggers, and Stefan Zimmer (2006). *Meillet aujourd'hui*. Leuven and Paris: Peeters.

Berman, Judith (1994). 'George Hunt and the Kwak'wala texts', *Anthropological Linguistics* 36.4: 482–514.

Berman, Judith (1996). 'The culture as it appears to the Indian himself: Boas, George Hunt, and the methods of ethnography', in George W. Stocking, Jr. (ed.), *Volksgeist as Method and Ethic*, 215–256. Madison: University of Wisconsin Press.

Bernstein, Bruce (1993). 'Roland Dixon and the Maidu', *Museum Anthropology* 17.2: 20–26.

Besant, Walter (1893). 'A first impression', *Cosmopolitan: A Monthly Illustrated Magazine* 15 (May–October 1893): 528–539.

Blackhawk, Ned, and Isaiah Lorado Wilner (eds) (2018). *Indigenous Visions: Rediscovering the World of Franz Boas*. New Haven: Yale University Press.

Bloomfield, Leonard (1924). Review of Saussure (1922 [1916]), *Modern Language Journal* 8: 317–319.

Bloomfield, Leonard (1926). 'A set of postulates for the science of language', *Language* 2.3: 153–164.

Bloomfield, Leonard (1933). *Language*. New York: Holt.

Bloomfield, Leonard (1944). 'Secondary and tertiary responses to language', *Language* 20.2: 45–55.

Boas, Franz (1887a). 'The occurrence of similar inventions in areas widely apart', *Science* 9.224 (20 May): 485–486.

Boas, Franz (1887b). Response to Mason 1887, *Science* 9.228 (17 June): 587–589.

Boas, Franz (1887c). Response to Powell 1887, *Science* 9.229 (24 June): 614.

Boas, Franz (1889). 'On alternating sounds', *American Anthropologist* 2.1: 47–54.

Boas, Franz (1893a). 'Ethnology at the exhibition', *Cosmopolitan: A Monthly Illustrated Magazine* 15 (May–October 1893): 607–609.

Boas, Franz (1893b). 'Notes on the Chinook language', *American Anthropologist* 6.1: 55–64.

Boas, Franz (1894). 'Classification of the languages of the North Pacific coast', *Memoir of the International Congress of Anthropology*, 339–346. (Reproduced in Stocking 1974a: 159–116.)

Boas, Franz (1895). 'The social organization and the secret societies of the Kwakiutl Indians', *Report of the United States National Museum for the year ending June 30, 1895*, 309–738. Washington: Government Printing Office.

Boas, Franz (1896). 'The limitations of the comparative method of anthropology', *Science* 4.103 (18 December): 901–908.

Boas, Franz (1899). 'Summary of the work of the committee in British Columbia', *Report of the British Association for the Advancement of Science for 1898*, 667–682. London: British Association for the Advancement of Science. (Reproduced in Stocking 1974a: 88–107.)

Boas, Franz (1900). 'Sketch of the Kwakiutl language', *American Anthropologist* 2.4: 708–721. (Reprinted in Stocking 1974a: 167–177.)

Boas, Franz (1904). 'The history of anthropology', *Science* (New Series) 20.512 (21 October): 513–524. (Reproduced in Stocking 1974a: 23–36.)

Boas, Franz (1907). 'The relationship of Tlingit and Athapascan', Letter dated 25 November 1907, from Boas to John R. Swanton, reproduced in Stocking (1974a: 180–181).
Boas, Franz (1910). 'Chinook', in Boas (1911–1941: vol. 1, 559–678).
Boas, Franz (1911). 'Introduction', in Boas (1911–1941, vol 1: 1–83).
Boas, Franz (ed.) (1911–1941). *Handbook of American Indian Languages*, 4 vols. Washington: Government Printing Office.
Boas, Franz (1912). 'Languages', in Hodge (1912: 757–759).
Boas, Franz (1917). 'Introductory', *International Journal of American Linguistics* 1.1: 1–8.
Boas, Franz (1920). 'The classification of American languages', *American Anthropologist* (New Series) 22.4: 367–376.
Boas, Franz (1924). 'The social organization of tribes of the north Pacific coast', *American Anthropologist* (New Series) 26.3: 323–332.
Boas, Franz (1925). 'Die Klassifikation der indianischen Sprachen', *Proceedings of the XXIe Congrès International des Américanistes, The Hague 12–16 August 1924*, 305–311.
Boas, Franz (1926). 'Additional notes on the Kutenai language', *International Journal of American Linguistics* 4.1: 85–104.
Boas, Franz (1929). 'Classification of American Indian languages', *Language* 5.1: 1–7.
Boas, Franz (1931). 'Notes on the Kwakiutl vocabulary', *International Journal of American Linguistics* 6.3/4: 163–178.
Boas, Franz (1932). 'Recent work on American Indian languages', *Science* (New Series) 75.1949 (6 May): 489–491.
Boas, Franz (1938). 'Language', in Franz Boas (ed.), *General Anthropology*, 124–145. New York: D. C. Heath.
Boas, Franz (1966 [1911]). Introduction to Handbook of American Indian Languages, in Boas and Powell (1966: 1–79). (Original in Boas 1911–1941: vol. 1, 1–83.)
Boas, Franz, and Ella Deloria (1939). 'Dakota grammar', *Memoirs of the National Academy of Sciences* (Second Memoir) 23: 1–183.
Boas, Franz, and John Wesley Powell (1966). Introduction to *Handbook of American Indian Languages/Indian Linguistic Families North of Mexico*, Preston Holder (ed.). Lincoln: University of Nebraska Press.
Boewe, Charles (1999). 'The Other Candidate for the 1835 Volney Prize: Constantine Samuel Rafinesque', in Leopold (1999), 267–303. Dordrecht: Kluwer.
Bogoraz, Vladimir (1899). 'Obrazci materialov po izučeniju čukotskago jazyka i fol'klora', *Izvestija Imperatorskoj Akademii Nauk* 10 (3).
Bogoraz, Vladimir (1901). 'Oblastnoj slovar' Kolymskago russkago narečija. Sbornik otdelenija russkago jazyka i slovesnosti', *Imperatorskoj Akademii nauk* 68 (4).
Bogoroditzky, Vasily (1909). *Opyt fiziologii obščerusskago proiznošenija v svjazi s èksperimental'no-fonetičeskimi dannymi*. Kazan: Tipo-litografija Imperatorskago Universiteta.
Bopp, Franz (1839). *Die Celtischen Sprachen, in ihrem Verhältnisse zum Sanskrit, Zend, Griechischen, Lateinischen, Germanischen, Litthauischen und Slawischen*. Berlin: Dümmler.
Böss, Otto (1961). *Die Lehre der Eurasier. Ein Beitrag zur russischen Ideengeschichte des 20. Jahrhunderts*. Wiesbaden: Harrassowitz.
Breton, Raymond (1665). *Dictionnaire Caraïbe-François, Meslé de quantité de Rémarques historiques pour l'esclaircissement de la Langue*. Auxerre: Bouquet.
Breton, Raymond (1667). *Grammaire Caraïbe*. Auxerre: Bouquet.
Briggs, Charles, and Richard Bauman (1999). '"The foundation of all future researches": Franz Boas, George Hunt, Native American texts and the construction of modernity', *American Quarterly* 51.3: 479–528.
Brinton, Daniel Garrison (1886). 'On polysynthesis and incorporation as characteristics of American languages', *Proceedings of the American Philosophical Society* 23.121: 48–86.
Broch, Olaf (1897). *Studien von der slovakisch-kleinrussischen Sprachgrenze im östlichen Ungarn*. Kristiana: Kommission Hos Jacob Dybwad.
Broch, Olaf (1903). *Die Dialekte des südlichsten Serbiens*. Wien: Hölder.
Broch, Olaf (1910). *Očerk fiziologii slavjanskoj reči*. Sankt Peterburg: Imperatorskaja Akademija Nauk.

Brøndal, Viggo (1935). 'Structure et variabilité des systems morphologiques', *Scientia*: 109-119. (Communication given at the Third International Congress of Linguists, Rome, 22 September 1933, cf. *Atti del terzo Convegno Internazionale dei Linguisti*, 146-148. Florence: Le Monnier; republished in Viggo Brøndal 1943, *Essais de linguistique générale*, 15-24. Copenhagen, Munksgaard.)

Brøndal, Viggo (1940). *Præpositionernes Theori. Indledning til en rationel Betydninsglære*. Copenhagen, Munksgaard. (French edition 1950.)

Bubrikh, Dmitry (1927). 'Kratkij otčet o lingvističeskoj ėkspedicii k Mordve letom 1927 g', *Doklady Akademii Nauk SSSR* 10: 205-209.

Bubrikh, Dmitry (1929). 'O vzajmootnošenijach russkogo i finskich jazykov', in Jiří Horák, Matija Murko, and Miloš Weingart (eds), *Ier Congrès des philologues slaves à Prague*. Praha: Státní tiskárna.

Buettner-Janusch, John (1957). 'Boas and Mason: Particularism versus generalization', *American Anthropologist* 59.2: 318-324.

Bulfinch, Chris (2017). '"Freakshow": The treatment of Ainu at Japanese World's Fair exhibits of 1893 and 1904', in *The Trinity Papers*. Trinity College Digital Repository, Hartford. https://digitalrepository.trincoll.edu/trinitypapers/50

Bunzl, Matti (1996). 'Franz Boas and the Humboldtian tradition: From *Volksgeist* and *Nationalcharakter* to an anthropological concept of culture', in George W. Stocking, Jr. (ed.), *Volksgeist as Method and Ethic: Essays on Boasian ethnography and the German anthropological tradition*. Madison: University of Wisconsin Press, 17-78.

Burke, Edmund (1790). *Reflections on the Revolution in France*. London: Dodsley.

Buschmann, Eduard (1856). 'Der Athapaskische Sprachstamm', *Abhandlungen der historisch-philologischen Klasse der Königlichen Akademie der Wissenschaften zu Berlin 1855*: 149-319.

Buschmann, Eduard (1859). *Die Spuren der aztekischen Sprache im nördlichen Mexico und höheren amerikanischen Norden. Zugleich eine Musterung der Völker und Sprachen des nördlichen Mexico's und der Westseite Nordamerika's von Guadalaxara an bis zum Eismeer.* [Abhandlungen der Königlichen Akademie der Wissenschaften zu Berlin, 2. Supplement-Band 1854.] Berlin: Königliche Akademie der Wissenschaften.

Byrne, James (1885). *General Principles of the Structure of Language*, 2 vols. London: Trübner & Co.

Campbell, Lyle, and William J. Poser (2008). *Language Classification: History and Method*. Cambridge: Cambridge University Press.

Cannizzo, Jeanne (1983). 'George Hunt and the invention of Kwakiutl culture', *Canadian Journal of Sociology and Anthropology/La Revue Canadienne de Sociologie et d'Anthropologie* 20.1: 44-58.

Cantineau, Jean (1955). 'Le classement logique des oppositions', *Word* 11.1: 1-9.

Cassirer, Ernst (1945). 'Structuralism in modern linguistics', *Word* 1: 99-120.

Castrén, M. Alexander (1849). *Versuch einer ostjakischen Sprachenlehre*. Sankt Peterburg: Imperatorskaja Akademija Nauk.

Castrén, M. Alexander (1854). *Grammatik der samojedischen Sprachen*. Sankt Peterburg: Imperatorskaja Akademija Nauk.

Charlevoix, Pierre-François-Xavier de (1744). *Histoire et Description générale de la Nouvelle France, avec le Journal historique d'un Voyage fait par ordre du Roi dans l'Amérique septentrionnale*, 6 vols. Paris: Ganeau.

Chevalier, Jean-Claude, avec Pierre Encrevé (2006). *Combats pour la linguistique, de Martinet à Kristeva: Essai de dramaturgie épistémologique*. Paris: ENS Éditions.

Chomsky, Noam (1957). *Syntactic Structures*. The Hague: Mouton.

Chomsky, Noam (1966). *Cartesian Linguistics: A Chapter in the History of Rationalist Thought*. New York: Harper & Row.

Cigana, Lorenzo (2014). 'La notion de "participation" chez Louis Hjelmslev: un fil rouge de la glossématique', *Cahiers Ferdinand de Saussure*, 67: 191-202.

Cigana, Lorenzo (2018). 'Dentro la lingua, sotto la logica', in Marcello Walter Bruno, Donata Chiricò, Felice Cimatti, Giuseppe Cosenza, Anna De Marco, Emanuele Fadda, Giorgio Lo Feudo, Marco Mazzeo, and Claudia Stancati (eds), *Linguistica e filosofia del linguaggio. Studi in onore di Daniele Gambara*, 133-148. Sesto San Giovanni: Mimesis.

Cigana, Lorenzo (2022), *Hjelmslev e la teoria delle correlationi linguistiche*. Roma: Carocci.

Cigana, Lorenzo (2023). 'Beyond linguistic languages. Glossematics and the origins of connotation', in Lorenzo Cigana and Frans Gregersen (eds.), *Structuralism as One - Structuralism as Many. Studies in Structuralisms*. Copenhagen: Det Kongelige Danske Videnskabernes Selskab.
Cigana, Lorenzo, and Polis Stéphane (2022). 'Hjelmslev, a forerunner of the semantic maps method in linguistic typology?', in Camiel Hamans (ed.), *The History of Linguistics and its Significance*.
Condillac, Etienne Bonnot de (1746). *Esai sur l'origine des connoissances humaines*, 2 vols. Paris: Mortier.
Condillac, Etienne Bonnot de (1775). *Cours d'étude pour l'instruction du Prince de Parme*, 16 vols. Parma: Imprimerie Royale.
Coseriu, Eugenio (1967). 'Georg von der Gabelentz et la linguistique synchronique', *Word* 23: 74-110.
Coseriu, Eugenio (1992 [1988]). *Einführung in die Allgemeine Sprachwissenschaft*. Tübingen: Francke.
Cowan, J Milton (1987). 'The whimsical Bloomfield', *Historiographia Linguistica* 14.1/2: 23-37.
Crantz, David (1765). *Historie von Grönland enthaltend die Beschreibung des Landes und der Einwohner &c*, 2 vols. Barby: Ebers.
Cuvier, Georges (1812). *Recherches sur les ossemens fossiles de quadrupèdes*, vol. 1. Paris: Deterville.
Cuvier, Georges (1816). *Le règne animal distribué d'après son organisation*, 3 vols. Paris: Fortin and Masson.
Dall, William H. (1887). 'Museums of ethnology and their classification', *Science* 9.228 (June 17): 587.
Darnell, Regna (1988). 'Daniel Garrison Brinton: The "fearless critic" of Philadelphia', Unpublished M.A. thesis, University of Pennsylvania Department of Anthropology. University Museum Publications No. 3.
Darnell, Regna (1990). 'Franz Boas, Edward Sapir, and the Americanist text tradition', *Historiographia Linguistica* 17.1-2: 129-144.
Darnell, Regna (1998). *And along came Boas: Continuity and revolution in Americanist anthropology*. Amsterdam and Philadelphia: John Benjamins.
Daston, Lorraine, and Peter Galison (2007). *Objectivity*. New York: Zone Books.
De Boer, Cornelis, van Ginneken, Jacobus, and van Hamel, Anton (eds) (1928). *Actes du premier Congrès International de Linguistes: à la Haye du 10-15 avril 1928*. Leiden: Sijthoff.
De Pauw, Cornelius (1768). *Recherches philosophiques sur les Américains, ou Mémoires intéressants pour servir à l'Histoire de l'Espèce humaine*, 2 vols. Berlin: Decker.
DeLancey, Scott (2004). 'Grammaticalization: From syntax to morphology', in Geert Booij, Christian Lehmann, Joachim Mugdan, and Stavros Skopeteas in collaboration with Wolfgang Kesselheim, *Morphology: An International Handbook on Inflection and Word-formation*, Vol. 2. Berlin and New York: Walter de Gruyter, 1590-1599.
Delbrück, Berthold (1901). *Grundfragen der Sprachforschung, mit Rücksicht auf W. Wundts Völkerpsychologie*. Straßburg: Trübner.
Derrida, Jacques (1967). *De la grammatologie*. Paris: Minuit. (English trans.: *Of Grammatology*, 2nd edition, Gayatri Chakravorty Spivak [trans.]. Baltimore: Johns Hopkins University Press, 1997.)
Destutt de Tracy, Antoine (1798). 'Mémoire sur la faculté de penser', *Mémoires de l'Institut national des Sciences et des Arts pour l'An IV. Sciences morales et politiques*, vol. I. Paris: Baudouin, 283-450.
Destutt de Tracy, Antoine (1801-1805). *Élémens d'Idéologie*, 3 vols. [Vols. 4-5 added in 1815.] Paris: Didot.
Dirr, Adolf (1928). *Einführung in das Studium der kaukasischen Sprachen*. Leipzig: Verlag der Asia Major.
Dixon, R. M. W. (1994). *Ergativity*. Cambridge: Cambridge University Press.
Dixon, Roland B., and A[lfred] L. Kroeber (1903). 'The native languages of California', *American Anthropologist* 5.1: 1-26.
Dosse, François (1991). *Histoire du structuralisme, I. Le champ du signe, 1945-1966*. Paris: Editions La Découverte. (English trans.: *History of Structuralism*, vol. 1: *The Rising Sign, 1945-1966*, Deborah Glassman [trans.]. Minneapolis: University of Minnesota Press, 1997.)
Dosse, François (1992). *Histoire du structuralisme, II. Le chant du cygne, de 1967 à nos jours*. Paris: Editions La Découverte. (English trans.: *History of Structuralism*, vol. 2: *The Sign Sets, 1967-present*, Deborah Glassman [trans.]. Minneapolis: University of Minnesota Press, 1997.)

Dunglinson, Robley (1844). *A Public Discourse in Commemoration of Peter Stephen du Ponceau, LL.D.* Philadelphia: American Philosophical Society.
Du Ponceau, Peter Stephen (1818). 'English phonology, or an essay towards an analysis and description of the component sounds of the English language', *Transactions of the American Philosophical Society* I: 228-264.
Du Ponceau, Peter Stephen (1819). 'Report [...] of the general character and forms of the languages of the American Indians' *Transactions of the Historical and Literary Committee of the American Philosophical Society* I: xvii-l.
Du Ponceau, Peter Stephen (1838a). *Mémoire sur le Système grammatical des langues de quelques nations Indiennes de l'Amérique du Nord.* Paris: Pihan de la Forest.
Du Ponceau, Peter Stephen (1838b). *A Dissertation on the Nature and Character of the Chinese System of Writing.* Philadelphia: American Philosophical Society.
Du Ponceau, Peter Stephen (1939). 'Notes and documents: The autobiography of Peter Stephen Du Ponceau', James Whitehead (ed.), *The Pennsylvania Magazine of History and Biography* 63.2: 189-227.
Du Ponceau, Peter Stephen (1999 [1825]). 'Essai de Solution du Problème proposé en l'année 1823 par la Commission de l'Institut Royal de France, chargée de la disposition du legs de M. Le Comte de Volney', in Leopold (1999), 37-79.
Durnovo, Nikolay [Nikolaj], Bohuslav Havránek, Roman Jakobson, Vilém Mathesius, Jan Mukařovský, Nikolay Trubetzkoy, and Bohumil Trnka (1929). 'Thèses présentées au Premier Congrès des philologues slaves', in *Mélanges linguistiques dédiés au Premier Congrès des Philologues Slaves.* Praha: Jednota Československých Matematiků a Fysiků, 5-29. (English trans.: 'Manifesto', in Marta K. Johnson [ed.], *Recycling the Prague Linguistic Circle.* Ann Arbor: Karoma, 1978, 1-31.)
Durnovo, Nikolay, N. N. Sokolov, and Dmitry Ushakov (1915). *Opyt dialektologičeskoj karty russkogo jazyka v Evrope: s priloženiem očerka russkoj dialektologii.* Moskva: Sinodal'naja tipografija.
Edelstein, Dan (2010). 'Introduction to the Super-Enlightenment', in D. Edelstein (ed.), *The Super-Enlightenment: Daring to Know too Much.* Oxford: Voltaire Foundation, 1-33.
Edwards, Ernst Richard (1903). *Étude phonétique de la langue japonaise.* Leipzig: Teubner.
Edwards, John (1823 [1778]). *Observations on the Language of the Muhhekaneew Indians*, John Pickering (ed.). Boston: Phelps & Farnham.
Egede, Hans (1745). *A Description of Greenland.* London: Hitch, Austen and Jackson.
Egede, Paul (1760). *Grammatica Grönlandica Danico-Latina.* Copenhagen: Kisel.
Egorov, Vladimir (1930). *Vvedenie v izučenie čuvašskogo jazyka.* Moskva: Centrizdat.
Elffers, Els (2012). 'The rise of general linguistics as an academic discipline: Georg von der Gabelentz as a co-founder', in Rens Bod, Jaap Maat, and Thijs Weststeijn (eds), *The Making of the Humanities*, vol. 2: *From Early Modern to Modern Disciplines.* Amsterdam: Amsterdam University Press, 55-72.
Eliot, John (1666). *The Indian Grammar Begun: or, An essay to bring the Indian language into rules.* Cambridge, MA: Marmaduke Johnson.
Eliot, John (1822). *A Grammar of the Massachusetts Indian Language*, John Pickering and Peter Stephen du Ponceau (eds). Boston: Phelps & Farnham.
E[lliott], A. M[arshall] (1892). 'Lebrija and the Romance future tense', *Modern Language Notes* 7/8: 485-488.
Emelyanov, Arkady (1927). *Grammatika votjackogo jazyka.* Leningrad: Leningradskij Vostočnyj Institut Imeni A.S. Enukidze.
Endzelīns, Jānis (1922). 'Des intonations lettonnes', *Revue des études slaves* 2: 56-68.
Endzelīns, Jānis (1923). *Lettische Grammatik.* Heidelberg: Carl Winter.
Evsevev, Makar (1928). *Osnovy mordovskoj grammatiki.* Moskva: Centrizdat.
Falk, Julia S. (2004). 'Saussure and American linguistics', in Carol Sanders (ed.), *The Cambridge Companion to Saussure*, 107-123. Cambridge: Cambridge University Press.
Fischer-Jørgensen, Eli (1966). 'Form and substance in glossematics', *Acta Linguistica Hafniensia* 10.1: 1-33.
Fischer-Jørgensen, Eli (1997). 'Hjelmslev et le Cercle Linguistique de Copenhague', in Alessandro Zinna (ed.), *Hjelmslev aujourd'hui. Semiotic and Cognitive Studies*, 27-36. Turnhout: Brepols.

Foley, William A. (1999). Review of *The Korowai of Irian Jaya*, by Gerrit van Enk and Lourens de Vries. New York: Oxford University, 1997, *Language in Society* 28.3: 470-472.

Formigari, Lia (2018). 'Wilhelm Wundt and the *Lautgesetze* controversy', *History and Philosophy of the Language Sciences*. https://hiphilangsci.net/2018/01/17/wundt-lautgesetze/

Fortes, Meyer (ed.) (1949). *Social Structure: Studies Presented to A. R. Radcliffe-Brown*. London: Oxford University Press.

Fortescue, Michael, Marianne Mithun, and Nicholas Evans (eds) (2017). *The Oxford Handbook of Polysynthesis*. Oxford: Oxford University Press.

Fortunatov, Filipp (1895). 'Ob udarenii i dolgote v baltijskich jazykach', *Russkij filologičeskij vestnik* 33: 252-297.

François, Jacques (2017). *Le siècle d'or de la linguistique en Allemagne de Humboldt à Meyer-Lübke*. Limoges: Lambert-Lucas.

Frazer, James (1911 [1890]). *The Golden Bough, a Study of Magic and Religion*, 3rd ed. London: Macmillan.

Fréret, Nicolas (1718). 'Réflexions sur les principes généraux de l'art d'écrire, et en particulier sur les fondemens de l'écriture chinoise', *Mémoires de l'Académie des Inscriptions et Belles-Lettres* VI: 609-634.

Friedrich, Janette (2000). 'Le recours de Humboldt au concept de "physionomie"', *Cahiers Ferdinand de Saussure* 53: 81-99.

Gabelentz, Georg von der (1881). *Chinesische Grammatik*. Leipzig: Weigel.

Gabelentz, Georg von der (1893). 'Baskisch und Berberisch', *Sitzungsberichte der königlich-preußischen Akademie der Wissenschaften zu Berlin*, 593-613.

Gabelentz, Georg von der (1894a). 'Hypologie [Typologie]: Eine neue Aufgabe der Linguistik', *Indogermanische Forschungen* 4: 1-7.

Gabelentz, Georg von der (1894b). *Die Verwandtschaft des Baskischen mit den Berbersprachen Nord-Africas, nachgewiesen von Georg von der Gabelentz*, Albrecht Graf von der Schulenburg (ed.). Braunschweig: Sattler.

Gabelentz, Georg von der (2016 [^{1}1891, ^{2}1901]). *Die Sprachwissenschaft, ihre Aufgaben, Methoden und bisherigen Ergebnisse*, Manfred Ringmacher & James McElvenny (eds). Berlin: Language Science Press. (1st and 2nd edition, Leipzig: T.O. Wigel Nachfolger).

Gadet, Françoise (1995). 'Jakobson sous le pavillon saussurien', in Michel Arrivé and Claudine Normand (eds), *Saussure aujourd'hui*, numéro spécial de *LINX*: 449-459.

Gallatin, Albert (1836). 'A Synopsis of the Indian Tribes of North America', *Transactions and Collections of the American Antiquarian Society* 2: 1-422.

Gallatin, Albert (1848). 'Hale's Indians of Northwest America, and Vocabularies of North America, with an Introduction', *Transactions of the American Ethnological Society* 2: xxiii-clxxxviii, 1-130.

Galton, Francis (1888-1889). 'Co-relations and their measurement, chiefly from anthropometric data', *Proceedings of the Royal Society of London* 45: 135-145.

Gardini, Francesco, Peter Arkadiev, and Nino Amiridze (2015). 'Borrowed morphology: An overview', in Francesco Gardini, Peter Arkadiev, and Nino Amiridze (eds), *Borrowed Morphology*, 1-23. Berlin: Mouton de Gruyter.

Gébelin, Antoine Court de (1773-1782). *Monde primitif analysé et comparé avec le Monde modern*, 9 vols. Paris: Boudet et al.

Gébelin, Antoine Court de (1774). *Histoire Naturelle de la Parole, ou Précis de l'Origine du Langage & de la Grammaire Universelle*. Paris: Boudet et al.

Georgievsky, Alexander (1928). *Russkie govory Primor'ja*. Vladivostok: Tipografija Gosudarstvennogo Dal'nevostočnogo Universiteta.

Gerullis, Georg (1930). *Litauische Dialektstudien*. Leipzig: Markert & Petters.

Ginneken, Jacob van (1933). 'La biologie de la base d'articulation', *Psychologie du langage—Journal de psychologie* 1-4: 266-320.

Givón, Talmy (1975). 'Serial verbs and syntactic change: Niger-Congo', in Charles N. Li (ed.), *Word Order and Word Order Change*. Austin and London: University of Texas Press, 47-112.

Goldsmith, John A., and Bernard Laks (2019). *Battle in the Mind Fields*. Chicago: University of Chicago Press.

Grasserie, Raoul de la (1889–1890). 'De la classification des langues. I. Partie: Classification des langues apparentees', 'II. Partie: Classification des langues non-apparentees', *Internationale Zeitschrift für Allgemeine Sprachwissenschaft* 4: 374–387; 5: 296–338.

Gray, Edward (1999). *New World Babel: Languages and Nations in Early America*. Princeton: Princeton University Press.

Gray, Louis (1939). *Foundations of Language*. New York: Macmillan.

Greenberg, Joseph H. (1966 [1963]). 'Some universals of grammar with particular reference to the order of meaningful elements', in Joseph Greenberg (ed.), *Universals of Language*. Cambridge, MA: MIT Press, 73–113.

Greenberg, Joseph H. (1974). *Language Typology: A Historical and Analytic Overview*. Berlin: De Gruyter.

Greenberg, Joseph H. (2005 [1966]). *Linguistic Universals with Special Reference to Feature Hierarchies*. Berlin and New York: De Gruyter.

Gregersen, Frans (1991). *Sociolingvistikkens (u)mulighed. Videnskabshistoriske studier i Ferdinand de Saussures og Louis Hjelmslevs strukturalistiske sprogteorier*, 2 vols. Copenhagen: Tiderne Skifter.

Gregersen, Frans, and Viggo Bank Jensen (2022). 'Worlds apart? Roman Jakobson and Louis Hjelmslev. History of a competitive friendship', in Lorenzo Cigana and Frans Gregersen (eds), *Structuralism as One - Structuralism as Many. Studies in Structuralisms*. Copenhagen: Det Kongelige Danske Videnskabernes Selskab.

Grégoire, Antoine (1899). 'Variation de la durée de la syllabe française', *La Parole* 1: 161–176.

Greimas, Algirdas Julien (1976). 'Entretien avec A. J. Greimas sur les structures élémentaires de la signification', in Frédéric Nef (ed.), *Structures élémentaires de la signification*, 18–26. Bruxelles: Editions Complexes.

Gruber, Jacob (1967). 'Horatio Hale and the Development of American Anthropology', *Proceedings of the American Philosophical Society* 111.1: 5–37.

Gurvitch, Georges (1955). 'Le concept de structure sociale', *Cahiers Internationaux de Sociologie*, Nouvelle série, 19: 3–44.

Gusdorf, Georges (1978). *Les Sciences humaines et la Pensée occidentale*, vol. VIII: *La conscience révolutionnaire. Les Idéologues*. Paris: Payot.

Haas, Mary R. (1976). 'Boas, Sapir, and Bloomfield', in Wallace L. Chafe (ed.), *American Indian Languages and American Linguistics: Papers of the Second Golden Anniversary Symposium of the Linguistic Society of America, held at the University of California, Berkeley, on November 8 and 9, 1974*, 59–69. Lisse: Peter de Ridder Press.

Hale, Horatio (1846). *United States Exploring Expedition during the Years 1838, 1839, 1840, 1841, 1842*, vol. VI: *Ethnography and Philology*. Philadelphia: Sherman.

Hale, Horatio (1883a). *The Iroquois Book of Rites*. Philadelphia: Brinton.

Hale, Horatio (1883b). 'Indian migrations, as evidenced by language', *American Antiquarian and Oriental Journal* 5: 18–28, 108–124.

Hale, Horatio (1885). 'On some doubtful or intermediate articulations: an experiment in phonetics', *Journal of the Anthropological Institute of Great Britain and Ireland* 14: 233–243.

Hale, Horatio (1886). 'The origin of languages, and the antiquity of speaking man', *Science* 8.186: 191–196.

Hale, Horatio (1890). *An International Idiom: A Manual of the Oregon Trade Language, or 'Chinook Jargon'*. London: Whitaker.

Harrington, Anne (1996). *Reenchanted Science: Holism in German culture from Wilhelm II to Hitler*. Princeton: Princeton University Press.

Harrington, John P. (1945). 'Boas on the science of language', *International Journal of American Linguistics* 11.2: 97–99.

Harris, Randy A. (2021). *The Linguistics Wars*, 2nd ed. Oxford: Oxford University Press.

Harvey, Sean P. (2015). *Native Tongues: Colonialism and Race from Encounter to the Reservation*. Cambridge, MA and London: Harvard University Press.

Haudricourt, André G., and Georges Granai (1955). 'Linguistique et sociologie', *Cahiers Internationaux de Sociologie*, Nouvelle Série, 19: 114–129.
Hawthorne, Julian (1893). 'Foreign folk at the fair', *Cosmopolitan: A Monthly Illustrated Magazine* 15 (May–October 1893): 567–576.
Heckewelder, John (1819a). 'An account of the History, manners, and customs of the Indian Nations who once inhabited Pennsylvania and the neighbouring States', *Transactions of the Historical and Literary Committee of the American Philosophical Society* I: 1–348.
Heckewelder, John (1819b). 'Words, phrases, and short dialogues, in the language of the Lenni Lenape', *Transactions of the Historical and Literary Committee of the American Philosophical Society* I: 451–464.
Heckewelder, John, and Peter Stephen du Ponceau (1819). 'A correspondence [...] respecting the languages of the American Indians', *Transactions of the Historical and Literary Committee of the American Philosophical Society* I: 351–448.
Henry, Victor (1883). *Étude sur l'analogie en général et sur les formations analogiques de la langue grecque*. Paris: Maisonneuve.
Hering, Ewald (1878). *Zur Lehre vom Lichtsinne*. Vienna: Gerold.
Herschel, John Frederick William (ed.) (2011 [1849]). *A Manual of Scientific Enquiry: Prepared for the use of Her Majesty's Navy and adapted for travellers in general*. Cambridge: Cambridge University Press.
Herskovits, Melville (1953). *Franz Boas: The Science of Man in the Making*. New York: Charles Scribner's Sons.
Heyse, Karl Wilhelm Ludwig (1856). *System der Sprachwissenschaft*, H. Steinthal (ed.). Berlin: Dümmler.
Hinsley, Curtis M. (2016). 'A visual interlude: Popular images of anthropology and its subjects at the fair', in Curtis M. Hinsley and David R. Wilcox (eds), *Coming of Age in Chicago: The 1893 World's Fair and the Coalescence of American Anthropology*, 239–260. Lincoln: University of Nebraska Press.
Hjelmslev, Louis (1928). *Principes de grammaire générale*. Copenhagen: Munksgaard.
Hjelmslev, Louis (1932). *Études baltiques*. Copenhagen: Levin and Munksgaards.
Hjelmslev, Louis (1935–1937). *La catégorie des cas. Étude de grammaire générale*, 2 vols. (Acta Jutlandica, 7.1 and 9.2). Aarhus: Aarhus Universitetsforlaget.
Hjelmslev, Louis (1937). 'La structure des oppositions dans la langue', *Onzième Congrès international de psychologie, Paris, 25–31 juillet 1937, Rapports et comptes rendus*, 214–242. (Reproduced in Cigana forthcoming.)
Hjelmslev, Louis (1938). 'Neue Wege der Experimentalphonetik', *Nordisk tidsskrift for tale og stemme* 2: 153–194.
Hjelmslev, Louis (1941). Review of Edward Sapir: *Glottalized consonants in Navaho, Nootka, and Kwakiutl*, *Acta Linguistica* 2.1: 61–66.
Hjelmslev, Louis (1942). 'Langue et parole', *Cahiers Ferdinand de Saussure* 2: 29–44.
Hjelmslev, Louis (1943). *Omkring sprogteoriens grundlæggelse*. Copenhagen: Munksgaard.
Hjelmslev, Louis (1946). 'Les degrés de comparaison', *Bulletins du Cercle Linguistique de Copenhague* 7: 14.
Hjelmslev, Louis (1959). *Essais linguistiques*. Copenhagen: Nordisk Sprog- og Kulturforlag.
Hjelmslev, Louis (1961). *Prolegomena to a Theory of Language*, Francis J. Whitfield (trans.). Madison: University of Wisconsin Press.
Hjelmslev, Louis (1970 [1938]). 'Essai d'une théorie des morphèmes', *Essais linguistiques* (Travaux du Cercle linguistique de Copenhague, 12), 152–165. Copenhagen: Nordisk Sprog- og Kulturforlag. (Reproduced in Hjelmslev 1959: 152–164.)
Hjelmslev, Louis (1970 [1939b]). 'La structure morphologique', *Essais linguistiques* (Travaux du Cercle linguistique de Copenhague, 12), 113–138. Copenhagen: Nordisk Sprog- og Kulturforlag.
Hjelmslev, Louis (1970 [1948]). '16.12.48. L. Hjelmslev: Le système d'expression du francais moderne (résumé)', *Bulletins du Cercle Linguistique de Copenhague 1941–1964* (8–31). Choix de communications et d'interventions au débat lors des séances tenues entre septembre 1941 et mai 1965, 217–222. Copenhagen: Akademisk Forlag.

Hjelmslev, Louis (1970 [1957]). 'Pour une sémantique structurale', *Essais linguistiques* (Travaux du Cercle linguistique de Copenhague, 12), 211-250. Copenhagen: Nordisk Sprog- og Kulturforlag.
Hjelmslev, Louis (1972 [1934]). *Sprogsystem og sprogforandring* (Travaux du Cercle Linguistique de Copenhague, 15). Copenhagen: Nordisk Sprog- og Kulturforlag.
Hjelmslev, Louis (1973 [1933]). 'Structure générale des corrélations linguistiques', *Essais linguistiques*, II (Travaux du Cercle linguistique de Copenhague, 14), 57-98. Copenhagen: Nordisk Sprog- og Kulturforlag.
Hjelmslev, Louis (1973 [1951]). 'Outline of the Danish expression system with special reference to the stød', *Essais linguistiques II* (Travaux du Cercle Linguistique de Copenhague, 14), 247-266. Copenhagen: Nordisk Sprog- og Kulturforlag.
Hjelmslev, Louis (1975). *Résumé of a Theory of Language*, Francis J. Whitfield (ed. and trans.). Copenhagen: Nordisk Sprog- og Kulturforlag.
Hjelmslev, Louis (1970 [1939a]). 'Note sur les oppositions supprimables', *Essais linguistiques* (Travaux du Cercle linguistique de Copenhague, 12), 82-88. Copenhagen: Nordisk Sprog- og Kulturforlag.
Hockett, Charles F. (1958). *A Course in Modern Linguistics*. New York: Macmillan.
Hodge, Frederick Webb (ed.) (1912). *Handbook of American Indians north of Mexico. Part 1*. Smithsonian Institution Bureau of American Ethnology Bulletin 30. Washington, DC: Government Printing Office.
Holmes, William H. (1893). 'The World's Fair Congress of Anthropology', *American Anthropologist* 6.4: 423-434.
Hopper, Paul J., and Elizabeth C. Traugott (2003). *Grammaticalization*, 2nd ed. Cambridge: Cambridge University Press.
Humboldt, Wilhelm von (1824). 'Über das Entstehen der grammatischen Formen und ihren Einfluß auf die Ideenentwicklung', *Abhandlungen der historisch-philologischen Klasse der Königlichen Akademie der Wissenschaften zu Berlin 1822-1823*: 402-430.
Humboldt, Wilhelm von (1905 [1820]). 'Über das vergleichende Sprachstudium in Beziehung auf die verschiedenen Epochen der Sprachentwicklung', in Albert Leitzmann (ed.), *Wilhelm von Humboldts Gesammelte Schriften*, vol. 4. Berlin: Behr, 1-34.
Humboldt, Wilhelm von (1988 [1836]). *On Language: The Diversity of Language-Structure and its Influence on the Mental Development of Mankind*, Peter Heath (trans.). Cambridge: Cambridge University Press. (English trans. of Humboldt 1998 [1836].)
Humboldt, Wilhelm von (1998 [1836]). *Über die Verschiedenheit des menschlichen Sprachbaues und ihren Einfluß auf die geistige Entwicklung des Menschengeschlechts*, Donatella Di Cesare (ed.). Paderborn: Schöningh. (English trans. in Humboldt 1988 [1836].)
Hurch, Bernhard, and Kathrin Purgay (2019). 'The Basque-Berber connection of Georg von der Gabelentz', in James McElvenny (ed.), *Gabelentz and the Science of Language*. Amsterdam: Amsterdam University Press, 57-97.
Hymes, Dell (1961). Review of Walter Goldschmidt (ed.), 'The anthropology of Franz Boas: Essays on the centennial of his birth', *The Journal of American Folklore* 74.291: 87-90.
Hymes, Dell, and John Fought (1981). *American Structuralism*. The Hague: Mouton.
Ivić, Milka (1970 [1963]). *Trends in Linguistics*. The Hague: Mouton.
Jacknis, Ira (1985). 'Franz Boas and exhibits: On the limitations of the museum method of anthropology', in George W. Stocking, Jr. (ed.), *Objects and Others: Essays on Museums and Material Culture*, 75-111. Madison: University of Wisconsin Press.
Jacknis, Ira (1991). 'George Hunt, collector of Indian specimens', in Aldona Jonaitis (ed.), *Chiefly Feasts: The Enduring Kwakiutl Potlatch*, 177-223. Seattle: University of Washington Press.
Jacknis, Ira (2016). 'Refracting images: Anthropological displays at the Chicago World's Fair, 1893', in Curtis M. Hinsley and David R. Wilcox (eds), *Coming of Age in Chicago: The 1893 World's Fair and the Coalescence of American Anthropology*, 261-336. Lincoln: University of Nebraska Press.
Jakobson, Roman (1923). *O češskom stiche preimuščestvenno v sopostavlenii s russkim*. Moskva: Gosudarstvennoe izdatel'stvo.
Jakobson, Roman (1928). 'Proposition 16', in *Actes du 1er Congrès international des linguistes, La Haye, du 10 au 15 avril 1928*, Leiden: Sijthoff, p. 18.

Jakobson, Roman (1929). *Remarques sur l'évolution phonologique du russe comparée à celle des autres langues slaves*. Praha: Jednota Československých Matematiků a Fysiků.
Jakobson, Roman (1931a). *K kharakteristike evraziiskogo iazykovogo soiuza* [For a characterization of the Eurasian language union]. Paris: Izdanie evrazijcev. (Reproduced, with slight modifications, in Jakobson 1971a: 144–201.)
Jakobson, Roman (1931b). 'Les unions phonologiques de langues', *Le Monde Slave* 1: 371–378.
Jakobson, Roman (1931c). 'O fonologicheskikh jazykovykh soiuzakh' [On phonological language unions], in *Evraziia v svete iazykoznaniia*, 7–12. Prague: Izdanie evrazijcev.
Jakobson, Roman (1932). 'Zur Struktur des russischen Verbums', *Charisteria Guilelmo Mathesio quinquagenario*, 74–84. Prague: Linguistický Kroužek.
Jakobson, Roman (1936). 'Beitrag zur allgemeinen Kasuslehre: Gesamtbedeutungen der russischen Kasus', *Travaux du Cercle Linguistique de Prague*, 6: 240–288.
Jakobson, Roman (1941). *Kindersprache, Aphasie und allgemeine Lautgesetze*. Uppsala: Almqvist och Wiksells Boktryckeri. (English trans: *Child Language, Aphasia and Phonological Universals*, The Hague: Mouton, 1968.)
Jakobson, Roman (1944). 'Franz Boas' approach to language', *International Journal of American Linguistics* 10.4: 188–195.
Jakobson, Roman (1958). 'Typological studies and their contribution to historical comparative linguistics', *Proceedings of the 8th International Congress of Linguists, Oslo*. (Reproduced in Jakobson 1971a: 523–531.)
Jakobson, Roman (1960). 'Linguistics and Poetics', in Thomas A. Sebeok (ed.), *Style in Language*, 350–377. Cambridge, MA: MIT Press.
Jakobson, Roman, counter-signed by N. S. Trubetzkoy, and Serge Karcevski (1971 [1928]). 'Proposition au Premier Congrès International de Linguistes: Quelles sont les méthodes les mieux appropriées à un exposé complet et pratique de la phonologie d'une langue quelconque?', in Jakobson (1971a: 3–6).
Jakobson, Roman (1971 [1929]). 'Romantické všeslovanství—nová slavistika', *Čin*, 31 October 1929, English trans. in 'Retrospect', in Roman Jakobson (ed.), in Jakobson (1971b: 711–712). (Original reproduced in Jakobson 2013–2014: 231–233.)
Jakobson, Roman (1971 [1931a]). 'Über die phonologischen Sprachbünde', in Jakobson (1971a: 137–143). (Original in *Travaux du Cercle Linguistique de Prague* 4: 234–340.)
Jakobson, Roman (1971 [1931b]). 'Principes de phonologie', in Jakobson (1971a: 202–220). (Original: 'Prinzipien der historischen Phonologie', *Travaux du Cercle Linguistique de Prague* 4: 247–267; revised version printed as appendix to N. S. Troubetzkoy, Principes de phonologie, ed. and trans. by J. Cantineau. Paris: Klincksiek, 1949.)
Jakobson, Roman (1971 [1938]). 'Sur la théorie des affinités phonologiques entre les langues', in Jakobson (1971a: 234–246). (Original in *Actes du 4e Congrès international de linguists, Copenhagen, 27 August–1 September 1936*, 48–58; revised version included as appendix 4 in Trubetzkoy 1986: 351–365.)
Jakobson, Roman (1971 [1939]). 'Les lois phoniques du langage enfantin et leur place dans la phonologie générale', in Jakobson (1971a: 317–327).
Jakobson, Roman (1971 [1956]). 'Two aspects of language and two types of aphasic disturbances', in Jakobson (1971b: 237–259). (Original in *Fundamentals of Language*. The Hague: Mouton, 1956.)
Jakobson, Roman (1971a). *Selected Writings*, vol. I. The Hague: Mouton.
Jakobson, Roman (1971b). *Selected Writings*, vol. II. The Hague: Mouton.
Jakobson, Roman (1971c). 'The Kazan' School of Polish linguistics and its place in the international development of phonology', in Jakobson (1971b: 394–428).
Jakobson, Roman (1979). 'The twentieth century in European and American linguistics: Movements and continuity', in Henry M. Hoenigswald (ed.), *The European Background of American Linguistics: Papers of the Third Golden Anniversary Symposium of the Linguistic Society of America*, 161–173. Dordrecht: Foris.
Jakobson, Roman (2013–2014). *Selected Writings*, vol. IX, Jindřich Toman (ed.). Berlin: Mouton de Gruyter.

Jakobson, Roman (2013–2014 [1929]). 'Über die heutigen Voraussetzungen der russischen Slavistik', in Jakobson (2013–2014: 215–230). (Original in *Slavische Rundschau* (Prague) 1: 629–646.)
Jakobson, Roman (2017 [1921]). 'L'influence de la révolution sur la langue russe', Stéphanie Cirac (trans.), in Archaimbault et al. (2017: 113–172).
Jakobson, Roman, and Claude Lévi-Strauss (1962). 'Les Chats' de Charles Baudelaire, *L'Homme* 2.1: 5–21.
Jakobson, Roman, and Claude Lévi-Strauss (2018). *Correspondance 1942–1982*, préfacé, édité et annoté par Emmanuelle Loyer et Patrice Maniglier. Paris: Seuil.
Jakobson, Roman, André Mazon, Sylvie Archaimbault, and Catherine Depretto (eds) (2017). *La langue russe, la guerre et la révolution*. Paris: Eur'Orbem éditions.
Jakobson, Roman, and Krystyna Pomorska (1980). *Dialogues*. Paris: Flammarion. (English trans.: Dialogues, Christian Hubert (trans.). Cambridge, MA: MIT Press, 1983.)
Jakobson, Roman, and Linda Waugh (1979). *The Sound Shape of Language*. Bloomington: Indiana University Press.
Jarvis, Samuel (1820). *A Discourse on the Religion of the Indian tribes of North America*. New York: Wiley and co.
Jeanpierre, Laurent (2004). 'Une opposition structurante pour l'anthropologie structurale: Lévi-Strauss contre Gurvitch, la guerre de deux exilés français aux États-Unis', *Revue d'Histoire des Sciences Humaines* 11: 13–43.
Jensen, Eva Skafte (2012). 'Markedness, participation and grammatical paradigms. Jakobson and Hjelmslev revisited', *Nordic Journal of Linguistics* 35.2: 145–168.
Jespersen, Otto (1924). *The Philosophy of Grammar*. London: George Allen and Unwin.
Jones, William (1787). 'The third Anniversary Discourse [On the Hindus], delivered 2 February 1786', *Asiatick Researches* I: 415–431.
Joseph, John E. (1990). 'Ideologizing Saussure: Bloomfield's and Chomsky's readings of the *Cours de linguistique générale*', in John E. Joseph and Talbot J. Taylor (eds), *Ideologies of Language*. London: Routledge, 51–78.
Joseph, John E. (1995). 'Natural grammar, arbitrary lexicon: An enduring parallel in the history of linguistic thought', *Language and Communication* 15.3: 213–225.
Joseph, John E. (1999). 'A matter of *Consequenz*: Humboldt, race and the genius of the Chinese language', *Historiographia Linguistica* 26.1/2: 89–148.
Joseph, John E. (2000). *Limiting the Arbitrary: Linguistic Naturalism and its Opposites in Plato's* Cratylus *and Modern Theories of Language*. Amsterdam and Philadelphia: John Benjamins.
Joseph, John E. (2001). 'The exportation of structuralist ideas from linguistics to other fields: an overview', in Sylvain Auroux, E. F. K. Koerner, Hans-Josef Niederehe, and Kees Versteegh (eds), *History of the Language Sciences: An International Handbook on the Evolution of the Study of Language from the Beginnings to the Present*, vol. II. Berlin & New York: Walter de Gruyter, 1880–1908.
Joseph, John E. (2002). 'How structuralist was "American structuralism"?', in *From Whitney to Chomsky: Essays in the History of American linguistics*, 157–167. Amsterdam and Philadelphia: John Benjamins.
Joseph, John E. (2010). 'Saussure's notes of 1881–1885 on inner speech, linguistic signs and language change', *Historiographia Linguistica* 37.1/2: 105–132.
Joseph, John E. (2012). *Saussure*. Oxford: Oxford University Press.
Joseph, John E. (2014). 'The wolf in itself: The uses of enchantment in the development of modern linguistics', in Rens Bod, Jaap Maat, and Thijs Weststeijn (eds), *The Making of the Humanities, III*. Amsterdam: University of Amsterdam Press, 81–96.
Joseph, John E. (2018). *Language, Mind and Body: A Conceptual History*. Cambridge: Cambridge University Press.
Joseph, John E. (2020). 'The agency of habitus: Bourdieu and language at the conjunction of Marxism, phenomenology and structuralism', *Language and Communication* 71: 108–122.
Joseph, John E. (2022a). 'The affective, the conceptual and the meaning of "life" in the stylistics of Charles Bally', *Language and Communication* 86: 60–69.

Joseph, John E. (2022b). 'Making grammars concrete again: Aurélien Sauvageot's *Esquisses* of Finnish and Hungarian', in Tim Denecker, Piet Desmet, Lieve Jooken, Peter Lauwers, Toon Van Hal, and Raf Van Rooy (eds), *The Architecture of Grammar: Studies in Linguistic Historiography in Honour of Pierre Swiggers*. Leuven: Peeters, 457–470.

Joseph, John E. (2023a). 'What structuralism is not', in Frans Gregersen, Lorenzo Cigana (eds), *Structuralism as One - Structuralism as Many. Studies in Structuralisms*. Copenhagen: Det Kongelige Danske Videnskabernes Selskab.

Joseph, John E. (2023b). 'Le dernier signifiant de Ferdinand de Saussure', in Frederico Bravo (ed.), *La double articulation ... on en crève! Repenser le signifiant*. Limoges: Lambert-Lucas.

Joseph, John E., Chloé Laplantine, and Georges-Jean Pinault (2020). 'Lettres d'Émile Benveniste à Claude Lévi-Strauss (1948–1967)', *Histoire Épistémologie Langage* 42.1: 155–181.

Joseph, John E., Nigel Love, and Talbot J. Taylor (2001). *Landmarks in Linguistic Thought II: The Western Tradition in the Twentieth Century*. London: Routledge.

Kalmar, Ivan (1987). 'The *Völkerpsychologie* of Lazarus and Steinthal and the modern concept of culture', *Journal of the History of Ideas* 48.4: 671–690.

Karadžić, Vuk (1898). *Srpski rječnik*. Beograd: U Štampariji Kraljevine Srbije.

Karcevsky, Serge (1927). *Système du verbe russe: essai de linguistique synchronique*. Prague: Legiografie.

Karcevsky, Serge (1929). 'Du dualisme asymétrique du signe linguistique', *Travaux du Cercle Linguistique de Prague* 1: 88–93.

Karcevsky, Serge (2000 [1927]). *Introduction au Système du verbe russe*, in Irina and Gilles Fougeron (eds), *Serge Karcevski. Inédits et introuvables*, 21–45. Leuven: Peeters.

Karlgren, Bernhard (1915). *Études sur la phonologie chinoise*. Stockholm: Norstedts.

Kettunen, Lauri (1926). *Untersuchung über die livische Sprache, Eesti Vabariigi Tartu ülikooli Tormetused* 8.3.

Khrakovsky, Viktor. (1969). *Iazykovye universalii i lingvisticheskaia tipologiia* [Language universals and linguistic typology]. Moscow: Nauka.

Kilarksi, Marcin (2021). *A History of the Study of the Indigenous Languages of North America*. Amsterdam and Philadelphia: John Benjamins.

Klaproth, Julius (1823). *Asia Polyglotta*, 1 + 1 vols. Paris: Schubart.

Klautke, Egbert (2013). *The Mind of the Nation*: Völkerpsychologie *in Germany, 1815–1955*. New York: Berghahn.

Knoop, Ulrich, Wolfgang Putschke, and Herbert Ernst Wiegand (1982). 'Die Marburger Schule: Entstehung und frühe Entwicklung der Dialektgeographie', in Werner Besch, Ulrich Knoop, Werner Putschke, and Herbert Ernst Wiegand (eds), *Dialektologie: Ein Handbuch zur deutschen und allgemeinen Dialektforschung*, vol. I. Berlin: De Gruyter, 38–92.

Kock, Axel (1901). *Die alt- und neuschwedische Akzentierung. Quellen und Forschungen zur Sprach- und Kulturgeschichte der germanischen Völker* 87.

Koerner, E.F. Konrad (1978 [1974]). 'Animadversions on some recent claims regarding the relationship between Georg von der Gabelentz and Ferdinand de Saussure', in E. F. Konrad Koerner (ed.), *Toward a Historiography of Linguistics: Selected Essays*. Amsterdam and Philadelphia: John Benjamins, 137–152.

Koerner, E. F. Konrad (1990). 'Wilhelm von Humboldt and North American ethnolinguistics: Boas (1894) to Hymes (1961)', *Historiographia Linguistica* 17.1-2: 111–128.

Koerner, E. F. Konrad (2002). 'On the sources of the "Sapir-Whorf hypothesis"', in *Toward a History of American Linguistics*, 39–62. London: Routledge.

Koerner, E. F. Konrad (2004). 'Notes on missionary linguistics in North America', in Otto Zwartjes and Even Hovdhaugen (eds), *Missionary Linguistics/Lingüística misionera: Selected papers from the First International Conference on Missionary Linguistics, Oslo, 13–16 March 2003* (= *Studies in the History of the Language Sciences*, 106), 47–80. Amsterdam and Philadelphia: John Benjamins.

Koerner, E. F. Konrad (2008). 'Hermann Paul and general linguistic theory', *Language Sciences* 30: 102–132.

Kohrt, Manfred, and Kerstin Kucharczik (2001). 'Die Wurzeln des Struckturalismus in der Sprachwissenschaft des 19. Jahrhunderts', in Sylvain Auroux, E. F. K. Koerner, Hans-Josef Niederehe, and Kees Versteegh (eds), *History of the Language Sciences*, vol. 2. Berlin: de Gruyter, 1719–1735.
Kopernicki, Izydor (1925). *Textes tsiganes*. Kraków: Nakładem Polskiej Akademiej umiejętności.
Košutić, Radovan (1919). *Grammatika russkago jazyka*. Petrograd: Tipografija Rossijskaja Akademija Nauk.
Kotvich, Vladislav (1929). *Opyt grammatiki kalmyckogo razgovornogo jazyka*. Rževnice u Pragi: Kul'turnych Rabotnikov v Čechoslovackoj Respublike.
Kowalski, Tadeusz (1929). *Karaimische Texte im Dialekt von Troki*. Kraków: Nakładem Polskiej Akademiej umiejętności.
Kroeber, A[lfred] L. (1909). 'The Bannock and Shoshoni languages', *American Anthropologist* (New Series) 11.2: 266–277.
Kroeber, A[lfred] L. (1913). 'The determination of linguistic relationship', *Anthropos* 8.2/3: 389–401.
Kurschat, Friedrich (1876). *Grammatik der litauischen Sprache*. Halle an der Saale: Verlag der Buchhandlung des Waisenhauses.
Kürschner, Wilfried (2009). 'Georg von der Gabelentz's manual for recording foreign languages (1892)—origins, aims, methods, effects', *Current Issues in Unity and Diversity of Languages, Linguistics Society of Korea*. Seoul: Dongnam, 3,897–3,920.
Kurylo, Olena (1929). 'Dešo do moldovans'koj dialektologii ta fol'kl'oristiki', *Zbirnik zachodoznavstva* 2: 215–222.
La Hontan, Baron Louis Armand de Lom d'Arce (1703). *New Voyages to North America*, 2 vols. London: Bonwicke et al.
Lagercrantz, Eliel (1923). *Sprachlehre des Südlappischen nach der Mundart von Wefsen*. Kristiana: Kommission Hos Jacob Dybwad.
Lagercrantz, Eliel (1926). *Sprachlehre des Westlappischen*. Helsinki: Suomalais-Ugrilainen Seura.
Lagercrantz, Eliel (1928). *Strukturtypen und Gestaltwechsel im Lappischen*. Helsinki: Suomalais-Ugrilainen Seura.
Langacker, Ronald W. (1977). 'Syntactic reanalysis', in Charles N. Li (ed.), *Mechanisms of Syntactic Change*, 57–139. Austin: University of Texas Press.
Laplantine, Chloé (2011). *Émile Benveniste, l'inconscient et le poème*. Limoges: Lambert-Lucas.
Laplantine, Chloé (2020). 'Le problème de Whorf', in Valentina Bisconti, Anamaria Curea, and Rossana De Angelis (eds), *Filiations, réceptions, écoles dans l'histoire des sciences du langage: avant et après Saussure*, 339–349. Paris: Presses de la Sorbonne Nouvelle.
Laplantine, Chloé (2022). 'Émile Benveniste, de la grammaire comparée à la poétique, en passant par le Canada et l'Alaska: une pensée par problèmes', in Ozouf S. Amedegnato (ed.), *Émile Benveniste, la croisée des disciplines*, 13–30. Limoges: Lambert-Lucas.
Larin, Boris (1926). 'Materialy po litovskoj dialektologii', *Jazyk i literatura* 1: 93–170.
Larsen, Svend Erik (1986). 'A Semiotician in disguise: semiotic aspects of the work of Viggo Brøndal', in Thomas A. Sebeok and Jean Umiker-Sebeok (eds), *The Semiotic Web*, 47–102. Berlin and New York: Mouton de Gruyter.
Larsen, Svend Erik (1988). 'Spænding og spændvidde—sider af dansk lingvistik i tredive', *Slagmark*, 11: 61–73.
Larsen, Svend Erik, and Raymon Nault (1993). 'Immanence and transcendence, Hjelmslev and/or Brøndal', in Michael Rasmussen (ed.), *Louis Hjelmslev et la sémiotique contemporaine* (Travaux du Cercle Linguistique de Copenhague, 24), 52–64. Copenhagen: Nordisk Sprog- og Kulturforlag.
Laruelle, Marlene (2008). *Russian Eurasianism: An Ideology of Empire*. Baltimore: John Hopkins University Press.
Laziczius, Gyula (1930). 'Egy magyar mássalhangzóváltozás phonológiája', *Magyar Nyelv* 26: 266–278.
Lehmann, Christian (2015 [1982]). *Thoughts on Grammaticalization*. Berlin: Language Science Press. (Original: Köln: Universität Köln, 1982.)
Lehr-Spławiński, Tadeusz (1929). 'Dzieje jezyków literackich slowianskich', *Lwowska Biljoteka slawistyczna* 9: 161–199.

Lehtisalo, Toivo (1927). *Über den vokalismus der ersten Silbem im Juraksamojedischen*. Helsinki: Suomalais-Ugrilainen Seura.
Leopold, Joan (ed.) (1999). *The Prix Volney. Volume II: Early Nineteenth-Century Contributions to General and Amerindian Linguistics: Du Ponceau and Rafinesque*. Dordrecht: Kluwer.
Leskien, August, and Karl Brugman (1882). *Litauische Volkslieder und Märchen: aus dem Preussischen und dem Russischen Litauen*. Strassburg: Trübner.
Lévi-Strauss, Claude (1949). *Les structures élémentaires de la parenté*. Paris: Presses universitaires de France. (English trans.: *The Elementary Structures of Kinship*, James H. Bell, John R. von Sturmer, and Rodney Needham [trans.]. Boston: Beacon Press, 1969.)
Lévi-Strauss, Claude (1951). 'Language and the analysis of social laws', *American Anthropologist*, New Series, 53.2: 155–163.
Lévi-Strauss, Claude (1963). *Structural Anthropology*, Claire Jacobson and Brooke Grundfest Schoepf (trans.). New York: Basic Books. (Translation, with additional content, of Lévi-Strauss 1974 [1958].)
Lévi-Strauss, Claude (1963 [1953]). 'Social structure', in Lévi-Strauss (1963: 277–323). (Original in Alfred Louis Kroeber, ed., *Anthropology To-Day*, 524–533. Chicago: University of Chicago Press.)
Lévi-Strauss, Claude (1974 [1945]). 'L'analyse structurale en linguistique et en anthropologie', in Lévi-Strauss (1974: 43–69). (Original in Word 1.1: 33–53.)
Lévi-Strauss, Claude (1974 [1949]). 'Introduction : histoire et ethnologie', in Lévi-Strauss (1974: 9–39). (Original: 'Histoire et ethnologie', *Revue de Métaphysique et de Morale* 54.3–4: 363–391.)
Lévi-Strauss, Claude (1974 [1954]). 'Place de l'anthropologie dans les sciences sociales et problèmes posés par son enseignement', in Lévi-Strauss (1974: 402–443).
Lévi-Strauss, Claude (1974 [1956]). 'Postface au chapitre XV', in Lévi-Strauss (1974: 379–401).
Lévi-Strauss, Claude (1974 [1958]). *Anthropologie structurale*. Paris: Plon. (English trans.: Lévi-Strauss 1963.)
Lévy-Bruhl, Lucien (1910). *Les fonctions mentales dans les sociétés inférieures*. Paris: Félix Alcan.
Lévy-Bruhl, Lucien (1922). *La mentalité primitive*. Paris: Félix Alcan.
Lévy-Bruhl, Lucien (1927). *L'âme primitive*. Paris: Félix Alcan.
Lewy, Ernst (1922). *Tscheremissische Grammatik*. Leipzig: Haessel.
Ljubischev, Aleksandr (1973). 'Moroznye uzory na steklakh: nabliudeniia i razmyshleniia biologa' [Frosty patterns on window panes: observations and reflections of a biologist], *Znanie—sila* 7: 23–26.
Ljubischev, Aleksandr (1977). 'Poniatie sistemnosti i organizovannosti (prevaritel'nyi nabrosok)' [The concept of systematicity and organization (preliminary outline)], *Trudy po znakovym sistemam* 9: 134–141.
López Yepes, Joaquín (1826). *Catecismo y Declaracion de la Doctrina cristiana, en lengua Otomí, con un Vocabulario del mismo idioma*. Mexico City: Valdés.
Lorentz, Friedrich (1903). *Slovinzische Grammatik*. Sankt Peterburg: Imperatorskaja Akademija Nauk.
Lorentz, Friedrich (1908). *Slovinzisches Wörterbuch*. Sankt Peterburg: Imperatorskaja Akademija Nauk.
Lorentz, Friedrich (1925). *Geschichte der pomoranischen (kaschubischen) Sprache*. Berlin-Leipzig: de Gruyter.
Losev, Aleksei F. (2003). *The Dialectics of Myth*, Vladimir Marchenkov (trans.). New York: Routledge.
Lowie, Robert H. (1944). 'Franz Boas (1858–1942)', *The Journal of American Folklore* 57.223: 59–64.
Lytkin, Georgij (1889). *Zyrjanskij kraj pri episkopach permskich i zyrjanskij jazyk*. Sankt Peterburg: Imperatorskaja Akademija Nauk.
Mackert, Michael (1993). 'The roots of Franz Boas' view of linguistic categories as a window to the human mind', *Historiographia Linguistica* 20.2/3: 331–351.
Mackert, Michael (1994). 'Horatio Hale and the Great U.S. Exploring Expedition', *Anthropological Linguistics* 36.1: 1–26.
Maistre, Joseph de (1980 [1821]). *Les soirées de Saint-Pétersbourg*. Paris: Ed. de la Maisnie.

Majeed, Javed (2018). *Colonialism and Knowledge in Grierson's Linguistic Survey of India*. London: Routledge.

Mallarmé, Stéphane (2003). *Igitur, Divagations, Un coup de dés*. Édition de Bertrand Marchal. Gallimard: Paris.

Marr, Nikolay (1926). *Abchazskij analitičeskij alfavit*. Leningrad: Leningradskij Vostočnyj Institut Imeni A.S. Enukidze.

Mason, Otis T. (1887). 'The occurrence of similar inventions in areas widely apart', [Response to Boas 1887a], *Science* 9.226 (3 June): 534–535.

Mason, Otis T. (1894). 'Ethnological exhibit of the Smithsonian Institution at the World's Columbian Exposition', *Memoirs of the International Congress of Anthropology 1894*, 208–216. Chicago: Schulte Publishing.

Matthews, Peter H. (1993). *Grammatical Theory in the United States from Bloomfield to Chomsky*. Cambridge: Cambridge University Press.

Maupertuis, Pierre-Louis Moreau de (1752 [1740]). 'Réflexions philosophiques sur l'Origine des Langues et la Signification des Mots', in *Œuvres de Mr. De Maupertuis*. Dresden: Walther, 353–368.

Mauro, Tullio de (1972 [1967]). 'Notes', in Tullio de Mauro (ed.), *Cours de linguistique générale* by Ferdinand de Saussure (cf. Saussure 1922 [1916]), 405–478. Paris: Payot.

Mazon, André (1920). *Lexique de la guerre et de la révolution en Russie (1914–1918)*. Paris: Champion.

McElvenny, James (2016). 'The fate of form in the Humboldtian tradition: the *Formungstrieb* of Georg von der Gabelentz', *Language and Communication* 47: 30–42.

McElvenny, James (2017a). 'Georg von der Gabelentz', *Oxford Research Encyclopedia of Linguistics*. DOI: 10.1093/acrefore/9780199384655.013.379.

McElvenny, James (2017b). 'Grammar, typology, and the Humboldtian tradition in the work of Georg von der Gabelentz', *Language and History* 60: 1–20.

McElvenny, James (2018a). *Language and Meaning in the Age of Modernism: C. K. Ogden and his Contemporaries*. Edinburgh: Edinburgh University Press.

McElvenny, James (2018b). 'August Schleicher and materialism in nineteenth-century linguistics', *Historiographia Linguistica* 45.1: 133–152.

McElvenny, James (2019). 'Alternating sounds and the formal franchise in phonology', in James McElvenny (ed.), *Form and Formalism in Linguistics*. Berlin: Language Science Press, 35–58.

McElvenny, James (2020). 'La grammaticalisation et la circulation internationale des idées linguistiques', in Jacques François (ed.), *Les linguistes allemandes du XIXème siècle et leurs interlocuteurs étrangers*. Paris: Éditions de la Société de Linguistique de Paris, 201–212.

McElvenny, James (2021). 'Language complexity in historical perspective: the enduring tropes of natural growth and abnormal contact', *Frontiers in Communication*. DOI: 10.3389/fcomm.2021.621712.

McNeely, Ian (2020). 'The last project of the Republic of Letters: Wilhelm von Humboldt's global linguistics', *Journal of Modern History* 92: 241–273.

Meillet, Antoine (1903). *Introduction à l'étude comparative des langues indo-européennes*. Paris: Hachette.

Meillet, Antoine (1905/6). 'Comment les mots changent de sens', *Année sociologique* 9: 1–38. (Repr. in Meillet 1921: 231–271).

Meillet, Antoine (1909). 'Sur la disparition des formes simples du préterit', *Germanische-Romanische Monatsschrift* 1: 521–526. (Repr. in Meillet 1921: 149–158.)

Meillet, Antoine (1912). 'L'évolution des formes grammaticales', *Scientia* 12: 384–400. (Repr. in Meillet 1921: 130–148.)

Meillet, Antoine (1913). 'Nécrologie: Ferdinand de Saussure', *École Pratique des Hautes Études, Section des sciences historiques et philologiques, Annuaire 1913–1914*. Paris: Imprimerie Nationale, 115–123.

Meillet, Antoine (1921). *Linguistique historique et linguistique générale*, vol. 1. Paris: Champion.

Meillet, Antoine (1921 [1906]). 'L'état actuel des études de linguistique générale' [Leçon d'ouverture du cours de Grammaire comparée au Collège de France, lue le mardi, 13 février, 1906], in Meillet (1921: 1–18).

Meillet, Antoine (1923). 'Le caractère concret du mot', *Journal de Psychologie Normale et Pathologique* 20: 246–258. (Repr. in Meillet 1936: 9–13.)

Meillet, Antoine (1928). 'N.S. Trubetzkoy, K probleme russkogo samopoznanija', *Bulletin de la Société de Linguistique de Paris* 28 (84): 51.
Meillet, Antoine (1928 [1918]). *Les langues dans l'Europe nouvelle*, 2nd ed. Paris: Payot.
Meillet, Antoine (1931). Review of Jakobson's K kharakteristke ...', *Bulletin de la Société linguistique de Paris* 32.3: 7–8.
Meillet, Antoine (1936). *Linguistique historique et linguistique générale*, vol. 2. Paris: Champion.
Meltzer, David J. (2010). 'When destiny takes a turn for the worse: William Henry Holmes and, incidentally, Franz Boas in Chicago, 1892–97', *Histories of Anthropology Annual* 6.1: 171–224.
Miletić, Ljubomir (1903). *Das Ostbulgarische*. Wien: Hölder.
Mladenov, Stefan (1915). 'Mekost'ta na s'glasnite ve b'lgarskite govori', *Godišnik na Sofijskija Universitet* 10–11.
Molina, Juan Ignacio (1808 [1776/1787]). *The Geographical, Natural, and Civil History of Chili*. Middletown: Riley.
Monboddo, James Burnet (1773). *Of the Origin and Progress of Language*, vol. I (of 6). Edinburgh and London: Kincaid & Creech/Cadell.
Moore, Omar Khayyam and David L. Olmsted (1952). 'Language and Prof. Claude Lévi-Strauss', *American Anthropologist*, 54.1: 116–119.
Moreira de Sousa, Silvio, Johannes Mücke, and Philipp Krämer (2019). 'A history of Creole Studies', *Oxford Research Encyclopedia of Linguistics*. DOI: 10.1093/acrefore/9780199384655.013.387.
Morpurgo Davies, Anna (1998). *History of Linguistics*, vol. IV: *Nineteenth-century linguistics*. London: Longman.
Moshkov, Valentin (1904). *Narečija bessarabskich gagauzov*. Sankt Peterburg: Imperatorskaja Akademija Nauk.
Mostaert, Antoine (1927). 'Le dialecte des Mongols Urdus (Sud)', *Anthropos* 21–22: 851–869.
Mugdan, Joachim (1985). 'The origin of the phoneme: farewell to a myth', *Lingua Posnaniensis* 28: 137–150.
Mugdan, Joachim (1986). 'Was ist eigentlich ein Morphem?' *Zeitschrift für Phonetik, Sprachwissenschaft und Kommunikationsforschung* 39: 29–43.
Mugdan, Joachim (2014). 'More on the origins of the term *phonème*', *Historiographia Linguistica* 41.1: 185–187.
Murdock, George Peter (1949). *Social Structure*. New York: Macmillan.
Murray, Stephen O. (1994). *Theory Groups and the Study of Language in North America: A Social History*. Amsterdam and Philadelphia: John Benjamins.
Neumeyer, Georg (ed.) (1875). *Anleitung zu wissenschaftlichen Beobachtungen auf Reisen*. Berlin: Oppenheim et al. (^{2}1888 [2 vols.], ^{3}1906 [2 vols.]).
Newmeyer, Frederick J. (1996). 'Has there been a "Chomskyan revolution" in linguistics?', *Language* 62: 1–19.
Nitsch, Kazimierz (1915). 'Dyalekty jezyka polskiego', in Jan Los and Henryk Ułaszyn (eds), *Język polski i jego historya II*, 238–466. Kraków: Nakładem Polskiej Akademii umiejętności.
Norde, Muriel (2009). *Degrammaticalization*. Oxford: Oxford University Press.
Normand, Claudine (2004). 'System, arbitrariness, value', in Carol Sanders (ed.), *The Cambridge Companion to Saussure*, 88–104. Cambridge: Cambridge University Press.
Osthoff, Hermann, and Karl Brugmann (1878). *Morphologische Untersuchungen auf dem Gebiete der indogermanischen Sprachen* 1.
Owen, Richard (1843). *Lectures on the Comparative Anatomy and Physiology of Invertebrate Animals*. London: Longmans Green.
Paasonen, Heikki (1901). *Tatarische Lieder*, Suomalais-ugrilaisen seuran aikakauskirja 19.2.
Paul, Hermann (1880). *Principien der Sprachgeschichte*. Halle an der Saale: Max Niemeyer. [*Prinzipien* in later eds.]
Pedersen, Holger (1916). *Russiske grammatik*. Copenhagen: G. E. C. Gad.
Perrot, Jean (2009). 'La carrière et l'œuvre d'Aurélien Sauvageot: engagement et retenue dans les options linguistiques'. *Études finno-ougriennes* 41: 9–25.
Peshkovsky, Aleksandr M. (1914). *Russkij sintaksis y naučnom osveščenii* [*Russian syntax in scientific light*]. Moscow.

Pickering, John (1820). *An Essay on a Uniform Orthography for the Indian Languages of North America, as published in the Memoirs of the American Academy of Arts and Sciences*. Cambridge, MA: Hilliard and Metcalf.
Pierronet, Thomas (1797). 'Specimen of the Mountaineer, or Sheshatapooshoish, Skoffie, and Micmac Languages', *Collections of the Massachusetts Historical Society* series 1, vol. 6: 16–33.
Pisani, Vittore (1959). 'Parenté linguistique', *Saggi di linguistica storica*, 29–42. Turin: Rosenberg and Sellier.
Plank, Frans (1991). 'Hypology, typology: The Gabelentz puzzle', *Folia Linguistica* 25: 421–458.
Pogodin, Alexander (1929). 'Trudy komissii po izučeniju plemennogo sostava naselenija SSSR i sopredel'nych stran: 15. Finno-ugorskij sbornik', *Slavia—Časopis pro slovanskou filologii* 8: 161–166.
Poirier, Guy (2016). 'Charlevoix, lecteur de Sagard', *Études littéraires* 47.1: 97–107.
Polivanov, Evgeny (1924). 'Vokalizm severno-vostočnych japonskich govorov', *Doklady Rossijskoj Akademii Nauk* 1: 105–108.
Polivanov, Evgeny (1928). *Vvedenie v jazykoznanie dlja vostokovednych vuzov* [Introduction to linguistics for orientalists]. Leningrad: Leningradskij Vostočnyj Institut Imeni A.S. Enukidze.
Polivanov, Evgeny (1929). 'Obrazci ne-iranizovannych (singarmonističeskich) govorov uzbekskogo jazyka', *Izvestija Imperatorskoj Akademii Nauk* 7: 511–537.
Poppe, Nicholas (1930). *Dagurskoe narečie*. Leningrad: Izdatel'stvo Akademii Nauk SSSR.
Porter, Theodore (1986). *The Rise of Statistical Thinking, 1820–1900*. Princeton, NJ: Princeton University Press.
Porzig, Walter (1924). 'Die Aufgaben der indogermanischen Syntax', in Johannes Friedrich, Johannes Baptista Hofmann, and Wilhelm Horn (eds), *Stand und Aufgaben der Sprachwissenschaft*, 126–151. Heidelberg: Carl Winter.
Powell, John Wesley (1877). *Introduction to the Study of American Languages, with Words, Phrases, and Sentences to be Collected*. Washington, DC: Govt. Printing Office.
Powell, John Wesley (1880). *Introduction to the Study of American Languages, with Words, Phrases, and Sentences to be Collected*, 2nd ed. Washington, DC: Govt. Printing Office.
Powell, John Wesley (1887). 'Museums of ethnology and their classification', *Science* 9.229 (24 June): 612–614.
Powell, John Wesley (1891). 'Indian Linguistic Families of America North of Mexico', *Seventh Annual Report of the Bureau of Ethnology to the Secretary of the Smithsonian Institution, 1885–'86*. Washington, DC: Govt. Printing Office, 1–142. (Reproduced in Boas and Powell 1966: 83–218.)
Prague Linguistic Circle (1931). 'Projet de terminologie phonologique standardisée', *Travaux du Cercle Linguistique de Prague* 4: 309–332.
Puech, Christian, and Annie Radzynski (1978). 'La langue comme fait social: fonction d'une évidence', [*Saussure et la linguistqiue pré-saussurienne*] *Langages* 49: 46–65.
Radcliffe-Brown, Alfred (1940). 'On Social Structure', *The Journal of the Royal Anthropological Institute of Great Britain and Ireland* 70.1: 1–12.
Radin, Paul (1919). 'The genetic relationship of the North American Indian languages', *University of California Publications in American Archaeology and Ethnology* 14.5: 489–502.
Radlov (Radloff), Wilhelm (1887). *Das türkische Sprachmaterial des Codex Cumanicus*. Sankt Peterburg: Imperatorskaja Akademija Nauk.
Ramstedt, Gustav John (1902). *Bergtscheremissische Sprachstudien*. Helsinki: Suomalais-Ugrilainen Seura.
Rasles [Râle], Sébastien (1833). 'A Dictionary of the Abnaki Language in North America', John Pickering (ed. and trans.), *Memoirs of the American Academy of Arts and Sciences*, New series, 1: 370–574.
Rasmussen, Michael (1987). 'Hjelmslev et Brøndal. Rapport sur un différend', *Langages* 86: 41–58.
Rischel, Jørgen (2001). 'The Cercle linguistique de Copenhague and Glossematics', in Sylvain Auroux, E. F. K. Koerner, Hans-Josef Niederehe, and Kees Versteegh (eds), *History of the Language Sciences: An International Handbook on the Evolution of the Study of Language from the Beginnings to the Present*, vol. II. Berlin: De Gruyter, 1790–1806.

Ritter, Carl. 1817. *Die Erdkunde im Verhältniss zur Natur und zur Geschichte des Menschen: oder allgemeine vergleichende Geographie, als sichere Grundlage des Studiums und Unterrichts in physikalischen und historischen Wissenschaften*. Berlin: Reimer.

Robins, Robert (1999). 'Du Ponceau and General and Amerindian Linguistics', in Joan Leopold (1999). Dordrecht: Kluwer, 1–31.

Rohner, Ronald P. (ed.) (1969). *The Ethnography of Franz Boas: Letters and Diaries of Franz Boas Written on the Northwest Coast from 1886 to 1931*. Chicago: University of Chicago Press.

Rousseau, Jean, and Denis Thouard (eds) (1999). *Lettres édifiantes et curieuses sur la langue chinoise, Humboldt/Abel-Remusat (1821–1831)*. Lille: Presses universitaires du Septentrion.

Rozwadowski, Jan Michał (1915). 'Historyczna fonetyka czyli głosownia jezyka polskiego', in Jan Łos and Henryk Ułaszyn (eds), *Język polski i jego historya I*. Kraków: Nakładem Polskiej Akademiej umiejętności, 289–422.

Sagard, Gabriel (1632). *Dictionnaire de la Langue huronne*. Paris: Moreau.

Samain, Didier (2020). 'Sinologie et typologie. Deux articles de linguisitique générale de Georg von der Gabelentz', *Histoire Épistémologie Langage* 42.2: 145–173.

Samoylovich, Alexander (1922). *Nekotorye dopolnenija k klassifikacii tureckich jazykov*. Leningrad: Leningradskij Vostočnyj Institut Imeni A.S. Enukidze.

Samuelian, Thomas J. (1981). 'The search for a Marxist linguistics in the Soviet Union, 1917–1950'. PhD thesis, University of Pennsylvania, Philadelphia.

Sandfeld, Kristian (1930 [1926]). *La linguistique balkanique, problèmes et résultats*. Paris: Champion. (Original in Danish, *Balkanfilologien*, 1926).

Sapir, Edward (1915). 'The Na-dene languages, a preliminary report', *American Anthropologist* 17.3: 534–558.

Sapir, Edward (1921). *Language: An Introduction to the Study of Speech*. New York: Harcourt, Brace and Co.

Sapir, Edward (1933). 'La realité psychologique des phonèmes', *Journal de Psychologie Normale et Pathologique* 30: 247–265. (Original English manuscript printed in David G. Mandelbaum [ed.], *Selected writings of Edward Sapir*, 46–60. Berkeley, CA: University of California Press, 1949.)

Saussure, Ferdinand de (1879). *Mémoire sur le système primitif des voyelles dans les langues indo-européennes*. Leipzig: B.G. Teubner.

Saussure, Ferdinand de (1922). *Recueil des publications scientifiques de Ferdinand de Saussure*, Charles Bally and Léopold Gautier (eds). Genève: Sonor; Lausanne: Payot; Heidelberg: C. Winter.

Saussure, Ferdinand de (1922 [1912]). 'Adjectifs indo-européens du type *caecus* "aveugle"', in Saussure (1922: 595–599). (Original in *Festschrift Vilhelm Thomsen zur Vollendung des siebzigsten Lebensjahres am 25. Januar 1912, dargebracht von Freunden und Schülern*, 202–206. Leipzig: Otto Harrassowitz.)

Saussure, Ferdinand de (1922 [1916]). *Cours de linguistique générale*, 2nd ed, Charles Bally and Albert Sechehaye (eds). Paris: Payot. (English trans.: *Course in General Linguistics*, Wade Baskin [trans.]. New York: Philosophical Library, 1959.)

Saussure, Ferdinand de (1997). *Deuxième cours de linguistique générale (1908–1909), d'après les cahiers d'Albert Riedlinger et Charles Patois/Saussure's Second Course on General Linguistics (1908–1909), from the notebooks of Albert Riedlinger and Charles Patois*, Eisuke Komatsu (ed.), George Wolf (trans.). Oxford & New York: Pergamon.

Saussure, Ferdinand de, and Émile Constantin (2005). Saussure, 'Notes préparatoires pour le cours de linguistique générale 1910-1911'; Constantin, 'Linguistique générale, cours de M. le professeur de Saussure 1910-1911', Daniele Gambarara and Claudia Mejía Quijano (eds). *Cahiers Ferdinand de Saussure* 58: 71–290.

Sauvageot, Aurélien (1992). *La structure du langage*. Aix-en-Provence: Publications de l'Université de Provence.

Savitzky, Pyotr (1921). 'Evropa i Evrazija', *Russkaja Mysl'* 1921 (1–2): 119–138.

Savitzky, Pyotr (1927). *Geografičeskie osobennosti Rossii*. Praga: Evrazijskoe knigoizdatel'stvo.

Savitzky, Pyotr (1928). 'O zadačach kočevnikovededenija', in Nikolay P. Toll (ed.), *Skify i gunny*, 83–106. Praga: Evrazijskoe knigoizdatel'stvo.

Savitzky, Pyotr (1929). 'Les problèmes de la géographie linguistique du point de vue du géographe', in *Mélanges linguistiques dédiés au Premier Congrès des Philologues Slaves*, 145–156. Praha: Jednota Československých Matematiků a Fysiků.
Schleicher, August (1859). 'Zur Morphologie der Sprache', *Mémoires de l'Académie Impériale des Sciences de St.-Petersbourg* I: 1–38.
Schleicher, August (1860). *Die Deutsche Sprache*. Stuttgart: Cotta.
Schleicher, August (1861–1862). *Compendium der vergleichenden Grammatik der indogermanischen Sprachen*. Weimar: Böhlau.
Schmidt, Wilhelm (1926). *Die Sprachfamilien und Sprachenkreise der Erde*. Heidelberg: Carl Winter.
Schuchardt, Hugo (1893). Review of Gabelenz (1893), 'Baskisch und Berberisch', *Literaturblatt für germanische und romanische Philologie* 14: 334–338.
Schuchardt, Hugo (1917). 'Sprachverwandschaft', *Sitzungsberichte der Berliner Akademie des Wissenschaften* 37: 518–529.
Selishchev, Afanasy (1921). *Dialektologičeskij očerk Sibiri*. Irkutsk: Gosudarstvennyj Irkutskij Univeristet.
Selishchev, Afanasy (1925a). 'Des traits linguistiques communs aux langues balcaniques', *Revue des études slaves* 5: 38–57.
Selishchev, Afanasy (1925b). 'Russkij jazyk u inorodcev Povolž'ja', *Slavia—Časopis pro slovanskou filologii* 4: 26–43.
Selishchev, Afanasy (1927). 'Russkie govory Kazanskogo kraja i russkij jazyk u čuvaš i čeremis', *Učenye zapiski Instituta jazyka i literatury RANION* 1: 36–72.
Sergyevsky, Maxim (1929a). 'Iz oblasti jazyka russkich cygan', *Učenye zapiski Instituta jazyka i literatury RANION* 3.
Sergyevsky, Maxim (1929b). 'Materialy dlja izučenija živych moldavskich govorov na territorii SSSR', *Učenye zapiski Instituta jazyka i literatury RANION* 3: 73–97.
Sériot, Patrick (1993). 'La double vie de Troubetzkoy, ou la clôture des systèmes', *Le gré des langues* 5: 88–115.
Sériot, Patrick (1996). *N. S. Troubetzkoy. L'Europe et l'humanité*. Liège: Mardaga.
Sériot, Patrick (2007). 'A quelle tradition appartient la tradition grammaticale russe?', *Langages* 167: 53–69.
Sériot, Patrick (2011). 'Vološinov, la philosophie du langage et le marxisme' [Théories du langage et politiques des linguistes], *Langages* 182: 83–96.
Sériot, Patrick (2014). *Structure and the Whole: East, West and non-Darwinian Biology in the Origins of Structural Linguistics*, Amy Jacob-Colas (trans.). Boston and Berlin: Mouton de Gruyter.
Shakhmatov, Alexey (1898). *Historická mluvnice jazyka českého: Napsal Jan Gebauer*. Sankt Peterburg: Imperatorskaja Akademija Nauk.
Shakhmatov, Alexey (1910). *Mordovskij etnografičeskij sbornik*. Sankt Peterburg: Imperatorskaja Akademija Nauk.
Sharaf, Galimdjan (1927). 'Paljatogrammy zvukov tatarskogo jayzka sravnitel'no s russkim', *Vestnik naučnogo obščestva tatarovedenija* 7: 65–102.
Shchepkin, Vyacheslav (1906). *Bolonskaja psaltyr'*. Sankt Peterburg: Imperatorskaja Akademija Nauk.
Shcherba, Lev (1915). *Vostočnolužickoe narečie*. Petrograd: Kollins.
Sinyavsky, Olexa (1929). 'Sproba zvukovoj charakteristiki literaturnoj movi', *Naukovi zapiski Charkivis'koj naukovodoslidgoj katedri movoznavstva* 2: 5–33.
Skalička, Vladimír (1934). 'Zur Charakteristik des eurasischen Sprachbundes', *Archiv orientální* 6: 272–274.
Smith, Andrew D. M., Graeme Trousdale, and Richard Waltereit (eds) (2015). *New Directions in Grammaticalization Research*. Amsterdam and Philadelphia: John Benjamins.
Smith, Murphy (1983). 'Peter Stephen Du Ponceau and his study of languages: A historical account', *Proceedings of the American Philosophical Society* 127.3: 143–179.
Solleveld, Floris (2019). 'Language, people, and maps: The ethnolinguistics of George Grierson and Franz Boas', *History of the Humanities* 4.2: 461–471.
Solleveld, Floris (2020a). 'Klaproth, Balbi, and the Language Atlas', in Émilie Aussant and Jean-Michel Fortis (eds), *History of Linguistics 2017: Selected papers from the 14th International Conference on*

the *History of the Language Sciences (ICHoLS XIV)*. Amsterdam and Philadelphia: John Benjamins, 81-99.
Solleveld, Floris (2020b). 'Expanding the comparative view: Humboldt's Über die Kawi-Sprache and its language materials', *Historiographia Linguistica* 47.1: 49-78.
Sommerfelt, Alf (1922). *The Dialect of Torr Co. Donegal*. Kristiana: Kommission Hos Jacob Dybwad.
Sommerfelt, Alf (1924-1927). 'Munster vowels and consonants', *Proceedings of the Royal Irish Academy* 37: 195-244.
Sørensen, Hans Christian (1949). 'Contribution à la discussion sur la théorie des cas', *Recherches structurales* (*Travaux du Cercle Linguistique de Copenhague* 5), 123-133. Copenhagen: Nordisk Sprog- og Kulturforlag.
Spang-Hanssen, Henning (1959). *Probability and Structural Classification in Language Description*. Copenhagen: Rosenkilde and Bagger.
Spitzer, Leo (1918). *Aufsätze zur romanischen Syntax und Stilistik*. Halle: M. Niemeyer.
Spitzer, Leo (1944). 'Answer to Mr. Bloomfield (*Language* 20.45)', *Language* 20.4: 245-251.
Steinthal, H. (1860). *Charakteristik der hauptsächlichsten Typen des Sprachbaues*. Berlin: Dümmler.
Steinthal, H. (1867). *Die Mande-Negersprachen psychologisch und phonetisch betrachtet*. Berlin: Ferdinand Dümmler.
Sternberg, Lev (1900). 'Obrazci materialov po izučeniju giljackago jazyka i fol'klora', *Izvestija Imperatorskoj Akademii Nauk* 13: 387-434.
Stieber, Zdzisław (1929). 'Ze studjów nad gwarami słowackiemi poludniowego Spisza', *Lud Słowiański* 1: 61-138.
Stockigt, Clara (2015). 'Early descriptions of Pama-Nyungan languages', *Historiographia Linguistica* 42.2/3: 335-377.
Stocking, George W., Jr. (1965). 'From physics to ethnology: Franz Boas' arctic expedition as a problem in the historiography of the behavioral sciences', *Journal of the History of the Behavioral Sciences* 1.1: 53-66.
Stocking, George W., Jr. (ed.) (1974a). *The Shaping of American Anthropology 1883-1911: A Franz Boas Reader*, New York: Basic Books.
Stocking, George W., Jr. (ed.) (1974b). 'Introduction: The basic assumptions of Boasian anthropology', in Stocking (1974a: 1-20).
Stocking, George W., Jr. (1974c). 'The Boas plan for the study of American Indian languages', in Dell Hymes (ed.), *Studies in the History of Linguistics: Traditions and Paradigms*, 454-484. Bloomington: Indiana University Press.
Sütterlin, Ludwig (1902). *Das Wesen der sprachlichen Gebilde: Kritische Bemerkungen zu Wilhelm Wundts Sprachpsychologie*. Heidelberg: Winter.
Sütterlin, Ludwig (1904). Review of Gabelentz, *Die Sprachwissenschaft* (1901 [1891]), *Literaturblatt für germanische und romanische Philologie* 25: 319-320.
Svyatopolk-Mirsky, Dmitrij Petrovič (1929). 'Nacional'nosti SSSR', *Evrazija* 23: 25-35.
Swadesh, Morris (1951). 'Diffusional cumulation and archaic residue as historical explanations', *Southwestern Journal of Anthropology* 7.1: 1-21.
Swanton, John R. (1911a). 'Tlingit', in Boas (1911-1941: vol. 1, 159-204).
Swanton, John R. (1911b). 'Haida', in Boas (1911-1941: vol. 1, 205-282).
Swanton, John R., and Franz Boas (1911). 'Siouan: Dakota (Teton and Santee dialects), with remarks on the Ponca and Winnebago', in Boas (1911-1941: vol. 1, 874-965).
Sweet, Henry (1900). *The History of Language*. New York: Macmillan.
Swiggers, Pierre (1994). 'Refraction et dépassement de l'Idéologie aux États-Unis: le cas de Peter S. Du Ponceau', in Brigitte Schieben-Lange et al. (eds), *Europäische Sprachwissenschaft um 1800*. Münster: Nodus, 39-64.
Swiggers, Pierre (1998). 'Americanist linguistics and the origin of linguistic typology: Peter Stephen Du Ponceau's "Comparative science of language"', *Proceedings of the American Philosophical Society* 142.1: 18-46.
Swiggers, Pierre (1999). 'Peter Stephen Du Ponceau's Mémoire sur le système grammatical des langues de quelques nations Indiennes de l'Amérique du Nord (1838): In search of a typology of grammatical form', in Leopold (1999: 100-129).

Synyavsky, Olexa (1929). 'Sproba zvukovoj charakteristiki literaturnoj movi', *Naukovi zapiski Charkivis'koj naukovodoslidgoj katedri movoznavstva* 2: 5–33.
Szinnyei, Josef (1922). *Finnisch-ugrische Sprachwissenschaft*. Berlin-Leipzig: de Gruyter.
Taylor, Talbot J. (1981). *Linguistic Theory and Structural Stylistics*. Oxford: Pergamon.
Techmer, Friedrich (1880). *Phonetik. Zur vergleichenden Physiologie der Stimme und Sprache*. Leipzig: Engelmann.
Tesnière, Lucien (1929). 'L'Accent slovène et le timbre des voyelles', *Revue des études slaves* 9: 89–118.
Thalbitzer, William (1911). 'Eskimo', in Boas (1911–1941: vol. 1, 967–1069).
Thomas, Lawrence L. (1957). *The Linguistic Theory of N. Ja. Marr*. Berkeley and Los Angeles: University of California Press.
Thomas, Margaret (2019). 'American structuralism', in Mark Aronoff (ed.), *Oxford Research Encyclopedia: Linguistics*. Published online at <https://oxfordre.com/linguistics/view/10.1093/acrefore/9780199384655.001.0001/acrefore-9780199384655-e-400>.
Thomsen, Vilhelm (1894). *Inscriptions de l'Orkhon*. Helsinki: Suomalais-Ugrilainen Seura.
Titchener, Edward B. (1898). 'The postulates of structural psychology', *Philosophical Review* 7.5: 449–465.
Titchener, Edward B. (1909). *Lectures on the Experimental Psychology of the Thought-Processes*. New York: Macmillan.
Toman, Jindřich (1994). *Letters and Other Materials from the Moscow and Prague Linguistic Circles, 1912–1945*. Ann Arbor: Michigan Slavic Publications.
Toman, Jindřich (1995). *The Magic of a Common Language: Jakobson, Mathesius, Trubetzkoy, and the Prague Linguistic Circle*. Cambridge, MA: MIT Press.
Tomson, Alexander (1927). 'Die Erweichung und Erhärtung der Labiale im Ukrainischen', *Zapiski istorično-filologičnogo viddilu Ukraïns'koï akademiï nauk* 13–14: 253–263.
Trabant, Jürgen (1986). *Apeliotes, oder Der Sinn der Sprache*. München: Fink.
Trabant, Jürgen (2012). *Weltansichten. Wilhelm von Humboldts Sprachprojekt*. München: Beck.
Trautmann-Waller, Céline (2006). *Aux origines d'une science allemande de la culture: Linguistique et psychologie des peuples chez Heymann Steinthal*. Paris: CNRS Éditions.
Tredyakovsky, Vasily (1849). 'Razgovor meždu čužestrannym čelovekom i rossijskim ob ortografii starinnoj i novoj i o vsem čto prinadležit' k sej materii', in Vasily Tredyakovsky, *Sočinenija* 3. Sankt Peterburg: Imperatorskaja Akademija Nauk.
Trnka, Bohumil et al. (1964 [1958]). 'Prague Structural Linguistics', in Josef Vachek (ed.), *A Prague School Reader in Linguistics*. Bloomington: Indiana University Press.
Trubetzkoy, Nikolay (1922). 'Essai sur la chronologie de certains faits phonétiques du slave commun', *Revue des études slaves* 2: 217–234.
Trubetzkoy, Nikolay (1923). 'Vavilonskaja bašnja i smešenie jazykov', *Evrazijskij vremennik* 3: 107–124. (English trans. In Trubetzkoy 1991: 147–160.)
Trubetzkoy, Nikolay (1924a). 'Langues caucasiques septentrionales', in Antoine Meillet and Marcel Cohen (eds), *Les langues du monde*, 327–342. Paris: Champion.
Trubetzkoy, Nikolay (1924b). 'Einiges über die russische Lautentwicklung und die Auflösung der gemeinrussischen Spracheinheit', *Zeitschrift für Slavische Philologie* 1: 287–319.
Trubetzkoy, Nikolay (1925). *Nasledie Chinghiz Khana* [The Legacy of Genghiz Khan]. Berlin. (English trans. in Trubetzkoy 1991: 161–232.)
Trubetzkoy, Nikolay (1927). *K probleme russkogo samopoznanija*. Paris: Evrazijskoe knižnoe izdatel'stvo.
Trubetzkoy, Nikolay (1929). *Polabische Studien*. Wien: Hölder-Pichler-Tempsky.
Trubetzkoy, Nikolay (1929). 'Zur allgemeinen Theorie der phonologischen Vokalsysteme', in *Mélanges linguistiques dédiés au Premier Congrès des Philologues Slaves*, 39–67. Praha: Jednota Československých Matematiků a Fysiků.
Trubetzkoy, Nikolay [Nikolai] (1931a). 'Die phonologischen Systeme', *Travaux du Cercle Linguistique de Prague* 4: 96–116.
Trubetzkoy [Troubetzkoy], Nikolay [Nikolai] (1931b). 'Phonologie et géographie linguistique', *Travaux du Cercle Linguistique de Prague* IV, 228–234. (Reproduced as an appendix to *Principes*

de phonologie de N. S. Troubetzkoy, J. Cantineau, ed. and trans. Paris: Klincksieck, 1986 [1949], 343–350.)
Trubetzkoy, Nikolay [Nikolai] (1939). *Grundzüge der Phonologie*. Prague. (English trans.: *Principles of Phonology*, Christiane A.M. Baltaxe [trans.]. Berkeley: University of California Press, 1969.)
Trubetzkoy, Nikolay [Nikolai] (1985). *N. S. Trubetzkoy's Letter and Notes*, Roman Jakobson (ed.). The Hague: Mouton.
Trubetzkoy, Nikolay [Nikolai] (1991). *The Legacy of Genghiz Khan and Other Essays on Russia's Identity*, Anatoly Liberman (ed. and trans.). Ann Arbor: Michigan Slavic Publications.
Trubetzkoy [Troubetzkoy], Nikolay [Nikolai] (2006). *Correspondance avec Roman Jakobson et autres écrits*, Patrick Sériot and Margarita Schoenenberger (ed. and trans.). Lausanne: Payot.
Tylor, Edward Burnett (1889). 'On a method of investigating the development of institutions; applied to laws of marriage and descent', *The Journal of the Anthropological Institute of Great Britain and Ireland* 18: 245–272.
Tynianov, Juri, and Roman Jakobson (1928). (Problemy izucheniya yazyka i literatury), (*Novyi LEF, New Left Front of the Arts*) 12: 36–37. (English trans.: 'Problems in the Study of Language and Literature', Richard De George [trans.], in Richard De George and Fernande De George (eds), *The Structuralists: From Marx to Lévi-Strauss*. New York: Anchor Books, 1972, 80–83.)
Uldall, Hans Jørgen (1967 [1957]). *Outline of Glossematics*. Copenhagen: Nordisk Sprog- og Kulturforlag.
Vendryès, Joseph (1979 [1921]). *Le langage, introduction linguistique à l'histoire*. Paris: Armand Colin.
Verlato, Micaela (2013). 'Wilhelm von Humboldt und die Erforschung nordamerikanischer Sprachen', in Micaela Verlato (ed.), *W. v. Humboldt, Nordamerikanische Grammatiken* [Schriften zur Sprachwissenschaft Vol. III.6]. Paderborn: Schöningh, 1–117.
Vincent, Nigel (1980). 'Iconic and symbolic aspects of syntax: Prospects for reconstruction', in Paolo Ramat et al. (eds), *Linguistic Reconstruction and Indo-European Syntax: Proceedings of the Colloquium of the Indogermanische Gesellschaft, University of Pavia, 6–7 September 1979*. Amsterdam and Philadelphia: John Benjamins, 47–68.
Virchow, Rudolf (1886). 'Gesammtbericht über die von der deutschen anthropologischen Gesellschaft veranlassten Erhebungen übe die Farbe der Haut, der Haare und der Augen der Schulkinder in Deutschland', *Archiv für Anthropologie* 16: 275–476.
Vladimirtzov, Boris (1929). *Sravnitel'naja grammatika mongol'skogo pis'mennogo jazyka i chalchaskogo narečija: Vvedenie i fonetika*. Leningrad: Leningradskij Vostočnyj Institut Imeni A.S. Enukidze.
Voegelin, Carl F. (1952). 'The Boas plan for the presentation of American Indian languages', *Proceedings of the American Philosophical Society* 96.4: 439–451.
Voegelin, Carl F. (1959). Review of Charles F. Hockett (ed.), *Eastern Ojibwa: Grammatical Sketch, Texts and Word List*. Ann Arbor, Michigan: University of Michigan Press, 1957, *Language* 35.1: 109–125.
Voegelin, Carl F., and Florence M. Voegelin (1963). 'On the history of structuralizing in 20th century America', *Anthropological Linguistics* 5.1: 12–37.
Vogel, Annemete von, and James McElvenny (2019). 'The Gabelentz family in their own words', in James McElvenny (ed.), *Gabelentz and the Science of Language*. Amsterdam: Amsterdam University Press, 13–26.
Volney, Constantin-François Chassebœuf [comte de] (1819). *L'alfabet européen appliqué aux langues asiatiques*. Paris: Firmin Didot.
Voloshinov, Valentin Nikolaevich (2010 [1929]). *Marxisme et philosophie du langage. Les problèmes fondamentaux de la méthode sociologique dans les sciences du langage*, nouvelle édition bilingue traduite du russe par Patrick Sériot et Inna Tylkowski-Ageeva. Limoges: Lambert-Lucas.
Vondrák, Václav (1924). *Vergleichende slavische Grammatik I*. Göttingen: Vandenhoeck & Ruprecht.
Vossler, Karl (1913). *Frankreichs Kultur im Spiegel seiner Sprachentwicklung*. Heidelberg: Carl Winter.
Vykypěl, Bohumil (2006). 'Hjelmslevs freie Gliederung', *Beiträge zur Geschichte der Sprachwissenschaft* 16.1-2: 179–194.
Wartburg, Walther von (1922–1967). *Französisches Etymologisches Wörterbuch*. Basel: R. G. Zbinden.
Waugh, Linda R., and Monique Monville-Burston (eds) (1990). *On Language: Roman Jakobson*. Cambridge, MA: Harvard University Press.

Wax, Murray (1956). 'The limitations of Boas' anthropology', *American Anthropologist* (New Series) 58.1: 63–74.
Weigand, Gustav (1909). *Linguistischer Atlas des Dacorumänischen Sprachgebietes*. Leipzig: Barth.
Weigand, Gustav (1913). *Albanesische Grammatik im südgegischen Dialekt*. Leipzig: Barth.
White, Leslie A. (1963). 'The ethnography and ethnology of Franz Boas', *Bulletin of the Texas Memorial Museum Bulletin* 6: 1–76.
Whitney, William Dwight (1867). *Language and the Study of Language: Twelve Lectures on the Principles of Linguistic Science*. New York: Scribner and Co.
Whitney, William Dwight (1874). 'The elements of English pronunciation', in *Oriental and Linguistic Studies*, vol. II, 202–276. New York: Scribner, Armstrong and Co.
Whitney, William Dwight (1875). *The Life and Growth of Language: An Outline of Linguistic Science*. London: King & Co.
Whitney, William Dwight (1881). 'On mixture in language', *Transactions of the American Philological Society* 12: 5–26.
Whitney, William Dwight (1898). *The Life and Growth of Language: An Outline of Linguistic Science*. New York: D. Appleton.
Whorf, Benjamin L. (1956). 'The relation of habitual thought and behavior to language', in John B. Carroll (ed.), *Language, Thought and Reality: Selected Writings of Benjamin Lee Whorf*. Cambridge, MA: MIT Press, 134–159.
Wichmann, Yrjö (1923). *Tscheremissische Texte*. Helsinki: Suomalais-Ugrilainen Seura.
Wiener, Norbert (1948). *Cybernetics, or Control and Communication in the Animal and the Machine*. Cambridge, MA: MIT Press.
Willems, Klaas (2019). 'Phenomenological aspects of Georg von der Gabelentz's *Die Sprachwissenschaft*', in James McElvenny (ed.), *Gabelentz and the Science of Language*. Amsterdam: University of Amsterdam Press, 99–129.
Wilner, Isaiah Lorado (2015). 'Friends in this world: The relationship of George Hunt and Franz Boas', in Regna Darnell, Michele Hamilton, Robert L. A. Hancock, and Joshua Smith (eds), *Franz Boas Papers*, vol. 1: *Franz Boas as a Public Intellectual—Theory, Ethnography, Activism*, 163–189. Lincoln: University of Nebraska Press.
Wolf, Eric (1982). *Europe and the People without History*. Berkeley and Los Angeles: University of California Press.
Wundt, Wilhelm (1886). 'Ueber den Begriff des Gesetzes, mit Rücksicht auf die Frage der Ausnahmslosigkeit der Lautgesetze', *Philosophische Studien* 3: 195–215.
Wundt, Wilhelm (1900). *Völkerpsychologie, eine Untersuchung der Entwicklungsgesetze von Sprache, Mythus und Sitte*, vol. I, *Die Sprache*. Leipzig: Engelmann.
Wundt, Wilhelm (^{3}1908 [^{1}1883, ^{2}1893–1894]). *Logik. Eine Untersuchung der Prinzipien der Erkenntniss und der Methoden wissenschafticher Forschung*, vol. III: Logik der Geisteswissenschaften. Stuttgart: Enke.
Yakovlev, Nikolay (1923). *Tablicy fonetiki kabardinskogo jazyka*. Leningrad: Leningradskij Vostočnyj Institut Imeni A.S. Enukidze.
Yakovlev, Nikolay (1928). 'Matematičeskaja formula postroenija alfavita', *Kul'tura i pis'mennost' Vostoka* 1: 41–64.
Yakovlev, Nikolay (1930). 'Kurze Übersicht über die tscherkessischen (adygheischen) Dialekte und Sprachen', *Caucasica* 6: 1–19.
Yokhelson, Vladimir (1898). 'Obrazci materialov po izučeniju jukagirskago jazyka i fol'klora', *Izvestija Imperatorskoj Akademii Nauk* 9.2.
Zeisberger, David (1827). *Grammar of the Language of the Lenni Lenape or Delaware Indians*, Peter Stephen du Ponceau (ed. and trans.). Philadelphia, PA: Kay.
Zelenin, Dmitry (1929). *Tabu slov u narodov vostočnoj Evropy i severnoj Azii*. Leningrad: Izdatel'stvo Akademii Nauk SSSR.
Zilberberg, Claude (1985). 'Connaissance de Hjelmslev: Prague ou Copenhague?', *Il Protagora* 25.7–8: 127–169.

Zilinsky, Ivan (1913). 'Proba uporjadkovannja ukraïns'kich govoriv', *Zapiski Naukovogo Tovaristva imeni Ševčenka* 117–118: 333–375.

Zipf, George (1949). *Human Behavior and the Principle of Least Effort: An Introduction to Human Ecology*. Cambridge, MA: Addison-Wesley.

Zipf, George (1965 [1935]). *The Psycho-Biology of Language: An Introduction to Dynamic Philology*. Cambridge, MA: MIT Press.

Zumwalt, Rosemary Lévy (2019). *Franz Boas: The Emergence of the Anthropologist*. Lincoln: University of Nebraska Press.

Index

Abel-Rémusat, Jean-Pierre, 18, 44
Abenaki language, 23, 39, 41, 42–3, 46
Adam, Lucien, 104
Adelung, Johann Christoph, 12, 19
Affinity, 105, 142, 147–9, 154–5
Ainu, 170
Algonkian languages, 29, 39–40, 72, 77, 80
Anthropology, physical, 96–7
Arabic, 72
Arbitrariness (of signs, etc), 15, 27, 68, 112–13, 142, 156
Armenian, 136–7, 190
Athabaskan languages, 61, 74, 75, 78–9, 80
Australian languages, 106

Bally, Charles, 3, 115–16, 117
Bantu languages, 72, 76, 144, 228
Basque, 90, 97, 106
Barr, Kaj, 207
Baudouin de Courtenay, Jan, 4, 138, 149, 180, 253
Behaviourism, 7
Benveniste, Émile, 109
Berber languages, 97
Berg, Lev, 152
Bloomfield, Leonard, 7–8, 65, 116
Boas, Franz, 7, 13, 28, 99–100, 270, 273, 276
Boasian trilogy, 57–8
Bopp, Franz, 14, 124–5
Bréal, Michel, 110
Brøndal, Viggo, 207–9, 214
Brugmann, Karl, 126
Bühler, Karl, 243–4
Bulgarian, 160, 169, 179
Burke, Edmund, 115, 156
Burmese, 105–6
Buschmann, Eduard, 26
Butrick, Daniel Sabin, 38
Byrne, James, 102–3

Cassirer, Ernst, 5, 150
Celtic languages, 133–4
Cherokee language, 38–9, 42
Cherokee syllabary, 25
Chinese, 18, 21, 22, 33, 48, 50, 71, 83, 101, 129, 132, 146
Chinook languages, 58, 67, 77, 78
Chinook trade jargon, 28
Chippeway, *see* Ojibwe
Chomsky, Noam, 7–9, 285–6
Chukchi, 77
Cohen, Marcel, 109
Coleridge, Samuel Taylor, 115
Condillac, Étienne Bonnot de, 16, 17
Copenhagen Linguistic Circle, 6
Coptic, 21
Correlation, 95–6
Cuvier, Georges, 92–3, 95–6, 105, 150, 153
Czech, 153, 155, 166–7, 169, 178, 183, 195

Danilevsky, Nikolay, 152–3
Danish, 170–2, 227–8
Delbrück, Berthold, 89–90
Derrida, Jacques, 4
Destutt de Tracy, Antoine, 17
Distinctive features, 4, 212–13
Dixon, Roland Burrage, 60, 70–1
Dorsey, James Owen, 70
Du Ponceau, Peter Stephen, 56–7
Dumézil, Georges, 109
Durkheim, Émile, 110–11, 114, 120, 123

Egede, Hans, 12, 21, 36
Eliot, John, 12, 19, 21
Ellipsis, 21–22, 31
English language, 136–7, 138, 144, 213, 227–8, 255
Ergativity, 90, 106
Eskimo, *see* Inuit
Estonian, 146, 170, 183

Eugenics, 96
Eurasianism, 141–2, 148, 161–2

Field work, 22–3
Finnish and Finno-Ugric languages, 80, 163, 171–2, 181–3, 187–8, 196–7, 213
Florovsky, Gregory, 141
Fortes, Meyer, 270
Frazer, James, 154, 164
French, 110–13, 114–15, 132, 134, 136, 138, 144, 221–2, 227, 255, 265

Gabelentz, Georg von der, 110, 116, 132
Galton, Francis, 95–6
Gatschet, Albert S., 70
Gauthiot, Robert, 109
Gébelin, Antoine Court de, 15–16, 34
General grammar, 14–16, 229
Georgian, 190
German and Germanic languages, 113, 131–3, 134, 135–6, 138, 171, 227–8, 265
Gilliéron, Jules, 91, 145
Goethe, Johann Wolfgang von, 151, 153
Grammaire générale, see general grammar
Granai, Georges, 269
Grasserie, Raoul de la, 94–5
Greek, 21, 117, 124, 127, 131, 133, 136, 160, 169, 228, 278
Greenberg, Joseph, 99–101
Greenlandic, 12, 21, 34, 36–7, 90, 106
Greimas, Algirdas J., 210
Grierson, George, 91
Grimm, Jacob, 14
Gurvitch, Georges, 269

Haida, 61, 64, 74, 77–9
Hale, Horatio, 13, 26–8
Halle, Morris, 8
Hamelin, Abbé, 23, 39
Hammerich, Louis Leonor, 207
Haudricourt, André-Georges, 269
Hebrew, 21
Heckewelder, John, 12, 19, 20, 22, 44
Henry, Victor, 126
Hervás y Panduro, Lorenzo, 20
Heyse, Karl Wilhelm Ludwig, 87, 93
Hjelmslev, Louis, 6
Hopi, 275
Horace, 128

Humboldt, Alexander von, 19–20
Humboldt, Wilhelm von, 13, 20, 28, 56, 64, 83–4, 86–7, 96, 99–101, 156
Hungarian, 120, 169, 183, 213, 228
Huron, *see* Wyandot

Idéologie, 14, 15, 17, 47
Incorporation, *see* polysynthesis
Indo-European, 25, 34, 58, 71, 78–80, 83, 94, 104, 114, 117–18, 126–7, 131–3, 250, 267
Inner form, 56, 61
Inuit, 25, 51, 74, 77
Iroquois languages, 29–30, 35, 40, 42, 44, 73

Jakobson, Roman, 2–4, 66–7, 214, 216–17, 230, 237–48, 268, 287
Japanese, 144, 146, 170, 175, 191
Jefferson, Thomas, 12
Jespersen, Otto, 208, 254

Kant, Immanuel, 115, 119–20
Karcevsky, Serge, 3, 145, 206, 211, 216–17, 225, 233–7
Khrakovsky, Victor, 142
Kroeber, Alfred Louis, 60, 70, 79
Kutenai, 73–4, 77–8
Kwakiutl, *see* Kwak'wala
Kwak'wala, 61, 63, 67, 75, 76, 78

Lahontan, Louis Armand de Lorme d'Arce Baron de, 29, 45
Latin, 21, 110, 112–13, 114, 117, 118, 127, 132–4, 136, 138, 213, 227, 239, 254, 278
Latvian, 144, 146, 171–2, 191
Lazarus, Moritz, 86, 89
Lenape, 12, 20–2, 24, 29, 34, 39, 41–2, 44, 49
Lévi-Strauss, Claude, 6–7, 268–71, 276, 281–2, 287
Levy-Bruhl, Lucien, 211
Lithuanian, 124, 131, 144, 146, 171–2, 191
Ljubishev, Aleksandr, 152, 155
Losev, Aleksei, 156

Maistre, Joseph de, 156
Malay languages, 88, 90, 105, 170
Mapuche, 21, 34, 37–8, 78

Markedness, 4, 210–11, 218–19, 238
Marr, Nikolay, 156
Martinet, André, 109
Marx, Karl, 283–4
Mason, Otis T., 53
Massachusett, 12, 21, 39, 41, 72
Maya, 78
Mazon, André, 272–3
Meillet, Antoine, 4, 85, 142, 149, 152, 162, 250, 267, 272–3, 278–9
Maupertuis, Pierre-Louis Moreau de, 15, 17–18
Molina, Juan Ignacio, 37
Mongolian, 188–9
Munda languages, 90, 105–6
Murdock, George, 270

Naturphilosophie, 142, 154, 156
Nebrija, 110
Neogrammarians, 4–5, 83–4, 85, 89, 93, 97–8, 111, 125–6, 156

Ojibwe, 21, 29–30, 39, 42, 72
Onondaga, 12, 20, 35
Osthoff, Hermann, 126
Otomi, 34, 41–2
Owen, Richard, 152, 154–5

Paul, Hermann, 89, 126
Pawnee, 73–4
Persian, 135, 104
Peshkovsky, Alekandr Matveevic, 216–17, 231–3
Phoneme, 3–4, 67, 126, 165–7, 269, 281
Phonetics, *see* phonology and phonetics
Phonology and phonetics, 23–4, 40–3, 67, 72–3, 93
Pickering, John, 12, 57
Pictet, Adolphe, 115
Pidgins and creoles, 104
Polish, 135, 144, 160, 166–7, 171, 174, 177, 213
Polynesian languages, 27–8
Polysynthesis, 11–13, 20–2, 26–7, 35–9, 47–50, 55–6, 73
Porzig, Walter, 160–1
Powell, John Wesley, 26, 53, 57, 59, 70
Potebnja, Aleksandr, 156

Prague Linguistic Circle, 2–3, 101, 207, 225
Prix Volney, 14–15, 24
Putnam, Frederic W., 52

Quechua, 41

Radcliffe-Brown, Alfred, 270
Radin, Paul, 60, 70–1
Râles, Sébastien, 43, 46
Ritter, Carl, 146
Romanian, 145, 155, 160, 180–1
Russian language, 126–7, 131, 135, 144, 153, 160, 162–3, 166–7, 173–6, 198–9, 238–9, 243

Sagard, Gabriel, 23, 45
Sahaptin, 77
Salish, 78, 80
Samoyed, 183–4
Sanskrit, 124, 132, 227
Sapir, Edward, 7, 13, 60, 64–5, 70, 79, 100, 270, 274, 289
Saussure, Ferdinand de, 3–4, 8–9, 66–8, 85, 86, 93, 109, 112–13, 115, 116, 117–18, 121, 122, 132, 158, 210–11, 231, 267, 273, 283, 296
Sauvageot, Aurélien, 120
Savitsky, Pyotr, 141, 146, 161–2
Schlegel, Friedrich von, 14, 20
Schleicher, August, 86, 101, 150
Schmidt, Wilhelm, 169–70, 274–5
Schoolcraft, Henry Rowe, 30
Schuchardt, Hugo, 97–8, 104, 149
Schulenburg, Albrecht von der, 82
Sechahaye, Albert, 3
Semitic languages, 78, 88, 105, 135
Sequoyah, 25
Serbo-Croatian, 160, 167–8, 172, 179
Shoshoni, 73–4, 77–8, 80
Sino-Tibetan, 90, 104, 105–6, 170
Sioux, 25, 29–30, 35, 61, 73, 75, 77–8, 80
Spanish, 110
Spitzer, Leo, 115–16
Stalin, Joseph, 156
Steinthal, Heymann, 56, 58, 64, 75, 86–7, 89, 100
Structuralism, American, 7–8, 66
Subordination of characters, 95

Sütterlin, Ludwig, 84, 89
Suvchinsky, Pyotr, 141
Synchronic analysis, 13, 27, 67–8

Tarde, Gabriel de, 110
Techmer, Friedrich, 93
Tesnière, Lucien, 109
Thai, 106
Tibetan, 90, 106
Titchener, Edward B., 2
Tlingit, 61, 64, 75, 78–9
Tone languages, 143–4, 146, 168, 170–2
Trubetzkoy, Nikolay, 2–3, 141, 145, 148, 153, 160, 162–4, 208, 214, 281
Tsimshian, 64, 67
Turanian languages, *see* Ural-Altaic languages
Turkish and Turkic languages, 72, 129, 184–7, 195–7
Tylor, Edward Burnett, 95

Ukrainian, 173, 176–8, 184, 198

Uldall, Hans Jørgen, 208
Ural-Altaic languages, 88, 162
US Exploring Expedition, 26–8

Vater, Johann Severin, 12, 19, 22, 44
Vendryès, Joseph, 109, 148, 253
Vietnamese, 106, 129, 132, 170
Virchow, Rudolf, 96
Völkerpsychologie, 86–7, 89
Voloshinov, Valentin, 274
Vossler, Karl, 274–5

Wartburg, Walther von, 274–5
Wenker, Georg, 91
Whitney, William Dwight, 26, 56, 78–9, 93–4, 98, 132
Whorf, Benjamin Lee, 7, 64, 274–6
Wiener, Norbert, 269
Wundt, Wilhelm, 89, 97, 129
Wyandot, 23, 43, 45–6

Zeisberger, David, 12, 19, 20, 24, 41, 44, 49
Zipf, George, 98